Pictorial
Travel Guide
of
Scenic America

by E. L. Jordan

HAMMOND INCORPORATED
MAPLEWOOD, NEW JERSEY
New York   Chicago   Los Angeles

Printing History:
    Hammond's Pictorial Travel Atlas of Scenic America — 1954, 1955, 1959, 1971
    Pictorial Travel Atlas of Scenic America: Bicentennial Edition — 1973, 1974
    Pictorial Travel Guide of Scenic America — 1976

Library of Congress Cataloging in Publication Data
Jordan, Emil Leopold, 1900-
    Pictorial travel guide of scenic America.

    First published in 1955 under title: Hammond's
pictorial travel atlas of scenic America.

    1. United States — Description and travel —
1960-   — Guide-books. I. Title.
E158.J82   1976   917.3′04′924   75-37581
ISBN 0-8437-3665-8

Foreword

Enjoying Scenic America is always an exciting experience. To see and examine it invites a comparison of almost unbelievable contrasts. America contains every type of scenic beauty encountered anywhere on earth: sky-high mountains and living deserts, white beaches and huge inland lakes, northern forests and southern palm groves, shiny glaciers and tropical islands. But to our forefathers this grandeur seemed immaterial for very practical reasons; the pioneers were absorbed in exploring and conquering the land, in taming and utilizing it. Only after the process of settling and civilizing had been accomplished did the scenic aspects of America come into their own. In our century the country has emerged as a huge travel and vacationland.

This transformation — a task of fabulous dimensions — has been performed by a host of people: railroad builders, highway engineers, airplane pilots, officials of national parks, rangers of forests and wilderness areas and innumerable others — among them, to a modest extent, the author and publisher of this book.

The purpose of the guide is twofold. In addition to offering pages of practical travel information, it dramatizes America as a unique travel land. With the combination of color photos, color maps and word pictures it attempts to show the complex and fascinating character and the infinite variety of the American landscape. By stressing the background and the appeal, the mood and the atmosphere of our country, the guide will enable the traveler to explore for himself both the momentary and the permanent values of travel in America and to discover the deep roots of our country and our nation — roots not anchored in Massachusetts and Oklahoma, or California and Florida, but stretching out in all directions and reaching far and wide from coast to coast.

When the original edition of the Travel Atlas appeared in 1955 one serious aspect of our environment had not yet entered the national consciousness — the problem of pollution. Today we are aware of it. To be sure, foul air and dirty rivers, dead fish and poisoned birds, junkyards and blatant neon signs are largely encountered in areas of concentrated industries and crowded populations, and the wide-open spaces of Scenic America are still fairly free of this plague. But if the drawbacks of modern technology occasionally spoil the traveler's enjoyment of nature, they will help to impress on him the overriding need for action on a national scale. Scenic America has to be kept clean, healthy and beautiful.

Princeton, N.J.   E.L.J.

Contents

Practical Hints on the Art of Travel

FREE, INDIVIDUALLY ROUTED ROAD MAPS

The most important map services are the following:

American Oil Motor Club, Travel Department, 111 West Jackson Street, Chicago, Ill., 60604.

Arco Travel Service, 600 Fifth Avenue, New York, N.Y. 10011; for motorists west of the Rockies: Arco Travel Service, 645 South Mariposa Street, Los Angeles, Calif. 90005.

Chevron Travel Service, 555 Market Street, San Francisco, Calif. 94120.

Citgo Touring Bureau, P.O. Box 2149, Houston, Texas 77001.

Exxon Touring Service, 800 Bell Street, Houston, Texas 77002.

Gulf Tourguide Bureau, 1375 Peachtree Street N.E., Atlanta, Ga. 30309; Gulf Building, 714 Main Street, Houston, Texas 77002; City Avenue and Schuylkill Expressway, Philadelphia, Pa. 19101; Gulf Building, Pittsburgh, Pa. 15219; 800 Bay Street, Toronto, Ontario, Canada.

Mobil Touring Service, 150 East 42nd Street, New York, N.Y. 16017.

Shell Touring Service, P.O. Box 2149, Houston, Texas 77001.

Sunoco Touring Service, P.O. Box 2149, Houston, Texas 77001.

Texaco Travel Service, 135 East 42nd Street, New York, N.Y. 10017; 312 South Michigan Avenue, Chicago, Ill., 60604; 1111 Rusk Avenue, Houston, Texas 77052; 3350 Wilshire Boulevard, Los Angeles, Calif. 90005; 1501 Canal Street, New Orleans, La. 70160.

SPECIAL TRAVEL PUBLICATIONS

By Hammond Inc., Maplewood, N.J. 07040: *Pictorial Travel Atlas of Scenic America; Hammond Road Atlas and Vacation Guide; Nature Atlas of America.*

By Rand McNally & Co., Chicago, Ill.: *Rand McNally Road Atlas;* see also under camping.

By Grosset and Dunlap, Inc., New York, N.Y.: *New Grosset Road Atlas.*

TRAVEL SERVICE ORGANIZATIONS

The following three organizations are best known. Current membership dues can be ascertained by writing to the respective headquarters.

American Automobile Association, 1712 G Street NW, Washington, D.C. 20006. Founded in 1902, the AAA consists of 840 clubs with approximately twelve million members. Their offices will plan any itinerary based on up-to-the-minute road information. The AAA field staff inspects thousands of hotels, motels, restaurants and campgrounds; only 17% qualify for AAA approval and listing. Computerized reservations are available. Emergency road service in case of breakdowns is provided by 26,000 officially appointed service stations. The association's publications include numerous maps, the AAA tour books (12 regional volumes covering the U.S. and Canada), two camping and trailering directories, booklets listing 26,000 garages for road service, a number of "Citibooks" covering individual cities in the U.S., and various smaller publications. The local offices will furnish additional information.

Exxon Travel Club, 800 Bell Ave., Houston, Texas 77002. This organization provides maps with individual travel routings, a travel atlas, six regional vacation guides with hotel and restaurant ratings and prices, low-cost accidental loss of life insurance, a $5000 bail bond and $200 arrest bond certificate, the travel magazine Vista/USA. Additional benefits include opportunities for low-cost buying and special value holidays.

National Travel Club, Travel Building, Floral Park, N.Y. 11001. This club is centered on travel in general, not specifically on automobile travel. To its members it offers travel accident insurance up to $15,000 ($30,000 the second year); a year's subscription to the magazine Travel; information about transportation, hotels, sightseeing, etc., in America and abroad; selected tours; discounts on books; road maps with individual routings; a guide to 2,500 English-speaking doctors and dentists around the world; a discount film library.

FOOD AND LODGING

Two different situations have to be considered. Those who wish to reach a certain goal in the shortest possible time will be disposed to stay overnight and have dinner at an inn of one of the national chains — Howard Johnson, Holiday, Ramada, Quality Courts, etc. These motels are conveniently located near the major highways. Those who travel in a leisurely fashion, intent on personal exploration, enjoying the Berkshires or the Ozarks or the Cascades or any other picturesque region away from turnpikes and heavy traffic, will find one of the practical guidebooks helpful. The Exxon Vacation Guides list hotels, motels and restaurants. Accommodations are rated in five categories (good, very good, excellent, superior and deluxe). Each guide contains an index to accommodations and restaurants. The Mobil Travel Guides list hotels, motels and restaurants; lodging and food are rated with one star meaning better than average to five stars marking the country's best eating places. Those relatively inexpensive restaurants which offer especially good value are listed with a check mark. One difficulty in preparing and keeping guides of this type up-to-date is the enormous size of our country.

Frequently it will happen that the attractive motel or the pleasant looking country inn where you would like to rest and enjoy a meal is not listed at all. In the United States it is simply impossible to be as all-inclusive as the European guides which deal with smaller countries.

The traveler's own judgment will always be decisive; motels recommended by the American Automobile Association and marked AAA will always be satisfactory and are preferred by most travelers. Reservations are generally not necessary if the arrival time is around five o'clock in the afternoon.

As far as meals are concerned, nationally famous restaurants in New York and Philadelphia, Chicago and New Orleans, San Francisco and other large cities are sightseeing and vacation attractions in themselves. In contrast, mass feeding is provided in the more heavily populated areas where national chains provide hamburgers, fried chicken and other simple dishes produced in large quantities at low prices. Throughout the country the food is quite good but monotonous, the same few standard dishes being offered everywhere.

However, there is a more imaginative minority of travelers who enjoy whatever traditional foods each region has to offer; for them, the consultation of a guidebook will be essential. A table of some famous regional dishes will be found on page 10.

CAMPING — TENT, TRAILER OR CAMPER

This form of vacation travel increases in popularity year after year, especially in the West where camping facilities are numerous. The sporting goods stores are able to fill every need in equipment, and supplies are usually available not far from the camping site.

The family car, usually a station wagon carrying the tent and other equipment, is gradually being replaced by the trailer or camper which eliminates the task of setting up quarters for the night. For camping travelers the following guidebooks are recommended:

Woodall's Trailering Parks and Campgrounds; this book lists campgrounds and trailer parks in the U.S., Canada and Mexico. It is published by Woodall Publishing Co. of Highland Park, Ill., and distributed by Simon & Schuster, 630 Fifth Avenue, New York 10020.

Rand McNally Campground and Trailer Park Guide; the book covers the U.S., Canada and Mexico with 18,000 listings: 8,000 private grounds, 3,500 national forests, 1,500 civic, county and city facilities and thousands of government campgrounds.

Rand McNally Western Campground and Trailer Parks; it describes 7,500 facilities in 13 states.

Camping Maps USA; Private Campgrounds USA; Camping Maps Canada. These maps can be ordered from the publisher, Camping Maps USA, Box 2652-T 7, Palos Verdes Peninsula, Calif. 90274.

STATE AND PROVINCIAL TOURIST AGENCIES

The following state and provincial agencies will be glad to provide travelers with illustrated folders on the sightseeing and sports attractions within their area. All have cooperated in this edition of the Travel Atlas by providing the most up-to-date material available; their assistance has been greatly appreciated.

UNITED STATES

Alabama Bureau of Publicity and Information, State Capitol, Montgomery, Ala. 36104.

Alaska Division of Tourism, Department of Economic Development, Pouch E, Juneau, Alaska 99801.

Arizona Department of Economic Planning and Development, Travel Information Section, 3003 North Central Avenue, Phoenix, Ariz. 85012.

Arkansas Parks, Recreation and Travel Commission, State Capitol, Little Rock, Ark. 72201.

California Office of Tourism and Visitor Services, 1400 10 St., Sacramento, Calif. 95814.

Colorado Division of Commerce and Development, Advertising and Publicity Department, 602 State Capitol Annex, Denver, Colo. 80203.

Connecticut Development Commission, Research and Information Division, State Office Building, Hartford, Conn. 06115.

Delaware State Division of Economic Development, 45 The Green, Dover, Dela. 19901.

Florida Department of Commerce, Division of Commercial Development, Collins Bldg., Tallahassee, Fla. 32304.

Georgia Department of Industry and Trade, Tourist Division, P.O. Box 38097, Atlanta, Ga. 30334.

Hawaii Visitors Bureau, 2270 Kalakaua Avenue, Honolulu, Hawaii 96815.

Idaho Department of Commerce and Development, State Capitol Building, Room 108, Boise, Idaho 83707.

Illinois Department of Business and Economic Development, 22 South College Street, Springfield, Ill. 62706.

Indiana Department of Commerce, Tourist Division, 333 State House, Indianapolis, Ind. 46204.

Iowa Development Commission, Tourism and Travel Division, 250 Jewett Building, Des Moines, Iowa 50309.

Kansas Department of Economic Development, State Office Building, Topeka, Kans. 66612.

Practical Hints on the Art of Travel

Kentucky Department of Public Information, Travel Division, Capitol Annex Building, Frankfort, Ky. 40601.

Louisiana Tourist Development Commission, Box 44291, Capitol Station, Baton Rouge, La. 70804.

Maine Department of Economic Development, Vacation Travel Promotion, State Capitol, Augusta, Maine 04330.

Maryland Department of Economic and Community Development, Tourist Division, State Office Building, Annapolis, Md. 21401.

Massachusetts Department of Commerce and Development, Division of Tourism, Government Center, Leverett Saltonstall Bldg., 100 Cambridge St., Boston, Mass. 02202.

Michigan Tourist Council, Suite 102, South Capitol Ave., Lansing, Mich. 48926.

Minnesota Department of Economic Development, Vacation Information Center, 57 West Seventh Street, St. Paul, Minn. 55102.

Mississippi Agricultural and Industrial Board, Travel Department, 1504 State Office Building, Jackson, Miss. 39205.

Missouri Tourism Commission, P.O. Box 1055, 308 East High Street, Jefferson City, Mo. 65101.

Montana Highway Commission, Advertising Department, Helena, Mont. 59601.

Nebraska Game, Forestation and Parks Commission, Information and Tourism, State Capitol, Lincoln, Nebr. 68509.

Nevada Department of Economic Development, Carson City, Nev. 89701.

New Hampshire Department of Resources and Economic Development, State Division of Economic Development, P.O. Box 856, State House Annex, Concord, N.H. 03301.

New Jersey Department of Labor & Industry, Division of Economic Development, Labor & Industry Bldg., P.O. Box 2766, Trenton, N.J. 08625.

New Mexico Department of Development, 113 Washington Ave., Santa Fe, N. Mex. 87501.

New York Department of Commerce, Travel Bureau, 112 State Street, Albany, N.Y. 12207.

North Carolina Department of Conservation and Development, Division of Travel and Promotion, P.O. Box 2719, Raleigh, N.C. 27611.

North Dakota Travel Department, State Capitol Building, Capitol Grounds, Bismarck, N. Dak. 58501.

Ohio Development Department, Travel and Tourist Div., 65 South Front Street, Box 1001, Columbus, Ohio 43215.

Oklahoma Industrial Development and Park Department, Division of Tourism & Information, Will Rogers Memorial Building, Oklahoma City, Okla. 73105.

Oregon State Highway Division, Travel Information Section, Highway Bldg., Salem, Oreg. 97310.

Pennsylvania Department of Commerce, Vacation and Travel Development Bureau, 406 South Office Bldg., Harrisburg, Pa. 17120.

Rhode Island Development Council, Tourist Promotion Division, Roger Williams Building, Hayes Street, Providence, R.I. 02908.

South Carolina Department of Parks, Recreation and Tourism, Travel Div., Box 1358, Columbia, S.C. 29202.

South Dakota Department of Highways, Travel Section, Pierre, S. Dak. 57501.

Tennessee Department of Conservation, Division of Tourist Information and Promotion, 2611 West End Avenue, Nashville, Tenn. 37203.

Texas Highway Department, Travel and Information Division, Austin, Texas 78701.

Utah Travel Council, Council Hall, Capitol Hill, Salt Lake City, Utah 84114.

Vermont Agency of Development and Community Affairs, Promotion and Travel, Montpelier, Vt. 05602.

Virginia Travel Service, Department of Conservation and Economic Development, 911 East Broad Street, Richmond, Va. 23219.

Washington Public Affairs Office, 14th and E NW, Washington, D.C. 20015.

Washington Department of Commerce and Economic Development, Tourist Promotion Div., General Administration Building, Olympia, Wash. 98501.

West Virginia Department of Commerce, Travel Development Div., State Capitol, Charleston, W. Va. 25305.

Wisconsin Department of Natural Resources, Vacation and Travel Service, Box 450, Madison, Wis. 53701.

Wyoming Travel Commission, 2320 Capitol Avenue, Cheyenne, Wyo. 82001.

CANADA

Alberta Government Travel Bureau, 1629 Centennial Building, Edmonton 15, Alta.

British Columbia Department of Travel Industry, Parliament Bldgs., Victoria, Br. Col.

Manitoba Department of Tourism & Cultural Affairs, Tourist Branch, Legislative Bldg., Winnipeg 1, Man.

New Brunswick Travel Bureau, Box 1030, Fredericton, N.B.

Newfoundland and Labrador Tourist Development Office, Confederation Building, St. John's, Newf.

Nova Scotia Travel Bureau, Department of Trade and Industry, Halifax, N.S.

Ontario Department of Tourism and Information, Parliament Bldgs., Toronto 285, Ont.

Prince Edward Island Travel Bureau, Charlottetown, P.E.I.

Province of Québec Department of Tourism, Fish and Game, Tourist Branch, Chemin Sainte Foy, Québec, Que.

Saskatchewan Department of Industry and Commerce, Tourist Development Branch, Power Building, Regina, Sask.

CAMERAS

Photography on a vacation trip is a wonderful pastime that will definitely enhance your travel enjoyment. By carefully focusing and framing in your camera viewer the sights that impress you most, and by jockeying for the best positions, the best light and the best background, you become much more conscious of the interesting and scenic features of your surroundings than as if you merely look and snap the shutter. Often your photo hobby will induce you to climb to some elevated vantage point which otherwise you would be too lazy to tackle, and a new panorama will reward you. For taking wildlife pictures — birds or wild animals at some distant point — a telephoto lens will be essential.

In showing travel slides at home after the journey is over, please use discretion. If you show only a restricted number of your very best slides that will be infinitely more enjoyable to your audience than showing all the 250 pictures you took while away, including the ones that are technically poor or near duplications.

BINOCULARS

Anyone interested in wildlife should take along a pair of good binoculars; the 7/35 type is popular and satisfactory for most regular purposes. Particularly in the western mountains where you can observe mule deer and elk, moose and bear, bighorn antelope and Rocky Mountain goats; along the Pacific coast where sea lions play on the rocks and innumerable varieties of sea birds fill the air; in Florida and in the southern mountains where song birds abound a handy pair of binoculars will greatly increase the pleasure of the journey.

WEATHER

Some of your travel experiences will be disappointing; in a fog or drizzling rain all scenic beauty is reduced to the vanishing point. If the tremendous climatic variety of our continent sometimes poses problems, they can always be solved with some common sense.

For instance, most people who have to cross the desert during the summer now travel at night. You may rest in an air-conditioned motel till midnight and then set out eastward through a pleasantly cool and possibly cold night, arriving at Salt Lake City in the morning. The sunrise over the desert is a splendid spectacle.

VARIETY AND SERENDIPITY

If your trip can include a boat excursion that will be a pleasant change. Opportunities are innumerable; almost every large lake, river or coastal body of water offers them. It may be a small fishing boat on a New Jersey inlet, or a floating raft in the Ozarks, or a seagoing steamer across Puget Sound to Victoria, or a ferry from Portland to Nova Scotia, or an excursion boat on the Mississippi, at St. Louis or New Orleans. If you are a sportsman you will stop where the trout fishing is good, or where you can get out to sea with the commercial fleet at daybreak and return in the afternoon with a couple of salmon. If you are a horseback rider, you will find innumerable opportunities for an afternoon ride over mountain trails or for pack trips of several days.

Sometimes local attractions are discovered unexpectedly. I remember coming upon a natural granite swimming pool near the lodge where we stayed in the Great Smoky Mountains, with crystal clear mountain water flowing through it, a forest of virgin hemlocks bordering its edges and a flock of great, brilliantly blue butterflies hovering above it.

With equal pleasure I like to think of the small canyon-bottom town of Ouray, Colorado, where we discovered an enterprise called Scenic Jeep Tours. In a sturdy, especially adapted jeep we were taken over old mining roads and through lonely ghost towns to the very roof of America, a unique experience.

I remember one afternoon when my family and I drove along the Columbia River Highway, headed for Portland. In spite of the grand vistas, heat and dust from new construction projects proved quite annoying. So a conference over a map and an interview with a gas station manager caused us to turn to the left into the Cascade Mountains. The road was very poor, but after 12 miles it ended at a small, blue mountain lake in which the snowy peak of Mt. Hood was mirrored in perfect stillness. A camp was available in a forest of huge Douglas firs; we stayed for five days.

Your personal attitude is the key to a successful vacation. If you take things the easy way, let the other members of your family have their turns at the wheel, if you are willing to put up with certain inconveniences and are inclined to see the humorous side of the little mishaps that are bound to occur, you will have mastered the art of travel. Bon voyage and happy landing.

America's Regional Foods

Some of the dishes listed in this table are strictly regional; she-crab soup, for example, can probably be obtained only in and around Charleston, S. C., and pollo relleno only in the Southwest. Other dishes have spread to many parts of the United States and Canada but still are especially delicious in their original regions.

NEW ENGLAND. Maine lobster; New England clam chowder; fish chowder; codfish cakes; salt codfish with pork scraps; clams steamed on hot rocks — the famous clam bake; local trout and salmon. Vermont turkey; wild duck; New England boiled dinner (corned beef, lean pork, quartered green cabbage, carrots, turnips, beets, potatoes, horseradish sauce, mustard pickles). Succotash; bean pole beans; baked beans and brown bread; Maine potatoes; baking powder biscuits; Parker House rolls; hot cakes with maple syrup. Indian pudding; maple sugar and maple syrup; Boston cream pie; squash pie; cranberry pie; huckleberry pie; apple and blueberry cobbler; country cider.

METROPOLITAN NEW YORK. The city has the country's most international cuisine. Excellent French, Italian, Spanish, Greek, German, Scandinavian, Swiss, Japanese, Chinese, Polynesian and Moroccan restaurants, to name a few, supplement those that provide standard American food. It is the birthplace of Manhattan clam chowder and the Manhattan cocktail.

PHILADELPHIA AND THE PENNSYLVANIA-DUTCH COUNTRY. Philadelphia snapper soup; Philadelphia pepper pot; scrapple (hog's head ground and yellow corn or oatmeal cut in thin slices and fried until crisp and brown); Lebanon sausage; headcheese; schnitz und knepp (dried apples, smoked ham, dumplings); hasenpfeffer (hare or rabbit meat); 7 sweets and 7 sours (apple butter, jam, spiced peaches, rhubarb, honey, chowchow, coleslaw, cucumber pickles, quince preserve, watermelon pickles). Reading pretzels; schmierkase; streuselkuchen (crumb cake); shoofly pie (molasses crumb pie); Philadelphia peach ice cream.

SOUTH. Pan-roasted oysters; fried soft-shell crabs; crab flakes Maryland; shrimp pie; green corn and shrimp pudding; she-crab soup. Diamondback terrapin stew; Virginia ham; Smithfield ham; Arkansas ham; Brunswick stew; hog jowl; Maryland fried chicken; squab pie; Kentucky burgoo (the famous dish for large outdoor gatherings requiring 600 pounds of lean soup meat, 200 pounds of fat hens and huge quantities of potatoes, onions, cabbage, tomatoes, carrots, corn, red pepper). Red beans and rice; black bean soup; hominy and butter; grits and gravy; beaten biscuits; hot breads; hush puppies; pecan pie; ambrosia; Florida oranges, grapefruits, avocados, papayas, mangoes, guavas. Mint juleps and planter's punch.

PUERTO RICO. Lechón asado (barbecued pig); arroz con pollo (chicken with rice); smothered young kid; kid fricassee; paella; asopao (a one-dish meal of rice with meat, shrimp, clams or other basic ingredients); pasteles (pastries filled with meat); plantains; sofrito, achiote, caldero (native seasonings). Flan (custard); guava shells in syrup with native cheese; papaya preserves in syrup; rum drinks.

MIDWEST. Great Lakes whitefish; Great Lakes perch; Minnesota pike; Michigan smelt; Indiana chicken potpie; Wisconsin roast goose; Chicago porterhouse or T-bone steak; Kansas City sirloin steak; pork loin roast with prunes; jellied pigs' feet; Dakota buffalo steak. In the German sections: sauerbraten, Wiener schnitzel, schnitzel à la Holstein; pig knuckles with sauerkraut; Kasseler rippchen (smoked rib chops); stuffed cabbage; blood sausage; tongue sausage; sauerkraut prepared with apples and caraway seeds; German potato salad; herring salad; apfelstrudel; apfelkuchen; pflaumenkuchen. In the Scandinavian sections: Swedish meatballs; Danish fricadellen; liver paste; smoked meats; cold fruit soups; Danish open sandwiches; Danish pastry; smorgasbord.

NEW ORLEANS AREA. Bayou oysters; oyster stew; oysters Rockefeller; crayfish; crayfish bisque; bouillabaisse; shrimp Creole; pompano; crab gumbo; jambalaya (rice with crab meat, shrimps, oysters, ham, sausages, pork, turkey, chicken); fried frog legs; chicken Creole; blanquette de veau; okra dishes; pommes soufflées. French omelet; brioches; Creole doughnuts; crêpes suzettes; cherries jubilee; café diable; pecan pralines.

SOUTHWEST. Chile con carne; pollo relleno (baked chicken with sharply seasoned ground beef); buffalo steak; tamales; tacos; frijoles; tortillas; enchiladas; pinto beans and barbecue sauce; sweet potatoes; yams.

SOUTHERN CALIFORNIA. Abalone; barbecued spareribs; Japanese sukiyaki; fresh vegetable salads; fresh fruit salads; various salad dressings, mostly with sweet overtones, like cream flavored and colored with berry juice; boysenberry pie; figs in syrup; fig pudding; date pudding.

SAN FRANCISCO AND THE NORTHWEST. Columbia salmon; smoked salmon; jerked salmon; abalone steak; crab meat flakes Lorenzo; broiled crab legs with butter; Dungeness crab; cioppino (the Italian version of bouillabaisse); oriental foods; various oriental teas; good local wines.

HAWAII. Oriental, especially Polynesian dishes; barbecued meats; tropical fruits, especially luscious pineapples; poi (taro root pounded to a paste with water and allowed to ferment); luau, the Hawaiian feast (piglets, chicken, bananas and other native foods baked in a sealed pit lined with hot volcanic stones); rum punch.

CANADA. The east coast of Canada enjoys the same seafood specialties that are popular in Maine; the world's largest lobster packing plant is located in St. Andrews in the province of New Brunswick. On the Pacific coast the luscious seafoods of San Francisco and Seattle are also available in Vancouver and Victoria. Québec has a wonderful French cuisine, and the British-Canadian sections are fond of roast beef, Yorkshire pudding and other English dishes.

Key to America's Regions

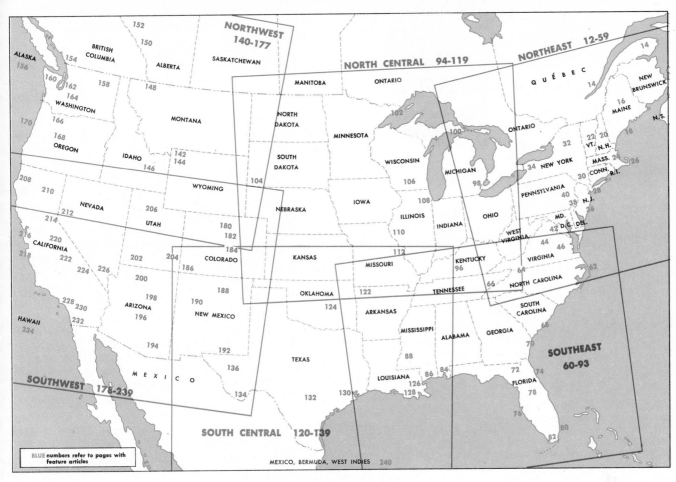

Sightseeing Guides

Northeast Map

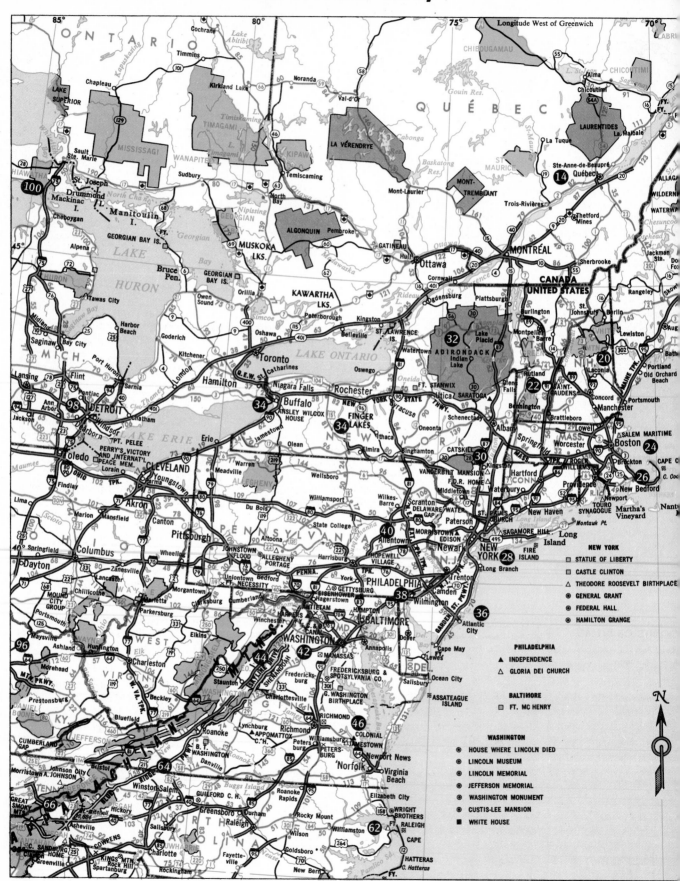

NEW YORK
☐ STATUE OF LIBERTY
☐ CASTLE CLINTON
△ THEODORE ROOSEVELT BIRTHPLACE
⊕ GENERAL GRANT
⊕ FEDERAL HALL
⊕ HAMILTON GRANGE

PHILADELPHIA
▲ INDEPENDENCE
△ GLORIA DEI CHURCH

BALTIMORE
☐ FT. MC HENRY

WASHINGTON
⊕ HOUSE WHERE LINCOLN DIED
⊕ LINCOLN MUSEUM
⊕ LINCOLN MEMORIAL
⊕ JEFFERSON MEMORIAL
⊕ WASHINGTON MONUMENT
⊕ CUSTIS-LEE MANSION
■ WHITE HOUSE

N

WHAT to SEE in the NORTHEAST REGION

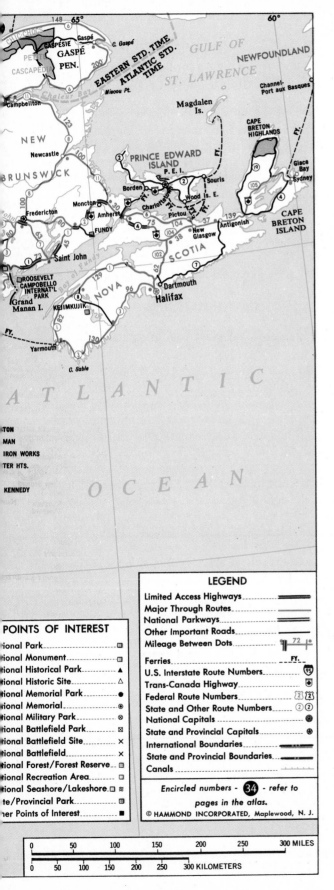

LEGEND

Limited Access Highways	═══
Major Through Routes	───
National Parkways	═══
Other Important Roads	───
Mileage Between Dots	72
Ferries	FY.
U.S. Interstate Route Numbers	(95)
Trans-Canada Highway	
Federal Route Numbers	23 23
State and Other Route Numbers	2 2
National Capitals	⊛
State and Provincial Capitals	⊛
International Boundaries	━━━
State and Provincial Boundaries	━━━
Canals	

Encircled numbers - **34** *- refer to*
pages in the atlas.

POINTS OF INTEREST

...ional Park	⊡
...ional Monument	⊡
...ional Historical Park	▲
...ional Historic Site	△
...ional Memorial Park	●
...ional Memorial	◉
...ional Military Park	⊗
...ional Battlefield Park	⊠
...ional Battlefield Site	×
...ional Battlefield	×
...ional Forest/Forest Reserve	▢
...ional Recreation Area	▢
...ional Seashore/Lakeshore	▢ ≈
...te/Provincial Park	▣
...er Points of Interest	■

TWO TO THREE WEEK TRIP THROUGH NEW ENGLAND. For a general introduction see pages 16-27, also sightseeing guide pages 48-59. Suggested route: New York City — Taconic State Parkway — the Berkshire Hills with their old forests and rushing brooks — Great Barrington and Stockbridge, typically historic and handsome New England towns — Bennington, Vermont, and Old Bennington, a veritable outdoor museum — through the lovely and unspoiled Green Mountains to Woodstock, Vermont, and the Laconia area on Lake Winnipesaukee, New Hampshire — interlude: a ride around the lake — north to the White Mountains with the cogwheel railroad to the top of Mt. Washington, the cable cars to the summit of Cannon Mountain, the huge stone profile called The Old Man of the Mountain and The Flume — Gorham, New Hampshire, and Bangor, Maine — Bar Harbor, a popular resort on Mt. Desert Island — Acadia National Park with Mt. Cadillac, with a fabulous view of Frenchman's Bay — Portland, Maine, with the Portland Head Light, a favorite object of photographers — boat ride to the islands in Portland's Casco Bay, a pleasant round trip — Boston may be included for a very worthwhile sightseeing tour, or it may be bypassed — New York City.

TWO TO THREE WEEK TRIP THROUGH NEW YORK STATE. For a general introduction see pages 28-35, also sightseeing guide pages 48-59. Suggested route: New York City — the Catskill Mountains, famous for their resort hotels — west to the Finger Lakes — Watkins Glen at the head of Seneca Lake with the picturesque Gorge Trail — Hammondsport on Keuka Lake, center of New York's wine region and site of many well-known wineries — Niagara Falls, the world's most famous cataract. The Canadian Falls are more spectacular than the American Falls — Fort Niagara — along Lake Ontario to the Thousand Islands, the 60-mile archipelago in the St. Lawrence River consisting of nearly 2,000 lovely, forested islands — across the spectacular and wild Adirondack Mountains to Lake Placid at the foot of Whiteface Mountain, a tourist resort and Olympic winter sports center — Ausable Chasm, the deep, picturesque canyon of the Ausable River — south along the shore of Lake Champlain to Fort Ticonderoga, a restoration of the French and later British fortress that was captured by the Green Mountain Boys — Lake George — Saratoga Springs, one of America's oldest spas, with hot springs, horse racing and an excellent summer festival of the performing arts — Albany — New York City.

TWO-WEEK TRIP THROUGH PENNSYLVANIA. For a general introduction see pages 38-41, also sightseeing guide pages 48-59. Suggested route: Philadelphia, birthplace of our nation. The old historic section around Independence Hall will stir your imagination — north to the Delaware Water Gap which cuts spectacularly through the Kittatinny Mountains — the Pocono Mountains with their clear pools and playful waterfalls — north along the Susquehanna River — west to Erie where the restored U.S.S. Niagara, Commodore Perry's flagship during his victorious battle on Lake Erie, may be inspected — Pittsburgh, no longer sooty and grimy, is a progressive steel and manufacturing center; Mount Washington offers a grand panorama of the Golden Triangle and the rest of the city — east to Gettysburg with the Gettysburg National Military Park, the battlefield of the Civil War — Lancaster, the heart of the Pennsylvania Dutch country with its neat farms, big red barns and farmers in traditional Amish clothes — Ephrata, a cloister built by the Seventh Day Baptists in 1732 — Valley Forge with the famous winter camp and Washington's headquarters — Philadelphia.

The St. Lawrence River

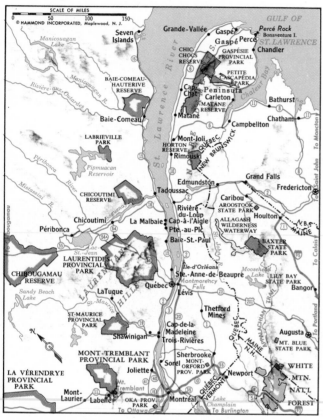

and views that encompass bays and shores, the Gaspé Peninsula will offer you many a reward. One of its most famous sights is the Percé Rock; facing the ocean toward the east, it stands in the blue waters like an oversized battleship. The scenery around the village of Percé belongs to America's most spectacular sights. A boat ride will take you to Bonaventure Island, a fascinating bird sanctuary for tens of thousands of gannets and gulls. The countryside here preserves a colorful peasant civilization from the French homeland: the bulky outdoor ovens in which delicious bread is baked; the large, good-natured dogs that pull carts heaped with vegetables; the piles of wood stacked high behind the houses for winter use; the frail horse buggies converging upon the village church on a Sunday morning; the crucifixes by the road; and the small country hotels where good meals are served.

SWANK AND WILDERNESS IN THE LAURENTIAN HILLS. Jumbled and without any regular pattern of orderly ranges, the Laurentians cover an enormous territory on the northwestern shore of the St. Lawrence. Cruises up the Saguenay River reveal a grandiose, lonely landscape of cliffs and forests; here you may see the river's famous school of white whales. Farther south, where a picturesque group of Laurentian hills touch the broad, lake-like St. Lawrence, the well-known summer resort of Murray Bay is flourishing. Its natural beauty has a French accent. Neither the government nor the mails know a place called Murray Bay; that name is merely a tradition. Officially the resort consists of three French Canadian towns with the romantic designations of La Malbaie, Cap-à-l'Aigle and Pointe-au-Pic. The showplace of the region is the Manoir Richelieu, a luxury hotel built on a cliff and offering its guests a stunning view of the 15-mile-wide river, all sports and a fabulous collection of Canadiana; 45 miles to the north it operates a camp from which 32 lakes may be fished. The inland Laurentians, with thousands of lakes and thousands of acres of forests, are both a lonely wilderness and an international playground with numerous hunting, fishing and skiing lodges, often built in a gaily colored French Canadian style. That does not mean that the hills are becoming crowded, it rather points up a typically Canadian resort specialty — the fine, comfortable hotel-lodge in an untamed, wild forest country. Snowmobile and skiing facilities are developed especially north of the two great cities. The Maple Leaf Trail is a unique 80-mile path for cross-country skiing, beginning at the logging town of Labelle and running southward through Mt. Tremblant, the ski resort.

GRAND WELCOME. There may be more central maritime approaches to America, but nowhere will the New World receive you in more grandeur. The ocean gradually narrows down to an inland sea, to blue waters surrounded by cliffs and hills, with immense black pine forests on the slopes and small, straight white church steeples in the tiny village ports. By the river's bank two great cities arise where the northern wilderness begins. This gateway is of huge proportions, and the traveler who wants to get acquainted with the St. Lawrence may easily spend his whole vacation on or near its shores. A leisurely ride around the Gaspé Peninsula alone will take a week, and many full days may be spent at Murray Bay and the Laurentians, in Québec and Montréal.

LA GASPÉ: REPLICA OF AN OLD FRENCH COUNTRYSIDE. If you like roads that run by the sea

THE ROCKS AND RAMPARTS OF QUÉBEC. Cities built on hills by the water are always spectacular, but

MAGNIFICENT GATEWAY to OUR CONTINENT

CANADIAN NATIONAL

Percé Rock, the famous landmark of the Gaspé.

CANADIAN PACIFIC

Québec City, America's outpost of French culture.

Québec has one advantage over such hilltown sisters as San Francisco or Rio de Janeiro: it is all of one piece, monolithic, easily encompassed by the human eye. There is the old town with its little crisscross streets along the river, and towering on the rock above stands the Château Frontenac. When Willa Cather, the poet, saw this picture gleaming at night with a million lights, it seemed to her like "an altar with many candles," like the vision of "a holy city in an old legend." To enjoy the majestic sweep of "the rock" and to view the picturesque Montmorency Falls, which are 100 feet higher than the drop of the Niagara, an excursion boat ride on the St. Lawrence is recommended. Getting acquainted with the old town and the ramparts — Québec is the only walled city in America — is a venture best performed on foot. From above and from the terrace surrounding it, the panorama is glorious from the Château Frontenac, the hotel that looks like a huge French castle. For exploring the upper town with its parliament building, monuments and gardens, an old-fashioned horse drawn calèche is usually hired, the driver ex-

plaining the sights or just chatting about his family. The city is altogether charming.

MONTRÉAL, A TWO-NATION COMMUNITY. This largest city of Canada is fascinating because of its contrasts. From Mount Royal, the green hill in the center of Montréal Island, you look into the vast, rich plains and feel, quite correctly, that you are in the center of a great inland empire. Then suddenly the big hull of an oceangoing liner or a huge tanker or a freighter from Liverpool or Rotterdam looms at the bend of the river, and you realize that this is also a great world port, 1,000 miles away from the ocean. Montréal is an ancient seat of religion and culture; it probably has more churches than any other American community and is the home of McGill University, one of the continent's leading universities. Yet Montréal lies on the edge of a wilderness that stretches uninterrupted to the North Pole. Among the new features of the town are the exhibition, "Man and His World," and Place Bonaventure, a huge trade and exhibition center.

15

Northwoods of Maine

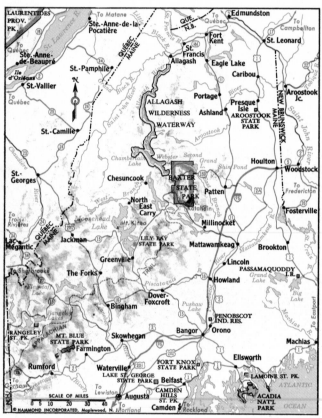

of his wilderness trip, a water body which cuts for 40 miles through almost trackless forests. About midway on its eastern side, Mount Kineo rises abruptly above the surface like a wounded giant cow moose lying by the shore, a striking comparison from Indian lore. Greenville at the southern end is a pleasant resort and outfitters' town, and in the north the portage to the West Branch of the Penobscot and the canoe trip to Chamberlain Lake are still a great experience in solitude and freedom. Chamberlain Farm where Thoreau borrowed some sugar is still there, ancient and weather-beaten but deserted. The decaying remnants of a lumber steamer in a shallow cove of the lake testify to the victory of nature over civilization. The rest of the trip, over Webster Lake and through the turbulent Webster Brook, through Second Lake and Grand Lake and down the East Branch of the Penobscot to Millinocket, is quite the same today as it was a century ago, or as it ever was. There are innumerable similar wilderness jaunts; best-known among them is the "Allagash Leap," which according to the guides in Greenville is "the finest canoe trip on the continent." It runs through solid deep forest, encompasses the eight remote Allagash lakes, includes some exciting examples of white water travel and is interrupted by few portages. The 94-mile canoe trail is permanently protected as the "Allagash Wilderness Waterway."

THE BIRD'S-EYE VIEW. One twentieth-century touch in the Northwoods is the presence of small planes that have become an accepted means of transportation. Such points as Greenville or Shin Pond northwest of Patten have become water airports. From there hunters and especially fishermen like to be flown to remote lakes which are not accessible by road and offer exceptional hunting and fishing. Also amateur nature photographers find such flights most rewarding. On clear days the deep green, endless expanse of forests and hills, the hundreds of shiny lakes and the blue mountain ranges far away on the horizon blend into an unforgettable panorama which Thoreau would have loved. Flying is also a lazy man's way of observing wildlife. Cruising above a mountain slope at a moderate altitude, one will come upon five or six bears grazing in the blueberry bushes and scattering in all directions. Two moose will stand in a little lake, their heads completely immersed in the water, searching for bottom plants and paying no attention to the big bird. Upon landing, an old red fox may watch you from a bushy peninsula, and a worried loon mother will take her two baby loons under her wings and dive with them out of sight. A look through your binoculars will confirm that the huge nest in a dead tree on a tiny island is occupied: a bald eagle family lives there. Ashore, a

SILENT LAKES AND INDIAN TRAILS. Since Thoreau wandered through the deep woods and canoed over the lonely lakes of northern Maine more than a hundred years ago, there have been some changes, but not in the way anticipated by Thoreau. He was afraid that settlements and towns would encroach upon the wilderness while in fact the woods and streams are lonelier than ever. They shelter more deer and bears, beaver and otters, foxes and wildcats than lived there in Thoreau's time, and the fishing about which he complained occasionally is infinitely better now because the lakes and brooks are stocked. Of course, the pines and balsam firs, the red spruces and hemlocks, the rock maples and aspen poplars are in their fourth or fifth growth now, but Thoreau saw little of the virgin giants himself; they were gone by 1857. On the whole he would still feel at home on Moosehead Lake, the starting point

THOREAU'S BELOVED WILDERNESS

Above: White birches blend with cool, blue lakes into a picture of our Northland.

Right: Blue lakes dot all of Maine, among them the lovely Rangeley group.

bed of bright scarlet cardinal flowers may welcome you. However, one warning is in order here: during the early summer the mosquitoes and flies are often most annoying.

THE MOUNT KATAHDIN STORY. The highest peak of Maine is Mount Katahdin, situated approximately in the center of the half circle described by Thoreau. It lies in Baxter State Park, one of New England's great fish and game preserves. With a height of 5,268 feet and a geographical location far east of New York, it is the first spot in the United States to be touched by the rays of the rising sun. No one has described the peak better than Thoreau: it is "a vast aggregation of loose rocks, as if at some time it has rained rocks, and they lay as they fell on the mountain, nowhere firmly at rest but leaning on each other, all rocking stones." There are a number of camps for vacationers at the foot of the mountain, and the ascent is neither easy nor difficult.

About Katahdin, the mountain god, the Abnaki Indians have an ancient tale: Once a beautiful girl who loved the mountain vanished while berry picking. She came back three years later with a handsome, strong boy who had eyebrows of stone. The camp buzzed with gossip, but nobody asked the indiscreet question. Later a famine descended upon the land, and the Abnaki would have perished if the boy had not shown supernatural powers and provided food. With his finger he pointed to a moose or a wild goose in flight, and the game's dead body fell to the ground. Gossip and insinuations became stronger, and finally the curious women made the tactless inquiry. "You fools," replied the angry and weary mother. "My boy is the son of Katahdin, sent to you to save you. But now your folly has destroyed his power." She took her child and wandered off toward the summit of the great mountain. The Abnaki, however, were doomed; white men came and robbed and killed them. It's a Lohengrin tale of the Northwoods.

The Maine Coast

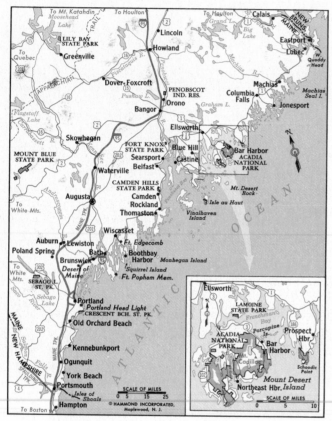

where Bowdoin College stands in a stately grove of cathedral pines and where Harriet Beecher Stowe wrote "Uncle Tom's Cabin," to Rockland, the great lobster harbor, the coast sends out into the sea a number of thin, long, rocky fingers, creating a thousand vacation spots of blue coves lined with granite and shaded by pines, with seals sunning themselves on the cliffs and birds singing in the trees. Boothbay Harbor has a varied resort life with summer theater and art exhibits, excursions to Wiscasset or to Fort Edgecomb, built about 1808, with a wonderful view of bays and woods; sails to Squirrel Island or Monhegan Island are popular. Camden (home of the original windjammer cruises), Belfast, Blue Hill and the large islands, all easily reached by bridges or by ferry, offer innumerable opportunities for individual exploration.

THE STEEPEST CAPES, THE DEEPEST HARBORS. The life of the shore comes to a grand crescendo in Mount Desert Island; this is the highest point on the Atlantic coast north of Rio de Janeiro, and the meeting place of the Temperate Zone and the Northern Zone. Its most picturesque part has been converted into Acadia National Park, created by purchases and donations of land, a monument to civic responsibility. A scenic automobile road leads to the summit of Mount Cadillac, so named in honor of the first owner of the island, Antoine de la Mothe Cadillac. From its peak, 1,532 feet high, you will see one of America's great land-and-ocean vistas; Frenchman Bay, deep enough for many of the biggest ocean vessels, lies below you; the Porcupine Islands look like ducks swimming out into the blue Atlantic. On the other side Katahdin, the great peak of the Northwoods, and the outline of New Hampshire's White Mountains will be visible on a clear day. The trails of the park will lead you to many a point where you stand on top of a cliff rising abruptly out of the sea, or to crystal-clear mountain lakes where wildflowers thrive between lichen-clad rocks. At migration time the land and sea birds of the north form mammoth congregations here.

J. P. MORGAN AND THE PIRATES. On the eastern shore of the island, Bar Harbor is Maine's most famous vacation spot. Once the pretentious summer outpost of eastern society, it is now one of the last resorts where dozens of huge Edwardian mansions are still kept up. Bar Harbor had its heyday when J. P. Morgan's yacht *Corsair* lay in the harbor, and the resort's Pot and Kettle Club represented 85% of America's wealth. A cruise through Mount Desert waters is strongly recommended; there is a northern frontier atmosphere over the cold, choppy waves, the lonely wooded islands, the seals and the porpoises, the ospreys and a rare bald

THE FOURTEENFOLD COASTLINE. If you fly from the northernmost to the southernmost point of the Maine shore, your speedometer will indicate that you have traveled less than 250 miles. If you sail along the coastline, you will ride for 3,500 miles. There is a geological explanation for this "folded" coast. A mountainous country has gradually sunk into the sea, the valleys have become inlets and bays and the outlying mountain peaks have turned into islands. This grandiose seascape begins with restraint at the southern end around the well-known resorts of Kennebunkport and Old Orchard Beach but gathers momentum at Portland. The white spray of the breakers that dashes over the granite cliffs of Portland Head Light has a wild, rugged power. A boat ride around Portland's Casco Bay has more amiable overtones. The rocky islands on which the boat calls are pleasant resorts. From Brunswick,

OUR MOST RUGGED STRETCH of ATLANTIC SHORE

Maine lobsters are preferred by gourmets.

Pemaquid Lighthouse mirrored in a tidal pool.

eagle surveying the scene from a high dead branch. One sight delights the imagination: every so often two granite promontories jut out into the ocean, thunderously sprayed with white foam, and between them, secretly tucked away between high granite walls, there lies a short, white sandy beach, a silent cove that is the perfect setting for a swords-and-treasure pirate story.

FROM THE SOUTH SEAS TO VACATION LAND. The Maine coast has more to offer than just natural beauty; about its piers and ports, its villages and towns there hovers that very real atmosphere that only history can create. It is a history far more fascinating than that of battles and diplomatic disputes: it is the true story of a worldwide shipping empire that is no more. America's first vessels were built here, on quiet coves, with native timber. White pine boards were the prime export article and could be sold at great profit even in jungle-covered Sumatra and Java. So Maine-made square-riggers with Maine captains and Maine crews carried their Maine lumber over the seven seas and came home from China and Hawaii, the East Indies and the South Seas with spices and silks and oriental wares. Sometimes one lucky trip made a man rich. In the 1820's Bangor was the world's leading lumber port, with a waterfront life that rivaled that of San Francisco's Barbary Coast in gold rush days. Then suddenly the great venture collapsed because of steamboats, the depletion of the forests and the lack of a populous hinterland. But there were still lobstering and fishing and farming, a good way of life, until in the twentieth century a new cash crop was thrust upon the coast — tourism. Natural scenic beauty, ideal fishing and sailing, fresh lobster dinners, and a native race of hardy and hearty Americans living along the coves and the docks combined to attract vacationers and travelers by the thousands. When the state introduced automobile license plates that proclaimed Maine as Vacationland, nobody protested but the undertakers. They did not think that such propaganda would be dignified on a hearse carrying a corpse to the cemetery; for them plates were made with the simple legend Maine.

19

The White Mountains

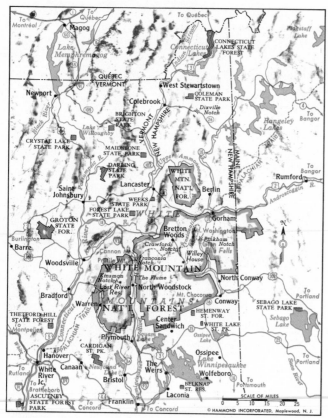

known since the days of exploration; and they towered in the heart of New England which in the nineteenth century was the most articulate section of the country.

COGS AND NOTCHES. The charm of the White Mountains lies in a perfect integration of civilization — little white churches, well-kept valley farms, neat villages gay with flowers — and nature in the grand manner — endless wooded hills, towering granite peaks, rushing mountain streams, sky-blue lakes. Today most visitors on a New Hampshire holiday cross and re-cross the White Mountains on various highways. After a ride through the foothills, the first group of famous sights is ready for inspection north of Woodstock around Franconia Notch (notch being the Yankee word for pass). There is the Flume, a deep canyon with vertical granite walls through which a cold mountain stream makes a spraying and gurgling 700-foot dash. The Lost River Reservation will take you into magnificent mountain scenery and through a series of caverns with such extravagant names as Cave of Lost Souls and the Judgment Hall of Pluto. Behind Profile Lake, 1,925 feet above the water, the rocky outline of the Old Man of the Mountain's stern face is clear and distinct, a landmark of New England and the inspiration of a classic. To get an impression of the surrounding mountainous countryside, a ride on the aerial tramway to the top of Cannon Mountain is recommended. This is a more conservative conveyance than the White Mountain chair lifts which serve sightseers in summertime and skiers during the winter. Proceeding in a northeasterly direction, Crawford Notch was the scene of New England's most famous landslide. The Willey cabin stood there; when in 1826 during a terrible storm the mountain behind gave way and roared down toward the farmhouse, the nine residents rushed out to seek shelter in the notch. All were caught in the maelstrom and literally ground to death while a boulder divided the slide just above the cabin and left it untouched. All would have lived had they stayed inside. The tragic irony of the incident has been recorded in a Hawthorne story. At Bretton Woods the famous Mt. Washington Hotel is decoratively surrounded by the Presidential Range, and nearby the cogwheel railroad to the summit of Mt. Washington may be boarded. Of the world's railways this is the oddest (its toy-like pusher-locomotives have tilted boilers to remain horizontal on a slope), the shortest (about 3 miles), and possibly the most expensive (if figured in cents per mile). It is also one of the oldest, opened in 1869, and one of the most ingenious; it was the first one to use the cogwheel principle which later was copied dozens of times in the Alps. On a clear day New England's tallest mountain (6,288 feet) offers a view of 150 miles in every direction.

"THE SECOND-GREATEST SHOW ON EARTH."

These were Mr. Barnum's words when he admired the view from the summit of Mt. Washington. Other celebrities were more subtle but not less lavish in their praise of New Hampshire's White Mountains. Thoreau and Agassiz, Daniel Webster and Washington Irving, Dana and Emerson traveled there and told the world; Hawthorne was inspired to write "The Great Stone Face" and Longfellow to compose his ode on "Chocorua's Curse"; Whittier penned his White Mountain Ballads, and others collected the Indian legends and the ancient stories about the ranges. At a time when America's other mountains just stood, the peaks of New Hampshire were glorified loudly throughout the land. The reasons for this early recognition were threefold: the White Mountains were indeed beautiful; they were easily accessible and, since on clear days they could even be seen from ships at sea, they had been

AMERICA'S FIRST HILLS and FOREST RESORT

It's a stormy peak, and the worst wind ever recorded anywhere on earth was recorded here. In April of 1934 it once blew at the rate of 231 miles an hour. Back at the base, you proceed through Crawford Notch around the range to Glen Ellis Falls and Pinkham Notch where an 8-mile toll road for automobiles leads to the top of Mt. Washington, with numerous hairpin turns that offer broad mountain vistas. Over various trails thousands of people climb to the summit. Throughout the White Mountains there are hundreds of miles of trails, supplemented by a chain of huts where simple food and lodging may be obtained along the trail. From Pinkham Notch on, the ride north leads into New Hampshire's forest primeval; at Dixville Notch the wilderness is pointed up by The Balsams, a large luxury hotel. The area from Conway to Berlin is a skier's paradise. The Nansen Ski Club of Berlin, established in 1872, is the oldest in the nation.

THE WREATH OF LAKES. It seems quite proper that these amiable mountains should be surrounded by groups of lovely lakes in whose clear waters wooded hills are mirrored. The scattering of small lakes and the Connecticut River in the west; the Connecticut Lakes in the north; Sebago and the Rangeley lakes of Maine; the myriad of New Hampshire lakes, including Winnipesaukee, the largest, and the Ossipees in the east; and lakes Squam and Newfound in the south combine to make a perfect stage for the Great White Hills. Winnipesaukee, an Indian name meaning the smile of the Great Spirit, has become a thriving tourist center. It has natural beauty with great expanses of blue water, a shoreline of 183 miles, 274 tree-shaded islands and the dark blue outline of the Presidential Range as a backdrop. Excursion boats tour the lake. At The Weirs there are water carnivals, outboard races and parachute jumps.

Fall in New Hampshire is a color festival.

Vacation fun at Lake Winnipesaukee.

NEW HAMPSHIRE DEPT. OF RESOURCES AND ECONOMIC DEVELOPMENT

TYLER PRESS-LACONIA, N. H.

The Green Mountains

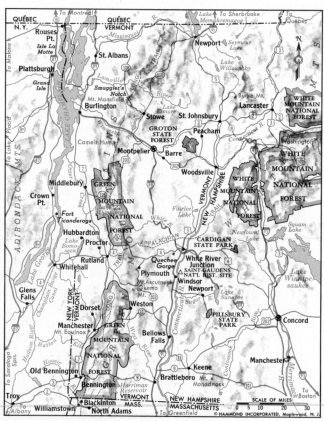

tangles set off by light hedgerows or heavy, golden-gray stone fences. In the valleys the gables of white farmhouses or white church steeples rise above green trees, and weathered covered bridges cross placid streams. This is not the wild, untamed beauty of the West, but a perfect harmony between soil and man, landscape and village; the Vermonters achieved it in only two centuries.

CATAMOUNT AND SMUGGLERS' NOTCH. No great cities intrude here. Driving to the capital, for instance, you see a golden dome suddenly emerging above the hills and trees, and you are at the state capital of Montpelier. In the south, Bennington is an interesting town, especially Old Bennington, which is west of the modern business district. It is a veritable outdoor museum with such attractions as the world's tallest stone battle monument, which towers 306 feet above the ridge of the hill. The First Congregational Church on the Old Burying Ground is one of New England's most beautiful buildings, and the Catamount Monument — the bronze figure of a large mountain lion — recalls tumultuous frontier days. This was the site of the Catamount Tavern whose sign was a stuffed catamount on a tall pole, the cat's wicked bare teeth facing the New York border. Here the Green Mountain Boys, excited by rum and hard cider, bragged that they could take Fort Ticonderoga from the British, which they did. To the north, Manchester is the foremost summer resort of the Green Mountains, a lovely spot for those who appreciate a quiet, cultured setting. A trip up the Mt. Equinox Skyline Drive, just west of Manchester, affords an excellent view of the surround-

Ancient covered bridges survive in Vermont.

"BEAUTIFUL, LOVELY, HARMONIOUS, EXQUISITE, GRACEFUL." These adjectives, descriptive of Vermont's Green Mountain landscape, do not come from the Chamber of Commerce but from Dorothy Canfield Fisher, the well-known writer who, as a Vermonter, should be inclined toward understatement. Perhaps it is for that reason that she calls the reader's attention to the fact that she does not say "sublime, magnificent, gorgeous or spectacular." Such words, she feels, should be reserved for the Rockies. Surely all visitors will agree with her, particularly those who do not just hurry through the Green Mountain country but stay for a while. The finest place to enjoy the essence of Vermont is the ridge of a hill pasture where you can sit down under a tall elm, with a "four town view" beneath. The horizon is a rhythmic chain of mountains. The fields and meadows are green and yellow rec-

22

STONE-FENCED PASTURES and ELM-SHADED FARMS

ing countryside. Burlington, partly a creation of those fascinating Vermont brothers Ethan and Ira Allen, lies on the three terraces of a mountain that faces Lake Champlain. On the highest level the campus of the University of Vermont offers a splendid panorama of the town and the broad expanse of the blue lake; beyond its waters the Adirondacks stand against the sky in light and dark blue sheets like a Chinese watercolor. Watching the sunset from here, William Dean Howells compared it to the sunset over the Bay of Naples, but he gave the crown to Burlington. To the east, Stowe has become the Green Mountains' ski center; it lies at the southern end of the Smugglers Notch Road, once a thoroughfare notorious for the duty-free importation of goods from Canada, and in the shadow of Mount Mansfield, with a height of 4,393 feet, the tallest peak of the chain. Ideal hill contours and plenty of snow combine with chair lifts, ski jumps and pleasant inns to make Stowe one of the most popular winter sports resorts in the East.

GRANITE, MARBLE, MAPLE SUGAR. Among the material contributions of these mountains to the country at large, granite and marble must be mentioned; both occur in seemingly inexhaustible quantities. Barre is the granite center and Proctor near Rutland the great marble producer; quarrying operations are fascinating to watch, and it is well worthwhile to visit one of the granite or marble "sheds," as the mills are called, to watch the sawing, carving and polishing of the stone. The Vermont stonecutters are interesting people: the granite workers are largely Scotsmen, who erected a fine statue

of Robert Burns in Barre, and among the marble cutters there are many Italian-Americans whose ancestors worked in Carrara, Italy; they are the descendants of quarrymen who shaped marble columns for the Forum of Augustus Imperator in Rome. Even better known than Green Mountain stone is Vermont maple sugar, although these days the production rather runs to maple syrup. The "harvest" begins in mid-March; a forty-year-old maple will yield ten gallons of sap annually.

CHARACTER RATHER THAN CASH. One of the best features of a Green Mountain vacation is the chance of getting acquainted with Vermonters. In their communities the latter never had a "gentry," and they never kept slaves, so they remained a very homogeneous group of American folks in the best and most democratic sense of the word. When one of their sons, Calvin Coolidge, was to take his presidential oath of office, he did so in Plymouth in the Coolidge homestead across the street from the family's general-store-and-post-office building. His father, a justice of the peace, officiated by the light of a kerosene lamp. Reporters from New York and Washington had to sleep on cots requisitioned from the jail that night — an arrangement reflecting a sense of fun. Such dry humor shines through numerous Vermont stories. An Iowa farmer, for instance, once watched a Vermont ploughman and remarked that at home in Iowa they would never bother to work a rock soil like that. "May be so," the Green Mountain man replied. "Sometimes I wonder myself how we make a living here and even save enough money to buy mortgages on Iowa farms."

The peace and silence of Cambridge, Vermont.

Vermont villages are often lively ski centers.

Boston

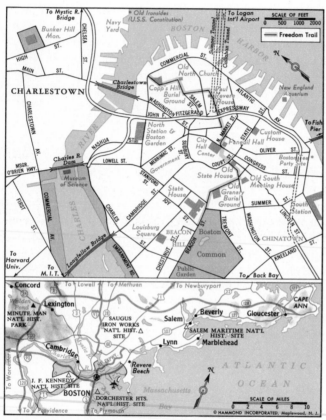

branch of his family and to the tenth that graduated from Harvard. There may be innumerable caricatures of stuffy and overly proper Bostonians, but it is because of their wealth, public spirit and cultural interest that Boston has one of the world's finest symphony orchestras, that its museums contain unique art treasures, that Harvard is our country's oldest, richest and most distinguished university and that Massachusetts Institute of Technology is one of America's leading engineering schools.

THE FREEDOM TRAIL. As a sightseeing town Boston is historic rather than scenic, although the approach from the sea presents the city quite handsomely, especially when the sun is setting behind the towering skyline. Since most of Boston's historic shrines are concentrated in the compact downtown district, it is recommended to see them on a walking tour which is marked by easily followed pointers. The "Freedom Trail" begins on Boston Common, the old cow pasture and training ground where stocks, pillory and gallows once stood. Your next step will be the "New" State House with its golden dome and its Hall of Flags; in the House of Representatives hangs the symbol of the coast — the Sacred Cod. The Old Granary Burial Ground is a hall-of-fame cemetery; you will see there the graves of Samuel Adams, John Hancock, Paul Revere and Peter Faneuil, the parents of Benjamin Franklin, and Mother Goose — a lady named Mary Goose. Old South Meeting House with its 180-foot steeple was the scene of violent revolutionary oratory, and the Boston Tea Party was planned there. The Old State House, dating from 1713, is an interesting historical and marine museum; the scene of the Boston Massacre is nearby. Faneuil Hall is a free meeting hall open to any group of citizens; many loud and angry protests against the British were voiced there. The weather vane of its steeple is a Boston curiosity: it represents a big grasshopper. The Paul Revere House, built c. 1677, is the oldest in Boston; with its overhanging second story and its diamond-shaped panes it is reminiscent of medieval England. The Old North Church was the lookout from which the British approach was signaled with the help of lanterns: "One if by land, and two if by sea, and I on the opposite shore will be." Ironically, the bells that hung above the warning lanterns are inscribed: "We are the first ring of bells cast for the British Empire in North America." Nearby, but not part of the Freedom Trail, is Copp's Hill Burial Ground.

SWAN BOATS AND OLD IRONSIDES. Another special Boston sight is the Public Garden with its labeled trees and bright flower beds. It is adjacent to the

A COMPLEX PERSONALITY. Ralph Waldo Emerson called Boston "the town which was appointed to lead the civilization of North America." Oliver Wendell Holmes felt that more than any other city "Boston has opened and kept open the turnpikes that lead straight to free thought and free speech and free deeds." Lincoln Steffens thought differently. "Boston," he wrote, "has carried the practice of hypocrisy to the nth degree of refinement and failure." Such conflicting views about "America's Mother of Freedom" are quite the rule, and the city's patterns are so complex that no mere visitor can hope to analyze the Boston spirit. The descendants of the Puritans are a small minority by now, but the Lowells and Reveres, Adamses and Cabots are still very much alive and strong in finance and politics. Former U.S. Senator Leverett Saltonstall, for instance, belonged to the twelfth generation of the American

NO LONGER the HUB, but STILL a CITY of CHARACTER

In Lexington, west of Boston, the Minute Man still stands on guard.

Faneuil Hall is a free meetinghouse; so many anti-British assemblies were held here before the Revolution that it is called the Cradle of Liberty.

Common on "made land" that was once a marsh along the Charles and is still called the Back Bay. A feature of the park is a ride on a swan boat. A ship of a different nature may be seen at the Navy Yard across the Charlestown Bridge: *Old Ironsides,* the U.S. frigate *Constitution,* may be inspected there, conserved in all its glory. Lovers of architecture will enjoy Beacon Hill, on Chestnut Street north of the Common, and Louisburg Square. The Boston "Brahmins" live or used to live here.

PHILOSOPHERS AND CAPTAINS COURAGEOUS.

Across the Charles River in Cambridge the Harvard Yard is well worth visiting; the University Museum's collection of glass flowers, authentic in every detail, and the Fogg Art Museum are famous. In Lexington, the pleasant suburb of Minuteman tradition, the Revolutionary War began, and at Concord Bridge the shot heard around the world was fired. Another of Concord's claims to fame can be read on the gravestones of its Sleepy Hollow Cemetery: Emerson, Thoreau, Alcott and Hawthorne are buried there. In its own way, Concord was once an American Florence or Weimar. Trans-

cendentalism and nature, Tanglewood Tales and Walden (the drowsy pond is not far from town) were then the topics of the day. North of Boston the city of Salem has the embarrassing memories of the witch trials — the house at 310½ Essex Street is still haunted by the witches' ghosts, they say — and the glorious memories of the clipper ship days. Its old sea captains' houses are, architecturally, among the country's finest buildings. The Maritime Museum and the House of Seven Gables of Hawthorne's classic are also located there. The rock-fringed harbor of Marblehead is the yachting capital of the Northeast; its winding streets are lined with elms and hollyhocks. Race Week at the end of July is a great water sports event. On Cape Ann, a resort area that combines ruggedness (huge boulders, promontories, coves) with gentleness (flowers, villas, woods), the city of Gloucester has been one of America's greatest fishing ports for 300 years. Its early sailors to the Grand Banks found a magnificent chronicler in Rudyard Kipling, whose "Captains Courageous" has become a classic. More than 10,000 Gloucester men who never returned from the sea are commemorated by a statue overlooking the harbor.

25

Plymouth and Cape Cod

Where British America began — a replica of the Mayflower *at Plymouth.*

THE GREAT ADVENTURE. Plymouth Rock is almost certainly a myth, not history. But that does not matter in the least. All Americans, who see the famous stepping-stone with the "1620" carved into it, feel that they are standing at one of the deep-reaching foundations on which America is built. This spot has been the scene of agony and humility, and for that we remember it proudly. At first only 17 men went ashore here, the others stayed aboard ship where snow covered the decks, and scurvy and ship fever raged. Between Christmas and March nearly half the company died. The Pilgrims had a few friends, though, and to one of them, the Indian chief Massasoit, a fine bronze statue has been erected on top of Cole's Hill near the Rock. But the true significance of this hill is expressed by its sculptured sarcophagus: to this spot the newcomers carried the corpses of their people at night, buried them secretly and planted corn on their graves. For terror was in their hearts, and they did not want the Indians to know that so many were dying. The cradle of the first white child born here, some rare old portraits and other interesting objects may be inspected at Pilgrim Hall. *Mayflower II,* a copy of the original ship of 1620, is docked nearby. Plimoth Plantation is a full-scale replica of the early Pilgrim colony.

THE YANKEE SPIRIT AND THE BOHEMIAN TOUCH. Cape Cod has the shape of a man's arm bent upward to show off its muscles. The arm is 65 miles long, 20 miles broad at the shoulder and 2 miles wide at the wrist. It is a seaside resort area that could hardly be improved upon: there are gleaming white dunes, lovely marshlands, dark evergreen forests, numerous inlets for sailing, and hundreds of freshwater lakes. Some stretches, particularly at the elbow, are bleak with high, lonely bluffs; others, especially on the south shore, are well-groomed with sea vistas framed in roses and tall trees, and with yacht clubs and golf courses. This sunny and breezy peninsula increases its regular population fivefold each summer, and since the visitors are the main source of income, a certain commercialism is unavoidable. To preserve the natural beauty of the beaches and seascapes, the cliffs and lighthouses, the Cape Cod National Seashore has been created, an area which will eventually include about 27,000 acres from Chatham to Provincetown. Such venerable old Cape towns as Sandwich (birthplace of the famous Sandwich glass, now a collector's item) and Barnstable, Woods Hole (a world center for oceanographic research) and Falmouth, Hyannis and Chatham still have a great deal of the genuine Yankee spirit. In contrast, Provincetown, at the tip of the peninsula, has a different though nonetheless intriguing atmosphere.

BEACHES, WHARVES and the WEB of HISTORY

Its regular population, the fishermen and storekeepers, are not to any extent of British-American stock but rather Portuguese from the Azores whose ancestors worked on Yankee whaling ships and settled here. The summer population is also different: it has been of an artistic bent ever since the first art school was opened there at the turn of the century. More than a dozen such institutions are in existence now, and inevitably the real artists have been joined by pseudo-artists, amateurs and hangers-on in search of the hippie life rather than art. The well-known playhouse also exerts a considerable influence on the summer colony, and the total result is that of an animated Greenwich Village.

FAMOUS VISITORS' ROSTER: FROM LEIF ERICSON TO EUGENE O'NEILL. You cannot see history, of course, but somehow it is in the air; the fact that history has often touched Cape Cod is one of the peninsula's main attractions. Long Viking ships with tall carved dragons on the bow may have landed at these shores half a millennium before Columbus officially discovered the New World. The man who charted the Cape's harbors in 1606 was Champlain. The name Cape Cod emerged from Bartholomew Gosnold's voyage in 1602. Captain John Smith visited the area in 1614. The Pilgrim Fathers, as everybody knows, landed in Provincetown before they settled across the bay at Plymouth. One of the early tourists on the Cape was Thoreau, and his report on what he saw is a classic. After that, the visiting celebrities were legion, from Daniel Webster to Grover Cleveland. In 1916 a future Nobel Prize winner, Eugene O'Neill, was living in an abandoned coast guard station near Provincetown, and one of his first plays, "Bound East for Cardiff," was staged in a fish house on a wharf. Since the drama takes place on a ship, and since the audience could hear the harbor water splash around the poles beneath their improvised theater, the realism was unsurpassed.

THE SHAPELY SEA WITCH. Of course, the Cape has also a wonderful folklore of its own. Many of its yarns run to the supernatural and the humorous. One of the most colorful, semi-legendary figures was Ichabod Paddock, the first great whaling captain. Once, when chasing whales near Nantucket, he noticed that a big bull whale seemed immune; no harpoon took hold. So the captain decided to investigate and swam through the huge throat of the beast into its stomach. To his surprise he discovered that a shapely young sea witch with red hair and green eyes lived there. She invited him to stay for the night, and he did. From then on he made his excursions into the bull whale two or three times a week until Mrs. Paddock decided to stop her husband's amorous aberrations. She persuaded another skipper to harpoon the whale with a sterling silver harpoon against which the witch was powerless. So the bull was caught and cut open. What they found inside were these ominous objects: a strand of red seaweed like a head of a woman's hair, two oval green beach plums, and two jellyfish the color of human flesh.

Cape Cod as Thoreau saw it. The Great Beach near Pamet.

New York City

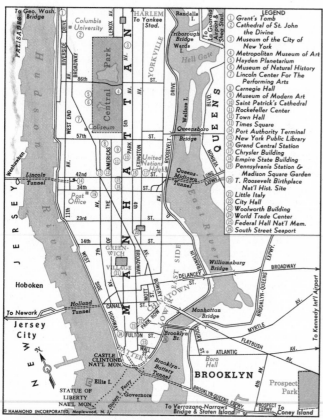

LEGEND

1. Grant's Tomb
2. Cathedral of St. John the Divine
3. Museum of the City of New York
4. Metropolitan Museum of Art
5. Hayden Planetarium
6. Museum of Natural History
7. Lincoln Center For The Performing Arts
8. Carnegie Hall
9. Museum of Modern Art
10. Saint Patrick's Cathedral
11. Rockefeller Center
12. Town Hall
13. Times Square
14. Port Authority Terminal
15. New York Public Library
16. Grand Central Station
17. Chrysler Building
18. Empire State Building
19. Pennsylvania Station & Madison Square Garden
20. T. Roosevelt Birthplace Nat'l Hist. Site
21. Little Italy
22. City Hall
23. Woolworth Building
24. World Trade Center
25. Federal Hall Nat'l Mem.
26. South Street Seaport

© HAMMOND INCORPORATED, Maplewood, N. J.

THE FIRST GLANCE. Libraries could be filled with the books, guides and articles that have been written about that "ragged purple dream, the wonderful, cruel, enchanting, bewildering, fatal, great city," as O. Henry expressed it. In the limited space available here we present only a few suggestions to the visitor who is interested in the atmosphere and the mood of the city rather than in a great many details. Your first impression of New York will be disheartening if you approach it by rail from the north through endless blocks of factories and tenements. It will be unfavorable if, en route to New York, you cross the Jersey meadows by train or car, and from the garbage dumps and the smoking factories a formidable stench assaults your nostrils. It will be a pleasant surprise if you ride on one of the parkways and out of a bright forest landscape you drive into a majestic river scene, the Hudson and

the Palisades to your right, the big city to your left. And it will be a vision of unearthly beauty if you approach New York from the sea and watch the skyline and the Statue of Liberty emerge from the morning mist.

THE SECOND GLANCE. For a general survey of the city two excursions are recommended. First take a trip to the top of one of the city's tallest buildings. From the 102nd story of the Empire State Building or the Observation Deck of the RCA Building you will have a stunning view of Manhattan. The World Trade Center, the world's tallest building until the completion of the Sears, Roebuck & Co. building in Chicago, will have an observation deck in 1974. Although, of course, New York is very much larger than the island, it is Manhattan's huge ship of rock below you that is the visitor's New York. This gigantic vessel, loaded with magnificent buildings and millions of human beings from every corner of the earth, points toward the ocean as if setting out on its journey into the future. Second, the circle tour by boat around Manhattan will offer you an obstructed view of many a famous "castle in the sky," will give you a feel of the harbor when you hear "the hoarse notes of the great ships in the river," and will give you a close-up view of New York's famous bridges, particularly the double-decked George Washington Bridge, the historic Brooklyn Bridge and, in the distance, the huge span of the Verrazano-Narrows Bridge.

STREETS THAT ARE IDEAS. The best sights are free in New York, as everywhere else. Just walk along the streets whose names are known around the world. Every avenue has a reputation of its own, and it is a pleasant pastime to check on it. Is Broadway, the stretch around Times Square, gaudy and vulgar? You look at the over-loud neon signs, the shooting galleries, the pornographic movies and the cheap souvenir stores, and you agree. Then you glance down one of Broadway's side streets in the theater district and read the famous names on marquee after marquee. You wind your way through the well dressed, festive crowds and cross the street between slowly moving taxis where a policeman on horseback surveys the scene like a general, and you will register your impressions as civilized and up-to-date. Is Fifth Avenue "like a smart woman, clad in the newest and most elegant raiment, perfumed and furred and bejeweled, modern and self-assured to her gleaming fingertips," as Silas Spitzer described it? Fifth Avenue names like Tiffany, Lord and Taylor, Van Cleef and Arpels, Bergdorf Goodman, the Plaza and a host of others have indeed a measure of glamour. Central Park is a resort in itself, and its southern part a favorite of camera enthusiasts. You can photograph its line of

AMERICA'S FABULOUS ISLAND

gleaming skyscrapers framed by the branches of elms and maples, or mirrored in a lake, or jutting out beyond rugged stone cliffs that seem to be transplanted from the Rockies. Then there are the foreign sections. Unfortunately, as time goes by and new American-born generations grow up, these neighborhoods lose more and more of their native flavor. Chinatown around Mott Street offers good Chinese food and oriental imports. The German section in Yorkville, at the eastern end of 86th Street, still has German cafés with Viennese waltzes, but there, as in the Italian and Spanish quarters, the food display is almost the only specialty left.

BUILDINGS THAT ARE SYMBOLS. Every visitor to New York is bound for Rockefeller Center, and rightly so. Its size is monumental; there are more than a million door keys, lush roof gardens, a theater seating 6,200 people, ten miles of underground corridors, and a variety of stores and restaurants, not to mention the skating rink and the Rockettes. This building complex is a truly American creation; it stands on land owned by a great university (Columbia) and was erected by the heirs of an oil magnate. Even more magnificent, architecturally and culturally, is the Lincoln Center for the Performing Arts with the Metropolitan Opera House, Philharmonic Hall, the Vivian Beaumont Theatre and other buildings. The center reflects America's artistic leadership which extends far beyond our borders over much of the globe. Also a tour of the United Nations buildings on the East River is a must. Camera buffs and harbor fans like the ferry ride to Staten Island. As to New York as the city of music, the drama, the opera, the nightclubs and of excellent eating places, the latest number of "Cue" or the "New Yorker" will furnish the desired information. Of the town's more than fifty museums the Metropolitan Museum of Art and the American Museum of Natural History are best-known. But whatever your special interest, whether it is numismatics or Indian totem poles, you will find a top-ranking museum collection of your hobby in New York.

The United Nations Building — center of the world.

The Hudson Valley

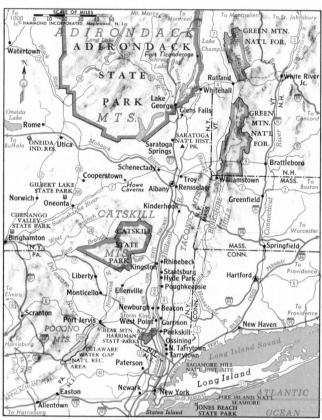

Excursion boats ply the Hudson River where Fulton's "Clermont" initiated steamboat travel some 170 years ago.

THE AMERICAN RHINE. The likeness between the Hudson and the great European artery has often been noted: the broad current, the mountain-lined banks, the pleasing perspectives at each bend, the sloping vineyards and the old legends and folk tales are of a similar nature. Around the turn of the century some wealthy shore proprietors carried the Old World touch even further and erected on the river's banks medieval castles of spurious antiquity; some built "ruins" on their estates as fitting ornaments for the hills by the water. Both the turrets and the ruins were a reflection of our new, uncultured wealth. In fact, the Hudson is as beautifully and interestingly American a river as can be found anywhere on the continent. On its rather short course it ties together two typically American elements: the wilderness and the metropolis, the untouched, primeval nature and the vanguard of civilization. It accomplishes this by

rising on the highest peak of the Adirondacks, Mt. Marcy, at Lake Tear-of-the-Clouds; by flowing between high mountains through a wild country of rocks and trees where only hunters and lumberjacks touch its shores; and by gradually maturing into a great river that forms the nation's busiest, skyscraper-studded port. Downstream where the piers, the transatlantic freighters and the smokestacks begin to crowd out nature, the river presents, as a last gesture of independence, a steep wall of rock: the rampart-like Palisades.

EXPLORING THE HUDSON VALLEY. It is easy enough to do so. On both banks of the river highways lead north to Saratoga and Lake George, the Adirondacks and Montréal. The Sleepy Hollow Restorations reflect the valley's history; they include Washington Irving's "Sunnyside" in Tarrytown, an idyll "as full of angles and corners as an old cocked hat"; Philipsburg Manor in North Tarrytown, an early trading center and the seat of an estate which once extended 20 miles along the river; and Van Cortlandt Manor, another historical Hudson River estate. Opposite Newburgh, the summit of Mt. Beacon is reached by an inclined railway.

30

A PEOPLE'S PLAYGROUND on a PATRICIAN RIVER

It offers a fine panorama of the Hudson Valley. Just south of Mt. Beacon, at Garrison, the beautiful mansion of Boscobel is the scene of a "sound and light" performance; it tells the story of the valley on Wednesday and Saturday evenings during the summer. The Hyde Park estate of the Roosevelts with the Franklin D. Roosevelt Library is the nation's storehouse of Rooseveltiana. Rhinebeck has a lovely distinction: it is America's violet capital, growing most of the violets marketed in this country; in springtime a veritable cloud of fragrance sometimes hovers over town and river. On the western bank north of the Palisades, Bear Mountain and Harriman State Parks are popular excursion goals. Farther north, the Storm King Highway and West Point offer some of the most magnificent views of the river, and beyond Kingston the Catskill Mountains beckon; there in the dark of the night Rip Van Winkle occasionally still bowls. Where picturesque ridges and wooded hills meet the swift waters arose the Hudson River School of Painting, whose members emphasized the wild romanticism of the river. Beyond Albany your road will leave the Hudson for a while near Saratoga Springs, one of America's oldest resorts. Its famous racetrack became popular after the Civil War. The spa and the mineral waters enjoy a wide reputation. The Saratoga Performing Arts Center is the summer home of the New York City Ballet and the Philadelphia Orchestra. You catch up with the Hudson at Glens Falls. In one way the river was more colorful a hundred years ago: it swarmed with sloops and schooners of varied types of sail and paddle-wheelers of every description. Today an occasional tanker, a barge or a rare white excursion steamer are the only craft enlivening its calm surface.

AN AMERICAN EPIC. The history of the valley is not exactly one of "riches to rags," but it began with a string of great land holdings in the feudal Old World manner and ended with a string of public parks along the lower river and of public camping grounds in the upper river country where people swim and play baseball, cook and picnic, relax for a day or vacation for a week. The democratic trend is new, though. For more than 200 years the aristocrats dominated the Hudson River scene: the Dutch patroons, people like the van Cortlandts and van Rensselaers, and the British lords of the manor who succeeded them, like the Livingstons and Morrises, built themselves imposing castles and ruled like absolute monarchs over their crude and not always compliant peasants. When the latter wasted their time by racing horses on the streets and their money by loitering in the low-ceilinged, small-windowed stone taverns instead of paying their rent, they were quickly thrown into debtor's prison. After the Revolution this feudalism vanished, and the wealthy merchants of New York built their fine country houses along the Hudson, large Victorian villas with superb views and patrician gardens. Most of these houses are still there, though no longer appreciated by some of their modern heirs, and often the mansions have been converted into schools, clubs or hospitals — institutions which together with the new parks finally turn the river's beauty over to the common man.

The lovely hills of the Headless Horseman — a famous resort area in the Catskill Mountains.

Our victory at Saratoga (1777) marked the turning point of the Revolution.

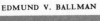

The Adirondacks

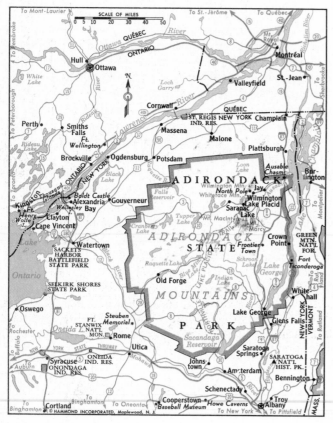

the 150-mile canoe route from Old Forge to Loon Lake. Here the Reverend William Henry Harrison Murray wrote his "Adventures in the Wilderness" in 1869, the first book to praise the wild beauty of the Adirondacks; it was so convincing that it resulted in the so-called Murray Rush, the beginning of the influx of tourists and sportsmen. To this day there are tracts so rugged that they could not be exploited by the lumber companies, and stands of hemlock, birch and spruce tower on the ridges in their primeval splendor. In the high-peak area, Frontier Town attracts the younger set. Toward the southeast on Lake Champlain, the restored Fort Ticonderoga with its heavy masonry walls, dark dungeon and big cannon presents an impressive contrast to the little wooden palisade forts of the frontier. It was built by the French in 1755, captured by the British in 1759, by the Green Mountain Boys in 1775, and recaptured by the British in 1777.

THE ST. MORITZ OF AMERICA. In the northern part of the Adirondacks a number of attractions draw thousands of visitors. Near Lake Champlain the Ausable Chasm is a deep gorge where walks may be enjoyed on galleries cut into the rock high above the Ausable River, and there are boat rides in the rushing current. To the west at Jay the Adirondacks present themselves in all their grandeur: their highest peaks — Whiteface, Wilmington, Marcy and MacIntyre — are towering around you. At Wilmington a serpentine toll road will take you to the top of Whiteface Mountain which is also a winter sports center. On a clear day the view encompasses Lake Champlain, the Green Mountains and the whole northern section up to Mt. Royal in Canada; the pall of smoke in the sky marks Montréal. At the foot of Whiteface, Lake Placid is a famous all-year resort; because of its fine hotels and its ideal winter sports facilities it has been called the St. Moritz of America. During the cold months Mirror Lake, in the center of the village, is a sight to behold in a mountain landscape of white snow and dark green forests. Conditions for skating, skiing, dogsledding and ski-joring are excellent, and its bobsled run is a unique feature; constructed for the 1932 Winter Olympic Games and maintained by the state, it descends for a mile with 16 curves, some with almost vertical banks. At times a speed of 90 m.p.h. has been approached. Saranac Lake, once a health center for TB patients, is now a pleasant tourist town.

NOT 1,000, BUT ALMOST 2,000. West of the Adirondacks, where Lake Ontario merges with the St. Lawrence River, there is a 60-mile archipelago of forested islands which enchanted even the Indians; they called it Mannitonna, "Garden of the Great Spirit." The French named it "Les Mille Isles" which survives in

NEW YORK'S BACKYARD. That a mountain wilderness should be found at the back door of the nation's greatest city seems strange to European visitors and quite normal to Americans who prize highly the side-by-side of urban civilization and untampered nature. North of New York City, around the headwaters of the Hudson, the Adirondack region contains five mountain chains which run parallel, about 8 miles apart. The main Adirondack range extends 100 miles from Lake Champlain to the Mohawk River; it is crowned by Mt. Marcy, at 5,344 feet the highest peak in the state; 2.27 million acres have been set aside as the Adirondack Forest Preserve to be forever kept as a wild forest land. There are almost 40 public camping grounds in the area, and 750 miles of hiking trails invite hikers. A favorite hunting and fishing area is the region of Blue Mountain and the Raquette lakes along Highway 28 which touches

ROOF of the EMPIRE STATE

"Thousand Islands." The exact number of islands is debatable; is a boulder with one nest of terns an island? In contrast, islands like Wolfe and Wellesley contain estates, clubs and golf courses. This is a great summer playground for lovers of boating; from the hundreds of island homes visiting and shopping has to be done over the intricate net of channels. It is also a paradise for anglers who fish for smallmouth bass, pike, or muskellunge. The currents here are still purest river water; for the St. Lawrence has a granite bottom and so many fresh underwater springs that its waters are renewed every six hours. Lately vacations on houseboats, personally owned or rented locally, have become popular. Tourists enjoy the islands from excursion boats out of Alexandria Bay or Clayton. They get a magnificent view of the archipelago from the 150-feet-high International Bridge. Also Kingston on the Canadian side offers fine land-and-water vistas. At this former capital of Canada the Royal Military College, Canada's West Point, and the restored Fort Henry are interesting.

ROMANTIC RUINS. Late in the nineteenth century the Thousand Islands were an exclusive playground for millionaires. But since the great democratization many of their castles have been converted, boarded up or torn down. The most famous one, Boldt Castle, which looks as if it had been transplanted from the banks of the Rhine, is actually falling into ruins. It was built though never finished by George Boldt, a hotel tycoon who liked to cruise between the islands on his yacht. On board he had a steward with a talent for new creations in cooking; one day the latter pleased his master's taste with a newly invented salad dressing and Mr. Boldt had it introduced at his luxury hotels. The names of both the concoction and the steward have become famous: Thousand Island Dressing and the legendary Oscar of the Waldorf.

EDMUND V. BALLMAN

Right: Small planes are a popular means of transportation for hunters and fishermen in the Adirondacks.

Below right: Even some of the smallest of the Thousand Islands are inhabited, at least at vacation time.

Below: The streams of the Adirondacks offer fishing in a setting of rugged beauty.

CHARLES G. LEES

Niagara Falls

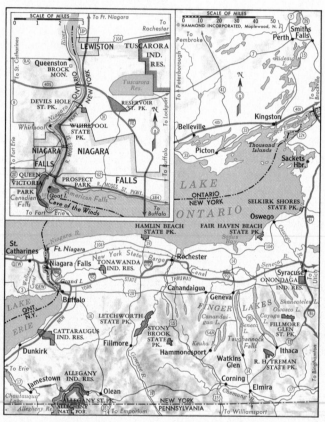

presses on these silent masses of water that suddenly burst into thunder and transform themselves into sheets and columns of spray as they crash into the cauldron 182 feet below. Touched by the sun with rainbow tints, they have stood the test of time and exploration. Many an eastern sightseeing attraction faded away when such wonders as Yellowstone and Grand Canyon were discovered. But the Niagara Falls have remained a wonderful, unmatched sight.

AN INTERNATIONAL PROJECT. Throughout most of the nineteenth century landowning interests exploited the sightseeing public, and not until 1885 did the State of New York succeed in creating a state park around the American Falls. Today the United States and Canada cooperate in presenting Niagara as exhaustively and attractively as possible. On the New York side Prospect Point is the spot from which most visitors have their first look at the 1,000-foot-wide American Falls directly below the ledge, at Goat Island, and the 2,500-foot-wide Canadian Falls beyond. Few realize how much bigger the latter are: 94 per cent of the flow passes over them, and only 6 per cent over the former. From the parking area elevators descend to a network of trails and bridges. The *Maid of the Mist,* a small steamer, takes visitors to all vantage points of the river, and the spray, the mist and the thunder are a good part of the fun. Hennepin Point, where Father Hennepin is said to have drawn his sketch, is the top of a 187-foot precipice, and Goat Island is a 70-acre public park between the American and Canadian falls. From Goat Island helicopter rides are available and you can reach the Cave of the Winds at the bottom of the cataract; rented rubber clothing — coat, hat and boots — will keep you from being drenched. A high-level view of the falls can be obtained from the 282-foot-high tower in Prospect Park.

NOT HEIGHT BUT POWER. When Father Louis Hennepin returned to his native Belgium in 1678, he was asked what in the New World had impressed him most. As an answer he showed a sketch of a gigantic double waterfall which, he said, the Indians called Niagara, i.e., "Thunder of Waters." The sketch was reproduced in a book some years later, and the fame of Niagara spread. Later visitors were more vociferous, and the Niagara Falls became, to the world at large, America's best-known natural phenomenon. It also became the world's standard to measure all other cataracts, no matter where they were. In such comparisons Niagara often seemed to emerge a poor second; the Yosemite Falls, for instance, were discovered to be eleven times as high. It was never the height that made Niagara great but its volume and the fantastic power behind it; somehow one feels that America's inland sea

QUEEN VICTORIA PARK. As nature has laid out the landscape, the real vantage point to view the spectacle is the Canadian shore of the river, and its man-made facilities are superior to those on the American side. From here you have a magnificent view of both falls, and you enjoy that view from a beautiful park with groves of tall trees and beds of fragrant flowers. At night floodlights of various colors play on the falls. This might seem a doubtful attempt at improving on nature, but it is done in a restrained, non-gaudy way and is quite effective. Three miles below the falls the sharp bend of the river creates a pothole whirlpool 1,754 feet wide. An aero car suspended by six cables takes passengers across the pool. Another vantage point to view the whirlpool is the Whirlpool State Park on the American shore. The Robert Moses State Parkway on the American bank of

34

THE MEASURE of ALL CATARACTS

CHARLES G. LEES

EDMUND V. BALLMAN

DOROTHY BACHELLER

Above: The Finger Lakes are one of the East's leading vacationlands, a region of gentle slopes and placid waters.

Above right: Among the numerous natural spectacles of our continent the Horseshoe Falls are still an unmatched sight.

Right: Niagara River Gorge is another landmark of the turbulent Niagara River.

the Niagara River leads to Fort Niagara, which was restored authentically in 1934 to its early eighteenth-century splendor. The gatehouse bears the fleur-de-lis coat of arms of the Bourbons.

THE HAND OF THE GREAT SPIRIT. On the way from Niagara Falls to the Atlantic coast you cross the Finger Lakes region, one of the most attractive sections of New York State. According to Indian lore the Supreme Being pressed his fingers into the soil, and the cavities filled with pure water. Appropriately, the six major lakes still keep their original Indian names: Canandaigua, Seneca, Cayuga, Keuka, Owasco and Skaneateles. This is not a lakes-and-forest wilderness but a lush, cultivated farm country of green hills and lovely valleys. Fields, pastures and vineyards descend to the broad, blue ribbons of the lakes, the green-yellow pattern punctuated by long bushy hedges, groves of trees, the thin threads of country lanes and summer camps ashore. One feature of the area is the abundance

of gorges, ravines and waterfalls. South of Rochester on the Genesee River is Letchworth State Park, the Grand Canyon of the East. Ithaca, at the head of Cayuga Lake and the seat of Cornell University, has several splendid chasms with cascades within its city limits, and nearby the Taughannock Falls make a 215-foot plunge. At the head of Seneca Lake, Watkins Glen State Park offers a 1½-mile climb up the Gorge Trail over 700 steps and numerous bridges to an altitude of 600 feet above the starting point. Auto racing on the Watkins Glen Grand Prix Race Course attracts thousands of tourists. For the summer visitors, water sports are the main attraction, and there are sailing regattas on Skaneateles and Seneca lakes. This region is also dotted with lush vineyards, and at Hammondsport such famous wine producers as Great Western, Taylor, Gold Seal and others offer tours of their wineries and samples of their wines. The Finger Lakes Wine Museum overlooks Lake Keuka; it is housed in a former winery with cellars deeply cut into the hillside.

35

The New Jersey Shore

a network of excellent highways. The resorts' attractions are man-made, and everyone finds something to his taste: amusement parks and taffy stands, luxury hotels and beach clubs, miles of boardwalks and saltwater swimming pools, first-run movie houses and piers with the most famous variety acts, name bands and nightclubs, and racetracks at Monmouth Park and Atlantic City. The centers of this resort life are Long Branch and Asbury Park, the metropolis of Atlantic City with its surging beach front of skyscraper hotels, Wildwood and the quieter Cape May, which has the charm of an old New England seaport. On the northern third of the shore some 20 resort towns have expanded so vigorously that they now form one continuous beach area from Atlantic Highlands to Seaside Park. Everywhere the atmosphere is democratic and without social snobbery; relaxed good will is in the air, and the sea breezes inject zest into life.

PRESIDENTS AND QUEENS. The Jersey shore claims to be the country's oldest seaside resort. When Henry Hudson sailed along this coast in 1609 vacationists could already be observed on the beaches: the Lenni Lenape Indians spent the warm season there, clamming and fishing. Philadelphia society summered in Cape May before George Washington was inaugurated president. Since the cape lies below the Mason-Dixon line, southern aristocrats poured in, too, and in 1847, when Henry Clay dazzled his female admirers on the beach, Cape May was America's leading resort. Presidents Lincoln, Grant, Pierce, Buchanan and Harrison vacationed there, but later in the century Long Branch, at the northern end, took over the distinction. It became the summer home of presidents Grant and Garfield, Hayes and Harrison. Lillie Langtry, Diamond Jim Brady and Lillian Russell turned the town into a showcase at the turn of the century. Woodrow Wilson was the last political celebrity to honor the Jersey shore as a summer resident. After that the Jersey coast turned from presidents to queens with a sigh of relief, and for over fifty years during a September pageant in Atlantic City the country's beauty queen has been crowned with the title of Miss America. For the winner the material awards are considerable, but the core of the prizes are scholarships, stepping-stones to advanced education and careers.

THE DEEP SEA AND THE HIGH SKY. Sportsmen and nature lovers will find the New Jersey shore with its numerous inlets and bays, its canals and islands equally rewarding. Bass fishing is popular, and off the Manasquan Inlet a famous mudhole is the place to troll for bluefish, tuna and bonito. Along the sheltered waters of the center where the tall red and white

MORE THAN MERE BEAUTY. The 125-mile-long shore from Sandy Hook to Cape May is neither the most glamourous nor the most picturesque coast in America. No palms or cypresses line the crest of its dunes, no granite rocks transform the onrushing breakers into spray. Yet, if blue water, white sand and pure ocean air were its only resources, it would probably not lure fifty million vacationers and visitors each year. It has other assets. One is its climate; the Gulf Stream, the great equalizer, flows by at a short distance. Those resorts which, like Atlantic City, lie on an island or a peninsula know no extremes in cold or heat waves. Another advantage is its mid-Atlantic location: it is the oceanic picture window for America's megalopolis, the densely populated, urbanized region which extends from Boston to Baltimore and Washington. From that area millions are siphoned to New Jersey's beaches by

PLAYGROUND and SANCTUARY

Barnegat Light towers above the sea as New Jersey's premier landmark, duck hunting is good in season. In its day the lighthouse warned all the ships at sea of the Barnegat Shoals, the ill-famed graveyard of many vessels. Toward the south the naturalist will encounter lovely landscapes among the dunes where the white untouched sand has been ruffled by the wind into varied, artistic, imaginative and ever-changing patterns. There is a great traffic of birds, with red-winged blackbirds rising from the marshes, ospreys building clumsy nests on poles, sandpipers inspecting the surf and terns darting over the crests of the waves. Near Atlantic City, at the bird sanctuary on Brigantine Island, such interesting species as the whistling swan and the snow goose can be observed at migration time. There is even virgin land left at the coast, a 10-mile strip of the Barnegat Peninsula, Island Beach State Park. Here yellow dunes contrast with dark cedars and pines and the bright green of the holly, the bayberries and beach plums.

Dune deer nibble at the beach heather and ocean birds congregate in masses. Cape May Point is a special haven for ornithologists; it is one of the foremost observation points for birds, and in season a bewildering variety of species pass by on their semi-annual migration.

THE QUIET BACKYARD. Behind the hustle and bustle of the seashore there is a great country of stillness, the Jersey Pine Barrens which you can cross by canoe on miles and miles of streams without seeing a soul; the clear water and the yellow sand, the pines and the birds are your only companions. Here the state owns its largest property, Wharton Forest in south-central New Jersey, an area of 155 square miles. Some 200 years ago a busy industrial oasis flourished among the pines, a center for the manufacture of iron and glass. The Batsto Village Restoration recalls that era, and the Batsto Nature Area preserves the present wilderness.

Right: Monmouth Park near Long Branch is a well-known racetrack along the Jersey shore.

Below right: Fishing for bass, bluefish and many other species is enjoyed by thousands of Jerseyites.

Below: The stately Barnegat Light played a vital role in sailing ship days.

HERBERT S. PIERCE

HERBERT S. PIERCE

DOROTHY BACHELLER

Philadelphia

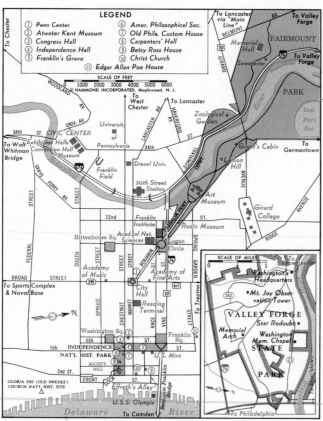

But the foremost reason why Americans have a friendly and respectful feeling for Philadelphia is historical: at the birth of the young republic the city acted as its godfather and godmother.

THE BICENTENNIAL CITY. On the 8th of July 1776, a boy climbed up a ladder and tore from Philadelphia's government building the coat of arms of the British king. With a shout of joy he threw it to the cheering crowd who in turn cast it into a fire while the Liberty Bell rang, summoning all citizens to the first public reading of the Declaration of Independence and proclaiming "Liberty throughout all the land unto all the inhabitants thereof." The building, known today as State House or Independence Hall, stands on Chestnut Street between 5th and 6th streets, on a small park that has been declared "a publick greene and walke forever." There everybody is welcome to enter and to see the fine, dignified room with the white panels and the crystal chandelier where the Second Continental Congress held its sessions. George Washington sat there, the only member wearing a military uniform, although Lexington and Concord had demonstrated that the fighting had started and that there was a war on. Jefferson squirmed in his seat while his colleagues picked at words, meanings and phrases of his masterpiece. His ruffled nerves were calmed by the jokes of old Dr. Franklin. In the same room the Constitution of the United States of America was written eleven years later. Here Alexander Hamilton pleaded for a strong central power, and James Madison proposed a government of three equal branches which would balance each other. In a world that has seen scores of constitutions adopted and abolished, changed and disregarded, the work of the men of Independence Hall has endured. We still uphold and cherish its original tenets. The prize exhibit of the house is the Liberty Bell whose ringing accompanied the birth of the nation. A "sound and light" spectacle called "the American Bell" is performed there nightly during July and August.

The streets around Independence Hall yield memories of the same era. Carpenters' Hall welcomed the First Continental Congress in 1774, and very appropriately so, for it was erected as an assembly place for builders. The Betsy Ross House, charming in its smallness and tidiness, saw the birth of the Stars and Stripes, at least according to tradition and to Mrs. Ross herself. In Christ Church on Second Street the pews of George and Martha Washington, and Betsy Ross and Robert Morris can be seen. Elfreth's Alley retains much of its colonial flavor and many of its colonial houses; it was a busy harbor street in the eighteenth century, full of the rattle of carts and the smell of rum, tea and spices. Even

SCRAPPLE AND BIDDLE. John Adams called Philadelphia "the happy, the peaceful, the elegant, the hospitable city," with the accent on the last adjective. For there he drank "Madeira at a great rate and found no inconvenience in it." Thackeray thought the town "grave, calm and kind." To Edward VII it was slightly confusing. "I met a very large and interesting family named Scrapple," he reported, "and I discovered a delicious native food they call Biddle." More factually, Philadelphia is one of the world's great ports, and so many factories are operating there that it is called the Nation's Workshop. Like every large city it has sorry tenements and endless rows of cheerless houses all built in the same dreary style. But it has also Fairmount Park, and a magnificent boulevard that connects the city hall with one of America's great art museums. Its symphony orchestra and its university have international status.

LIBERTY BELL and VALLEY FORGE

Independence Hall, our country's most historic shrine.

the open gutter in the center is preserved, a reminder of the yellow fever plagues that at times decimated the town's people. Finally, there is the city-owned chain of colonial mansions in Fairmount Park along the Schuylkill River, gems of architecture like Sweetbrier and Lemon Hill. The park's zoological garden has a superb wild animal collection.

THE PRACTICAL PHILOSOPHER. To a surprising degree Philadelphia is still the city of Benjamin Franklin, America's first figure of international stature. If he could visit his city today, he could still enter his pew in Christ Church; he would, of course, love the science museum called Franklin Institute in his honor; he would be surprised (or perhaps he wouldn't) at observing his lightning rods on the city's skyscrapers, at his chairs, with small tables attached, in all schools, and at his bifocals on the noses of distinguished elderly gentlemen who attend the meetings of his American Philosophical Society on Independence Square. He founded that oldest learned body himself, just as he organized the first fire

company and the first public library.

THE VALLEY OF DESTINY. On the road from Philadelphia to Pittsburgh the old residential area called "The Main Line" has become so well-known for pleasant, prosperous middle class living that it is now a veritable symbol of suburbia. In its western part one of America's great shrines is located: Valley Forge, now a state park where visitors may see the breastworks of the camp, the reconstructed huts of the Continental Army and the small, rural stone house where General Washington had his headquarters. Perhaps it is a sign of maturity that we should have preserved this monument to an American defeat and to the darkest hour in the life of the nation, for we feel that nothing will endure and stay dear to our hearts that is not born in agony and sacrifice. And there is another thought: not only Washington was at Valley Forge but also von Steuben, and Lafayette and Pulaski stayed nearby; they showed the way. This was to become, in time, a Nation of Nations.

39

Lovely Hills of Pennsylvania

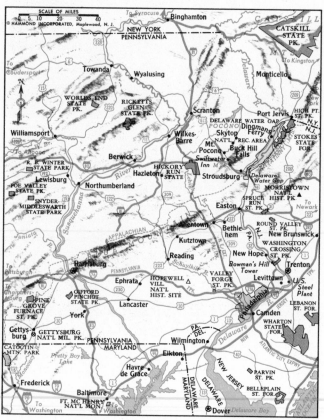

creations of nature. The inscription of the old Swiftwater Inn, which has been in business since 1778, seems to summarize the pleasant vacation atmosphere of the area: "Rest ye Bones/Tickle ye Palate/and nae Rob ye Wallet." As mere samples, some highlights from the eastern part of the state are presented here.

THE SUSQUEHANNA. The river's upper reaches where it rushes through mountain gorges are a stretch highly prized by fishermen because of its bass, perch and walleyed pike. The current meanders southward and at Wyalusing flows around a fascinating piece of history: the French Asylum. A colony of aristocratic refugees from the French Revolution was established here in 1793 in grand style. Its center, la Grande Maison, was probably the largest log house ever built in America with two stories and 8 fireplaces, large glass windows, broad piazzas and French furniture. There were 60 similar houses, all overwhelmingly elegant for the American backwoods, and visited by such celebrities as Louis Philippe, later King of France, and the master politician Talleyrand. The site, selected for its natural beauty, can be seen from Highway 6; a marker overlooks the settlement of which nothing remains but the foundations of la Grande Maison. The river proceeds through the once great anthracite country of Wilkes-Barre and Berwick. Some collieries are open to visitors, an interesting experience. At Northumberland the West Branch of the Susquehanna joins the main stream after having traversed a stretch of grouse, quail and pheasant country. At Harrisburg you will have a fine view of the river while crossing it on the turnpike bridge. Its blue waters flow around tree-covered islands with the state capitol in the background. From here on the river broadens out into a string of wide, glistening lakes.

A PATTERN OF ITS OWN. If you draw a map of Pennsylvania showing nothing but her rivers, your drawing looks like a Japanese screen on which three bizarre but pleasing willow trees are painted: to the left the Allegheny and Monongahela unite in the Ohio; to the right the Delaware winds its course; and the center is filled with the meandering branches of the Susquehanna. With their numerous tributaries these rivers form a cobweb of bright waterways which embrace tree-clad mountains in a rugged landscape or irrigate immaculately kept farms. Lakes and waterfalls are judiciously distributed here and there with the result that the whole state is a grand vacation and resort country, not in the spectacular sense of our western scenery but as a beautiful, quiet, prosperous hill and valley land with rich traditions, a great history and a harmonious integration of the works of man with the

THE DELAWARE. Pennsylvania's eastern boundary river tumbles down from the Catskills in many lovely cascades, and between Port Jervis and the Delaware Water Gap, where it cuts through the Kittatinny Mountains, it parallels the Pocono Mountains. This is the heart of the resort area with such well-known summer and winter vacation spots as Mt. Pocono, Stroudsburg and Skytop. Both the Buck Hill Falls, which plunge for 50 feet into a deep green pool, and Dingmans Falls near Dingmans Ferry, which tumble for 177 feet over rocks and boulders between spray-drenched ferns and moss, are exquisite. Between Easton and Washington Crossing the narrow road which squeezes its way between the old, abandoned canal and the steep mountainside is one of the most beautiful in the East, particularly in the fall. It leads through quiet villages, past colonial stone houses and along the rows of old elms

WINDING RIVERS, WOODED RIDGES, THRIVING FARMS

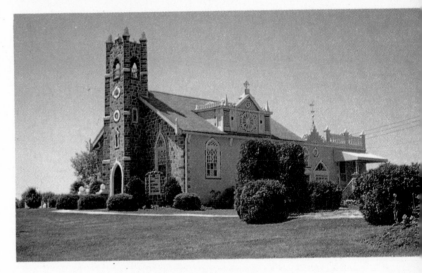

DOROTHY BACHELLER (3)

Above: Typical for many Pennsylvania-Dutch farms are the large and often superb stables, barns and silos while the owner's residence remains small and modest.

Above right: The tools and implements of the early Pennsylvania-Dutch settlers are exhibited at the Farm Museum in Lancaster, Pa.

Right: Pennsylvania-Dutch churches are as neat and well maintained as Pennsylvania-Dutch farms. The roof window has the shape of a "hex wheel."

that form a line of gothic arches on the dam between the green canal and the blue river; it rambles through the picturesque artists' colony at New Hope, offers a grand vista of the river valley from Bowman's Hill Tower and proceeds to Washington Crossing where a dramatic moment of our history is commemorated in state parks both on the New Jersey and Pennsylvania sides. A pavilion exhibits the famous Leutze painting of the daring venture, and although the picture was conceived on the Rhine and shows the Stars and Stripes prematurely by a few years, it is a popular piece of Americana.

"BUMP, THE BELL DON'T MAKE." This is supposedly the sign a Pennsylvania Dutch housewife will hang at her door if the bell is out of order. "The off is all" means vacation is over. It's funny little phrases like these through which the Pennsylvania Dutch have become widely known and, since they are the first ones to relate such gems, have endeared themselves to the American sense of humor. But it is also worthwhile to

visit their rolling country in southeastern Pennsylvania where on the world's second best soil (the best is in Belgium) they have erected impressive, spic and span farms with huge red barns that bear white hex wheels to keep out witches. The district extends around Bethlehem, Allentown, Reading and Lancaster; Lancaster's central market is a famous institution where Amish farmers with beards and low-crowned black hats and less conservative Mennonites sell schnitz and shoefly pies, scrapple and calves' heads, dandelion greens and sticky buns. The Pennsylvania Dutch, really Pennsylvania Germans, began to arrive in the late seventeenth century and continued coming during the eighteenth. They are hard-working, God-fearing and prosperous, defenders of the simple life and of Biblical traditions. The men still wear black coats, the women bonnets and long dresses, and the children are small replicas. Being master farmers, they introduced crop rotation and fertilization long before the rest of the country and kept their soil rich and productive for ten generations.

Washington, D.C.

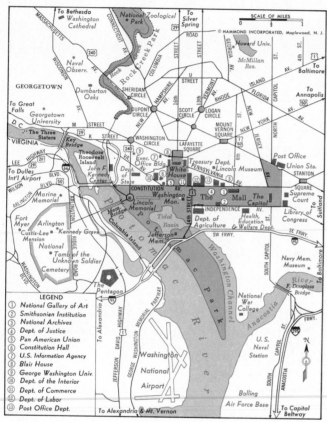

LEGEND
1. National Gallery of Art
2. Smithsonian Institution
3. National Archives
4. Dept. of Justice
5. Pan American Union
6. Constitution Hall
7. U.S. Information Agency
8. Blair House
9. George Washington Univ.
10. Dept. of the Interior
11. Dept. of Commerce
12. Dept. of Labor
13. Post Office Dept.

"BRIGHTEST STAR OF THE CONSTELLATION THAT ENLIGHTENS THE WORLD." With these words the Marquis de Lafayette referred to the city of Washington when he visited there in 1824. His listeners smiled skeptically at his French politesse. For Washington was a rather wretched village, its few big buildings far apart, its Greek temple facades unfinished, its streets impassable after a rain and its swamps breeding mosquitoes. The world at large paid no attention whatever to any enlightenment that might have originated in the American capital. But the marquis was a better prophet than his doubters. Washington did become a bright and beautiful city, and it did assume world leadership although that preeminence was never sought. The eyes of the world are on it, and so are the eyes of America. Particularly in spring everybody seems to be there, and the thousands of parents who

take their wide-eyed offspring from one hallowed place to another are a reassuring sight; high school youngsters arrive by the busload from all over the nation. They find the city a thrilling, concrete illustration to school books and civics lessons.

LEGISLATIVE, JUDICIAL, EXECUTIVE. The sightseeing excursion usually begins where the nation's laws are made, at the Capitol. After inspecting the Victorian splendor of the building itself, a visit to the gallery of the lower or the upper house of Congress offers the familiar sight of a speaker before empty seats, with two or three congressmen chatting casually and a few others reading the morning paper. This sight shocks foreign visitors, but in the U.S. everybody knows that Congress does its work not on the floor but in committee rooms and in its office buildings reached by miniature subways. To the east, the Library of Congress is not only a fantastic collection of 16 million printed items but also an historical museum where Jefferson's rough draft of the Declaration of Independence and other priceless documents may be viewed. The original Constitution and the Bill of Rights are exhibited at the National Archives. Next to the Library the judicial power of the land has its seat and symbol. Built in gleaming white marble, the Supreme Court Building has been called Washington's best adaptation to the Classical style. The public is admitted to most rooms and, if you can attend a session of the court, the personalities of the judges and the splendid surroundings will probably interest you more than the trial on hand. From the Capitol, Pennsylvania Avenue leads to the White House. You will walk through the East Room where Mrs. Adams, first occupant of the premises, hung her wash and where formal receptions are now held while Gilbert Stuart's Washington looks down from the wall. You will see the rooms in which the world's leaders are entertained, and you will conclude that the elegant simplicity of the White House has stood the test of time better than the nineteenth-century pomp of the congressional rotunda and wings. When George Washington discussed the executive mansion with Major L'Enfant, creator of the city's plan, the general specified for it "the sumptuousness of a palace, the convenience of a house, and the charm of a country seat." Certainly it has all of that, to this very day.

THREE MEN — THREE SHRINES. Three outstanding attractions of the Washington scene are the Washington Monument, the Lincoln Memorial to the west, and the Jefferson Memorial to the south. It has been said that all three shrines somehow seem to reflect the personalities of the great Americans they honor: Washington's 555-foot column is solid, reliable, unshakable.

SPLENDID SETTING for a POWER CENTER

It hardly ever sways, even in a gale; the view from its top embraces the city, the Potomac, Arlington Cemetery where President Kennedy is buried, and the Pentagon — an excellent orientation point. The Lincoln Memorial is the most touching of the three; its statue is a masterpiece by Daniel Chester French. Perhaps Lincoln's face and figure are idealized, but no visitor can escape the hushed feeling: I am in the presence of a great man, the American who lived "with malice toward none, with charity for all . . ." The Jefferson Memorial is a creation of beauty; it is as urbane and gentlemanly as the liberal aristocrat it glorifies, a symbol of the statesman who swore "eternal hostility against every form of tyranny over the mind of man." The setting at the Tidal Basin is magnificent, especially at cherry blossom time.

ALONG THE MALL. On the Mall, the boulevard between the Capitol and Washington Monument, are located so many museums and sightseeing attractions that you will have to make a choice according to your taste. On the north side the National Gallery of Art presents a superb collection of paintings and sculptures in a magnificent setting; the entrance hall with its fountain and black marble columns is especially striking. Two blocks down the Mall, at the Department of Justice Building, an FBI tour begins at approximately every quarter hour, and no show in Washington is more dramatic and thrilling. Around the corner on Tenth Street, Ford's Theatre, where Lincoln was murdered, is now a Lincoln Museum. Back on the Mall and across the avenue, the Smithsonian Institution is the number one attraction for all who love to see the historical exhibit of outdated machinery, the original "Spirit of St. Louis," the thousand inventions and relics, the wax statues of all first ladies wearing their inaugural gowns, the ship models, and the army uniforms since the Revolution. Finally, on the Ellipse south of the White House, the building of the Pan American Union is a great showplace. Spectacularly it makes us aware of the huge double continent on which we live.

Designed by John Russell Pope in the classical style beloved by Jefferson, the Jefferson Memorial is one of Washington's most impressive buildings. It honors the statesman who had sworn "eternal hostility against every form of tyranny over the mind of man."

J. WARING STINCHCOMB

Skyline Drive

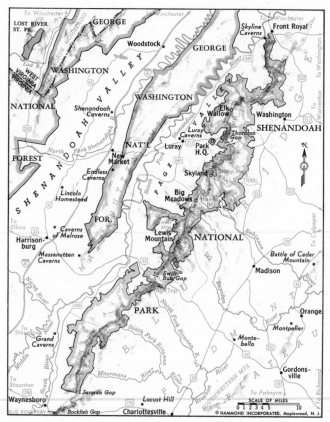

hills and old forests that culminate in the Great Smokies. But the former is a small oasis in the busy expanse of Atlantic civilization. Whether you look into the Piedmont plateau toward the ocean or into the fertile Shenandoah Valley to the west, you see a carpet of green and yellow squares, the fields and pastures of rich farmlands. Villages and church steeples, a bridge over the silver band of a river or the metallic gleam of a railroad track indicate the presence of busy human life. At night the twinkling lights of the valley look like reflections of the starry sky, and the Indian word Shenandoah becomes a most appropriate name. It means "Daughter of the Stars." On clear days the outlines of larger cities can be distinguished, and some maintain that from a certain point the Washington Monument obelisk in the nation's capital can be spotted — it is about 75 miles away. From New York and the large cities of Pennsylvania and Ohio the park can be reached in a day. Shenandoah National Park is about 80 miles long but only 2 to 13 miles wide. Its mountains are of medium height (3,000 to 4,000 feet), and the pines, cedars, beeches and maples are mostly second growth. But there are some virgin hemlock groves, some huge ancient oaks and the gray skeletons of dead chestnuts. In spring the blossoms of the dogwood and the redbuds splendidly cover slope after slope, and in the fall the blazing colors of the foliage seem especially rich and warm.

"HEART OF THE WORLD." The National Park, which did not come into existence until 1935, was created by buying privately owned lands, and about 600 mountain families had to move out of the area. They sold their quit-claims willingly, for nobody had to wander far; there were more of the beloved hills nearby. Freeman Tilden reports the reaction of an old mountaineer named Hezekiah, who could tell by the smell in which valley any batch of "corn likker" had been made. He would have liked to stay but "never believed in bein' agin the government." Signing the transfer papers, he admitted that he had not read them. "I reckon I could of," he said, "if I hadn't lost my specs. I allus said these hills would be the heart of the world." A few old mills and mountain cabins are preserved in the park, and occasionally a marker points out the name of a family that had lived in a certain "holler" and how many children they had raised in their circular little valley. But all this is not just history; a short drive along one of the side ridges, or still better a horseback ride or a hike will soon bring you to log cabins perched on steep hillsides, to friendly country stores with round iron stoves in the center and to berry patches where blue-eyed children gather supplies for the canning season. There is an excellent network of

THE "HIGH" WAY. Between two broad plains the Blue Ridge Mountains hug the ground like the skeleton of a huge, prehistoric monster, and the Skyline Drive finds its way along the crest of the backbone. Ordinarily automobile roads follow the valleys and, if in mountainous country, they climb over passes, they wind their way down again as fast as they can. Not so the Skyline Drive. Whether it is the world's only exception to the rule is hard to determine, but its more than 100-mile-long course from Front Royal to Rockfish Gap along the backbone of the Blue Ridge Mountains is unique. There is a succession of wide views from 75 "overlooks," now to the left, now to the right, and sometimes a turnout offers a grand panorama both to the east and to the west. The continuation of the Skyline Drive, the Blue Ridge Parkway, is also a mountaintop road, but there is a marked difference. The latter leads into the lonely

DOUBLE-VISTA ROAD in SHENANDOAH NATIONAL PARK

The Shenandoah Valley as seen from the Skyline Drive looks like a haven of peace and plenty.

trails easily accessible from the Drive. A section of the Appalachian Trail runs through the park the whole length of the Skyline Drive. On the western slope are the spectacular Luray Caverns; for the visitors an eerie, bell-like tune is played on the cave's rock formations.

STORY AND HISTORY. Ever since Governor Spotswood and his Knights of the Golden Horseshoe rode over the ridge to get a glance at the unknown West beyond, American history has centered around these mountains. In whatever direction the traveler may look there are mementos of George Washington and Thomas Jefferson, James Madison and Patrick Henry, George Rogers Clark and Sam Houston, Stonewall Jackson and Phil Sheridan. The villages and towns of the whole region abound with local history and mountain lore, and such characters as Bert Lynch, the bully of the mountains, and Brother Billy Patterson, the new preacher, are wonderful protagonists of the tough and gentle life in the hills of bygone days. The two had

quarreled and, before fighting it out in the open, Brother Patterson had pleaded for a reconciliation. It was rejected; all the bully conceded was time for a short prayer. So the parson knelt down and with a loud voice addressed himself to the Great Father. "O Lord, Thou knowest that when I killed Bill Cummings and John Brown and Jerry Smith and Levi Bottles, that I did it in self-defense. Thou knowest, O Lord, that when I cut the heart out of young Slinger and strewed the ground with the brains of Paddy Miles, that it was forced upon me and that I did it in great agony of soul. And now, O Lord, I am about to be forced to put in his coffin this poor, miserable wretch who has attacked me here today. O Lord, have mercy upon his soul and take care of his helpless widow and orphans when he is gone." The parson concluded his service with a vigorous song:

> "Hark from the tombs a doleful sound;
> Mine ears attend the cry . . ."

He looked around. Bert, the bully, was disappearing in a cloud of dust.

Colonial Virginia

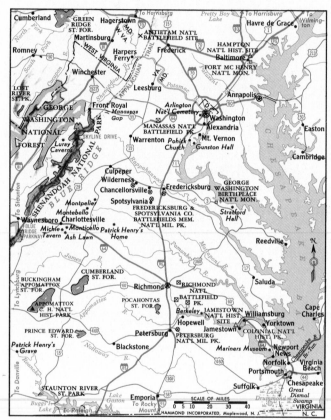

turist in America. He kept elaborate notes, corresponded with other farmers, including Thomas Jefferson, about his experiments, introduced crop rotation, operated a smokehouse, dairy, distillery and grist mill and had his products shipped, in his own schooners, to the market ports. When Frederick the Great sent him a sword and Lafayette presented him with the keys to the Bastille, he felt honored. But he enjoyed it just as much when the Agricultural Society awarded him a prize "for raising the largest jackass."

WILLIAMSBURG: MUSEUM OR LIVING PAST?

Among European journalists who visit America, it is the fashion to call the restored capital of colonial Virginia "just a replica." Such an opinion is based on a misconception. For the layout of the streets and some of the town's finest colonial structures, like the Wren Building of the College of William and Mary and the lovely Bruton Parish Church, are the originals. The other buildings are erected, with absolute authenticity, on the original foundations. The result is as genuine as most of Europe's often repaired and restored historic shrines. Another complaint states that Williamsburg is commercialized. On this point there is also an answer. The men who planned the restoration had to decide whether they wanted a hushed museum or a living recreation of the past where visitors could not only see how the governor lived and where the bigwigs of the council met, but also how eighteenth-century boots and perukes were made, where modern Americans could sample the delicious foods of Old Virginia and smoke the long colonial clay pipes. The latter course was chosen, and

George Washington Birthplace National Monument east of Fredericksburg reflects friendliness and patrician dignity.

ORIENTATION. Historic shrines are so abundant in the state of Virginia that for travel purposes a certain organization seems advisable. Three areas are particularly close to the hearts of all Americans: (1) Mount Vernon, which is usually visited from Washington, D.C., (2) The Tidewater area of Williamsburg, Jamestown and Yorktown and (3) in the foothills of the Blue Ridge Jefferson's Monticello, Ash Lawn and the University of Virginia at Charlottesville.

WASHINGTON'S REALM. Those of us who for the first time see the fine colonial mansion of Mount Vernon, with its elegant cupola and curving arcades in a splendid hill setting with broad lawns sloping down to the Potomac, think of this estate as the home of the great general, statesman and father of our country. Yet it was rather George Washington the farmer who lived there, whose ambition it was to become the leading agricul-

46

M. WOODBRIDGE WILLIAMS — NAT'L PARK SERVICE

"THE COMMON GLORY"

millions of Americans have responded enthusiastically.

ALONG DUKE OF GLOUCESTER STREET. When you arrive in Williamsburg, you are advised to visit first the official orientation center where by means of films and slides you will be shown the role of Williamsburg in American history and the fascinating story of the restoration. After that you will inspect the Governor's Palace, a showplace more sophisticated and elegant than the White House; it saw splendid parties with as many as 200 guests. You will like the dignified Capitol, the Raleigh Tavern where Phi Beta Kappa was founded, the fine private homes, the Guardhouse and the Public Gaol, always guided by well informed local ladies or gentlemen in the proper costume of the day. You will visit the apothecary and the other shops and perhaps attend a service at Bruton Parish Church or eat Brunswick Stew at Chowning's Tavern.

JAMESTOWN AND YORKTOWN: COLONIAL BEGINNING AND ENDING. Easily reached from Williamsburg are Jamestown, one of the points where America began, and Yorktown, where the Revolutionary War ended with our victory. In Jamestown Festival Park you will inspect the full-sized replicas of the *Susan Constant,* the *Discovery,* and the *Godspeed;* it will seem like a miracle that these tiny ships crossed the ocean safely and brought 104 immigrants to their new home. There is a restoration of Britain's first enduring colony in the New World, with half-timbered walls and thatched roofs not unlike those of Old England. To the east of Williamsburg, Yorktown lies picturesquely on a 50-foot bluff on the south side of the York River. In addition to the battlefield, Grace Church and several other historical buildings in the Colonial National Historical Park are worth visiting.

THE SPIRIT OF JEFFERSON. Toward the western end of the state where the Blue Ridge looms in the distance, near the pleasant town of Charlottesville, the spirit of Thomas Jefferson lives on in his beloved Monticello. It is a delight to visit because more intensely than any other great estate it bears the personal imprint of its owner: the hilltop view and the decorations betray his artistic taste; the Classical touches on the house and the formal gardens reflect his classical education; the well balanced organization of the layout is an image of his orderly mind; the clever devices and inventions which fill the house (a pulley clock indicating even the days of the week, a disappearing bed, dumbwaiters, a duplicate writing machine, unusually designed chairs and tables) indicate his typically American predilection for gadgets and improvements; and the fields, pastures, orchards, the brickyard, carpentry shop and nail factory were the fruits of his enterprising spirit. To the visitor the estate reveals the real and human side of a man who, as the author of the Declaration of Independence, has become a legendary figure. Near Monticello, Monroe's mansion, Ash Lawn, is much less pretentious; Michie Tavern built prior to 1740 is nearby. In Charlottesville the University of Virginia has one of the country's finest campuses designed by Jefferson himself; he considered the founding of the university his noblest accomplishment.

The Governor's Palace in Williamsburg was once America's most elegant building.

Glassblowing and similar trades have been revived at Jamestown in the same manner in which they were practiced in colonial days.

GAIL HAMMOND

M. WOODBRIDGE WILLIAMS — NAT'L PARK SERVICE

Sightseeing Guide

CONNECTICUT

Connecticut does not offer any spectacular sights but has a lovely atmosphere of its own created by old trees, velvety village greens, fine homes and white beaches.

THE COAST OF CONNECTICUT. In the industrial city of Bridgeport Seaside Park has a beach of several miles, and the P. T. Barnum Museum of Circus Life is worth seeing. Mr. Barnum's last home is located here. In adjoining Stratford the Judson House of 1723 is noted for its fine antique furniture and fireplaces, and the American Shakespeare Festival Theatre, modeled after London's Old Globe, is a famous cultural center. In New Haven on the Yale University campus the Peabody Museum of Natural History and the Gallery of Fine Arts are open to the public. Also in New Haven is the Winchester Gun Museum, located on Winchester Avenue. East Haven boasts of the Branford Trolley Car Museum which exhibits all types, from a primitive horsecar to a luxurious electric parlor car. In the town of Guilford the Whitfield House, which was one of the first stone houses built in America, is now a museum. The Nathaniel Allis House on Madison's lovely village green is also a museum. On the Connecticut River, Essex is a matchless colonial river port with winding narrow streets, big shade trees and the mansions of retired sea captains. New London, the largest seaport of the state, is the seat of the U.S. Coast Guard Academy and a submarine base is nearby. Old Lyme and Old Saybrook are picturesque ports. Mystic, with its restored old seaport and its living museum of the sea, is a fascinating tourist goal. Among its outdoor exhibits of historic craft are the wooden whaling ship *Charles W. Morgan* and the square-rigger *Joseph Conrad*. Among Mystic's old houses, the Denison Homestead of 1717 was occupied by eleven generations of the Denison family, and today it is a museum of New England home life. Stonington, near the Rhode Island state line, has many old homes of former sea captains.

THE INTERIOR OF CONNECTICUT. The Danbury Fair is one of the major fairs in the East. In Litchfield the historic Tapping Reeve Law School with its early lawbooks is a landmark in the development of law education in America. Old Newgate Prison near East Granby is open to the public; it was a rather barbaric Revolutionary jail and before that a copper mine. Hartford, the state capital, is also "the insurance capital of America." Guided tours to the dome of the State Capitol offer a broad panorama. Noted among the city's historic houses are those of Harriet Beecher Stowe and Mark Twain. The Wadsworth Atheneum is a fine art museum. Nearby in Bristol the American Clock and Watch Museum presents the history of clockmaking in the United States. To the northeast, at Storrs, is the University of Connecticut. Between Hartford and the Massachusetts state line the tobacco fields covered with white cloth are an unusual sight; outside wrappers for cigars are raised here. In Farmington the Whitman saltbox house of 1660 is now a colonial museum. In nearby Wethersfield the Webb House of 1752 was the meeting place of Washington and Rochambeau; they discussed strategy for the Revolutionary War. Middletown is the seat of Wesleyan University; a prized exhibit of the Wesleyan Library is the manuscript of Albert Einstein's Theory of Relativity.

DELAWARE

NORTHERN DELAWARE. In Claymont, near the Pennsylvania state line, the old Swedish Blockhouse, a remnant of the Swedish settlement of 1654, still stands. Wilmington, the capital of the DuPont industrial empire, has a number of sightseeing attractions of historical interest. A state park preserves the site of Fort Christina at The Rocks, where the Swedes landed in 1638, the first permanent white settlement on the Delaware River. Nearby Old Swedes Church of 1698 is Wilmington's oldest public building and one of the oldest Protestant churches in America. The lovely stone building was erected by masons from Philadelphia, and for the glass work a glazier was imported from Holland. The DuPont Winterthur Museum, housing one of the world's great antique collections and surrounded by fabulous gardens, and Brandywine Creek State Park along the river are worth visiting. Newark is the home of the University of Delaware. On the west bank of the Delaware New Castle is a charming outdoor museum of colonial days. The village green is shaded by stately trees and faced by the Dutch House, dating from the 1650's, the courthouse and the Amstel House, now a museum. On the third Saturday each May, "A Day in Old New Castle" is celebrated, with all colonial buildings open to visitors. Dover, the tree-shaded capital, also has a lovely colonial atmosphere. The State House is the country's second oldest state capitol still in use.

SOUTHERN DELAWARE. Lewes is a busy port for fishing and pleasure craft. The Dutch landed there in 1631 and established the Zwaanendael colony, which was destroyed by Indians less than a year later. The event is commemorated by Zwaanendael House, a museum built like the town hall of Hoorn, Holland, in an adapted Renaissance style. Rehoboth Beach and Bethany Beach are favorite summer resorts for Washingtonians escaping the heat of the national capital.

MAINE

VACATIONLAND MAINE possesses about 17 million acres of forest land (almost 80% of its surface), 3,500 miles of coastline, innumerable islands, more than 2,200 lakes and over 5,000 streams. It is one of the few American states that remains truly close to nature. Fewer than a million people live in an area about as large as the other five New England states combined.

THE COAST OF MAINE. A general view of the Maine coast is presented on page 18. At the southern end of the coast the resort of York has restored its one-room schoolhouse of 1745. Old Orchard Beach, one of America's oldest seaside resorts, has 7 miles of sandy bathing beaches; its amusement park caters to youthful visitors. Portland with its island-studded bay is described on page 18. Among its fine old homes is the Wadsworth-Longfellow House where the poet spent his boyhood. Bowdoin College is located in the pleasant town of Brunswick. From the high bridge over the Kennebec River the well-known shipyards of Bath can be seen; they perpetuate an old Maine industry that flourished along the coast in sailing ship days. Near the tree-shaded resort town of Wiscasset, Fort Edgecomb is an octagonal blockhouse with a view of blue inlets, rocky islets and wooded peninsulas. Boothbay Harbor, the popular summer resort, attracts many artists. Twenty miles out in the ocean, Monhegan Island is reached in summer by a trip from Boothbay Harbor. The excursion to the small island — it is 2½ miles long and 1 mile wide — is well worthwhile. Rockland is a great lobster port; its Farnsworth Art Museum houses a fine collection of paintings of the Maine scene. Camden can be called an ideal summer resort with the sea and a busy, landlocked harbor at its feet, and lovely hills with wide maritime views at its back. Its "windjammer cruises" are conducted on old coastal schooners converted for the purpose. In Searsport, the Penobscot Marine Museum keeps alive the memory of the days when Maine was a maritime power. Nearby Fort Knox still looks grim with its granite walls and heavy cannon. Bar Harbor and Acadia National Park with Cadillac Mountain are described on page 18. The fishing town of Eastport is appropriately named, for it is the easternmost city of the United States. The coastal tides are powerful there, rising and falling about 18 feet. In nearby Quoddy Village an attempt was made to harness the tides for the generation of electricity, but the project was abandoned. St. Croix Island National Monument in the St. Croix River commemorates the first European settlement on the Atlantic Coast north of Florida.

WESTERN MAINE. The Rangeley Lakes are a chain of sparkling blue waters lined with scented pine forests and surrounded by sweeping hills. The best way of getting acquainted with the area is a 50-mile-long canoe trip from Rangeley village to Upton; it takes a week of paddling over the lakes and streams. As almost everywhere in the interior of Maine, salmon and trout are most highly prized by fishermen. Sebago Lake, large in itself, is connected with Long Lake and thus forms a 42-mile waterway.

CENTRAL MAINE. Augusta on the Kennebec River is the state capital. Fort Western, built in 1754 as a stronghold against the Indians, is a historical museum now. North of Augusta, the Belgrade Lakes are a favorite playground. Within their area are Winslow with Fort Halifax, a blockhouse of hand-hewn timbers, and Waterville with Colby College. To the north Skowhegan on the rushing Kennebec is a tourist town, and the nearby resort of Lakewood is famous for its summer theater. Bangor, once the world's leading lumber port with a Barbary Coast of its own, is a quiet commercial center today. With its many old established businesses catering to logging camps and outfitting sport camps, it has a northern frontier atmosphere of its own. North of Bangor in the town of Orono is located the University of Maine. Close-by is Old Town, seat of a nationally known canoe factory which is open to visitors. Many of the skilled craftsmen are Indians from the reservation on the island in the Penobscot River; they perpetuate an art which the white man learned from their forefathers. In central Maine rock hounds have fun searching for gold, beryl, garnet, topaz or tourmaline; a hammer and a small pick are the only tools necessary.

NORTHERN MAINE. On pages 16-17 the Northwoods of Maine as well as Baxter State Park and Mount Katahdin are described. The latter is the northern terminus of the Appalachian Trail, which follows the principal eastern and southern ranges and ends on Springer Mountain in Georgia. The Maine potato country around Presque Isle and Fort Kent in Aroostook County is not particularly scenic. However, its rolling hills and huge potato fields, when in bloom, have a quiet charm of their own.

MARYLAND

The most outstanding geographical factor in the life of Maryland is Chesapeake Bay, which provides the state with thousands of miles of waterfront and square miles of inland water. Consequently Maryland's opportunities for swimming, fishing, boating and yachting are excellent.

EASTERN SHORE OF MARYLAND. Wye Oak at Wye Mills is a white oak, the state tree of Maryland, and one of the largest in America. The tree, which grows in a state park, is believed to be over 400 years old, has a circumference of more than 21 feet and a spread of 165 feet. Ocean City is a popular bathing resort and a deep-sea fishing center; several hundred white marlin are caught each year. Princess Anne, one of the state's earliest settlements, has several churches dating back to the 1700's, avenues of big trees and old, dignified homes. Here and there along the shoreline of the Chesapeake Bay side of the Delmarva Peninsula mountainous piles of oyster shells can be seen, reflecting one of the region's major industries. The center of oyster fishing and crabbing is the city of Crisfield, self-styled "Seafood Capital of the U.S." Its lively dock area, built on "the residue of 70 years of oyster shucking," has the salty flavor of the sea.

CENTRAL MARYLAND. Havre de Grace, at the Susquehanna River Bridge, is a widely known racing resort. Upstream, the Conowingo Dam forms a 14-mile-long lake with good perch and bass fishing. In the Baltimore suburb of Towson, at the Hampton National Historic Site, the eighteenth-century Hampton House is open to visitors. Baltimore, one of America's top ranking ports, has been called "a blend of northern industry and southern charm." Founded as a tobacco depot in 1729, it launched the U.S. frigate Constellation, became the birthplace of the "Star-Spangled Banner" and erected the first Catholic cathedral in the United States. Large numbers of clipper ships were built here so skillfully that the expression "a Baltimore clipper" stood for excellence. The world's first telegraph message was received here. Baltimore is the seat of Johns Hopkins University, and of Johns Hopkins Hospital and Medical School, both world famous institutions. During the twentieth century Baltimore attracted a great many industries, including metal, chemical and food processing enterprises, but it still retains an air of graciousness. It has an impressive skyline and narrow cobblestone alleys on the waterfront, fine mansions and row upon row of identical red brick houses with marble entrance steps. The star-shaped Fort McHenry, whose flag inspired the writing of the "Star-Spangled Banner," is a national monument. The flag, of outsize proportions, was made by Mary Pickersgill in the Flag House, now a historical museum. Other sightseeing attractions are the Washington Monument, the Walters Art Gallery, the Baltimore Museum of Art, the Shot Tower and the Pimlico Race Track. Frederick, west of Baltimore, possesses several historic shrines: the Barbara Fritchie Home — a reproduction housing a museum, the grave of Francis Scott Key, and to the north, historic Catoctin Furnace. South of Frederick the Water Gardens are beautiful when their aquatic plants are in bloom. Near Boonsboro, with its Crystal Grottoes, and Sharpsburg is a great historic area. On the Antietam Battlefield the bloodiest single-day battle of the Civil War was fought. Washington Monument State Park is not far to the north. The Great Falls of the Potomac are a spectacular cataract about 15 miles upriver from Washington, D.C. A scenic park surrounds the 200-foot gorge with the 35-foot waterfall. In this same area the old Chesapeake and Ohio Canal is restored for canoeing and fishing. Among the world's farm experts Beltsville is well-known as the seat of the National Agricultural Research Center. In the neighboring town of College Park the campus of the University of Maryland is located. During the eighteenth century Annapolis was a gay and gracious residential town of rich tobacco planters. Today it still has a colonial atmosphere, but it is primarily a political and educational center. The State House, built in 1772, is the oldest American capitol still in use. The campus of the U.S. Naval Academy is impressive and fairly breathes America's great naval traditions. St. John's College is an outstanding small liberal arts college which grew out of King William's School, the first free school in Maryland. Of the city's lovely colonial homes, the Hammond-Harwood House is open to the public. Just northeast of Annapolis the Chesapeake Bay Bridge is a structure of excellent modern design; with a length of more than 7 miles, it is one of the longest overwater steel bridges on earth. To the south, in St. Marys City, a replica of the original state house may be seen; Maryland was founded there.

WESTERN MARYLAND. North of Cumberland a famous pioneer route to the west (now Highway 40) passes through the Cumberland Gorge, with walls up to 1,000 feet high. The western handle of the state, the area around Oakland, is Maryland's mountain playground. The attractions include the large, man-made Deep Creek Lake, Swallow Falls State Forest, Herrington Manor and New Germany state parks.

MASSACHUSETTS

EASTERN MASSACHUSETTS. Boston's Museum of Fine Arts at 465 Huntington Avenue owns one of the world's finest collections of oriental art. Fenwood, the palatial home of the Isabella Stewart-Gardner Museum with art objects from six centuries, has a courtyard famous for its profusion of flowers. The Museum of Science with its do-it-yourself exhibits fascinates the younger set. On the Harvard campus in Cambridge the Busch-Reisinger Museum shows Northern European art from the Middle Ages to the twentieth century. In Larz Anderson Park in Brookline the Antique Auto Museum offers nostalgic reminiscences. In Quincy, south of Boston, the mansion of the Adams family is a National Historic Site, and in the southwestern suburb of Dedham the Fairbanks House of 1636 is one of the oldest frame buildings in America; family heirlooms of eight generations are on display. Concord of Thoreau and Emerson fame, Salem with the House of Seven Gables, Marblehead with its rock-lined harbor and Gloucester of "Captains Courageous" are described on page 25. Rockport on Cape Ann is an artists' colony. In Amesbury the homestead of John Greenleaf Whittier, the Quaker poet, may be inspected. Between Boston and Plymouth, in the town of Duxbury, the John Alden House of 1653 is preserved by his descendants as a museum. Plymouth and Plymouth Rock are described on page 26. At Bourne, at the entrance to Cape Cod, a replica of the Aptucxet Trading Post, first building on the cape, is open to visitors. Cape Cod and Provincetown are described on pages 26-27. In Fall River the battleship *Massachusetts* is permanently docked as a state war memorial. In New Bedford the Whaling Museum exhibits a model of the whaling bark *Lagoda*. South of Cape Cod the triangular island of Martha's Vineyard is a scenic summer resort of high cliffs and landlocked ports, old towns and lovely flowers. Big game fishing is excellent here, and every fall the Striped Bass and Bluefish Derby is held, attracting throngs of sportsmen. Nantucket is probably America's most famous North Atlantic island; it is an early nineteenth-century whaling community. When the bottom fell out of the whaling business because of the discovery of petroleum, the isolated island could not attract other industries. Progress passed it by and Nantucket stayed as it was to the delight of present-day vacationers who enjoy the cobblestone streets, the rambler roses, the horse drawn coaches and the mansions of rich whaling captains long dead. The white beaches, the moors, the cranberry bogs and the Scotch heather add to Nantucket's allure.

CENTRAL MASSACHUSETTS. In Sudbury, west of Boston, the Wayside Inn of 1686 is still operated as a hostelry; it is immortalized by Longfellow in his "Tales of a Wayside Inn." In North Oxford, below Worcester, the birthplace of Clara Barton, founder of the Red Cross, is open to visitors. Nearby Old Sturbridge Village is a replica and living museum of a New England country town in the early nineteenth century. Life of that day is reenacted in some thirty shops, mills, and homes, a church and a general store. North of Worcester, in Harvard, the four Wayside Museums are reminders of New England's history; one is Fruitlands, the farm establishment of the New Eden colony of A. Bronson Alcott. The colony's goal was a new social order, community living without exploiting man or animal. The second museum is the Shaker House with relics of an unusual religious settlement. A picture gallery and an Indian museum are the third and fourth components of the group.

WESTERN MASSACHUSETTS. The Berkshire Hills are a charming combination of peaceful, green scenery and a strong cultural tradition which is maintained to this day. The mountains are not high — the tallest peak, Mt. Greylock, attains a height of under 3,500 feet — but they are steep and varied, covered with dense woods and traversed by rushing brooks. This is an area of quiet towns with attractive village greens and well-kept estates. There are resorts in and around Great Barrington, Stockbridge, Lee, Lenox and Pittsfield. At Williamstown, where Williams College is located, the Mohawk Trail begins. Skiing is popular here. The Berkshires are rich in literary traditions. Hawthorne lived at Tanglewood and Melville wrote "Moby Dick" near Pittsfield. Thoreau climbed Mt. Greylock, and Oliver Wendell Holmes enjoyed cool summers in the hills. Today many creative writers and artists live in the Berkshires, and of the area's cultural institutions the annual Berkshire Music Festival is to America what the Salzburg Music Festival is to Europe. On the Tanglewood Estate near Lenox a rare blend of excellent symphonic music, performed mainly by the Boston Symphony Orchestra, and wonderful scenery — a green valley, a blue lake and a horizon of distant ridges — may be enjoyed. The Berkshire Playhouse at Stockbridge and the Jacob's Pillow Dance Festival at Lee are celebrated institutions. The Pioneer Valley is the broad valley of the Connecticut River east of the Berkshire Hills. Beginning in the north, in the village of Northfield, the first American Youth Hostel was founded. Amherst is the seat of Amherst College and the University of Massachusetts. In Northampton, Wiggins Tavern and the Smith College campus are sightseeing attractions. Near the industrial city of Springfield (also a great arsenal of weapons with an Army Museum), the village of Storrowtown is a colonial restoration.

NEW BRUNSWICK, CANADA

SOUTHERN NEW BRUNSWICK. The southwestern coast of New Brunswick attracts many painters. There are beautiful resorts like St. Andrews, a golfers' favorite. Islands like Campobello and Grand Manan are popular vacation areas; the latter's towerlike cliffs rise from the ocean for hundreds of feet, a metropolis of thousands of sea gulls and strayed tropical birds. The sturdy boats, the cod and lobster fisheries, the young sailors, the women gathering dulse (an edible seaweed) — all these sights create a fascinating local atmosphere. On the feast day of St. John the Baptist in 1604, Champlain landed and properly called the river St. John. The first English settlement was made before 1765 and the city of St. John was incorporated in 1783 by expatriated royalist settlers from New England. The outstanding feature of the harbor is the tide which rises to an average height of 30 feet. At low tide the fishing schooners at the

NORTHEAST REGION

Market Slip Pier lie in the mud. A phenomenon caused by the huge tides is that of the Reversing Falls, where the waters of the St. John River gush in a torrent either down or up according to the outgoing or incoming tide. King Square Park and the historic New Brunswick Museum are other attractions. To the northeast Fundy National Park rises from the bay. Although the shore of the park is of rugged grandeur, the interior is sylvan and hilly, and an idyll of mixed forests and small lakes. Near Sackville Fort Beauséjour National Historic Park commemorates the French-English struggle for the possession of Canada; the old French fort was begun in 1751. Shediac is a popular seaside resort offering fine swimming and excellent sailing conditions in Northumberland Strait, where normally the ocean water is pleasantly warm. Fredericton is the small but dignified capital of the province, with impressive legislative buildings, a cathedral and the University of New Brunswick. On the St. John River, Fredericton is the gateway to the great fishing and hunting regions of the province, and just above the town a salmon pool is famous among sportsmen.

NORTHERN NEW BRUNSWICK. In the huge, roadless forest and hill country of the province, the Plaster Rock-Renous Game Refuge is one of North America's great preserves. Here roam the black bear, the moose, the white-tailed deer, and smaller fur bearers such as mink, muskrat, red fox, raccoon, beaver, otter, wildcat, lynx and weasel. In the northwestern corner of the province Edmundston is the supply center for the St. John River Valley which extends through the western part of New Brunswick. The broad river, the hilly banks with wide views, the prosperous villages with their large apple orchards (their McIntosh apples are famous), the lush meadows and stands of trees create a lovely landscape of peace and plenty. The river may be crossed on the world's longest covered wooden bridge at Hartland.

NEWFOUNDLAND, CANADA

For geographic reasons, sportsmen rather than sightseers visit this rocky island, the thirteenth largest in the world. Its many rivers, particularly the Humber, Portland Creek and the Serpentine, offer excellent fishing. The island's rocky shores are studded with picturesque fishing villages where millions of silvery cod dry on rickety scaffolds. St. John's, the capital, is an interesting typically northern city with whale, seal and cod fisheries. At the northern tip of the island, at L'Anse-au-Meadow, the authentic remnants of a Viking settlement have been discovered, proving the existence of a temporary European colony 500 years before Columbus.

NEW HAMPSHIRE

NORTHERN NEW HAMPSHIRE. In the northern corner of New Hampshire near the Canadian border the Connecticut Lakes region is a famous hunting and fishing wilderness. In the early 1800's this area was disputed territory; for a while the local backwoodsmen rejected both Canadian and United States sovereignty in favor of an independent republic. At Dixville Notch The Balsams is a resort in a vast mountain and forest country.

THE WHITE MOUNTAINS. America's first mountain resort area, including Mt. Washington, the Old Man of the Mountain, the Flume and other famous sightseeing spots, is described on pages 20-21. All of these points are within the White Mountain National Forest. The rim of the forest around Berlin is a popular ski area. On the southern fringe of the forest the new winter resort of Waterville Valley draws many skiers annually.

Bethlehem is a lively resort; the Magic Mountain Express leads to the top of Mt. Agassiz where there is an observation platform. South of the forest, Wonalancet is the home of the Chinook Kennels where powerful huskies from the Arctic are trained; to the east, North Conway is a ski center with a skimobile to the summit of Mt. Cranmore.

CENTRAL NEW HAMPSHIRE. This is the region of the great blue lakes of which Winnipesaukee is the largest, described on page 21. To the northeast, Ossipee Lake and the Mystery Pond are both tourist spots, and the latter provides rides with glass bottom boats. Squam Lake and Newfound Lake are popular water sports centers. The Polar Caves near Plymouth are an interesting maze of tunnels and caverns. Hanover is a lovely New England college town, tree-shaded, dignified and friendly. Dartmouth College, founded as an Indian school, is the intellectual center of the region. The impressively modern Orozco frescoes are an unexpected sight in the traditional building of Baker Library. The Dartmouth Winter Carnival, held each February, is one of the country's best known winter festivals. Its snow and ice sculpturing contest often creates wonderful lifelike statues. South of Hanover near Plainfield the Saint-Gaudens National Historic Site preserves the studio, the burial place and a number of works of the famous sculptor. Southwest of Lake Winnipesaukee, near Franklin, the Daniel Webster Memorial exhibits mementos of Webster's life in the modest birthplace of this famous New England statesman. West of Franklin Lake Sunapee is a recreational area with a gondola lift to Mt. Sunapee. In Newport the Clock Museum has a collection of old and rare clocks.

SOUTHWESTERN NEW HAMPSHIRE. The Franklin Pierce Homestead in Hillsboro shows interior decorations of the times of the 14th president of the United States; the mansion's scenic wallpaper is a conversation piece. Peterborough is a cultural center. The MacDowell Colony, named for the composer Edward MacDowell who is buried there, provides for its members an opportunity for creative composing, writing or painting in peaceful, sylvan surroundings. The Goyette Museum contains an especially fine collection of early Americana. Three miles east Pack Monadnock Mountain in Miller State Park offers a panorama of the hills of New Hampshire, Vermont and Massachusetts. Mt. Monadnock itself lies west of Peterborough. From the peak of this isolated 3,166-foot-high mountain all six New England states are supposedly visible on a clear day. To the south near Rindge, home of Franklin Pierce College, the Cathedral of the Pines is a beautiful evergreen sanctuary.

SOUTHEASTERN NEW HAMPSHIRE. Concord's state capitol is built of Vermont marble and fine-grained granite from neighboring quarries. In the nineteenth century a local manufacturing specialty of the city became world famous — the Concord Coach. Old models of these sturdy and elegant coaches are exhibited in New Hampshire at various tourist centers. To the south at the Amoskeag Falls of the Merrimack River Manchester is the state's largest city. To the south at Hudson an animal farm is open to visitors, and here wild animals are raised and trained for zoos and circuses. Durham, to the northeast, is the seat of the University of New Hampshire. South of Durham Exeter is another educational center, the home of Phillips Exeter Academy. Portsmouth, New Hampshire's only seaport, had its great days early in the nineteenth century when its seaborne trade brought wealth to its merchants and shipowners, when John Paul Jones' *Ranger* was built there. Captain Jones stayed at the boarding house which is now the headquarters of the Historical Society. Among the other fine buildings — some of them open to the public — are the Moffat-Ladd Home with its splendid staircase and St. John's Church which owns such relics as an organ built in England in 1710, an ancient bell recast by Paul Revere and one of the four "Vinegar Bibles." The town's narrow streets preserve a colonial atmosphere. South, along the shore, are the resorts of Rye and Hampton beaches.

NEW JERSEY

New Jersey is called the Garden State, an appellation which is quite correct. It is also called the Mosquito State, but the mosquito control agencies have done much to control their numbers. It should certainly be called the Highway State because of its excellent network of highways; it is the crossroads between the North and South and connects New York and Philadelphia. The Garden State Parkway, the New Jersey Turnpike and U.S. Highway 1 manage some of the heaviest traffic in the world. The visitor who approaches New York by car from the New Jersey side and rides over the multiple highway ribbons which twist and loop above, below and alongside each other, will somehow feel that he is motoring in an East Coast Los Angeles.

Northern New Jersey. High Point State Park in the northernmost corner of New Jersey offers a broad view of the wooded Delaware valley; its altitude of 1,803 feet makes it the highest point in the state. The adjoining Stokes State Forest is a popular camping area. At Hamburg the fairytale Gingerbread Castle appeals to all children. East of Hamburg Greenwood Lake, which lies half in New York state, is 7 miles long and surrounded by hills as high as 700 feet. It is a picturesque and popular vacation spot, as are all the lakes of northern New Jersey, particularly lakes Mohawk and Hopatcong. East of Greenwood Lake Ringwood Manor State Park preserves a fine old manor house whose wealth was derived from an iron furnace operating nearby. In Paterson the first successful submarine is displayed in Westside Park; it was built here by J. P. Holland, pioneer designer of our earliest submarines. The historic duel between Aaron Burr and Alexander Hamilton occurred in Weehawken near the bottom of the Palisades below the marker on Hudson Boulevard. In the suburban area of Newark, West Orange is the home of the Edison Museum; it displays the original models of many of Edison's inventions as well as his desk and library. Eagle Rock is a famous lookout point over the metropolitan area and the New York skyline. Newark, the largest city in New Jersey, is part of a huge urban area including Jersey City, Hoboken and a dozen additional communities ranging from lovely hill and garden suburbs in the Oranges to manufacturing cities near the Hudson. Newark is an important communications center, a seaport and has a large airport serving both New Jersey and New York City. West of Newark is historic territory, with innumerable mementos of the American Revolution. In the center of Springfield there is a fine old white church near which the Battle of Springfield was fought. When the Revolutionary troops lacked gun wadding, Pastor James Caldwell did not hesitate to haul out the hymnbooks and use them for this patriotic purpose. In Morristown National Historical Park the Ford Mansion, George Washington's headquarters during the winters of 1777 and 1779, is an important museum now. The Continental Army campgrounds at Jockey Hollow, reconstructed Fort Nonsense and the Wick House may be inspected. In the hills near the Delaware River the ruins of the ancient blast furnace at Oxford

are interesting. The iron works furnished cannon balls both for the Revolutionary and the Civil wars. At the Pennsylvania state line the famous Delaware Water Gap is a highlight of the lovely Delaware valley; the highway passes through the gorge across from Pennsylvania.

Central New Jersey. In Elizabeth is Boxwood Hall, the mansion of Elias Boudinot, first President of the Continental Congress; the plain wooden house stands on East Jersey Street beside tall, modern office buildings. Edison operated his first large experimental laboratory in Menlo Park, and there the electric lamp was invented. As a memorial to this event the 134-foot Edison Tower is crowned with a huge replica of the original incandescent lamp bulb. New Brunswick and Princeton circumscribe the state's foremost area of higher education and research. New Brunswick is the seat of Rutgers University — colonial college, land grant college and state university in one; on its main campus the 1810 Queen's Building is a historic landmark. The university's agricultural experiment station is one of the leaders in the field, and its Institute of Microbiology is a world center for research in antibiotics. Princeton, a lovely, tree-shaded town with fine old mansions in large gardens, is the home of Princeton University, famous for its scientific research and its Woodrow Wilson School, training center for future diplomats and administrators. The campus is magnificent. Its Nassau Hall of 1756 played an important role during the Revolutionary War; it served as the home of the first state legislature and of the Continental Congress, as a hospital and even as a battlefield when a decisive struggle ended within its walls. The Institute of Advanced Studies, where internationally known scholars are at work, and the Westminster Choir College have their homes in Princeton. Flemington is well-known for pottery and glass works and interesting shops. One of the most daring deeds of the Revolutionary War is commemorated by the famous painting, "Washington Crossing the Delaware." The painting was created on the Rhine, and it shows the stripes and stars which did not exist at the time of the crossing, but this has not detracted from its effectiveness. The spot where the crossing occurred is now known as Washington Crossing State Park. Trenton, the state capital, has an attractive complex of modern state buildings, including offices, the state library and the state museum. The Trent House of 1719 is open to visitors. The Old Barracks, an architectural gem erected in 1758 for colonial troops, housed British, Hessian and American soldiers. It is now a museum. To the east near Freehold the old Tennent Church of 1751 and the Molly Pitcher Well mark the field of the Battle of Monmouth of 1778. Along the coast the Atlantic Highlands offers a splendid marine view over Sandy Hook and Raritan Bay, the new Gateway National Recreational Area. The resorts along the coast are described on pages 36-37.

Southern New Jersey. Burlington is the hometown of James Fenimore ("Leatherstocking") Cooper and Captain James ("Don't give up the ship!") Lawrence. The Cooper birthplace is a museum of antique costumes, period furniture and manuscripts. The Lawrence home contains mementos of the naval hero of the War of 1812. In Camden, across the Delaware from Philadelphia, the Walt Whitman House at 330 Mickle Street is now a museum. The poet lived here from 1884 to 1892, the last 8 years of his life, and his grave is nearby. The Salem Oak at Salem is a magnificent, centuries-old tree under which the Quakers used to barter with the Indians. The southern shore of New Jersey, including Atlantic City, Barnegat Lighthouse, Island Beach and Cape May are described on pages 36-37.

NORTHEAST REGION
NEW YORK

EASTERN NEW YORK. The skyline of New York City rivals the Grand Canyon as the American sight best known to the entire world. A description of New York City is found on pages 28-29. As an educational center New York is the home of some of the most distinguished and interesting universities: Columbia, NYU, the urban City University, Fordham, Manhattan College, and the New School for Social Research. Family sightseeing in Manhattan includes a boat trip to the Statue of Liberty or round the island, the Central Park or Bronx Zoo, the Empire State Building or the World Trade Center. Greenwich Village with its youth culture, its unusual shops and cafés is a tourist attraction. For more information on any aspect of the city write to the New York Convention and Visitors Bureau, 90 East 42nd Street, New York 10017. Across from Manhattan on the west bank of the Hudson River, Palisades Interstate Park consists of spectacular cliffs of diabase reaching a height of about 500 feet. When trap rock quarries threatened to destroy the cliffs, gifts of land and cash by J. P. Morgan, John D. Rockefeller, Jr., the Harriman Family and others made the creation of the park possible. Of the various beaches of the metropolitan area Jones Beach on Long Island is probably the world's largest bathing resort. Yet it is one of the cleanest and most pleasant Atlantic resorts. It consists of 2,413 acres with miles of beaches, facilities for all kinds of sports, a mile-long boardwalk, bathhouses, restaurants and a marine theater. To the east Fire Island National Seashore is a 32-mile-long barrier beach, much of it undeveloped. Southampton is a fashionable resort 110 miles east of the city, with elegant summer residences, historic houses and expensive shops. Some of these homes date back to the seventeenth century. Montauk Point is the eastern end of the island, a popular surf fishing, deep-sea fishing and sailing area. Sterling Forest Gardens, 35 miles northwest of New York City near Tuxedo Park offers splendid flower gardens, lakes, fountains, porpoise and animal shows and rides on exotic animals. The sightseeing attractions of the Hudson Valley are described on pages 30-31. Bear Mountain, crossed by the Appalachian Trail, and Harriman state parks on the west bank offer miles of hiking trails and a trailside museum. During the winter the area is a popular skiing center. The Storm King Highway and West Point, the seat of the U.S. Military Academy, are mentioned on page 31. Inland from West Point, Goshen has a track famous for harness races; it is the home of the Hall of Fame of the Trotter. Newburgh is picturesquely located on bluffs above the broad Hudson. During the Revolutionary War it was Washington's headquarters for 16 months. In the Hasbrouck House where the general stayed his famous letter opposing monarchy for the United States was written; the house is a museum now. North of Newburgh the Catskill Mountains are a lovely region of wooded hills rising to elevations of a little over 4,000 feet, lonely trails and panoramic views. The area abounds with luxurious hotels some of which have become internationally known. The Catskill Game Farm raises animals for zoological gardens, from donkeys and ostriches to llamas and bison. Other attractions in the Catskill area are the Belleayre Ski Center with a 3,000-foot chair lift, and 3,213-foot-tall Mt. Utsayantha, accessible by toll road, is near Stamford. The Hudson estate of Hyde Park is the birthplace of Franklin D. Roosevelt. In Albany the State Capitol and the Philip Schuyler Mansion are interesting. The observation tower of the State Office Building offers a panorama of the city. The new mall of tall modern buildings will be magnificent when it is finished. Opposite Albany in Rensselaer is Fort Crailo (1642). This is believed to be the birthplace of "Yankee Doodle." A British officer watching American militiamen riding by found their appearance humorous, and he wrote down the words of the famous song. Saratoga Springs is described on page 31; east of town are Saratoga Lake and Saratoga National Historical Park, where the turning point of the American Revolution occurred. West of Saratoga Springs, the Petrified Gardens exhibit plants which grew there when the sea covered the valley eons ago. To the west, Gloversville is America's glove manufacturing center; plant tours can be arranged. In Johnstown the colonial mansion of the Mohawk Valley leader Sir William Johnson is a museum now. In Auriesville near Amsterdam the National Shrine of the North American Martyrs is on the site of St. Isaac Jogues' martyrdom in 1646. The Howe Caverns near Cobleskill, which offer a boat ride on a river 200 feet underground, are a popular tourist attraction. Cooperstown on Otsego Lake of Leatherstocking fame is the home of James Fenimore Cooper; his house exhibits folk art and historical items. There are also a Farmers' Museum and the Baseball Hall of Fame; baseball was supposedly invented in Cooperstown. At Dolgeville the Beaversprite Sanctuary is a colony of tame beavers; they can be watched working in the late afternoon.

NORTHEASTERN NEW YORK. At Glens Falls on the Hudson River, Cooper's Cave was made famous by Cooper's "Last of the Mohicans." Lake George is a long-established recreational area and one of the loveliest spots in the state; 32 miles long, it is surrounded by wooded mountains and dotted with green islands and white sailboats. From Bolton Landing and Lake George village tour boats circle the lake. All winter sports flourish in the area. Near Lake George village Gaslight Village recreates the Gay 90's. At Pottersville the Natural Stone Bridge arches 62 feet above the Schroon River in a 180-foot span. The restored Fort Ticonderoga with its superb view of Lake Champlain is described on page 32. At the Crown Point Reservation, also on Lake Champlain, are the ruins of two forts built in colonial times. To the north, the Ausable Chasm near Keeseville is the spectacular canyon of the Ausable River; see page 32. A description of the Thousand Islands of the St. Lawrence River can be found on pages 32-33. To the south near Carthage, the Natural Bridge Caverns, 1,000 feet underground, may be inspected by boat. Syracuse, an industrial center, is the seat of Syracuse University and of a French fort in replica which dates back to the very first attempt to settle central New York. The Finger Lakes region has been described on page 35. Near Waterloo the Scythe Tree is an oddity and a symbol; a Balm of Gilead tree has grown around the scythes which the farm boys hung on the tree branches when they left for the Civil War and World War I. South of the Finger Lakes, the Corning Glass Center displays the 20-ton glass disk cast for the telescope of Mount Palomar in California. The famous crystal sculptures of Steuben glass are also created at the center. Both the glass factory and the museum are open to visitors. Southwest of the Finger Lakes, the Hammondsport-Naples-Urbana region is one of America's leading wine and champagne producers. At Ithaca, on Cayuga Lake, is Cornell University. On the campus of Elmira College near the Pennsylvania state line Mark Twain's study, shaped like the pilot-house of a riverboat, is preserved. Rochester is a world center for the manufacture of photographic and optical goods. The Eastman Kodak plants may be seen on guided tours, and the Photo Museum at the George Eastman House has interesting items. The Xerox Square Exhibit Center has scientific and cultural exhibits. The city is also the seat of the University of Rochester, the well-known Eastman School of Music, the

Rochester Symphony Orchestra and the beautiful lilac gardens in Highland Park.

WESTERN NEW YORK. Farther south, at the Pennsylvania state line, Rock City offers a broad view of the surrounding country from huge rock formations. To the west Panama Rocks is an erupted ocean floor with gorges and crevices. On the lake with the same name, Chautauqua is the seat of the Chautauqua Institution and its program of adult education. Once a nationwide organization, it is now restricted to the summer resort of Chautauqua proper. Buffalo, New York's second largest city, has an interesting waterfront on Lake Erie, with huge grain elevators, wharves and ships. The Peace Bridge to Canada, the Albright-Knox Art Gallery and the Museum of Science in Humboldt Park are other attractions, and the city is also the seat of the Buffalo unit of the State University of New York. Niagara Falls and Fort Niagara are described on pages 34-35.

NOVA SCOTIA, CANADA

SOUTHERN NOVA SCOTIA. Halifax, the capital of the province was founded in 1749. In Canada's history it played a leading part, for it has the country's oldest Protestant church (St. Paul, built in 1750) and was the site of Canada's first printing press (1751), which printed Canada's first newspaper in 1752. It had Canada's first public school, first public gardens, first dockyard and the first post office. It was a garrison and fortress from the beginning and still is the principal base of Canada's fleet. For a magnificent view of Halifax harbor visitors ride to the highest hill in the city which is crowned by the Citadel, a squat, gray fort that has never been attacked. At the southern end of the city's peninsula Point Pleasant Park has several old forts and historic structures like the Martello Tower, which was built by Queen Victoria's father, the Duke of Kent, in 1796. North West Arm, a 3-mile inlet, is an ideal harbor for yachts, canoes and other pleasure craft. From the National Memorial Tower in Fleming Park a superb view of the city may be enjoyed. Downtown, Province House is an impressive structure. Halifax is also the home of Dalhousie University. To the southwest Lunenburg is a picturesque fishing port; one of its schooners, the *Bluenose,* won international fame as the North Atlantic champion. Deep-sea fishing flourishes all along the coast, and the annual International Tuna Cup Match, held at Wedgeport on the southern coast, attracts thousands of sportsmen. A current off the coast called Soldier's Rip is an especially productive fishing ground. Port Royal National Historic Park on the Bay of Fundy honors a unique event in Canada's history in the reconstructed Habitation, a fortified trading post erected by Champlain and De Monts in 1605. Nearby, at Annapolis Royal, Fort Anne National Historic Park contains the restored fort, a museum and a historical library. On the Minas Basin Grand Pré Memorial Park is a popular recreational area. The Bay of Fundy, by the way, has the world's highest tides, sometimes measuring up to 53 feet.

NORTHERN NOVA SCOTIA. Every July thousands flock to the Scottish Highland Games in Antigonish. Leaving the mainland you will enter Cape Breton Island, the northern part of the province. In its center a cluster of beautiful lakes impressed the first French settler deeply, particularly at sunset; he called the lakes Bras d'Or, Arms of Gold. There at Baddeck is located the summer home of the inventor of the telephone, Alexander Graham Bell; a modern museum explains his experiments in aerodynamics. Sydney, Nova Scotia's third largest city, is both an industrial city (coal and steel) and a popular summer resort. Twenty-three miles to the south the Fortress of Louisbourg

National Historic Park preserves the ruins of one of the most impressive military establishments on the American continent. The walled city of Louisbourg erected by the French early in the eighteenth century is being restored. In the north Cape Breton Highlands National Park is a landscape of solitary grandeur and is touched on three sides by the scenic Cabot Trail. Both freshwater and saltwater fishing are good in the park, and the east coast offers a special treat to deep-sea fishermen. Ingonish and Neil Harbour are the centers of the swordfishing industry.

ONTARIO, CANADA

EASTERN ONTARIO. The "greatest ship highway in the world" is the Soo Canal between Sault Ste. Marie in Ontario and the city of the same name in Michigan. Watching the traffic in the canal is a great sightseeing attraction; one of the huge locks is located in Canada. The whole area is described on pages 100-103. On the northern shore of Lake Huron Manitoulin Island is the largest freshwater island on earth. Georgian Bay is an immense arm of Lake Huron, with a shoreline of hundreds of sheltered bays and an archipelago of more than 40,000 islands along its eastern coast. Rocky capes, sandy bars, wooded islands, picturesquely winding channels and myriads of fish in the sparkling waters make this region a wonderful summer playground. Georgian Bay Islands National Park consists of approximately 50 islands, of which Beausoleil is the largest. This region was Huronia, the ancient home of the great Huron Indian federation which was almost annihilated by the Iroquois. Near Midland, on the south shore of Georgian Bay, the Indian village and Jesuit Mission of St. Ignace was burned and destroyed in the massacre of 1649, an event which is commemorated today in the Martyr's Shrine of Midland. To the southwest at Stratford the Stratford Shakespeare Festival is famous for its annual midsummer season of excellent dramatic performances of plays by Shakespeare and, occasionally, of other classical or modern dramas. Art exhibitions are held in conjunction with the festival which draws thousands of visitors from Canada and the United States. At the southwestern tip of Ontario Windsor is located on the left bank of the Detroit River opposite America's automobile capital. Windsor plays a similar role in Canada. Point Pelée National Park is the most southerly point of Canada. If you fly directly westward on the park's latitude you will land in California — a surprise to those who think of Canada in terms of the far north. Point Pelée's broad, sandy beaches and shady groves of maple trees, oaks and red cedars have indeed a southern charm. The park is also a fascinating bird sanctuary on one of the continent's principal bird migration routes. Thousands of Detroiters and Windsorites enjoy the park during the summer. To the east the Niagara Falls are described on page 34; the Canadian sector of the falls is larger in volume and more beautiful than the American part and the shore park of the Canadian city of Niagara Falls offers the best view of the great natural spectacle as a whole. To the north Toronto is built on a slope below a plateau which gradually rises from Lake Ontario to a height of 300 feet. It is the capital of Ontario, essentially a British-Canadian community. The old Parliament buildings in Queen's Park are of red sandstone, and the new additions are of blue dolomite. In contrast are the beautiful curves of the new City Hall on Civic Square. There are 69 other parks, among them Exhibition Park, which houses the annual Canadian National Exhibition. The city's seat of higher learning is the University of Toronto. St. Lawrence Islands National Park is the Canadian section of that most picturesque region usually called the Thousand Islands, described on pages 32-33. The Canadian park consists of a mainland area and 17 islands whose granite and limestone cliffs rise from the blue channels; everywhere there are groves of birch, pine, oak and maple. The islands are equipped with wharves, and many have bathing beaches and camping facilities. The drive northeastward along the St. Lawrence Seaway, a system of canals, locks and power plants opening the Great Lakes to ocean commerce, passes through a region of scenic beauty, historic interest and recreational facilities. Overlooking the St. Lawrence River at Prescott, Fort Wellington National Historic Park preserves an impressive fortress which was erected during the War of 1812. The pentagonal earthworks enclose a massive stone building with walls 4 feet thick. To the north Ottawa is located on the right bank of the Ottawa River on a chain of hills which rises from the riverbank to an altitude of 135 feet. The scenery is beautiful, and from the Parliament buildings one can clearly see the Chaudière Falls with their clouds of spray. The Rideau Canal separates the city into an Upper Town (largely English), and a Lower Town (largely French). As the capital of Canada, Ottawa possesses imposing Victorian Gothic-style government buildings, most of them erected on Parliament Hill in 1860. Besides the legislative buildings, the Royal Mint, the National Museums of Man and Natural Science, the National Art Gallery, the War Memorial and the Dominion Observatory are tourist attractions. The mansions of the governor general and the prime minister in suburban Rockliffe Park, and the campus of the University of Ottawa are also of interest. Nearby Lake Deschênes is a summer resort, and skiing in the Laurentian Hills to the north is a favorite winter sport. West of Ottawa Algonquin Provincial Park comprises 2,910 square miles of unspoiled natural beauty. It is a sanctuary for deer, moose and beaver, with numerous lakes and streams. Campsites and accommodations are available.

WESTERN ONTARIO. Lake of the Woods, on the Manitoba border, is a great resort area with Kenora, "Queen of the North," at its center. This playground offers thousands of square miles of island-studded lakes and woods, and too many delightful bays and inlets to be counted. From small boats and big cruisers visitors fish for muskies and lake trout, walleyes and smallmouth bass. Just east the Rainy Lake-Fort Frances region is a vast tract of evergreen forests with the earmarks of a true wilderness. There are hundreds of lakes which have no names; in fact their exact number is not known either. The district has been described as "the greatest canoe country in North America." Quetico Provincial Park and Superior National Forest on the United States side of the border form a huge water and woods wilderness ideal for canoeing; parts of it are a forest primeval of white pines. It is a rugged and beautiful country for experienced "voyageurs." On the shore of Lake Superior the city of Thunder Bay (formerly Fort William and Port Arthur) is the starting point for the great hunting and fishing wilderness. But at the same time it is also the trading center of the busy Thunder Bay region which produces gold, silver, iron and grain. The city's waterfront with miles of bustling docks, wharves and the continent's biggest grain silos is interesting to watch.

PENNSYLVANIA

EASTERN PENNSYLVANIA. Philadelphia is a historical, industrial and cultural center, the Bicentennial City of the United States; it is described on pages 38-39. The American sanctuary of Valley Forge is pictured on page 39. The Pennsylvania Turnpike runs from the Delaware River for 327 miles across the state to the Ohio border. The first of America's cross-country toll roads, it is still considered the most spectacular one, with long tunnels leading through mountain ranges, and connecting the New Jersey and Ohio turnpikes. East of Philadelphia, on a peninsula in the Delaware River near Tullytown, William Penn's summer home, Pennsbury Manor, has been reconstructed. The scenic road along the Delaware leads from Washington Crossing to the picturesque artists' colony of New Hope and beyond. This setting of a quiet canal, great shade trees, bridges and solid fieldstone houses is Old Pennsylvania at its best. The same pleasant atmosphere prevails in Doylestown, where the Mercer Museum of the Bucks County Historical Society exhibits the early settlers' tools in fully equipped colonial shops. Near Kennett Square, not far from the Delaware state line, Longwood Gardens is a fabulous estate of Wilmington's DuPont family. A spectacular park with a 3-acre conservatory and lovely fountains is open to the public. Brandywine Battlefield State Historical Park is near Chadds Ford. The Pennsylvania Dutch country and Lancaster with its famous farmers' market are described on page 41. The Pennsylvania Farm Museum of Landis Valley near Lancaster illustrates interestingly the civilization of the Pennsylvania Dutch (actually Germans) since 1710. Northeast of Lancaster the Ephrata Cloister has been restored and welcomes visitors; the buildings, erected in 1732, were occupied by a group of monastic Seventh Day Baptists who wrote and composed their own sacred hymns. Near Baumstown, not far from Reading, the Daniel Boone Homestead has been restored on the site of the pioneer's birthplace; it is a stone house with some early furnishings. At Hopewell Village National Historic Site an eighteenth-century iron making village comes to life. The Trexler-Lehigh Game Preserve which maintains herds of bison, elk and other game animals is located at Schnecksville near Allentown. Bethlehem is famous on several counts: it is the seat of a great steel industry, the home of the excellent Bach Choir and its annual Bach Festival, and Lehigh University is located there. Originally a Moravian settlement, Bethlehem still preserves several ancient Moravian buildings like the Bell House, Brethren's House, Gemein House and Old Chapel. At the Delaware Water Gap the river cuts through the Kittatinny Mountains, creating a deep, 3-mile gorge; this is a gateway to the Pocono Mountains and Stroudsburg, a popular vacation area described on pages 40-41. The Pocono Wild Animal Farm near Stroudsburg exhibits mountain goats and llamas, kangaroos and deer. In the Wilkes-Barre — Scranton district some companies offer guided tours into the anthracite coal mines.

CENTRAL PENNSYLVANIA. Throughout central Pennsylvania numerous limestone caverns are open to the public. Near the New York state line the Tioga Point Museum at Athens displays Indian and frontier relics. To the south Eagles Mere is a popular summer resort on Eagles Mere Lake. At Sunbury on the Susquehanna River, the site of Fort Augusta is marked by a museum and a model of the fort. Hershey, east of Harrisburg, is one of America's chocolate centers, with a well-known hotel, huge rose gardens, golf courses and an amusement park; the chocolate plant is open for inspection. Harrisburg, the state capital, is described on page 40. Near the Maryland state line on Highway 194 between Hanover and Littlestown, the stables of the Hanover Shoe Company Farms may be visited; famous trotters are raised there. Abraham Lincoln's "Gettysburg Address" at the dedication of part of the battlefield as a military cemetery marks the outstanding event in the history of Gettysburg National Military Park. Today almost 30 miles of roads wind their way past markers and monuments, breastworks and artillery. The Eternal Light Peace Memorial and the High Water Mark Monument, at the point of the farthest Confederate advance, are outstanding. An observation tower overlooks the battlefield and a cyclorama painting illustrates the details of the most important battle of the Civil War. Guided tours are available. The park has a lovely hill and woodland setting, and the old town of Gettysburg does not seem to have changed much since the fateful July of 1863. The Eisenhower Farm is close by. One of the landmarks of American railroading is the horseshoe curve near Altoona; the tracks form a big U on their way through the Alleghenies. To the northeast State College is the home of Pennsylvania State University. Tourists interested in airplane construction may visit the Piper Aircraft Corp. plant near Lock Haven. In a picturesque setting in the north central part of the state, the Pine Creek Gorge is a thousand feet deep and about 50 miles long; it is called the Grand Canyon of Pennsylvania. Surrounding the chasm are Colton Point State Park and Leonard Harrison State Park with recreational facilities and lookout points high above the canyon.

WESTERN PENNSYLVANIA. Kane is known for its Lobo Wolf Park; the large, fierce beasts and a number of Arctic wolves may be seen in a fenced-in preserve where they roam freely. At Johnstown an inclined plane railway carries visitors and cars to a 500-foot summit which offers a broad panorama of the city. Near the West Virginia state line 11 miles southeast of Uniontown, Fort Necessity has been reconstructed at the site of the first battle in which young George Washington took part. The burial place of General Braddock is nearby. At New Geneva, Friendship Hill is a museum containing many historical documents. It was formerly the home of Albert Gallatin, one of our first secretaries of the treasury. Pittsburgh is one of the world's great steel and manufacturing centers; it is a bright community today, as cheerful and healthy as any city its size. Historically it developed from Fort Duquesne, later Fort Pitt, at the confluence of the Monongahela and the Allegheny rivers which form the Ohio. The peninsula is the Golden Triangle, Pittsburgh's business district. The rest of the city has spread to the surrounding hills, and a unique communications system negotiates rivers and ridges. There are 18 bridges, several tunnels and a number of inclines, cable cars that lift people and cars to the tops of the hills. Mt. Washington Incline, across the Monongahela from the Golden Triangle, rises to a height of 400 feet and offers a fine panorama. In the Oakland district the University of Pittsburgh has an unusual campus; its 42-story Cathedral of Learning is an impressive skyscraper. Nearby are the Stephen Collins Foster Memorial, which honors the Pittsburgh-born composer of America's favorite folk tunes, and the Carnegie-Mellon University. Other outstanding sites are the Buhl Planetarium and Institute of Popular Science, the Allegheny Observatory in Riverview Park, the Syria Mosque, and Schenley Park, with an excellent botanical conservatory. To the northwest at Ambridge the once flourishing communal Christian settlement of the Harmonists, Old Economy, may be visited; it consists of the 35-room Great House, the granary, music hall and other structures filled with early nineteenth-century relics. Pymatuning Reservoir is a large, man-made body of water with a 78-mile shoreline. The surrounding state park is popular for fishing and water sports in summer and for skating and iceboating in winter. In the northwestern part of the state, particularly in Cook Forest State Park, large stands of virgin timber and abundant wildlife still remain. At Titusville, the Drake Well Memorial Park has been established around the world's first well that was drilled for oil, produced oil and initiated a new industrial era. Colonel Drake's primitive

apparatus and some of his papers and personal belongings may be seen in the museum. On Presque Isle in Lake Erie, opposite the city of Erie, the obelisk of the Perry Monument commemorates Perry's victory in the Battle of Lake Erie. The commodore's reconstructed flagship, *Niagara,* may be inspected at at the foot of State Street.

PRINCE EDWARD ISLAND, CANADA

Of all Canadian provinces, Prince Edward Island is the smallest and one of the loveliest. The whole island is a beautiful park, with a lacy shoreline of tidal streams, lagoons and inlets, with gently rolling hills, prosperous farms, lush forests and picturesque red sandstone cliffs in the south. In 1534 Jacques Cartier described the island as "the fairest that may possibly be seen, and full of beautiful trees and meadows." After more than four centuries the explorer's endorsement is still valid. There is only one city on the island, Charlottetown, capital of the province. It is picturesquely located at a spot where three rivers merge into a fine harbor. At Province House in the Confederation Chamber was held the meeting which led to the Union of Canada. Fathers of Confederation Memorial Centre includes a theater, an art gallery, a museum and a library. St. Dunstan's University and Prince of Wales College have combined to form the University of Prince Edward Island. North of Charlottetown Prince Edward Island National Park is a 25-mile coastal strip on the Gulf of St. Lawrence, a fine smooth sandy beach of reddish color set off by sand dunes and red sandstone cliffs. Some sections are well forested, and stands of white birches and dark spruces have a northern beauty of their own. All sports are available, but swimming, sailing and fishing in the many sheltered bays are most popular. There are numerous picturesque and idyllic fishing villages on the island, as for instance Mount Carmel in the southwestern corner. It is an Acadian settlement which seems to have been transplanted from Brittany not hundreds of years ago but yesterday. Traditional handicrafts flourish, particularly the making of hand-hooked rugs with gay patterns. The Dominion Experimental Fox and Mink Ranch at Summerside is open to visitors.

QUÉBEC, CANADA

SOUTHERN QUÉBEC. Entering the Province of Québec from New England, visitors will find in the Eastern Townships much the same landscape as south of the border, with pleasant forests, hills and lakes. One of the largest lakes of the region, Memphremagog, is partly in Vermont, partly in Québec. Sherbrooke, the "Queen of the Eastern Townships," has a spectacular location on the scenic slopes of two rivers, the St-François and the Magog. To the west Fort Chambly National Historic Park, 20 miles from Montréal, contains a stone fort of 1711. Some of its massive walls are the originals, and there are a display room and a small theater. Not far away, 12 miles south of St-Jean, in Fort Lennox National Historic Park are the remains of one of Canada's largest old fortresses, first built in 1759 by the French to stop the advance of the English from the south. The present fortified buildings, the ramparts and the 60-foot-wide moat date from 1819.

THE ST. LAWRENCE VALLEY OF THE PROVINCE OF QUÉBEC. Montréal, Canada's largest metropolis and home of the permanent exposition "Man and His World" (an outgrowth of Expo '67), is described on page 15. Among the city's famous buildings are the magnificent Cathedral of Notre-Dame-de-Montréal and the Château de Ramezay, across from city hall, which was the palace of the French governors of New France. The city's subway offers the world's quietest ride, for the trains run on pneumatic tires. The Place des Arts is a cultural center where symphonic music, opera and ballet flourish, and McGill University and the University of Montréal are notable institutions of higher learning. To the northeast on the St. Lawrence River Trois-Rivières has very old traditions. The city was founded as a trading post in 1634, and many of its streets are as winding and narrow as they were when laid out hundreds of years ago by pioneers from Normandy and Brittany. Trois-Rivières is one of the world's greatest pulp and paper manufacturing centers. Québec, the capital of the province, is described on pages 14-15. Its walls, citadel and city gate are favorites of photographers. Among the historic buildings are the Convent of the Ursulines, the church of Notre-Dame-des-Victoires and the Basilica of Notre-Dame of 1647. Laval University is the leading French university in North America. Québec is also a haven for gourmets; the city's French restaurants are generally excellent. A sound and light spectacle called "Journey into the Past" is offered on summer nights at the Parliament Building. Below the city the Île-d'Orléans shelters the most picturesque old French farmhouses with walls three feet thick. A few miles north of Québec Ste-Anne-de-Beaupré is a widely known shrine whose basilica is dedicated to Ste. Anne, mother of the Virgin Mary. It is sometimes called the Lourdes of America because many miraculous cures have been reported there. Farther north on the left bank of the St. Lawrence the fashionable summer resort of Murray Bay with the Manoir Richelieu is described on page 14. On the same page is the description of the Gaspé Peninsula. The Gaspésie Provincial Park is the home of a herd of caribou.

QUEBEC'S NORTH COUNTRY. The huge mountainous area of the Laurentian Hills has been developed into a great ski center with all winter sports facilities and the cross-country Maple Leaf Trail. The Saguenay River region is usually enjoyed from a steamboat. At the mouth of the river, shielded by a rocky promontory, Tadoussac has a unique history. It was not only one of the first French trading posts in America, but it also played an important part in the history of the Indians. Long before the sixteenth century Indians from as far north as Hudson's Bay and from as far south as Florida gathered here for a great barter fair and festival. Proceeding upriver to Bagotville, today's boats move between canyon walls over 500 feet high. Cape Trinité and Cape Éternité are huge rocks rising precipitously from the water. River cruises may be taken from Montréal or Québec, and steamboat trips from Tadoussac. The area is also accessible by highway. At the western end of the Saguenay region the Lac St-Jean area was a lonely backwoods country not so long ago; today it is an industrial empire sparked by one of the biggest hydroelectric developments in America. Plants have been established there for smelting ores, manufacturing aluminum and making pulp and paper. But the lake is large, and there are still plenty of opportunities for fishermen. The sportsmen's specialty is ouananiche, landlocked salmon, reputedly the finest fighter in North American fresh water. The port of Sept-Îles (Seven Islands) near the mouth of the St. Lawrence River is the terminal of a 360-mile-long railroad that connects the deepwater port with the vast iron ore deposits in the interior at Schefferville and Wabush. On the right bank of the river St-Jean — Port Joli is Canada's folk art center, a colony of painters and wood-carvers, coppersmiths and engravers. The town's religious carvings decorate numerous churches in Canada and elsewhere.

RHODE ISLAND

NORTHERN RHODE ISLAND. Providence, the capital of the state with the longest name (Rhode Island and Providence Plantations) and the smallest area, is particularly attractive around College Hill where the beautiful campus of Brown University is located. Its John Carter Brown Library owns a splendid collection of early Americana. Fine old residences reflect the wealth of the seaport turned industrial center. The slender spired First Baptist Meeting House, long used for Brown University commencements, is one of the city's loveliest buildings. Roger Williams Park has lovely rose gardens, flower displays and the Betsey Williams Cottage which is a museum for colonial furniture. The Old Slater Mill in nearby Pawtucket, erected beside the Blackstone River in 1793, is the birthplace of the cotton textile industry in America; primitive eighteenth-century machines are displayed and demonstrations of textile making are given in the ancient frame building.

SOUTHERN RHODE ISLAND. At Bristol, on the eastern shore of Narragansett Bay, Colt Drive in Colt State Park is a scenic waterfront road on the former large Colt estate. Newport, one of the last resorts, had its heyday around the turn of the century. The expression "the 400" as a symbol of social prominence originated there because Mrs. William Astor's ballroom held exactly 400 guests. Today the pompous "cottages," pretentious copies of European palaces costing $2 or $3 million when they were built 80 or 90 years ago, can best be seen on an 11-mile loop drive called the Ten-Mile-Drive. This takes the sightseer past the most spectacular estates such as the Breakers of the Vanderbilts, the Marble House and Belcourt Castle. Hikers will find the Cliff Walk beautiful; it follows the shore for three miles between velvety lawns and masses of rocks and boulders sprayed with salty foam. In many ways the historic old port city is more interesting than the millionaires' palaces. Around Washington Square with the Commodore Perry Statue such buildings as the old City Hall of 1761, the Old Colony House and the Redwood Library, one of the country's earliest, reflect the city's historical and cultural importance. The oldest Jewish congregation in America was founded in this town when Jews from the Netherlands settled there in 1658. They built the Touro Synagogue, the first one on this continent, in 1763. At the edge of Touro Park the Old Stone Mill is an impressive circular fieldstone structure of medieval appearance; its origin is unknown. The theory of Viking origin has been discredited now. It fired the imagination of Longfellow and James Fenimore Cooper, who mentioned it in their writings. Newport's Coasters Harbor Island is the birthplace of the nation's naval training. On the western shore of Narragansett Bay, Wickford is an attractive old village with a marina. A trading post of 1679, Smith's Castle, has been restored. Near Wickford Junction the South County Museum exhibits colonial crafts and Americana. Saunderstown, to the south, maintains the Gilbert Stuart birthplace as a memorial to the famous colonial portrait painter. South of Kingston, home of the University of Rhode Island, and Narragansett, Scarborough and other state beaches are recreational areas. Block Island may be reached by ferry from Providence, Newport, Point Judith or New London. It is a summer resort and deep-sea fishing center, especially for swordfish and tuna.

VERMONT

NORTHERN VERMONT. The pleasant Vermont town of St. Albans was the scene of one of the most daring raids of the Civil War. A troop of Confederates invaded Vermont from Canada, took the town, looted the bank of $200,000 — and vanished back into Canada. St. Albans Bay is noted for excellent bass and perch fishing. Burlington and the University of Vermont are described on page 23. South of Burlington, the Shelburne Museum is one of the country's most outstanding outdoor exhibits of Americana, including an old ten-wheel locomotive, a lighthouse and the side-wheel steamer *Ticonderoga*. A ferry ride on Lake Champlain is recommended, and sportsmen will find the lake a good fishing ground for pike, perch and bass. Along the wooded and hilly lakeshore there are numerous popular vacation spots. To the east Stowe is Vermont's great ski resort (see also page 23); it lies in the shadows of Mt. Mansfield, the highest peak in the state. The summit may be reached by toll road or gondola lift. To the north the highway runs through a spectacular gap at the base of Mt. Mansfield called Smugglers Notch. Elm-shaded St. Johnsbury lies in the center of the maple sugar country, and the Maple Grove Maple Museum is a tourist attraction. The city's natural science museum has a good display of the state's fauna and flora. North of St. Johnsbury an area of dozens of lakes invites sportsmen and vacationers. Lake Memphremagog which is partly in Canada is the largest.

CENTRAL VERMONT. The Long Trail of the Green Mountains runs the whole length of the state. Montpelier's capitol is built of Vermont granite. The town possesses several interesting historical relics, among them the first printing press brought to the colonies. Barre is the world's leading producer of monument granite; the operation of the quarries on Millstone Hill is a fascinating spectacle (see also page 23). West of Barre around Waitsfield the Green Mountain area is a popular all-year resort. Middlebury is a fine old town, the seat of Middlebury College whose foreign language schools are nationally known. Rutland and nearby Proctor are famous for their marble quarries and finishing plants; in Proctor the exhibit of the Vermont Marble Company is most interesting (see also page 23). Rutland is the seat of the Green Mountain Club which maintains trails in the mountains. In South Woodstock, east of Rutland, the Green Mountain Horse Association opens and maintains marked bridle paths. One outstanding breed, the Morgan Horse, is a product of Vermont. East of Woodstock the Quechee Gorge is a mile-long chasm; the Ottauquechee River flows 165 feet below the highway bridge of U.S. 4. Plymouth, the birthplace of Calvin Coolidge, has been mentioned on page 23.

SOUTHERN VERMONT. In Weston, the Vermont Country Store has been restored as an emporium of the 1890's; it sells Vermont specialties and attracts large numbers of tourists. To the southwest, near the resort of Manchester, the Skyline Drive is a scenic toll road to the summit of 3,816-foot-high Mount Equinox. Near modern Bennington, Old Bennington, with its museum and monument, is a historical reminder of Ethan Allen, the Green Mountain Boys, the Catamount Tavern and the Battle of Bennington (see also page 22). Brattleboro is picturesquely located on the Connecticut River; the town was once noted as a producer of organs. In nearby Marlboro the annual Marlboro Festival attracts the world's leading musicians; it has become one of the country's outstanding annual musical events. Nearby Mt. Snow is the major ski resort of southern Vermont.

VIRGINIA

The best time to visit Virginia is spring, when the whole state sparkles brightly with flowers. Garden Week in Virginia, held every year during the last week of April, presents the Old Dominion at its best; many interesting antebellum homes with colorful gardens are open to visitors. Circulars with all details may be obtained from the Garden Club of Virginia, Jefferson Hotel, Richmond, Virginia.

TIDEWATER VIRGINIA. Alexandria, a few miles south of Washington on the western bank of the Potomac, preserves a dignified colonial atmosphere. General George Washington attended Christ Church, was present at the planning of the French and Indian campaign at Carlyle House, Braddock's quarters, and ate and drank at Gadsby's Tavern. The Masonic National Memorial Temple is dedicated to him. Mount Vernon, the plantation homestead and burial site of George and Martha Washington, is described on page 46. Manassas National Battlefield Park commemorates 2 Civil War battles and lies about 25 miles southwest of Washington. To the south Fredericksburg is a shrine of American history. George Washington went to school there for a short time, and the home of his mother Mary is furnished as it might have been in her day. His sister, Betty Washington Lewis, lived at Kenmore, a stately colonial mansion, now a museum. In Fredericksburg the James Monroe Museum and Memorial Library houses the law offices of James Monroe; they contain various Monroe relics, including the desk on which the fifth president of the United States wrote the Monroe Doctrine. Fredericksburg and Spotsylvania National Military Park commemorates four major battles of the Civil War which were fought there between 1862 and 1864. Gun pits, trenches, markers, the building in which General Stonewall Jackson died and a museum with relief maps, diorama and gun collections may be inspected. To the east, near Colonial Beach, the George Washington Birthplace National Monument has been established; the Memorial Mansion is open to visitors. Nearby Stratford Hall is the birthplace of three famous Lees, General Robert E. Lee, and Richard Henry and Francis Lightfoot Lee, both signers of the Declaration of Independence. Across Chesapeake Bay, on the open Atlantic coast, Chincoteague Island is a hunting and fishing resort. An interesting wilderness touch is provided by a herd of wild ponies which roams the salt marshes; every year in July a "pony penning day" is held. Chincoteague connects with Assateague Island National Seashore, which includes a wildlife refuge. Recrossing Chesapeake Bay to Mathews and Gloucester counties, the numerous daffodil farms with their acres of blossoms are a sight to behold in springtime. To the west Richmond, the capital of Virginia, was originally built on seven hills by the James River; it has now spread over a large area on both sides of the river. It is a modern industrial city and a great historic center. The State Capitol, designed by Thomas Jefferson, was the scene of the treason trial of Aaron Burr and later became the home of the Confederate Congress; there General Robert E. Lee took over the command of Virginia's Confederate forces. The old White House of the Confederacy is now the Confederate Museum. In 1775, in Richmond's St. John's Church, Patrick Henry coined the challenging words "Give me liberty or give me death." Other attractions are the home of the great jurist John Marshall, the Virginia Museum of Fine Arts, the Edgar Allen Poe Museum in the city's oldest house, the Carillon Tower in William Byrd Park and the bright gardens of Maymont Park. Tourists interested in Virginia tobacco and the manufacture of cigarettes may take a guided tour through the plants of the American Tobacco Co. or Philip Morris, Inc. South of Richmond, Petersburg National Battlefield includes parts of 7 Civil War battlefields lying southeast of the city. Restored Williamsburg and the Colonial National Historical Park, including Jamestown and Yorktown, has been described on page 47. At the mouth of the James River Newport News is a busy shipbuilding city; the Mariners

NORTHEAST REGION

Museum has an outstanding collection of ships' models, maritime prints, and nautical documents. The city's favorite bathing resort is Buckroe Beach in adjoining Hampton. Across Hampton Roads the sailors' center of Norfolk is the gateway to the famous hunting regions of the Back Bay (waterfowl) and the Dismal Swamp (small game animals); it is also the starting point for 25 miles of fine beaches. Virginia Beach with its white sands, 6 miles of beaches, fine hotels and elegant clubs is one of the best known resorts on America's Atlantic coast. One of the area's unmatched facilities is the 17½-mile-long tunnel-bridge that connects with Cape Charles and the North; it is one of the world's most impressive toll roads.

CENTRAL VIRGINIA. The Great Falls of the Potomac, north of Washington, D.C., are described under Maryland. In Winchester, the office of young Washington may be inspected; he used it when he worked as a surveyor for Lord Fairfax. The Skyline Drive and Shenandoah National Park are described on page 64. In the Shenandoah valley near the Skyline Drive, a number of limestone caves may be visited on guided tours; the more important ones are Crystal, Skyline (near Front Royal), Shenandoah, Endless (near New Market), Grand (near Waynesboro), Massanutten and Luray. The Luray Caverns are especially well-known. In the Shenandoah valley at Mt. Solon the Natural Chimneys are seven huge rock towers rising above the plain in Natural Chimneys Regional Park. The birthplace of Woodrow Wilson in Staunton is open to visitors. East of the Skyline Drive, Charlottesville with the University of Virginia, Thomas Jefferson's Monticello, Monroe's Ash Lawn and the old Michie Tavern are described on page 47. South of Charlottesville the Appomattox Court House National Historical Park has been established at the site of General Lee's surrender to General Grant; the McLean House, where the truce terms were drafted, has been restored. At the North Carolina state line, the city of Danville is noted for its old established tobacco auctions, which are held from mid-September to the winter months.

WESTERN VIRGINIA. Near the West Virginia border, Hot Springs is a fashionable resort with the traditional Homestead Hotel, an old established spa and convention site. The city of Lexington in the Shenandoah valley is the burial place of two southern heroes, Robert E. Lee and Stonewall Jackson. This "shrine of the South" is also the home of Washington and Lee University and Virginia Military Institute. South of Lexington the Natural Bridge is a huge stone arch 215 feet above Cedar Creek; it has been a famous sightseeing spot since the days of George Washington. During the summer a sound and light pageant is performed there every night. The Blue Ridge Parkway connects the Skyline Drive with the Great Smoky Mountains in North Carolina; it is described on pages 64-65. At Roanoke, modern commercial center of western Virginia, the scenic drive to Mill Mountain is pleasant. From the park on the summit a fine panorama of the city, the Blue Ridge and the Allegheny Mountains may be enjoyed. A 100-foot neon star on the mountainside above the city is visible for 50 miles. Booker T. Washington National Monument, near Roanoke, is the birthplace of the famous teacher and founder of Tuskegee Institute. At mile post 176 of the Blue Ridge Parkway the restored Mabry Mill demonstrates the small mountain industries of the pioneer south. Fairy Stone State Park is located just east. At Pocahontas on the West Virginia state line the Exhibition Mine may be visited; all mining operations are explained. Near the Tennessee border, Abingdon is a center for arts and skills of the southern mountains, for pottery making, weaving and wood

carving; its Barter Theater is nationally known. Every mid-August an Arts and Crafts Festival and a Barter Theater Festival are held. To the west the Natural Tunnel in a state park near Clinchport provides space for a small river and a railroad track; the tunnel can be reached on a trail. Nearby at Big Stone Gap the Southwest Virginia Museum depicts the story of the region in historic relics.

WEST VIRGINIA

NORTHERN WEST VIRGINIA. Morgantown is the home of the University of West Virginia. In the narrow northern panhandle between Pennsylvania and the Ohio River, Moundsville is the site of one of the country's largest Indian burial mounds; the structure measures 900 feet in circumference and is 79 feet high. The interior has been excavated and may be inspected by visitors. Oglebay Park in the hilly, wooded countryside near the industrial city of Wheeling, offers all sports facilities, an historical and regional museum, and summer performances of plays, musicals and concerts.

EASTERN WEST VIRGINIA. Harpers Ferry, at the junction of the Shenandoah and Potomac rivers in the eastern panhandle, was the scene of John Brown's antislavery raid in 1859. The engine house which served Brown and his men as a fort until his capture there is now a museum on Old Arsenal Square. Nearby Charles Town, founded by George Washington's brother Charles, is a lovely city of fine old homes and big shade trees. Seven of its elegant houses were built by Washington's relatives. To the northwest Berkeley Springs has been a health resort with medicinal mineral springs since the days of the Revolution. To the south Cacapon State Park is a popular recreational area; from Prospect Rock four states may be seen on a clear day. Lost River State Park can be reached by a scenic skyline drive. To the west the restored Fort Ashby was built at the command of George Washington. Monongahela National Forest is a huge wooded area along the eastern border of the state. In the mountains near the Virginia state line the Smoke Hole Cavern, Seneca Caverns and Seneca Rocks are tourist attractions. In the limestone caves guided tours are available. Seneca Rocks consist of glistening white sandstone towers that rise spectacularly to 1,000 feet.

SOUTHEASTERN WEST VIRGINIA. White Sulphur Springs is one of America's famous resorts, and its Greenbrier Hotel is a fabulous hostelry. The spa was the outstanding social center of the wealthy planters of the South before the Civil War, and the summer seat of several nineteenth-century presidents. It is still a fashionable vacation spot. Neighboring Lewisburg is a leisurely county seat. Its shady lanes, colonial homes, Old Stone Church of 1796, built of limestone blocks, and the General Lewis Inn with its collection of pioneer guns, pokers and warming pans combine to create an atmosphere of the Old South. The West Virginia State Fair is an important local event.

WESTERN WEST VIRGINIA. In Parkersburg on the Ohio River the City Park is noted for its pioneer museum and its lily pond. Farther south, also on the Ohio, Point Pleasant commemorates its battle of 1774 with a tall stone shaft and a log house museum displaying pioneer relics. In Charleston the State Capitol is crowned with a 300-foot-high gilded dome. To the southeast New River Gorge and Hawks Nest State Park are a picturesque recreation area. At the Virginia state line near Bluefield, Pinnacle Rock State Park is located in the wooded mountains.

Southeast Map

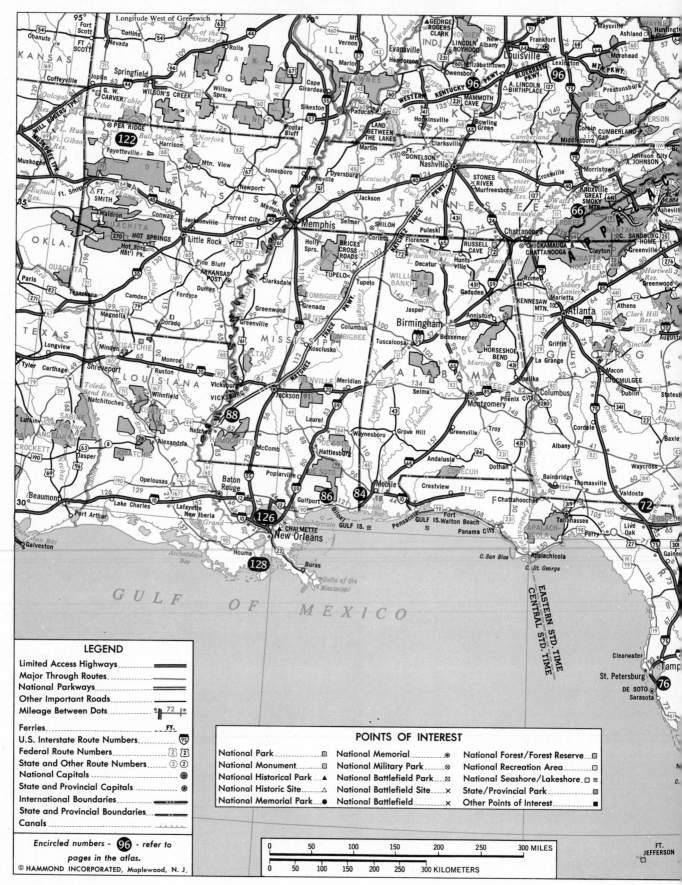

LEGEND

Limited Access Highways	
Major Through Routes	
National Parkways	
Other Important Roads	
Mileage Between Dots	72
Ferries	FY.
U.S. Interstate Route Numbers	95
Federal Route Numbers	2 21
State and Other Route Numbers	2 2
National Capitals	⊛
State and Provincial Capitals	⊛
International Boundaries	
State and Provincial Boundaries	
Canals	

Encircled numbers - 96 - refer to pages in the atlas.

© HAMMOND INCORPORATED, Maplewood, N. J.

POINTS OF INTEREST

National Park ⬛	National Memorial ⊚	National Forest/Forest Reserve ⬛
National Monument ⬛	National Military Park ⊗	National Recreation Area ⬛
National Historical Park ▲	National Battlefield Park ⊠	National Seashore/Lakeshore ⬛ ≈
National Historic Site △	National Battlefield Site ×	State/Provincial Park ⬛
National Memorial Park ●	National Battlefield ×	Other Points of Interest ■

0	50	100	150	200	250	300 MILES

0	50	100	150	200	250	300 KILOMETERS

WHAT to SEE in the SOUTHEAST REGION

TEN-DAY TRIP THROUGH THE BLUE RIDGE AND SMOKY MOUNTAINS. For a general introduction see pages 64-67, also sightseeing guide pages 90-93. Suggested route: Washington, D. C. — Front Royal at the northern end of the Skyline Drive — Shenandoah National Park with panoramic views and mementos of Appalachian mountain life — Waynesboro — Roanoke — Blue Ridge Parkway, crossing the ancient Daniel Boone wilderness. The road is spectacular in spring when thousands of rhododendrons are in bloom; at the Parkway Craft Center (mile 294) mountain crafts are sold, and at the Brinegar Cabin (mile 238½) mountain textiles can be inspected and bought — Asheville, North Carolina, hometown of one of America's great novelists, Thomas Wolfe — Biltmore House, south of Asheville, built by George Vanderbilt, is an immense and pretentious chateau; Grove Park Inn, constructed of big boulders, was a hangout of Ford, Firestone, Edison, Taft and Theodore Roosevelt at the turn of the century — Waynesville — Cherokee, an Indian village where the local Cherokees carry on a flourishing trade with traditional Indian crafts. Great Smoky Mountains National Park, a beautiful mountain forest with huge trees alive with birds and animals, including considerable numbers of bears. A ride to the summit of 6,642-foot-tall Clingman's Dome is recommended — Gatlinburg, Tennessee, with a skylift to the top of Crockett Mountain. At Homespun Valley Mountaineer Village square dances are performed and the distilling of moonshine whiskey is demonstrated — Knoxville, the starting and finishing point of the 100-mile Loop Drive through the Great Smokies — Oak Ridge, one of the country's great scientific research centers, with the American Museum of Atomic Energy — White Sulphur Springs, West Virginia, one of America's oldest spas — Washington, D.C.

THREE-WEEK TRIP THROUGH FLORIDA. For a general introduction see pages 72-83, also sightseeing guide pages 80-93. Suggested route: Jacksonville, Florida, with tropical flower displays in Oriental Gardens — St. Augustine, oldest European city in the United States — Marineland of Florida with entertaining porpoise shows and oceanic outdoor museum — Daytona Beach. Its auto races, once held on its hard packed beach sands, are now run on its International Speedway — Silver Springs. The crystal clear springs may be inspected from glass bottom boats — Ocala with its thoroughbred horse farms — Orlando, a lovely garden city, with Walt Disney World, a super edition of Disneyland — Winter Haven. The thrilling water ski shows at Cypress Gardens are nationally famous — Lake Wales with the Bok Singing Tower — Cape Kennedy (Canaveral) with the John F. Kennedy Space Center; the 30-mile spaceport tour is interesting — Vero Beach with Dodgertown, winter home of the Los Angeles Dodgers — Palm Beach, the fashionable winter resort with exotic shops and art studios. The mansion of Henry Flagler, the resort's founder, is a museum now — Fort Lauderdale, the Venice of America — Miami, with Seaquarium, Serpentarium, Parrot Jungle, Monkey Jungle — Miami Beach with its row of skyscraper hotels along the waterfront — Key West, with the homes of Hemingway and Audubon, is at the end of one of the world's longest highway bridges. Everglades National Park, our only tropical wildlife sanctuary — Naples — Sarasota, with its Jungle Gardens, the Ringling Circus Museum and the magnificent Ringling Art Museum, is the winter quarters of the world's greatest circus — St. Petersburg. Its Sunken Gardens display exotic flowers. Tarpon Springs, famous for sponge fisheries — Jacksonville.

Kitty Hawk and Roanoke Island

THE VIRGINIA DARE TRAIL. Two events of world history took place along this scenic highway, one a tragedy — the first English settlement in America — and the other a modern achievement — the first flight of an airplane. The trail starts at Elizabeth City, a pleasant town at the eastern edge of the Great Dismal Swamp, which at one time was the spooky refuge of runaway slaves and desperate fugitives from justice but is now a haven for wildlife. Over the so-called floating road the highway proceeds through swampy woodlands which in spring are fragrant with honeysuckle and yellow jessamine, and then runs in a southeasterly direction along Currituck Sound. This body of water is a favorite spot for migratory waterfowl; the whistling swan, which breeds in Alaska, winters here. At Point Harbor you cross the Wright Memorial Bridge, the spot of confluence of four great sounds: Roanoke, Croatan,

Currituck and Albemarle; you are now on "the outer islands."

MAN LEARNS TO FLY. Behind the dunes, shaded by wind-twisted trees, there is a village with the strange name of Kitty Hawk, according to legend referring to the mosquito hawks that are frequent there in season. It was in the summer of 1900 that the postmistress of the village received a letter postmarked Dayton, Ohio, in which one Wilbur Wright and his brother Orville inquired about the topography of the Kitty Hawk dunes because they planned to carry out a number of "kite-flying experiments." The postmistress' husband, Captain W. J. Tate, gave all the requested information and later, when the Wrights arrived, acted as their host. For three years the brothers worked at their experiments; the great moment came when they equipped their glider with a gasoline motor. Four epochal flights followed on December 17, 1903, with the brothers alternating as pilots; the first covered 120 feet in 12 seconds, the fourth 852 feet in 59 seconds. The news made headlines all over the world. To commemorate this feat, the Wright Memorial Monument was erected on top of Kill Devil Hill, surrounded by a park. It is an impressive 60-foot-high tower of granite from Mount Airy and has an inner chamber that contains a model of the original plane and the busts of its inventors. The inscription honors the Wrights' genius, resolution and unconquerable faith. To the north a granite boulder marks the exact spot where the first heavier-than-air flying machine left the ground and actually flew.

THE LOST COLONY. The road now resembles a hook, passes through the hunting and fishing resort of Manteo and ends at Fort Raleigh, "the Cittie of Ralegh" in what was then the colony of Virginia. After an abortive attempt in 1584-1585, Governor John White arrived there in 1587, established friendly relations with the Indians and prepared a settlement. On August 18 of that year the governor's daughter, who was married to Ananias Dare, gave birth to a child who was appropriately christened Virginia Dare, the first white child of English parents born in America. A week after the christening White sailed back to England for additional supplies, but because of the wars with Spain could not return until 1591. He landed at Fort Raleigh, ready to celebrate the fourth birthday of his granddaughter, but to his horror found the colony of 116 men, women and children missing. The deserted place was still "very strongly enclosed with a high palisade of great trees." On a large tree he discovered a spot where the bark had been removed, and the mysterious word CROATOAN was carved in capital letters. The settlement was abandoned "without any sign or cross of

TWO MILESTONES of the WESTERN WORLD

The Bodie Island Lighthouse at Cape Hatteras saved many a vessel from shipwreck at this maritime graveyard.

distress." The governor was puzzled as there was no evidence of a violent struggle, and to this day we are puzzled about the fate of the first Anglo-Americans. John White was a careful official who returned to England with minute drawings of what he had seen, so that the present reconstruction of blockhouses and palisades is an authentic reproduction of the 1585 original. A great attraction during the summer months is the picturesque pageant "The Lost Colony" which is performed in an open-air theater.

SHIP'S GRAVEYARD. The southward continuation of the ride to Cape Hatteras used to be a perilous undertaking for even adventurous drivers. But now a safe road leads to the Cape Hatteras National Seashore, which includes the outer bank islands of Bodie, Hatteras and Ocracoke. It preserves, for the people's enjoyment, 45 square miles of virgin beach, white dunes shifting into fantastic shapes and throwing strange shadows and blue or green waters lining the narrow strip of sand on both sides. Across Oregon Inlet the highway runs all the way south to Hatteras Light, the 193-foot tower that is spirally painted in black and white. No longer in service, it stands at the most treacherous spot of the Atlantic coast. Even now numerous ship skeletons can be seen protruding from the sand. During the sailing ship era this beach was a veritable graveyard, feared by sailors throughout the world. Salvaging was an important business, and there are gruesome tales from the early days when some salvagers were not above interfering with fate: a stormy night, a strategically placed lamp, a shipwreck — and

The Wright Brothers National Memorial. In 1903 an airplane was a "flying machine."

plunder. In 1966 the outer bank islands south of Hatteras were transformed into the Cape Lookout National Seashore.

WEATHERED, BRONZED, INDEPENDENT. One of the largest communities is Hatteras, an old fishing village. Some of the inhabitants believe that they are the descendants of shipwrecked English sailors. Their speech is picturesque: "If you're scunnered, don't fault me" means "If you are angry, don't blame me."

63

Blue Ridge Parkway

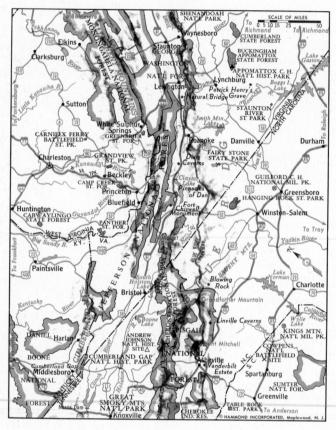

basswood, gum and buckeye, sourwood, persimmon and dozens of other species produce an arboreal variety unknown elsewhere. Various types of pines and hemlocks, while in the minority, are also evident, and the cuts and fills of the parkway have been planted with native shrubs. From early spring into summer a splendid array of blossoms accompanies the traveler: the beeches show their tan and the maples their red flowers early; the redbuds, the dogwoods and the azaleas follow suit; the mountain laurel blooms brightly in June, and the rhododendron may be admired even in July and August. Another popular travel season is in the fall when the gold and scarlet of the slopes rivals the autumn foliage of New England. All this natural beauty can be enjoyed from a modern highway unspoiled by advertising posters and hot dog stands. However, it is suggested that upon entering the parkway you secure a guide circular which has information on motels and restaurants just off the parkway.

A GIANT OUTDOOR CONCERT HALL. Statistically it would be difficult to prove that more songbirds per square mile live in our southern mountains than elsewhere on this continent, but on the strength of personal experience there seems to be no doubt about it. Bluebirds and thrushes, orioles and mockingbirds fill the forest with exuberant song. There are so many bright red cardinals — year-round residents in the hills — that both Virginia and North Carolina have honored the cardinal as the official state bird. The mountain people love the birds too, and Jean Thomas tells of an old lady who lived alone in a cabin and refused to sell her stand of black walnut trees. "Be gone," she told the agent of the lumber company, "I don't want to be scrouged by your racket-makin' contrapshuns under my very nose." After many promises and concessions she came out with her most important reason for refusal: "Such as that skeers off the birds in the forest," she stated.

DOVE IN THE WINDOW AND SWING YOUR CORNER LADY. The farther south the parkway takes you, the higher the mountains become and the wilder the scenery. On the road to Mount Mitchell, with a height of 6,684 feet the tallest peak east of the Mississippi, you pass through landscapes of alpine character. At the foot of the mountain the Craggy Gardens should be seen in spring when their huge rhododendron displays are in bloom. Near the end of the parkway the pleasant resort town of Asheville will greet you. Every August a Mountain Folk Festival keeps alive the old songs and square dances and displays the century-old crafts and skills with ax, saw and knife that have flourished in the hills as a matter of necessity and self-

THE GREAT HARDWOOD TRAIL. A green forest sanctuary once familiar only to the southern mountain people has been opened to all Americans by the Blue Ridge Parkway. This mountaintop route connects Shenandoah National Park and Great Smoky Mountains National Park, the gateway to the very heart of the southern hills. In a world of valley roads the drive of 469 miles along breezy ridges with broad vistas is an exhilarating experience. After passing Roanoke, Virginia, you realize at once that the wide valleys of farms and towns that follow the Skyline Drive on both sides have receded into the distance. Instead, the "hollers" your eyes meet here are deep and often narrow, and from their green funnels a bluish mist will rise in the morning. The soil here is a sandy carboniferous loam, and in it the finest stands of hardwoods in the United States grow. White oaks and poplars, tall tulip trees and fragrant

THROUGH an AMERICAN SANCTUARY

The Blue Ridge Parkway crosses the world of the old-time mountaineers. With the Skyline Drive it offers nearly 600 miles of top-of-the-range riding.

sufficiency. These include the carving of wooden bowls and trays as well as the shaping of utensils and pieces of furniture. The handwork of the women is also a living art; lace is crocheted in the seashell, acorn or cloverleaf pattern. You may choose homemade quilts from such famous models as nine patch, dove in the window or double wedding ring. For 200 years the mountain people lived in their own, isolated world — simple and proud, poor and self-assured, illiterate and hospitable and, above all, independent and freedom loving. So fond were they of their mountain forests that they did not join the great westward trek of the nineteenth century. But now the singing contests, the folk dance festivals and handicraft fairs are establishing the contact between their small world and the great outside. This does not necessarily mean a loss. There is a good chance that many of the old traditions will survive; ballad making and ballad singing, for instance, have

adapted themselves to a new century. There is even a ballad now on the great artery that opened the heart of the green hills to the American people at large, the Skyline Drive and the Blue Ridge Parkway. The poem does not claim to be literature, but with the clarity of a backwoods ballad it describes the purpose of the ridge-road system more forcefully than an engineer's report. Here is a sample of it: "The builders of this skyline drive/Have filed no patent right/That they improved upon God's plan/Nor have more power and might;/But they have seen His handiwork/This panoramic view/Have paved this road to ease the load/Of all the world and you." (George A. Barker).

Near Asheville the Vanderbilt palace, Biltmore, a pompous French castle in a gentle American landscape, is a tourist attraction. To the west, the Shining Rock Wild Area in Pisgah National Forest is popular with botanists and lovers of wildflowers.

Great Smoky Mountains and TVA

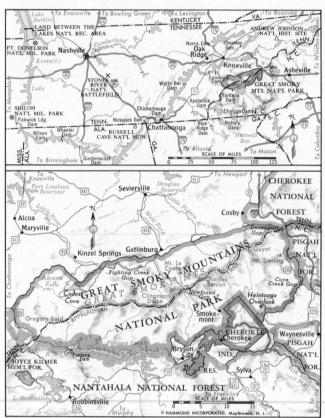

Replicas of pioneer cabins show the life-style of the early settlers.

finest lookout points are easily accessible. Clingmans Dome, at 6,642 feet the highest of the range, can be reached by a scenic highway, and with hikers Mount Le Conte is most popular. From these vantage points the blue haze, the "smoke" of the Great Smokies, can be observed. Copious rainfall wets the ground from which light mists rise here and there in curving wreaths. If a sudden burst of sunlight strikes the forest floor a column of steam swirls up as if released from a boiler. Unusual is the occurrence of "balds," treeless spots on the ridges. Wildlife is abundant, and while the black bears are not quite as numerous as in Yellowstone Park, it is just as dangerous to feed them.

THE CHEROKEE TRAGEDY. This green sanctuary is the ancient home of the Cherokees, one of the most advanced of all Indian tribes. De Soto reported that they lived in log houses and tilled the soil; they were friendly with the early white settlers, and the great chief Sequoyah created the Cherokee alphabet of 86 characters. Many of the tribe learned to read and write. But in spite of their peaceful ways the shout "Run the redskins out!" grew louder and louder, especially when gold was discovered on their land in 1829. It was largely a false alarm, but the gold diggers and land-grabbers succeeded with their scheme. In 1838 the U.S. Army drove the Cherokees from their mountains, westward to Oklahoma, during the coldest winter months. One-fourth of the Indians perished on the march. But large numbers did not obey and for years hid in the mountains, outcasts in their own land, until they were finally granted permission to stay and an eastern Cherokee reservation was organized. Their descendants still live there, and their handicrafts are a tourist attraction. Near their town of Cherokee there is the open-air Mountainside Theater where, against a background of native hills and trees, the drama of the

BLUE HAZE OVER TALL WOODS. Although the Great Smoky Mountains lay within 600 miles of many of the major population centers of the United States, they remained an unknown wilderness to the world at large until the first decades of the twentieth century. Even now a large part of the forests in the Great Smoky Mountains National Park are virgin timber. They are a sea of trees of incredible variation — 130 native species and 1,300 varieties of flowering plants. Mountain laurels and rhododendrons, magnificent at blossom time, form impenetrable thickets called "slicks" or "hell." To enter Joyce Kilmer Memorial Forest, under ancient, sky-high hemlocks and gigantic tulip trees with green Gothic arches high above and no underbrush to block the view, is like walking through a cathedral. The mountains themselves are the highest east of the Rockies, with 16 peaks taller than 6,000 feet; yet the

A VIRGIN FOREST and a VALLEY LABORATORY

Sixteen peaks of the Great Smokies are taller than 6,000 feet. The name Smokies refers to the blue haze that hovers above the mountains.

Cherokees is enacted nightly except Sunday during the summer months.

THE LONG RIFLES. The drama of the white man in these mountains is equally stirring. The English, Scottish and Scotch-Irish peasants who drifted into the valleys in the 1700's thought they had reached paradise: here complete freedom reigned without tax collectors, police sergeants, recruiting officers, or poaching laws. They could fish and hunt and talk and sing to their hearts' content. Life was poor but free, and corn, they discovered with joy, made both good bread and good whiskey. Their descendants are still there, all around the edges of the park, and they have changed little. They still live in log cabins that sometimes can be reached only on foot or on horseback; their tools and utensils are mostly homemade; they are masters in woodcraft, and their products are by no means restricted to their own simple needs. Some mountain lodges have each guest room furnished in a different native wood, done by local craftsmen with excellent workmanship. They are expert marksmen and like to use the long rifles of their ancestors; many do not know how to read and write, but they are natural-born storytellers and ballad singers, fiddlers and folk dancers. To call their speech Elizabethan is perhaps an exaggeration, but they certainly speak a colorful, archaic English. The name of a local flower is Hearts-abustin-with-love, and the surrounding landscape abounds with imaginative appella-tions like Charlie's Bunion (bunion — big toe), Chunky Gal Mountain and Fighting Creek Gap.

A NEW WAY OF LIFE. Six thousand tons of water fall annually on every acre of the Great Smokies. In a thousand creeks the water rushes down to form the Tennessee River and in the process carries along good soil. Erosion and floods used to be the characteristics of the river. Then a grand network of dams was conceived to end the waste and the damage, and during President Franklin D. Roosevelt's first term the Tennessee Valley Authority was created for the purpose of "maximum flood control, maximum development of the river for navigation, maximum generation of electric power — proper use of marginal lands, proper methods of re-forestation — and economic and social well-being of all the people." The valley was turned into a huge technical, economic and social laboratory, and on the whole the experiment seems to have succeeded. When TVA began, less than three per cent of the farms of the region used electricity; now the electrification is practically complete. Kerosene lamps and wood stoves have disappeared and with them many fine old folkways and traditions. Whether the march of progress is always a blessing is a purely academic question; some say it can't be stopped. But the traveler to the Great Smokies will find it interesting to visit Fontana Dam, the highest east of the Mississippi, and Oak Ridge, the research center with the American Museum of Atomic Energy.

Charleston, S.C.

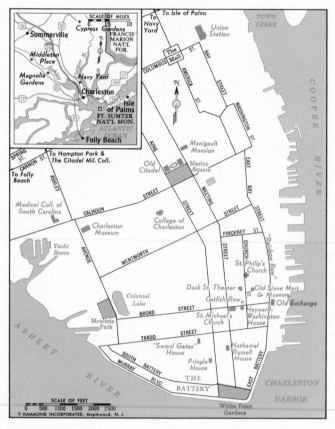

THE TRAVELING BELLS. Those northerners and westerners who from novels and stories have formed a romantic and picturesque concept of the South should visit Charleston. There, more than anywhere else, their vision will be confirmed. The stately eighteenth-century homes, the balconies of wrought iron and the French windows, the graceful porticos and the carved doorways, the waving palmettos and the moss-draped live oaks, the servants' quarters and the old wharves — all these ingredients blend into a charming, colorful picture of the historic South. The spirit is there too, for the people of Charleston feel a deep love and fervent loyalty toward their city. They have been compared to the Chinese, for "they eat rice and worship their ancestors." Rice was the crop that made Charleston rich.

Along the Battery there are fine patrician homes with a broad view of the harbor. Rainbow Row looks like a stage setting; it is a row of delicately tinted houses along

the East Bay waterfront, once a street where sailing vessels from the seven seas tied up. There are various fine churches in town, and the oldest ones have experienced incidents of storybook quality. At St. Michael's the church bells attained celebrity status: they crossed the Atlantic five times. Cast in London and installed in Charleston, they were pillaged by the British during the Revolutionary War and shipped to England. Later a loyal Charlestonian discovered them in London and sent them back to Charleston. During the Civil War the bells were partially destroyed; after the war ended the pieces were dispatched to London to be recast in the original form. In due time they were returned and ever since have been a part of Charleston's life.

Lovers of antiques and artistic interiors, particularly of the pre-Civil War period, will find a visit to the Charleston Museum rewarding; built in 1773, it is the oldest in the country. During the spring festival many old mansions are opened to the public, and several houses may be visited throughout the year: the Manigault Mansion, the Heyward-Washington House and the Nathaniel Russell House. The Dock Street Theatre occupies the site of a playhouse opened in 1736. A full-scale replica of the Confederate submarine *Hunley* can be seen at Church and Broad streets.

THE CHARLESTON CIVILIZATION. The historical background of this cultured American scene is as cosmopolitan as can be imagined. The first settlers were small sugar planters from Barbados; then a number of capitalists arrived, and with the help of especially trained Gullah Negroes introduced the highly profitable rice culture and a truly baronial plantation system. French Huguenots, among them excellent artisans, found refuge and prosperity in the city. However, life was not always a bed of roses; storms, hurricanes and at least one earthquake hit the town and the surrounding countryside. The Spaniards attacked, the French were repulsed, and the British invaded the stronghold. Pirates boldly displayed the skull and crossbones in the harbor but were not always successful. For their benefit a row of gallows once stood on the Battery, and their bodies swayed in the breeze as a warning. During the years before the Civil War the "Charleston Civilization" was at its height. Charlestonians looked down on New York and Boston as rather barbaric settlements and oriented their lives toward Paris. A good deal of French was spoken in town, and exquisite art objects and elegant gowns were imported from France. Here the War Between the States began when, as everybody knows, the Confederate cannons fired their shots at Fort Sumter in Charleston Harbor.

PORGY AND BESS. But Charleston has never been

THE STORYBOOK SOUTH

just a white man's town. Once the Negro population was its largest segment, and to this day it exercises a far-reaching influence. Remarkably uniform in appearance, the Charleston Negroes are descendants of the Gullahs, and they speak primarily what is called the Gullah dialect. It has a soft charm of its own and quite a strange vocabulary; to outsiders it is often unintelligible — a fact which adds an exotic touch to the scene. The numerous Negro street vendors will not only sell their flowers, fish and other wares, but advertise them loudly in a colorful singsong: "Porgy walk, Porgy talk, Porgy eat with knife and fawk; Porgee-e." Porgy's Catfish Row was immortalized by author DuBose Heyward; Gershwin's classic folk opera "Porgy and Bess," performed by excellent Negro casts, took the fame of this Charleston street to New York, London, Berlin and Paris. Charleston's Old Slave Mart and Museum traces the cultural history of the American Negro.

Right: The well kept, traditionally elegant waterfront of residential Charleston.

Below right: With 25 acres of old azalea and camellia bushes, the Magnolia Gardens are a sight of unsurpassed beauty.

Below: Charleston's fortunes, made from rice plantations and in shipping, built elaborate mansions.

THE MAGNIFICENT GARDENS. One of the first projects carried out by the early settlers of Charleston was a community garden. This love of bright flowers has survived, and today thousands of visitors descend upon the Charleston region every spring for the purpose of enjoying its famous plantings: the thickets of white, yellow, pink, red and purple azaleas, the many varieties of camellias, the magnolias and other blossoms. Among the various old plantation gardens that are open to the public and can be reached easily by car from Charleston, three are outstanding and are classed among the loveliest in the world: Magnolia Gardens, with its 25 acres of azaleas and camellias; Middleton Place, the first landscaped gardens in America, laid out in 1741 on the huge plantation of Henry Middleton, president of the Continental Congress; and Cypress Gardens, a former rice plantation where visitors may ride in boats through the arched avenues of tall trees.

GAIL HAMMOND

SOUTH CAROLINA DEPT. OF PARKS, RECREATION AND TOURISM

SOUTH CAROLINA DEPT. OF PARKS, RECREATION AND TOURISM

Savannah and the Golden Isles

South. The Low House, another Classic Revival structure, was built by a family of Savannah cotton factors. Thackeray the poet stayed in that house twice, in 1855 and 1856; Robert E. Lee visited there in 1870, and in 1912 Mrs. Juliette Gordon Low founded, in the same building, a movement which grew into the Girl Scouts of America. In the old days popular construction materials were rough red brick brought as ballast in sailing ships, or gray brick from the kilns of a plantation nearby.

A SISTER OF CHARLESTON. In many ways Savannah seems to be related to her northern neighbor Charleston. It has the same old magnolia trees, the exuberantly blossoming azaleas, the great mansions that blend into the so-called romantic South, and the same ancestor worship, social exclusiveness, cultivation of good manners and friendliness. If Charleston for two centuries preserved an ancient African civilization in its Gullah dialect and tradition, Savannah did the same with its Geechee Negro speech and songs. Both cities have their picturesque street vendors who with a loud singsong, intelligible only to the local residents, offer their glistening fish, Southern vegetables and bright flowers. In one point, however, there is a difference: Savannah has not "gone overboard" — as a leading citizen expressed it — to turn itself into a tourist attraction as Charleston supposedly has done for some time.

LIKE THE DECK OF A SQUARE-RIGGER. To many visitors the most intriguing section of Savannah is the waterfront portion called Factors' Walk. Here a line of old red brick warehouses faces the Savannah River as four- or five-story buildings; on the land side they appear as two-story structures on a broad, tree-shaded esplanade that runs on a high bluff. However, between the avenue and the warehouses a narrow alley or court ambles along, about halfway between the street level and the river level. It has a cobblestone wall on the avenue side, and above the alley little wooden bridges cross from the storehouses to a wooden walk running along the row and connecting the small bridges. The whole arrangement is reminiscent of the catwalks of the large vessels of the sailing ship era, which have been revived on modern tankers. In its heyday, Factors' Walk was a center of world commerce, and from there the first seagoing steamship, the *Savannah,* crossed the Atlantic Ocean in 1819. The Trustees Garden, site of an experiment in producing silk and now a restored residential area, is also worth seeing. In tune with this background you may dine at the Pirate's House or the Pink House.

THE CLASSIC TOUCH. Green is Savannah's color if seen from the air, and the name of Forest City is well justified. For there are trees everywhere, and—a unique urban feature—24 little parks called squares are strewn throughout the old section of this lovely city. General Oglethorpe wanted it that way when he laid out the town in 1733 in accordance with a sketch he found in the book, "Villas of the Ancients," written by an Englishman named Robert Castell, who died in a debtor's prison — ironically so because the Georgia experiment was supposed to improve the lot of men thrown into that type of jail. Savannah's regular layout, inspired by Roman models, is not the only classical touch; the city boasts of a number of fine old residences erected in the style of the Classic Revival: the Telfair House which, as the Telfair Academy of Arts and Sciences, contains one of the finest art galleries in the

OYSTER ROASTS AND SAND SAILING. From the Savannah River to the Florida state line a string of

THE SEA, TRADITION and WILDERNESS

CECIL W. STOUGHTON — NAT'L PARK SERVICE

SAVANNAH AREA CHAMBER OF COMMERCE

CECIL W. STOUGHTON — NAT'L PARK SERVICE

Above: Georgia's well preserved Fort Pulaski was named in honor of the Polish patriot who was killed at the siege of Savannah during the Revolution.

Above right: At this stately home, built by the influential Low family, the Girl Scouts of America movement was founded in 1912.

Right: The British Fort Frederica once protected a thriving seaport town which has vanished without traces.

islands separates the mainland from the ocean; all have the same scenic character: they are flat, covered with fine stands of live oaks, magnolias, cedars and pines, and are crossed by saltwater creeks. The Spaniards under Pedro Menéndez de Avilés, founder of St. Augustine, discovered the isles and took possession of them. "The Golden Isles of Guale," named after the local Indian chief, are also known as the Sea Islands. Early in the eighteenth century the pirate Blackbeard had his hideout there, and a generation later a British victory at the Battle of Bloody Marsh established British rule in that part of America. In contrast to this martial past, the islands' presence is peaceful and wholly dedicated to recreation and pleasure. Tybee Island is the favorite beach resort of Savannah, and on its broad white sands a local specialty flourishes: the oyster roast. In a small oven or in a pit the oysters are roasted, opened speedily, dipped into a sharp sauce and eaten without the benefit of a fork. To the south Jekyll Island, St. Simons Island

and its close neighbor, Sea Island, can be reached by road. Here are wonderful stands of old live oaks (the first fleet of the United States was built of St. Simons oak, including *Old Ironsides,* the frigate *Constitution),* of white oleanders and pink crepe myrtles, with gleaming beaches and stretches of the deep blue sea. The overgrown ruins of the British Fort Frederica on St. Simons Island tell a pathetic story: the fort once protected within its walls a seaport of 1,500 inhabitants, a town of which only the ruins remain. On Sea Island sand sailing on especially designed craft is a favorite of the numerous honeymooners. South of St. Simons Island, Jekyll Island has undergone a thorough democratization. Once an ultra-exclusive winter resort club belonging to such legendary characters as J. P. Morgan, William Rockefeller, William K. Vanderbilt and Cyrus McCormick, it is now a state park. Most of the other Golden Isles are a lonely wilderness of lush vegetation; only a few black families live there.

71

Okefenokee and Suwannee

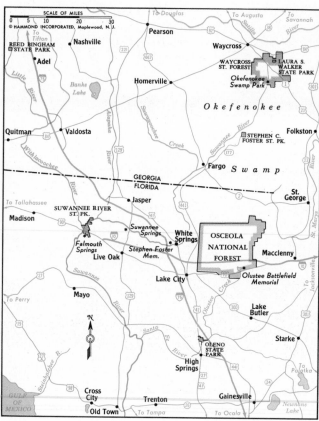

toes will annoy you on the cypress boardwalks provided for visitors. Penetrating the thicket in one of the shallow, light pole boats is an experience without parallel. Wherever you look you are surrounded by a motionless mirror of water which reflects the blue sky, the white clouds and the tall, unkempt trees. In this scene of untamed, unfinished wilderness thousands of water lilies float in splendid perfection. You will ride on one of the boat runs, i.e., the channels meandering between clumps of trees and underbrush; in the veritable maze of these runs you could lose your way easily. One phenomenon of Okefenokee is called the blow-up — decaying vegetable matter frequently generates gases which force a stretch of bottom vegetation to the surface; there it becomes a floating island of perhaps 100 square feet and, on its travels, gathers grass, briars, weeds and seeds. Its journey continues until the float is anchored by a clump of trees; sometimes it becomes firm, but just as often it never solidifies and sways and trembles at the slightest provocation. However, there are also firm islands with a sandy base, and one of them is even enchanted. A party of Indians once landed there and was welcomed by beautiful girls who treated them to marsh eggs, corn pone and fancy grapes. When the banquet was at its height, the girls announced that their jealous husbands would now drown the visitors in the swamp. The visitors left hastily, and ever since parties of Seminoles have tried to rediscover the island.

A SAFE RETREAT FOR BIRDS AND BEARS. Around noon the silence is almost incredible, yet there is life. Alligators float in green bays like ten- or twelve-foot logs; turtles sunbathe on a stump. A raccoon sleeping in the fork of a tree seems to wink at you; on a tangle of roots and cypress knees a cottonmouth water moccasin lies neatly coiled. An egret stands motionless in the center of a small prairie, and a heron rises from a cove with a quiet grace. At sundown, however, a nightly concert begins. The frogs account for the upper registers, the bull alligators roar the basso parts, and additional sound effects are provided by splashing water birds, hooting owls and the occasional spine-chilling screech of a wildcat. All this night music blends into a rumbling symphony called "the booming of the swamp." You will probably not encounter any panthers or otters, but you may meet one of the Okefenokee bears. One of the park patrolmen had the same amusing experience on more than one occasion: a bear had climbed high up a tree, picking berries or grapes from vines. The ranger would glide nearer, avoiding all noises, and then suddenly burst out with a startling yell. Each time the bear had the same reaction; he let go and through the crashing branches dropped into the water with a loud splash, drenching the boat. Then he would stumble ashore and

LOST WORLD. America has her massive mountains, her big rivers and her great desert. She also has her huge swamp, properly called Okefenokee, that is Trembling Earth, comprising some 700 square miles in southern Georgia and northern Florida. Most of it is in a National Wildlife Refuge accessible from the north at Waycross (Okefenokee Swamp Park, a state park adjacent to the Refuge), from the west at Fargo, and from the east at Folkston; guides and boats are available and, at Swamp Park, electric boats also. As a rule, swamps are dismal places and hardly an attraction for travelers, but Okefenokee has a different character. It lies at an altitude of 120 feet; its waters well up from hundreds of springs and are pure and transparent until they reach the cypress groves which color them dark. The swamp is not stagnant but has a slow, steady flow, and therefore it does not breed malaria, and few mosqui-

THE INDIANS' "TREMBLING EARTH"

vanish in the thicket. Former park manager Bill Edwards reported that he and a ranger spent a night in a swamp shack which they suspected to be the hideout of alligator poachers. For hours they waited silently in their ambush, then footsteps were heard, and a black outline appeared in the door. The ranger switched on the flashlight. There, on its hind legs, stood a huge black bear filling out the whole frame. It was difficult to say who was more excited, the bear who grunted threateningly, or the men who crouched in a corner. Finally the beast turned and sauntered away, angrily slapping the bushes.

"WAY DOWN UPON THE SUWANNEE RIVER." In 1889 a lumber company built a canal into the eastern part of Okefenokee in order to float out cedar and cypress logs. After the waterway had been completed at great cost, it was discovered, to everybody's consternation, that the logs floated the wrong way, i.e., to the west. The company went bankrupt, and upon investigating the phenomenon it was found that Okefenokee is the source of the Suwannee River, which drains the swamp waters off in a southwesterly direction. A number of boat runs unite and form the riverbed; at first the pace of the new stream is slow, but when it crosses into Florida it becomes a swift current and its boulders suggest a mountain brook. The banks are high limestone ridges covered with cedar forests. After flowing through a lonely wilderness for miles, the river touches a very civilized spot, the old Florida spa of White Springs. This is a shady village with late Victorian overtones, at one time known as Rebels' Refuge, where a number of planters from Georgia found a safe refuge for their families and slaves during the Civil War. White Springs boasts of a Stephen Foster Museum in Stephen Foster Memorial Park, for his "Old Folks at Home" made the Suwannee one of America's famous rivers. Oldtimers insist that Stephen Foster visited the region in the 1850's, but history knows that he didn't. Old-fashioned riverboats will take you down the river.

Foster's memory is kept alive at the Stephen Foster Memorial at White Springs.

Stephen Foster's song made the Suwannee River famous. He himself had never been there.

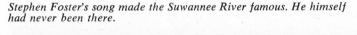

St. Augustine

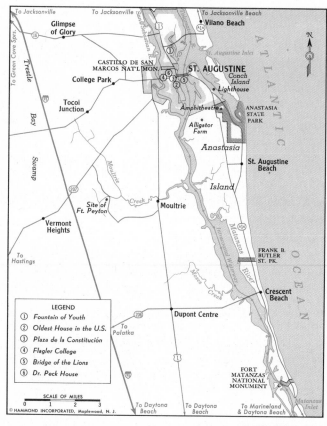

LEGEND
1. Fountain of Youth
2. Oldest House in the U.S.
3. Plaza de la Constitución
4. Flagler College
5. Bridge of the Lions
6. Dr. Peck House

SCALE OF MILES
0   1   2   3
© HAMMOND INCORPORATED, Maplewood, N. J.

ECHOES OF THE SPANISH MAIN. In the pageant of American history the city of St. Augustine plays a small but spectacular part: it is our country's contact with the Spanish Main. It has the same kind of Castilian fortress, with moat and steep walls and corner turrets, that is encountered in San Juan, Puerto Rico, and Havana, Cuba, and the same kind of cathedral. It also can boast of all those swashbuckling deeds and events that made the Spanish Main such a colorful corner of the earth. St. Augustine had its conquistadores: in 1513 Ponce de Leon landed there and spent five days searching for the miraculous Fountain of Youth, and the Spanish admiral Menéndez de Avilés took possession of the land for Castile in 1565. He named the settlement in honor of St. Augustine, on whose day — August 28 — he first sighted Florida. Like so many towns on the Main, St. Augustine had its own massacre. A French

fleet under Jean Ribaut approached to attack and sack the city when a hurricane blew the ships out to sea, and the 350 surviving Frenchmen found themselves shipwrecked at nearby Matanzas Inlet. When the Spaniards arrived, the French surrendered unconditionally and nearly all were murdered promptly, not for being French but for being Protestants. The town suffered from pirates; the worst of them was Sir Francis Drake, who plundered and burned it. The Spaniards, who had fled to the woods, then returned and rebuilt their settlement. One integral part of the Spanish colonial system was the establishment of Indian missions, and St. Augustine became the headquarters of a chain of forty of them, reaching as far west as Pensacola. In the middle of the eighteenth century the British moved in; the next flag to fly over St. Augustine was that of the short-lived Republic of Florida. In 1821 the United States took over and has stayed there ever since, with the exception of the Civil War years which furnished the city with its fifth official flag, that of the Confederacy.

CATHEDRALS AND PATIOS. This wonderful storybook history has not vanished from the face of the city, and traces of the days of the Spanish Main's glory are preserved. One fortunate circumstance was the occurrence of a building material more durable than timber — coquina. As this is a limestone composed of prehistoric seashells, it is readily available along the coast and has helped to preserve a unique heritage. St. Augustine's most photographed item is the Oldest House in the United States, on St. Francis Street. First built in the late 1500's, the wooden second story rests on a thick coquina wall, and the crushed coquina floors, the handhewn cedar beams, the low ceilings and the massive fireplaces are reminiscent of the Middle Ages. At Treasury and St. George's streets the Dr. Peck House is most interesting; the original building was erected about 1600 and was used by the Spanish royal treasurer; the

Castillo de San Marcos, Spain's picturesque contribution to St. Augustine.

74

A MELLOW TOWN, a SWASHBUCKLING LEGEND

FLORIDA DEVELOPMENT COMMISSION

The castle still evokes memories of the Spanish Main, of Ponce de León and the conquistadores.

FLORIDA NEWS BUREAU

A remnant of the Middle Ages — the oldest house in the U.S., built in the late 1500's.

present building was erected after 1702. The patio contains a collection of rare plants, including frankincense and Mexican coral trees. Inside there are fine nineteenth-century mahogany furnishings, carved four-poster beds and ancient oil paintings; the treasury room preserves two relics that reflect medieval barbarism pure and simple: two horrible figures, half ghouls, half apes, that were used by the Spanish Inquisition to intimidate the poor wretches before the tribunal. The Cathedral of St. Augustine, begun in 1793, has a coquina front and a gable extended into a belfry in the style of the missions of our Southwest. At the Plaza de la Constitucion in the center of town, the Public Market is a "new" structure, dating from 1824; the "old" building had stood on the same site since 1598. The Ponce de Leon Hotel, now Flagler College, which introduced St. Augustine to the country at large as a winter resort, is a kind of historic shrine now.

THE SPANISH CASTLE. Castillo de San Marcos, formerly named Fort Marion in honor of General Francis Marion, "the Swamp Fox," was started in 1672. Negro slaves and Indian hostages, soldiers and citizens dug the moat, ferried the coquina blocks from Anastasia Island to the building site and labored for two generations before the fortress was completed. The "hot shot oven" is still preserved in the eastern earthworks; in it cannonballs were heated and fired red hot into pirate and enemy ships, causing spectacular fireworks.

There are hardly any descendants of the builders of the castle alive today, but Spanish tradition has been carried on by a large group of immigrants from Minorca who arrived in 1767; although they have resided there for more than 200 years, local guidebooks refer to them as the town's largest foreign group.

PORPOISE ACROBATS. The coast road to the south leads over the Bridge of the Lions to Anastasia Island. At St. Augustine Beach the "new" lighthouse dates from 1874; the "old" signal tower was reported in 1586 by Sir Francis Drake as standing on the same spot. The Alligator Farm with thousands of specimens of all sizes is a local curiosity. Seventeen miles south of St. Augustine the studios of Marineland are a great coastal attraction. Deep-sea life is maintained in circular and rectangular oceanariums, and through portholes the daily routines of sharks and porpoises, sawfish and devilfish, giant green turtles and shrimps may be observed. Since the water is changed six times every 24 hours, and since cleaning crews in divers' suits are always at work, the water is wonderfully clear. At six shows daily trained porpoises and whales perform tricks and leap high out of the water, receiving bits of fish from the keepers' hands as a reward. There are also splendid sea gardens where brilliant tropical fish swim between coral and algae, and on the surface penguins walk around as if they were the duly appointed inspectors of the establishment.

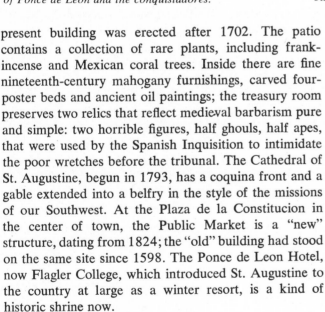

Sarasota, St. Petersburg, Tarpon Springs

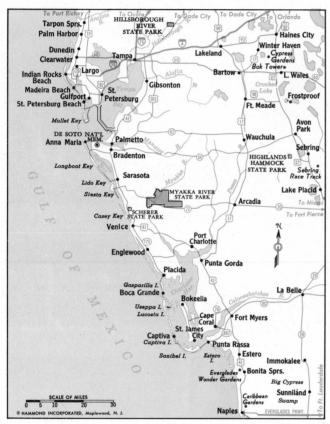

Titian and Tintoretto, Raphael and Rembrandt and many others. Its larger-than-life-size Rubens' sketches which were patterns for tapestries are a treasure that only the Louvre at Paris can match. Another prize exhibit is the Asolo Theater, built in Italy in 1798; its fabulous interior was transported to Sarasota in 1949 and has won wide recognition as the State Theater of Florida. Don't fail to visit the John and Mabel Ringling residence overlooking Sarasota Bay. It's a palace, a flamboyant circus man's vision of a castle come true. Finally there is The Circus Hall of Fame, a unique and exciting exhibit of Circusiana, including two miniature scale models of a circus show — one set up under canvas, the other set up in a train and ready to travel. The retired specimens of old parade wagons with their gilded carvings are as baroque as the Rubens' paintings; one of the bandwagons, the "Two Hemispheres," used to be drawn by a team of forty horses. Just south of Sarasota, the town of Venice is the new winter headquarters of the Ringling Brothers & Barnum and Bailey Circus, the "Greatest Show on Earth." For the price of admission, people from 50 states walk around leisurely and admire the long lines of shiny railroad cars that take the circus all over the country, look at the tigers and lions in the menagerie, watch 30 elephants going through their routines, observe a ten-horse act in training, pass some circus folk conversing in German or Italian or Thai, and spend an afternoon with the pleasant feeling of having seen the circus backstage.

SUNSHINE INSURANCE. One city that does not want to be baroque is St. Petersburg. Quiet and pleasant, it used to cater to those who have done their life's work and wish to enjoy their declining years, but now it welcomes people of all ages, especially the young. To be sure, there is still the Three-Quarter-Century Club whose members are at least 75 years old, but they are young at heart and organize dances, theatricals and contests. The town's principal commodity is sunshine, and any day on which the sun fails to appear before 3 o'clock, the whole edition of the afternoon paper is given away free. That happens about five times a year. The prettiest parts of the Sunshine City are the parks and boulevards along Tampa Bay, with harbor, yacht basins and the famous municipal pier. Here fishermen try their luck from special balconies, and pelicans and gulls wheel around screaming for tidbits. In the late afternoon the fishing boats return, the prize catch — perhaps a big tarpon — proudly displayed hanging from the mast. A visit to the Sunken Gardens is recommended; exotic tropical flowers from all over the world are displayed there. At Derby Lane greyhound races offer an opportunity to win or lose money, and at

THE RINGLING BROTHERS AND PETER PAUL RUBENS. The general assumption that the central west coast of Florida is quieter and less hectically pleasure-bound than the east coast is correct; yet the gulf shore offers some fascinating experiences. Sarasota, for instance, is a most attractive town, with its municipal pier, its causeway to Longboat and Lido keys, and its lovely white beaches where the trees creep up almost to the water's edge. Downtown you may see big league baseball players who make Sarasota their spring training center. Sarasota Jungle Gardens and Floridaland are other attractions. This town was the home of the world's leading circus family, the Ringlings, who left their mark here, sometimes in surprising ways. In an area of shuffleboards and trailer camps there is suddenly the John and Mabel Ringling Museum of Art, one of the world's great collections of baroque paintings, with works by

FLORIDA'S PICTURESQUE WEST COAST

Tarpon Springs sponge fishermen carry on an ancient Greek trade.

A touch of Renaissance Italy. The gardens of the John and Mabel Ringling Museum of Art.

St. Petersburg Beach rare, colorful fish may be watched at Neptune Reef. Performances of porpoises and sea lions are staged at the Aquatarium.

A BIT OF GREECE: AMERICA'S SPONGE CAPITAL. Driving north, past the attractive waterfront of Clearwater, you will soon find yourself in one of America's most interesting towns, Tarpon Springs. Here the descendants of Greek sponge fishermen, who for thousands of years had practiced their difficult trade in the Aegean Sea, carry on the ancient craft in the New World. On the docks of the Anclote River the colorful boats and the Greek waterfront life may be watched. The Greek language is heard here, delicious Greek honey and almond confections may be sampled, and a demonstration boat trip down the river with a diver descending to the bottom and emerging with a cluster of sponges is an interesting excursion. If you are lucky, you may witness the return of the sponge fleet, perhaps at Easter time. The whole community is then assembled to greet the brightly painted boats that bear the names of Greek gods or of Greek national heroes. The Stars and Stripes and the blue and white Greek pennants flutter in the wind, the diving suits dangle from the masts like grotesque scarecrows, and the decks are piled high with the harvest of sponges. There is the laughter of welcome on the wharves, and music and excitement. The sponges are sold at auction in the courtyard of the Sponge Exchange. The community preserves many colorful Old World ceremonies like the blessing of the departing boats, or Greek Cross Day when a priest of the Greek Orthodox Church releases a white dove and throws into the water a gold cross which is retrieved by young divers, or the Easter festival with its candlelight service and roast lamb and rice dinners. The interior of the Church of St. Nicholas is faced with marble donated by the Greek government.

77

Florida's Heartland

near the town of Ocala, surpasses them all. Here 150 natural springs flow into a common basin, and, from an easily visible cove 65 feet long and 12 feet high, up to 800 million gallons of water gush to the surface every day. Visitors may swim there and enjoy the limestone-filtered water which is so clear that light is broken into prismatic colors. In 80 feet of this iridescent current all bottom plants are clearly seen from glass-bottom boats, and the life of numerous fishes, turtles and shrimps can be observed. At Ross Allen's Reptile Institute snakes are "milked" for the manufacture of an anti-snakebite serum.

THE CITY THAT LOOKS LIKE A PARK. Southeast of Ocala, Orlando is one of America's most attractive residential cities. Subtropical gardens, parks and boulevards display their camphor trees and live oaks, palms from many corners of the earth and winter-blooming flowers. The foliage is green, the brick pavement red, the surface of the lakes sparkling blue. The town has also many cultural attractions, among them fine theaters with Broadway plays, good bookstores and a widely acclaimed symphony orchestra. Academic life centers around nearby Rollins College. Aware of these advantages, Orlandians derive the name of their city from Orlando, the hero of "As You Like It." Just southwest, Walt Disney World is the big eastern brother of California's Disneyland; it is the newest entertainment center and a conservation experiment of gigantic proportions.

CINERAMA SCENERY. When the producers of the first giant screen motion picture looked for samples of spectacular American scenery, they went to the Cypress Gardens near Winter Haven, south of Orlando. There a wild swamp adjacent to Lake Eloise has been turned into a tropical park; its masses of blooming azaleas, camellias and gardenias are planted around placid lagoons in which old, moss-festooned cypresses are mirrored. Attractive girls in period costumes help to create a make-believe atmosphere of the Old South, and a thrilling performance of water-ski acrobatics is a great drawing card.

CARILLONS AND NIGHTINGALES. A few miles to the south, near Lake Wales, a 325-foot hill called Iron Mountain rises above the surrounding valleys. There the early settlers discovered a large boulder surrounded by 13 smaller stones, a symbol of the sun and the 13 moons of the Indian year. Since time immemorial this crest had been a sanctuary, and it still is, thanks to a thought of the Philadelphia publisher Edward Bok who established here his Mountain Lake Sanctuary. The Bok Singing Tower is a famous Florida sight, and

A CRYSTAL COVE OF 150 SPRINGS. "Florida Cracker" is a very respected name in the central part of the state. It implies the genuine, original, native Floridian spirit, in marked contrast to that of the southern part of the peninsula where the Yankees prevail. This heartland comprises the citrus belt, with lush orange and grapefruit groves rising to little hills, descending to small lakes and climbing back to gentle ridges. These plantings are clean and neat, and beautiful and fragrant at blossom and at harvest time. Occasional stretches are monotonous, but then again there are breathtaking spots where deep blue views are framed by tall live oaks or cypresses decorously draped with Spanish moss. Much of this section lies on top of a thick layer of porous limestone which stores huge masses of water; consequently there are 27 big and numerous small springs in that area, but Silver Springs,

ORANGE GROVES and WALT DISNEY WORLD

rightly so. The far-away loneliness of earlier years is gone now, with an ever-increasing influx of visitors, but the spire itself retains its beauty and dignity, "its feet in flowers and its brow in the sun." Built of steel and faced with coquina rock from the coast and pink marble from Georgia, it rises for 205 feet, overlooking 30 lakes. Its metal work, its marble carvings, its friezes and colorful ceramics blend into a perfect setting for one of the finest carillons in existence. The 71 bells — the largest weighing 11 tons — are tuned in a chromatic scale over 4½ octaves, and their music harmoniously merges with the breeze. In the surrounding garden a profusion of azaleas and callas, iris and amaryllis blossoms among the trees, and more than a hundred species and varieties of birds have found a safe home there. Especially introduced are European nightingales which outsing even our mockingbirds.

CITRUS FRUIT AND BRAHMA COWS.

Lakeland, to the southwest, is a busy center of large groves which produce a large part of the nation's citrus crop. Visitors soon discover that the connoisseur does not just buy oranges but Temple or Parson Brown, Pineapple or King or Valencia, Satsuma or Lue Gim Gong. It is interesting to visit a packing house and watch the cleaning and sorting. East and west of Lake Wales the cow country of Florida begins. There in the palmetto flatlands with a scanty growth of grass a sturdy breed of cattle with an outlandish ancestry flourishes. The original stock had been imported by the Spaniards long before the Pilgrims landed at the Rock. The cows were so scrawny that as late as the turn of this century they only reached the size of a small donkey and were the laughingstock of western cattlemen. Then hump-backed Brahma bulls from the East Indies were introduced, and the resulting strain is a healthy meat animal.

SPACEPORT.

Travelers on the way to southern Florida are advised to stop at Cape Canaveral (Cape Kennedy), approximately halfway down the Atlantic coast. There various tours are available, among them the 30-mile spaceport tour of Merritt Island. Visitors get a view of the 52-story-high Vehicle Assembly Building and of various interesting spaceport exhibits.

The Singing Tower is the focal point of Mountain Lake Sanctuary, a unique place of beauty and peace.

Against a background of tropical wonder, Florida Cypress Gardens offer great aquatic shows.

THE MOUNTAIN LAKE SANCTUARY

FLORIDA CYPRESS GARDENS

Florida's Gold Coast

were at work; they imported brightly blossoming decorative plants and fine tropical fruit trees, adapting them to the climate and improving them, until today Florida's royal palms are taller and straighter than those of Brazil, and her mangoes surpass their progenitors in southern Asia. This collaboration of nature and man resulted in attracting such numbers of winter residents and tourists that statistically speaking the Gold Coast has become the greatest resort playground on earth.

PALM BEACH AND THE OLD RICH. In 1878 the Spanish bark *Providencia* was shipwrecked off a Florida island and its cargo of coconuts was washed ashore. Many of the nuts took root; others were picked up by the few settlers and planted here and there. Fifteen years later the coco palms had transformed the sandbar into a lovely island suggesting the South Seas, and Henry M. Flagler, the Florida railroad tycoon, set out to develop it into a winter colony for the very rich. Philadelphia society in particular moved in, building fabulous waterfront estates. Palm Beach is still an exclusive resort of inherited wealth although there, too, a new day is dawning and quite a few of the palaces are boarded up or torn down. The Flagler mansion is a museum now. The sightseeing visitor will enjoy greatly the eighteen-mile-long island which in some spots is only 500 feet wide. The stately Royal Palm Way with its double row of royal palm columns connects Lake Worth with the ocean. Via Mizner and Via Parigi are narrow streets or courts paved with flagstones and open only to pedestrians. With their exotic shops and art studios, open-air cafés and patio restaurants of international cuisine, these vias will give you the illusion of being on the Riviera or Capri.

A MAN-MADE SPECTACULAR. Some 80 years ago, when the U.S. was well settled and even the Pacific shore cities had passed their early youth, the southeastern coast of Florida was a wilderness of lonely dunes and palmetto thickets, mangrove forests and swamps infested with snakes, alligators and mosquitoes. Then suddenly a burst of energy changed the scene; the railroad pushed south, engineers built canals, dams, causeways, bridges and artificial islands, and architects laid out new cities. To this day the photogenic beauty of the Gold Coast — the pastel-colored, palm-shaded villas by blue canals, the city's skyline above the flat shore, the white yachts in the basin — is purely man-made although, of course, the basic ingredients have always been there: the sun, the crystal clear air, the white beaches and the azure blue Gulf Stream. In addition to the builders, the biologists and horticulturists

MIAMI AND THE NEW RICH. In contrast to Palm Beach, Greater Miami (Miami and Miami Beach) is the winter haven of the big spenders, of show business stars, fashion merchants, TV producers, radio commentators and gossip columnists. The row of hundreds of sybaritic waterfront hotels in Miami Beach is not duplicated anywhere else on this planet; each hostelry has its swimming pool and private beach, terrace and sundeck, cabanas and a sea-view platform for midday dancing outdoors, and its own nightclub. On the whole, resort life does not lean heavily on sports but runs to sunbathing, swimming, long siestas, elaborate dining, extensive nightclubbing and romancing. Sightseers will find the Miami Bayfront Park and the municipal yacht basin interesting. Excursion boats will take you over Biscayne Bay to lush artificial islands and through quiet man-made canals where the estates of celebrities will be pointed out. Glass bottom boats will show you the "sea

RIVIERA of the NEW WORLD

Miami is the one American resort that is known all over the world.

gardens" where brightly colored tropical fish dart from coral formations and sea plants, and deep-sea fishing boats are available to those who would like to write home about catching a sailfish or a barracuda. In Coral Gables the campus of the University of Miami is in tune with the area. In Hialeah the Hialeah Park racetrack is famous both for the huge sums of money placed there in bets and for its beauty: 300 pink flamingos wade placidly through an artificial lake in plain view of the grand-stand. Informative entertainment is provided by the Miami Seaquarium, the Miami Serpentarium, the Monkey Jungle and the Parrot Jungle. The Miami Beach Garden Center displays rare orchids, anthuriums and ferns.

LAGOONS AND ISLETS. Between Palm Beach and Miami, resorts like Hollywood and Boca Raton are fashioned after the Miami pattern, while the city of Fort Lauderdale is a great water sports center. Natural and man-made islands are surrounded by miles of rivers, lagoons, inlets, canals and waterways, and the effect is that of a bright, modern Venice. The city's harbor, Port Everglades, has become a major point of departure for Caribbean cruise ships. Between Miami and Key Largo there are only 50 miles, but they lead from Florida at its gaudiest to Florida at its quietest, to fishing coves, rickety piers, rusty anchors, wind-blown beachcomers' shacks and old-time saloons. The 100-mile-long chain of islands called the Florida Keys is connected by the Overseas Highway, and a ride to Key West is one of America's outstanding travel experiences. Key West is a picturesque "Caribbean" city that in the early 1800's prospered on vessels shipwrecked on the outlying reefs; salvaging the cargoes was a profitable and adventurous business. Of particular interest on its present-day water-front are the turtle kraals. The Conch Tour Train will take you around the city, past the Ernest Hemingway Home and Museum and the Audubon House.

The Everglades

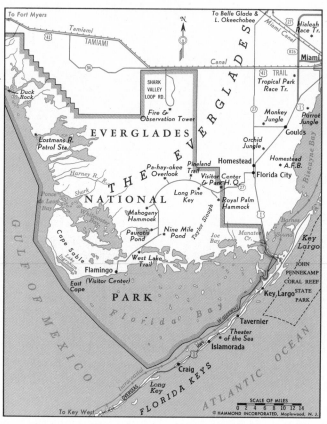

THE RIVER OF GRASS. To classify the Everglades is difficult; to describe them is easy. The southernmost part of the Florida peninsula consists of two mildly elevated ridges along the two coasts where the great resorts have been built with their skyscraper hotels and luxury stores. Between these two narrow ridges there is a broad groove extending from Lake Okeechobee to Florida Bay at the southernmost tip of land — a wide expanse of untouched, empty wilderness, half dry and half wet, half soil and half water, a continent in the process of emerging. Much of it looks like a prairie of grass, but it is an extraordinary kind of grass, six, seven, and in spots eight feet tall. Its blades are sharp and cut like saws — hence the name saw grass, and crossing it is an exasperating task. It is also a river: the water does not flow in one wide, open stream but it meanders slowly and silently around millions of blades from Lake Okeechobee to the ocean. Here and there natural canals wander aimlessly over the landscape. During the winter months the groove seems to be dry, but still there is the river; below the surface it seeps through the mud, always in the same direction. During recent years recurrent long droughts accompanied by fires have caused damage to the park's wildlife and considerable worry about the future of the Everglades.

The river of grass is dotted with hundreds of tree islands called hammocks, their graceful palms or grotesque Caribbean pines rising over thickets of lush vegetation. The archipelago of green islands, the waving grass and the white clouds sailing in the trade winds present themselves best from Highway 27 which turns south from the Tamiami Trail out of Miami. The Royal

A walkway through swampy territory serves as an observation platform.

A UNIQUE NATURE EXHIBIT. That our countryside prides itself on towering peaks and glistening glaciers, on blooming deserts and huge canyons, on primeval forests and rugged coasts is taken for granted. But that among the sights to be enjoyed there is also a tropical jungle, with fantastic fauna and flora and the largest mangrove forest in the Americas, is a crowning glory. Since the Everglades have become a National Park, this virgin land will retain its unusual personality and develop according to its own laws. The nucleus of the park was Royal Palm State Park, originally established as a wildlife sanctuary by the State Federation of Women's Clubs. Geographers will object to the term "tropical" and forestry experts to the word "jungle." Yet the meteorologists consider the climate tropical, and the botanists and zoologists find that its plant and animal life is, to a considerable extent, tropical.

SANDY GATES

A FRAGMENT of the EARTH on the THIRD DAY of CREATION

CECIL W. STOUGHTON — NAT'L PARK SERVICE

The graceful lookout tower on the Shark River adds a modern touch to the unspoiled nature of the Everglades.

NATIONAL PARK SERVICE

Alligators are the most spectacular inhabitants of the Everglades.

Palm Ranger Station is a central attraction, for its Anhinga Trail, a boardwalk into Taylor Slough, leads into a living primeval world.

THE BIRDS AND BEASTS. A log drifting in the swampy water turns out to be a camouflaged alligator; suddenly and smoothly it slides into a school of garfish which churn the water in panic. Watching the spectacle are a few American egrets, their snowy white bodies and S-shaped necks balanced on thin, black legs; some stately herons and cranes wade through the shallows in search of their dinner; an anhinga and a white ibis with black wing tips fly by with clumsy, primeval grace. In the park there are also crocodiles, distinguished from the blunt snouted alligators by their long, tapered noses.

The Everglades is one of the last refuges for another creature of antediluvian appearance — the sea cow or manatee, a large, harmless mammal. It grows to a weight of almost 1,500 pounds on a diet of sea grass plucked from the bottom of shallow bays; the female nurses her baby upright in the water, exposing head and shoulder, clasping her infant with her flippers and nursing it serenely. Such a scene is said to be the origin of the ancient mariners' tales of mermaids in Florida waters. Along the ocean huge loggerhead turtles, weighing up to 300 pounds, build their nests, especially on the beaches toward Cape Sable where some of America's most magnificent shells may also be found. Snakes abound, and with their flaming colors and strange patterns offer a weird beauty of their own — diamondback rattlers and cottonmouth, indigo and green water snakes, king snakes and bright-colored coral snakes.

But no cautious visitor will be harmed.

It seems strange that the low, warm and watery Everglades should shelter the same group of animals that inhabits the dry, high and cold regions. Deer, bears, wildcats and panthers splash through the tepid streams, raccoons climb into treetops to catch the cool trade winds, and otters, playful, nonchalant and unafraid, have a wonderful time. Visitors who are interested in fishing may take the marl-surfaced highway toward Lake Ingraham. There and in neighboring Flamingo boats may be rented. Fishing is fine, and the varieties are endless, but the coveted prize is the tarpon, the large, spirited game fish with the shiny, silvery scales.

BIRDS THAT BUILD A TOWER AND TREES THAT KILL. Large areas of the park are and should be practically inaccessible, leaving undisturbed the haunts of rare, beautiful birds like the bald eagle, the roseate spoonbill, the bronze turkey and others. The huge rookeries of the more common pelicans and cormorants, limpkins and ducks, egrets and gallinules are an incredible bedlam of noise and excitement during the nesting season. A mass of white ibises rising from their nests in a circling flight and forming a "tower" is a sight to behold. At Duck Rock, a little key inside the park on the Gulf Coast, as many as 50,000 of these ibises may be seen roosting during the summer months.

Tree lovers will visit the Gumbo Limbo Trail, also near the Royal Palm Ranger Station, to study the vegetation of the typical hammock, from the tamarind tree and the wild coffeebush to the cabbage palm and the strangler fig which embraces a host tree and strangles it.

83

Mobile and the Azalea Trail

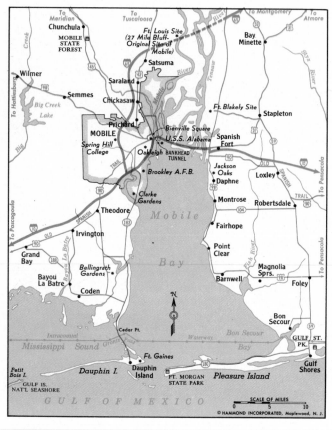

times stated, the small sister of New Orleans. It is rather the old lady across the bay who taught the infant on the Mississippi how to grow up, Southern style.

NO LONGER POOR, AND GLAD OF IT. Indian troubles, hurricanes, conflagrations, yellow fever epidemics — Mobile had its share of all of them. But, while after the Civil War many Southern centers languished, Mobile shipped cotton to the world at large and organized the lumber industry in its hinterland. Later on steel and iron from Birmingham floated down the river in barges and was reshipped from Mobile to foreign ports. Paper mills moved in, shipbuilding flourished, and the Bankhead Tunnel under the Mobile River facilitated communications to the east. Today Mobile is a prosperous international port with a future, and because it is well-to-do, it gladly preserves its past. It has a unique method of doing so: whenever an ancient structure is demolished, the weathered old bricks and particularly the iron lacework are saved and used again in new construction. This adaptation of the old to the new works very well, and the modern city preserves many a genuine French and Spanish touch; on Bienville Square the live oaks, the bright flowers and the splashing fountain suggest a relaxed calm. The battleship *Alabama,* docked along Battleship Parkway, is a state shrine open to the public.

BOEUF GRAS, JUG BANDS AND JUBILEE. Where was Carnival first celebrated in America? In Mobile, to be sure. The Gulf Coast was a howling wilderness in 1704, but the Casket Girls had just arrived, and so everybody dressed in fancy clothes for the Masque de St. Louis. In 1711 this annual affair was renamed Boeuf Gras. When it shifted from New Year's Eve to Shrove Tuesday, it became Mardi Gras. It is still the great event of community merrymaking, with parades, floats, and balls presided over by Emperor Felix. The black people have their own picturesque procession, and the jug bands that appear all over town on that occasion are a local curiosity: two boys accompany their street singing with a guitar and a contraption consisting of a washboard, a frying pan, a coffeepot and an ancient auto horn. Another "Jubilee" is provided by nature, usually on the eastern shore of the bay in late summer. Early in the morning a cry is heard along the bay: "Jubilee, Jubilee!" and as the news travels up the streets, people appear with baskets and wheelbarrows, and laughing and shouting they race to the bay. What has happened? The commotion means that hundreds of thousands of fish of all descriptions, from flounders to shrimps, have flung themselves on the shore, and innumerable seafood dinners may be had for the picking. There is no scientific explanation for the phenomenon, just the theory of a

THE GRANDMOTHER OF NEW ORLEANS. On the first document to bear the name "America" — Waldseemüller's map of 1505 — the outline of Mobile Bay is clearly drawn. The Spaniards explored it, and the first settlement was made in 1559. Had it lasted, Mobile would have in her hands the tourist trump card which is now played by St. Augustine, the oldest city in the United States. But the settlement on Mobile Bay was abandoned, and not until 1699 was a new colony established on Dauphin Island. In 1702 the colony was moved to Fort Louis de la Mobile. It was there that the first cargo of Casket Girls arrived, 23 poor but decent young women from Canada. Within a month 22 had husbands; one was hard to please. In 1710 the settlement was transferred to the present site of Mobile and in 1721 received a cargo of 600 Africans who became slaves. All this makes it clear that Mobile is not, as is some-

ALABAMA'S WORLD PORT

The striking Bellingrath Gardens are a memorial to the wife of Walter Bellingrath, a Coca-Cola tycoon.

"tidal spasm." According to James Street, "Some say the fish just go crazy. Anyway, the people do."

BLOSSOMS BY THE BAY. The question "Who started the Southern flower craze?" — if craze is the right word for so pleasant an enthusiasm — is difficult to answer. But Mobile has an excellent claim to this title. For it was Mobile that imported in 1754 the first azalea from France and has pampered, improved and crossbred the plants until today you can admire there every imaginable type, from 120-year-old azalea trees that are giants 35 feet tall to oriental miniatures that are midgets. For one March week every year thousands of visitors descend upon Mobile to enjoy the Azalea Trail, 35 miles of streets blazing with flowers, with all gardens along the route open to the public. The trail starts out from Bienville Square, and the markers are followed easily. Official guides are available, usually pretty girls from town; to outsiders their lush Alabama accent alone is worth the fee. The next goal of most visitors lies about 20 miles to the south: the magnificent Bellingrath Gardens where a quarter million azaleas cover 800 acres. Owner of this spectacle is the Coca-Cola Bellingrath family; their mansion emphasizes the Gulf Coast style with wrought iron railings and an iron lace patio. The gardens are in bloom all year, with a succession of roses, laurel, sweet olive, gardenias, crepe myrtle, oleander, allamanda and hibiscus.

THE HAUNTED BAYOU. Not far from Bellingrath, near the village of Irvington, a fascinating short trip is recommended: follow the road along Bayou la Batre — an old Spanish highway that was paved with crushed white shells; the oaks shading the dark waters were standing when the Spaniards came, when Laffitte used the inlet as a hideout, and when the buccaneer La Mas spent his last years in a cabin by the bayou. He had "waded the decks deeply in gore" and was the source of gruesome tales. His final days were disturbed, he complained, by the phantom of a mounted Spaniard galloping over the oyster-shell road, red sparks pouring from his mouth. The rider had seduced a French girl, and with his sword her father had pierced the Spaniard's throat.

85

Mississippi's Playground

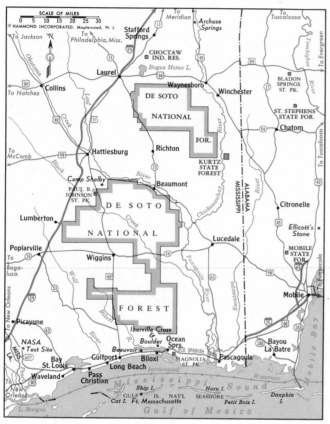

THE LUSH AND BREEZY SHORE. Through arches formed by oaks and cypresses, catalpa and tulip trees you look out on the calm, glistening Gulf. The scent of magnolia and oleander is in the moist, mild air. Mockingbirds sing in the crepe myrtle trees and pelicans land on the water's mirror with a splash. Lilies, roses, honeysuckle and jessamine blossom in sight of the beach, and the smell of the sea and the fragrance of the flowers blend into a rich, exuberant atmosphere. The white 40-mile seawall and the ancient live oaks where Indian tribes used to hold meetings; the shore road that used to be the Spanish Trail; the stories of pirates and adventurers, of French blades and Spanish poniards; the small shipyards where wooden craft are built; the food stands that advertise giant shrimps, gumbo and jambalaya; and the black street vendors singing "Oyster ma-an from Pass Christi-a-an" — all this is Mississippi's

Gulf Coast. It consists of seven cities, six of them pleasant old resorts: Pascagoula, Ocean Springs, Biloxi, Pass Christian, Bay St. Louis, Waveland and one — much newer — Gulfport.

BEES AND CRABS. The waters of Mississippi Sound are calm because a row of islands several miles offshore breaks the pounding waves; the only winds they cannot mitigate are the hurricanes. The islands themselves are low sandbars, with patches of an evergreen shrub called titi; when the latter blossoms in April there is such a sweet heavy fragrance in the wind that the fishermen can smell it far out on the Gulf. The myriads of honeybees and the white sand crabs that race over the dunes seem to be the only living creatures there. Opposite Pass Christian some islands are completely covered with shells and produce small, sweet oysters. Ship Island, opposite Gulfport, is rich in history and legend and is the site of the Civil War Fort Massachusetts.

THE SINGING RIVER. It sounds like a swarm of bees, or like a honey locust, and can best be heard on a hot summer evening. From the fish docks of Pascagoula, the old Gulf town, one can hear the strange sound of the Pascagoula River which has been singing this same song from time immemorial. Spanish records of the seventeenth century mention it, but it is as much of a puzzle today. Scientific explanations do not exist, only theories: it may be natural gas escaping, or the rolling of sand on the slate bottom, or a cave sucking in a current. Only the Indians know the true reason: once upon a time the Pascagoulas found themselves hopelessly surrounded by the Biloxis, their archenemies. They would not think of surrender but chose suicide instead. From a great water oak on the shore they walked into the river with joined hands, chanting their song of death until the last body had vanished in the dark current. But their voices were never hushed; they are humming on, just as the old water oak still stands on the riverbank. In American naval history the Battle of Pascagoula turned out to be a brilliant victory of good sense for all concerned. A local boy, David Farragut, who had grown up on a plantation near the Singing River, returned as a famous Yankee admiral during the War Between the States, took New Orleans and approached Pascagoula to effect a military occupation. Outside the port he was met by a fleet of small craft of every description manned by the admiral's old playmates and school friends. The reception was terrific; joy and emotions ran high, and what might have been a bloody encounter ended as the biggest fish fry in the history of the Gulf Coast. West of Pascagoula, the restful city of Ocean Springs is the original Biloxi, first capital of French Louisiana.

A STRING of SEVEN PEARLS

TORCHES AT EBB TIDE. During dark spring evenings the shallow waters at Biloxi are aglow with light; you'd think of fireflies in a pasture rather than of torches on the sea. Men are "gigging" here for flounders. Two by two, they wade through the water, their lights in one hand, their spears with long, narrow tips in the other. Heads bent, they look for flounders half-buried in the sand, spear them, throw them into a basket, and late at night return in a torchlight parade. The fishermen here are mostly Austrians, Czechoslovakians, Poles and Yugoslavs, and as they all possess a certain natural gaiety, they fit well into this country of French, Spanish and Negro traditions. A fiesta atmosphere hovers over Biloxi, which once was the fashionable rendezvous of the Southern haut monde and still is a lively resort with Victorian charm.

THE WHITE CROSS. In 1699 the French under d'Iberville landed near Biloxi, erected a white cross and took possession of the land for their king and their God. On that same bay beneath a white cross, on the Sunday preceding the 15th of August, all the deep-sea fishing boats, freshly painted and bedecked with gay pennants, are anchored there. The chants begin at midnight, and mass is held with all the magnificence of the Roman Catholic ritual; priests visit each boat to bless the crew, sprinkle drops of holy water on the planks and pray for the men's safety and prosperity during the new season. At dawn the boats set out for the open sea. Near Biloxi the shore estate of Beauvoir was the last home of Jefferson Davis, the Confederate president. Gulfport is a planned port city of twentieth-century vintage. Pass Christian, formerly the most beautiful of the "Seven Pearls" with aristocratic Greek Revival homes under old live oaks, was largely destroyed in 1969 by the 30-foot tidal waves of hurricane Camille. Bay St. Louis was formerly as exclusive as Pass Christian across the bridge, but it is now a gay, popular middle class resort. Waveland, near the Louisiana state line, is a haven for summer commuters from New Orleans. Its Pirate House is linked, though somewhat tenuously, with Jean Laffitte, the buccaneer.

The Gulf of Mexico produces fine shrimps in quantity, and Mississippi's shrimp boats haul in big catches.

SHOSTAL ASSOCIATES

Natchez to Vicksburg

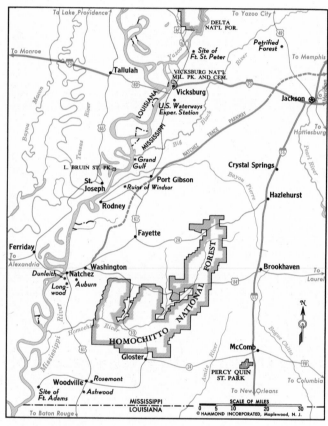

of azaleas are in bloom, the "Confederate Pageant" is performed in the evening, and in tableaux crinolined Southern belles with Dresden-china complexions accept the adoring smiles of dashing young officers of the Confederate Army. Every year in March Natchez offers the most spectacular revival of an era in which planters were colonels, young women had a romantic bent, and at the drop of a pin men defended their honor on the dueling ground.

ROYAL SPLENDOR. The mansions which were completed in and around Natchez just before the War Between the States are of a magnificence that is not matched by other Southern cities with similar traditions, such as New Orleans, Savannah or Charleston. Stanton Hall, for instance, has ceilings 22 feet high, mantles carved of Carrara marble and huge doors of mahogany. Tall mirrors, bronze chandeliers and exquisite furniture were purchased in France and Spain, and a sailing vessel was chartered which brought the treasures across the Atlantic and up the Mississippi directly to the Natchez waterfront. Of the numerous showplaces only a few can be mentioned here: Rosalie, on the site of old Fort Rosalie where an Indian massacre took place in 1729, its living room furniture appropriately carved of rosewood; Bontura, with its lovely lace ironwork, erected by a wealthy Portuguese merchant; Greenleaves, whose bird patterned china was painted by Audubon; the Elms, Arlington, Dunleith, and Auburn. Outside of Natchez to the south, Longwood is an unfinished monstrosity of oriental splendor; the eight-sided six-story structure was under construction when the War Between the States began. The workmen dropped their tools to join the army, and the house was never completed. Even if you cannot come to Natchez in March, a visit at any other time is recommended; quite a few homes are open the year round.

PILGRIMAGE CITY. "Why not let some less fortunate folks, even if they are Yankees, see the wonderful heritage we have here in our refined old homes?" That was the convincing argument with which the Garden Club of Natchez persuaded the owners of the fine old plantation houses to open their gates and display their treasures to the public during the Natchez Pilgrimage each March. The year was 1931, the depression hitting the bottom, and many of the old estates were in a state of dilapidation. The idea of the Garden Club was gladly accepted as both idealistic and practical; the admission fees were to be used for the purpose of restoration and maintenance. The project turned out to be a great success, and today the Natchez Pilgrimage is almost a national institution. There not only will you see the actual settings of our Southern novels, but ladies in antebellum hoop skirts will greet you at the doors. Acres

PLANTERS, GAMBLERS, RIVER PIRATES. On Jefferson Street, the King's Tavern (the oldest house in the city) and Ellicott's Inn (also called Connelly's Tavern) are mementos of another Natchez. That the town on the bluffs should have developed into one of the country's most refined and cultured centers of well-mannered and gracious living while below along the waterfront Natchez-Under-the-Hill carried on at its gaudiest and wickedest seems an ironical coincidence. For many years during the flatboat and steamboat eras the lower town swarmed with flatboatmen and deckhands, Kentuckians and Acadians, Indians and half-breeds, highwaymen and river pirates, perfumed quadroons, imposters and gamblers. Bars and gambling houses did a booming business while flatboats were tied to the shore twelve or fourteen deep for a two-mile

ROMANTIC ANTEBELLUM COUNTRY

stretch. Sailing vessels from Liverpool or Genoa docked at the wharf. But only part of the customers arrived on the river; even more men galloped into town on horseback, their money belts bulging, their weapons ready, the groups keeping close together to discourage holdups. For all flatboatmen sold their cargoes downstream in Natchez or New Orleans along with the boat itself, and traveled back on the notorious Natchez Trace. That historic road is now transformed into the Natchez Trace Parkway, leading to Nashville, Tennessee. Instead of soldiers and adventurers, flatboaters and highwaymen, modern tourists use it and stop at the Tupelo Visitors Center to see the documentary film "Path of Empire."

HIGH BLUFFS ABOVE THE MISSISSIPPI. On the way north you will ride through the old plantation country. Near Port Gibson, on a bluff overlooking the Mississippi, the spectacular ruins of Windsor stand out against the sky: 22 tall stone columns of Corinthian elegance, deserted and overgrown — a sad memorial.

Seventy-one miles north of Natchez, the city of Vicksburg is a spot of scenic beauty. Built on high bluffs that rise 200 feet above the river, it lies in a countryside of terraces, ravines, caves and a tangled vegetation that is almost jungle-like. The city's great moment in American history had been, of course, the 47-day siege and defense of the town in 1863, an event that is remembered in the Vicksburg National Military Park, organized "to preserve the history of the battles and operations on the ground where they were fought." The park of 1,330 acres is well laid out and marked, and the military leaders are honored in 3 equestrian statues, 19 memorials, and about 150 busts and relief portraits. Another interesting institution near Vicksburg is the U.S. Waterways Experiment Station, a hydraulic research laboratory investigating problems of drainage and flood control. Here is a scale model of a 600-mile stretch of the Mississippi River, including all tributaries, and all natural conditions like the flow of water and the runoff from rainfall are authentically recreated.

Right: Dunleith in Natchez, built in 1847, is a typical square plantation house with Doric columns.

Below right: Connelly's Tavern, the town's oldest house, is said to have been a boisterous and wicked place in the days of the flatboatmen.

Below: Stanton Hall. A sailing vessel was chartered to bring decorative treasures from Spain and France to Natchez.

Sightseeing Guide

ALABAMA

NORTHERN ALABAMA. The Muscle Shoals area near Florence contains several TVA dams (Wilson and Wheeler) and lakes created by the Tennessee River. Lakes Wilson and Pickwick are popular for fishing, boating and camping. East of Florence the city of Huntsville is the home of the George C. Marshall Space Flight Center, a fascinating institution open to visitors. The development of rocketry may be observed at the Space Orientation Center. The Saturn and other boosters, a full size replica of the spacecraft used by America's first astronauts, the firing panel for launching Explorer I, a satellite exhibit and and other displays may be viewed there. Russell Cave National Monument near Bridgeport was a home for Stone Age man.

CENTRAL ALABAMA. Birmingham, the Pittsburgh of the South, is the center of a steel industry based on local iron, coal and limestone deposits. From Red Mountain the statue of Vulcan, Roman god of the forge, overlooks the city; mounted on a 124-foot tower, it is the largest iron statue on earth. Tuscaloosa on the Black Warrior River is the seat of the University of Alabama. Montgomery, the state capital, is a city of traditional Southern dignity. It was the first capital of the Confederacy; on the capitol grounds the first White House of the Confederacy is preserved as a historic shrine and museum. Tuskegee Institute, two miles from Tuskegee, is one of the country's best known predominantly Negro schools. The names of two outstanding Negro leaders are linked with it — Booker T. Washington, its founder, and George Washington Carver, the great scientist whose researches helped to bring revolutionary changes to Southern farming.

SOUTHERN ALABAMA. Mobile with its Azalea Trail and the Bellingrath Gardens are described on pages 84-85. From the eastern terminal of the causeway across Mobile Bay, the Eastern Shore Dogwood Trail is spectacular at blossom time, some dogwood trees are 30 feet tall.

FLORIDA

NORTHERN FLORIDA. Jacksonville is the gateway to Florida and is its financial and commercial metropolis. The Oriental Gardens have beautiful displays of tropical flowers throughout the year, and 40 miles of pleasant beaches attract tourists and vacationists. The St. Johns River is a famous fishing ground, particularly in its upper reaches. St. Augustine, the oldest city in the United States, and Marineland, the unique aquarium and outdoor museum of oceanic life, are described on pages 74-75. White Springs, an old Southern spa on the Suwannee River, with its memorial to Stephen Foster, is also described on page 73. Tallahassee, the capital of Florida and the seat of Florida State University, is surrounded by fine old plantations antedating the Civil War. The Alfred B. Maclay Gardens State Park near Tallahassee is worth visiting, and the Wakulla Springs are a crystal clear body of water. In Pensacola the ruins of the Spanish Fort San Carlos of 1698 look out on a fine natural harbor. The town is perhaps best known for its naval air base, one of the country's largest. Across the bay, on Santa Rosa Island, Pensacola Beach is a lively Gulf Coast resort.

CENTRAL FLORIDA. In Gainesville the University of Florida is located; interesting plantations of Chinese tung trees are nearby. Near the residential town of Ocala, Florida's Silver Springs is one of the state's major sightseeing attractions. It is described on page 78. Another tourist spot is Ross Allen's Reptile Institute. Almost as impressive as Silver Springs is the resort of Rainbow Springs near Dunnellon. The daily flow of clear water is nearly 500 million gallons, and unusual species of underwater plant and animal life may be seen there. On the east coast of central Florida, Daytona Beach is a year-round resort; on its beach a stretch of sand is so hard packed that at low tide automobile driving is possible there. Speed records have been set on that beach by racing experts. To the south, Cape Kennedy (Cape Canaveral) is America's spaceport and is described on page 79. Sanlando Springs, south of Sanford, is another of central Florida's big, gushing springs. Orlando, a beautiful garden city and cultural center, is described on page 78. Near Orlando the new Walt Disney World comprises 43 square miles but only 100 acres are allotted to the "Magic Kingdom," the theme of the park. A further 2,500 acres are set aside for recreation and housing, including the new town of Lake Buena Vista, and 5,000 acres of Reedy Creek Swamp are maintained as a conservation area protecting the lives of panthers and bears, alligators and turtles, cranes and eagles. The whole project has been organized to avoid environmental damage. On the central west coast of the state, Homosassa Springs offers "Nature's Giant Fish Bowl" and, to the south is the bubbling Weeki Wachee Spring. The major towns and resorts of Florida's west coast are described on pages 76-77: Tarpon Springs, the Sponge Capital of the World; St. Petersburg; Sarasota with its Jungle Gardens, the Ringling Museums and the circus winter quarters in nearby Venice. St. Petersburg and Sarasota are connected by the Sunshine Skyway, a long, majestic bridge across Tampa Bay. In Tampa the section called Ybor City is fascinating; it was founded by Cuban and Spanish cigar makers and preserves the Spanish language and Spanish customs, and offers excellent Spanish food. Busch Gardens, with its African animals and bird shows, is popular. Lakeland, which has 13 lakes within its city limits, is a center of the citrus industry. Two of Florida's main attractions, the Cypress Gardens near Winter Haven and the Bok Tower near Lake Wales, are described on pages 78-79. East of Lake Wales, on the east coast, the McKee Jungle Gardens near Vero Beach are well-known.

SOUTHERN FLORIDA. Lake Okeechobee, a near circle with a diameter of 31 miles, is the largest natural body of fresh water not only in Florida but also in the country. On its southwestern shore the town of Clewiston is both a resort and an interesting market center for the cane sugar and winter vegetable area around Lake Okeechobee. Swamp buggy and airboat rides to various swamp sanctuaries are available. On the southwest coast the lively resort town of Fort Myers is America's City of Palms. Its First Street offers an imposing view — the country's longest avenue of Royal Palms. Thomas Edison spent his winters in Fort Myers and conducted a number of experiments there. Near Fort Myers, Cape Coral Gardens display 40,000 rosebushes. At night rising and falling columns of water blend with music and colored lights in a spectacle called Waltzing Waters. Florida's Gold Coast on the eastern shore is described on pages 80-81: Palm Beach, the society resort; Fort Lauderdale, an Eden for all water sports; Miami and Miami Beach; Coral Gables with the campus of the University of Miami; the Overseas Highway; the picturesque keys and Key West. The Seminole Indian Village offers a tourist version of native Indian life. The fascinating Everglades National Park, which preserves the only subtropical plant and animal jungle life in the United States, occupies the southern tip of Florida; it is described on pages 82-83. In Fort Jefferson National Monument, the abandoned fortress on Garden Key of the Dry Tortugas can be reached only by a seagoing boat or seaplane.

SOUTHEAST REGION

GEORGIA

NORTHERN GEORGIA. Augusta, the important cotton center, is also a mecca for golf enthusiasts. Every spring the Masters Invitational Tournament is held at the Augusta National Golf Club. Athens is the seat of the University of Georgia, the oldest chartered state university in the United States. Atlanta, the capital of Georgia, is a rather young city which developed rapidly as a railroad center. It was burned to the ground by General Sherman on his march to the sea but recovered quickly. Today Atlanta's interests are not only industrial and political but also educational; it is the seat of Georgia Institute of Technology, Georgia State University, Morehouse College, and Atlanta University, and Emory and Oglethorpe universities are nearby. Among the local attractions, a huge 50-foot-high painting of the Battle of Atlanta in the Cyclorama Building of Grant Park is widely known. The new Atlanta Memorial Arts Center on Peachtree Street, a magnificent building complex with facilities for symphony concerts, opera, drama and ballet performances, is nationally admired. It is also the home of the High Museum and School of Art. A network of viaducts half a century old has been transformed into Underground Atlanta, with gaslighted cobblestone streets, gourmet restaurants, sidewalk cafés and boutiques. Across the Chattahoochee River Six Flags over Georgia is a fantasyland-entertainment park with a historical theme. One of America's beloved folklore figures originated in Atlanta — Uncle Remus. The home of his creator, Joel Chandler Harris, has been restored and is a museum now at 1050 Gordon Street, S. W. Sixteen miles to the east of Atlanta Stone Mountain has been transformed into a most spectacular memorial of the Confederate cause, showing the monumental figures of President Jefferson Davis and generals Lee and Stonewall Jackson riding across the face of the monolith. There are also a cable car to the top of Stone Mountain, a showboat on Stone Mountain Lake, a 12-story carillon, a game ranch, a plantation complex, scenic railroad and museums. Northwest of Atlanta near Cartersville the Etowah Indian Mounds, erected between A.D. 1000 and 1500, are an impressive monument of a vanished Indian culture. The park museum contains Indian mortuary figures painted white. The Chickamauga Battlefield in the northwest corner of the state commemorates the battle that took place there in 1863. Springer Mountain is the southern terminus of the Appalachian Trail which begins at Mount Katahdin in Maine. The famous Georgia marble quarries at Tate are fascinating; both the quarries and the plants which cut and polish the marble may be visited on guided tours.

THE COAST OF GEORGIA. Savannah and the Golden Isles are described on pages 70-71; the latter include the lovely resorts of Sea Island, St. Simons Island and Jekyll Island State Park. Guarding the entrance of the port of Savannah, Fort Pulaski is a well preserved fortress which was shelled in the Civil War; it is a national monument now. Brunswick is Georgia's central market for shrimps and crabs.

CENTRAL GEORGIA. Near Macon Ocmulgee National Monument preserves the remains of six successive Indian cultures; among the relics are ceremonial mounds and a council chamber. Warm Springs, where President Franklin D. Roosevelt died, became nationally known for both its beneficial treatment of victims of polio and for the personal interest the president took in the development of the health resort. Franklin D. Roosevelt State Park at Warm Springs is traversed by a scenic highway (State 190) which runs along the ridge of Pine Mountain in the foothills of the Appalachians. Callaway Gardens is a magnificent preserve of wildflowers and natural woodlands, with a bird study trail and a ski pull for water skiers on Robin Lake. Columbus, an industrial city, is the site of Fort Benning, the largest infantry post in the country. Visitors are welcome.

SOUTHERN GEORGIA. The fascinating, jungle-like wilderness of that huge swamp, the Okefenokee National Wildlife Refuge, is described on pages 72-73. The Georgia Veterans Memorial State Park is situated near Cordele. To the south, near the Florida state line, Thomasville is a winter resort famous for its roses. Its annual rose show in April is magnificent. Many fine old antebellum estates surround the town.

MISSISSIPPI

NORTHERN MISSISSIPPI. John W. Kyle State Park overlooks Sardis Lake, a reservoir with an area of 110 square miles where water sports facilities are available. East of the dam in Oxford the University of Mississippi is located. The home of William Faulkner, novelist and Nobel Prize laureate, is also in that Southern community.

CENTRAL MISSISSIPPI. East of Laurel, the industrial and oil center of the state, a popular recreational area has been created around Bogue Homo Lake near the De Soto National Forest. In Jackson, the state capital, both the old and the new capitols are of interest; the former is Mississippi's most distinguished historic building. The Classical Revival style governor's mansion at the city's busiest corner was headquarters for both Grant and Sherman. Trenches which were part of the city's Civil War fortifications can still be inspected. Vicksburg, with the National Military Park and the U.S. Waterways Experiment Station, and Natchez, with its lovely antebellum plantation homes, are described on pages 88-89.

SOUTHERN MISSISSIPPI. The Mississippi Gulf Coast, with its lively resorts along the old Spanish Trail from Bay St. Louis to famous Biloxi and historic Pascagoula, is described on pages 86-87. At Bay St. Louis a 10-mile sand beach has been pumped into the Gulf to join the man-made beaches of adjoining Harrison County. The 36 miles of unbroken superb beaches are known as the Gulf Coast Riviera. In Biloxi the handsome lighthouse was not built but fabricated of cast iron in 1848. The Gautier House, the Red Brick House with slave quarters and the Old Magnolia Hotel of 1844 are distinguished historical buildings. On the industrial side, shrimp and oyster canning plants are interesting and may be visited. Near Gulfport Marine Life offers a porpoise show.

NORTH CAROLINA

THE COAST OF NORTH CAROLINA. The Wright Brothers National Memorial, Fort Raleigh National Historic Site on Roanoke Island and Cape Hatteras National Seashore are described on pages 62-63. Edenton on Albemarle Sound, site of the Edenton Tea Party, is a fine old town with colonial homes and public buildings. In New Bern, near the mouth of the Neuse River, Tryon Palace is the early colonial capitol, now restored. In Wilmington, North Carolina's largest port, tourist attractions are the U.S.S. *North Carolina* Battleship Memorial, the Burguin-Wright House (Cornwallis' Headquarters) and Greenfield Gardens. To the north of the city is Moores Creek National Military Park, commemorating a Revolutionary War battle. South of the city, Airlie Gardens and Orton Plantation gardens are famous for their beauty. The innumerable sounds and inlets of the coast offer good fishing. Freshwater lakes also are available; Mattamuskeet Lake, near Pamlico Sound, is the largest natural lake with a surface of approximately 100 square miles.

PIEDMONT OF NORTH CAROLINA. In the southern tier of the state, Charlotte is the seat of the Mint Museum of Art. To the east, at Gaddy's Wild Goose Refuge in Ansonville visitors are welcome to watch the thousands of birds during the season which lasts from October to spring. Farther to the east, Pinehurst and Southern Pines are famous mid-South resorts with magnificent golf courses and all facilities for equestrian sports; steeplechases and horse shows are annual events. In Fayetteville the Old Slave Market is an impressive building with tower and arcades. In the northern tier, or Piedmont, Winston-Salem is said to be the world's largest tobacco manufacturing center, where Camels and other cigarettes are made. Both the factories and the tobacco auctions are interesting. Old Salem preserves a number of restored colonial buildings of the Moravian community of 1766, including the home Moravian Church and God's Acre (the graveyard), Single Brothers' House, the Salem Tavern and the Wachovia Historical Society Museum. North of the city, Pilot Mountain offers a broad panorama, with a toll road leading to the summit of the solitary pinnacle; Hanging Rock State Park is a recreational area. East of Winston-Salem, Greensboro is the site of Guilford Court House National Military Park, with monuments and a museum honoring the Revolutionary battle. Nearby Sedgefield is a popular resort. To the east Chapel Hill is the seat of the University of North Carolina. Of special interest on the campus are the Coker Arboretum and the Morehead Planetarium. Durham, the town where Chesterfields and other brands are manufactured, is the seat of Duke University. On the beautiful campus the chapel's campanile with a 50-bell carillon is a landmark; the Sarah P. Duke Memorial Gardens are lovely. Raleigh, the state capital, has a number of attractions: the State Capitol built of local granite, North Carolina State University, home of the first nuclear reactor installed on a college campus, and the tiny frame building where the 17th president of the United States, Andrew Johnson, was born. On the state fairgrounds, the J. S. Dorton Arena is one of America's most striking modern structures.

WESTERN NORTH CAROLINA. The spectacular Blue Ridge Parkway is described on pages 64-65. At mile 285 the parkway is crossed by the road of Daniel Boone's westward trek; through the gap in the mountains he used to take settlers into the wilderness of Kentucky. At various points of the parkway local products may be inspected; at mile 238½ at the Brinegar Cabin there are weaving demonstrations; at mile 294, at the Parkway Crafts Center in Moses H. Cone Memorial Park, mountain crafts are demonstrated; and at mile 331 the Museum of North Carolina Minerals is an exhibit of surprising variety. At Mount Airy, near the Virginia state line, the open-faced granite quarry is one of the largest on earth; visitors are welcome. South of the parkway Blowing Rock offers a wide mountain view. The unusual name is derived from the air currents that form in the flume between the walls of the mountain; a piece of paper or a feather thrown into the gorge is blown back by the wind. An old-time narrow-gauge railroad takes railway buffs on trips. During the summer in nearby Boone the Daniel Boone Amphitheater presents the open-air drama, "Horn in the West," in a natural setting of hills and trees. To the southwest the resort of Linville offers a number of tourist attractions: Linville Caverns just east of the parkway, Linville Falls and Gorge and Grandfather Mountain, which has an abrupt rise of 5,964 feet but may be scaled on an automobile toll road. Another mountain peak reached by a

side road from the Blue Ridge Parkway is Mt. Mitchell, with an elevation of 6,684 ft. the highest summit east of the Mississippi. North of Asheville, the Craggy Gardens contain a spectacular stand of purple rhododendron; some bushes are 12 feet tall. The resort town of Asheville and Biltmore, the 250-room Vanderbilt estate, are described on page 65. The boyhood home of the famous novelist Thomas Wolfe is in Asheville at 48 Spruce Street. Among Asheville's handicraft specialties are hearthbrooms, homespuns and dogwood jewelry. Carl Sandburg Home National Historic Site, a farm at Flat Rock, was occupied by the poet from 1945 until his death in 1967 at the age of 89. In Pisgah National Forest on former grounds of the Biltmore estate is the site of the first forestry school in the United States; as a memorial, an old-time logging camp with museum and demonstration camp is reconstructed there. East of Asheville, in Chimney Rock Park, Lake Lure with Hickory Nut Gorge and Chimney Rock are tourist attractions; the latter is a 300-foot boulder, with an elevator to take visitors to the top. South of Asheville, a number of resorts are popular with winter guests from the Deep South: Waynesville, Hendersonville, Saluda, Tryon (famous for fine handweaving), Brevard (home of a summer music festival) and Highlands. Near Highlands are the Bridal Veil Falls; a visitor can drive his automobile right under the rushing waterfall. Between Highlands and Cashiers a toll road leads to the summit of Whiteside Mountain (4,930 ft.). Great Smoky Mountains National Park and the Cherokee Reservation are described on pages 66-67; at the Mountainside Theatre in Cherokee the outdoor drama "Unto These Hills" is enacted during the summer. Fontana Dam, the world's fourth highest and a part of the TVA system, creates a 30-mile-long reservoir with good fishing facilities. Fontana Village is a resort. Hot Springs, north of Great Smoky Mountains National Park, has been a popular spa since Indian days.

SOUTH CAROLINA

THE COAST OF SOUTH CAROLINA. Charleston, one of America's "character towns," and the famous Cypress, Magnolia and Middleton gardens with their acres of blossoming azaleas and camellias are described on pages 68-69. At Fort Sumter, where a Confederate shell started the Civil War, the fort's history is presented in dioramas; the fort can be reached by boat leaving from the municipal yacht basin. Edisto Beach State Park with its beach of white sands and waving palm trees is a popular recreation spot 50 miles southwest of Charleston. Beaufort County is an exceedingly picturesque area, consisting largely of 65 islands. Its attractions include several historic ruins of churches and fortifications. Among these, Fort Frederick, erected in 1731, was built of tabby, a building material of shells, lime and sand. The city of Beaufort has some fine colonial buildings like the St. Helena Church and many stately antebellum residences. The neighboring island of St. Helena has a large population of Gullah Negroes, said to be the purest African stock in America. Parris Island is a U.S. Marine Corps Training Station; visitors are welcome. Hilton Head Island boasts of 12 miles of beautiful beach and a shooting preserve where bobwhite are hunted on horseback or from horse buggies. On the coastal highway north of Charleston, near the town of McClellanville, is Hampton Plantation with its pillared mansion, the home of Archibald Rutledge, the poet. Between McClellanville and the ocean, the Cape Romain National Wildlife Refuge has been established. South of Georgetown the Belle Isle Gardens are admired for their huge live oaks spreading their branches over beds of bright flowers. North of Georgetown the state-owned Brookgreen Gardens are interesting. The park contains an impressive avenue of gigantic, moss-hung live oaks, formal boxwood gardens, a noted outdoor collection of sculptures and a game preserve. Nearby Murrells Inlet is popular with fishermen; soft-shell crabs, oysters and clams are abundant, and drift fishing on the Gulf Stream nets marlin and dolphin, amberjack and cobia. To the north, Myrtle Beach fringed by live oaks and palms is the area's outstanding seaside resort.

CENTRAL SOUTH CAROLINA. In Columbia the State Capitol is a historical landmark. When General Sherman shelled the building in 1865 his artillery left in the walls holes and scars now covered with bronze stars; the Confederate Relic Room contains historical collections. Columbia is also the site of the University of South Carolina and of Woodrow Wilson's boyhood home. Between the low coastal country and the uplands of the Piedmont, the sand hills in the Long Leaf Pine Belt are a region where all equestrian sports are cultivated. Camden is one of the oldest mid-Southern winter resorts; horse shows and polo matches are important events, and the Springdale Course is noted for steeplechase racing. Near Sumter the Swan Lake Gardens and the Dunndell Gardens with their large displays of Japanese iris are tourist attractions. To the south, at Summerton, the Fort Watson Memorial honors the storming of the British fort by General Francis Marion, the Swamp Fox. At Orangeburg the Edisto Gardens include large stands of wisteria and azaleas, a rose test garden and facilities for picnicking. Aiken calls itself the polo capital of the South; like Camden, it is a resort for horse lovers. Polo ponies, hunters and jumpers are trained there, and the surrounding parks and forests offer quiet roads for horseback riding and horse-and-buggy driving. North of Aiken in Edgefield, Oakley Park is an antebellum residence filled with family heirlooms; it is open to visitors. Not far from McCormick, near the Georgia state line, the John de la Howe State School is a unique institution. Founded in 1797, this manual training school teaches cooking, dairying and other trades; visitors are welcome. In the south-central part of the state Lake Marion and Lake Moultrie are highly appreciated by fishermen. Landlocked striped bass is caught there throughout the year; other fish in plentiful supply are crappie, bream and black bass.

NORTHERN SOUTH CAROLINA. Lancaster is the reputed site of Andrew Jackson's birthplace. King's Mountain National Military Park near Gaffney commemorates a Revolutionary War victory in 1780 when regular British troops surrendered to American frontiersmen. The park offers a ridge drive past markers and monuments, and the museum contains a diorama of the battle. Cowpens National Battlefield is also nearby. North of Greenville, Caesars Head is a rock rising 1,200 feet above the Saluda River, with a lookout platform and a recreational area. Table Rock State Park is another popular goal. At Clemson, near the Georgia border, Fort Hill on the campus of Clemson University was the home of John C. Calhoun. The stately plantation mansion still contains many of its original furnishings; visitors are welcome.

TENNESSEE

EASTERN TENNESSEE. The Great Smoky Mountains National Park, which lies partly in North Carolina and partly in Tennessee, is described on pages 66-67. The scenic loop drive through the Great Smokies, a 100-mile excursion, starts at Knoxville. The popular resort of Gatlinburg is the northern gateway to the Great Smoky Mountains. From the main street tourists travel by sky lift to the top of Crockett Mountain.

Homespun Valley Mountaineer Village demonstrates mountain skills and crafts, even the making of moonshine whiskey. A favorite goal of mountain climbers is Mt. Le Conte, at a height of 6,593 feet one of the highest peaks east of the Rockies. Knoxville is the supply depot for the eastern Tennessee mountains and the nerve center of the TVA system. Visiting engineers from every corner of the world study the huge Tennessee Valley rehabilitation project with a view of applying similar methods at home. Knoxville is also the seat of the University of Tennessee. The nearby TVA lakes — Norris and Fort Loudoun, Watts Bar, Douglas and Cherokee — are excellent fishing grounds. Norris Dam, north of the city, was the first TVA dam to be completed, in 1936. The lake formed by the dam is a vacation area, with Norris Dam and Big Ridge state parks offering all water sports facilities. Norris Freeway leads to a lookout peak offering a fine view of the dam and the lake. In nearby Oak Ridge the American Museum of Atomic Energy has exhibits explaining the work of the famous Oak Ridge Laboratory. For a broad panorama of Chattanooga on the Georgia state line, ride to the summit of 2,225-foot-high Lookout Mountain either by car on a scenic highway or by incline railway. On top of the mountain, Point Park, the Rock City Gardens and the Lookout Mountain Caverns with Ruby Falls are sightseeing attractions. Bloody battles were fought there during the Civil War, and monuments mark the battlefields. From what is now Chickamauga and Chattanooga National Military Park, General Sherman started his notorious march to the sea. On the other side of the Tennessee river canyon, Signal Mountain is a lookout point high above the picturesque countryside; the mountain is so-called because of the Indian smoke signals which once emanated from there. Nearby Chickamauga Lake, one of the TVA reservoirs, offers all water sports.

WESTERN TENNESSEE. In Nashville the State Capitol on Cedar Knob affords a good view of the city. An authentic reproduction of the Parthenon in Athens has been erected in Centennial Park; it contains an art gallery. Fort Nashborough, the frontier post from which Nashville developed, has been reconstructed. Vanderbilt University, Tennessee State University and Fisk University, the latter one of America's largest predominantly Negro colleges and home of the famous Jubilee Singers, are located in Nashville. The city's Grand Ole Opry House is a nationally known institution, and the local recording studios have made Nashville the world center for recorded country and western music. Twelve miles east of Nashville, Andrew Jackson's home, The Hermitage, is not only a historic shrine but also one of the country's most distinguished mansions. The original furnishings are still there, and the garden is preserved as it existed in "Old Hickory's" day. Both the general and his wife Rachel are buried there. In the northwestern corner of the state, Reelfoot Lake is a region of wild and eerie beauty; during the New Madrid earthquake of 1811 a cypress forest was half submerged, creating a fantastic lake 14 miles long. Huge beds of lotus flowers and water lilies add colorful touches. Fishing for all mid-continent species is said to be wonderful there, and duck hunting is popular. Memphis markets one-third of the nation's cotton and is considered by many the most typical Southern city. Two of its institutions have become famous: the Memphis Cotton Carnival, held every May, and Beale Street, home of the "Memphis Blues." Two stern-wheelers operate tourist excursions on the Mississippi. In Shiloh National Military Park, near the meeting point of Tennessee, Mississippi and Alabama, markers and a museum commemorate the bloody Battle of Shiloh in 1862.

North Central Map

POINTS OF INTEREST

National Park............................ ▫	National Memorial..................... ⊛	National Forest/Forest Reserve... ▫
National Monument.................... ▫	National Military Park................ ⊗	National Recreation Area............ ▫
National Historical Park............. ▲	National Battlefield Park............ ⊠	National Seashore/Lakeshore... ▫ ≈
National Historic Site................ △	National Battlefield Site............. ✕	State/Provincial Park................. ▪
National Memorial Park............. ●	National Battlefield.................... ✕	Other Points of Interest............ ▪

WHAT to SEE in the NORTH CENTRAL REGION

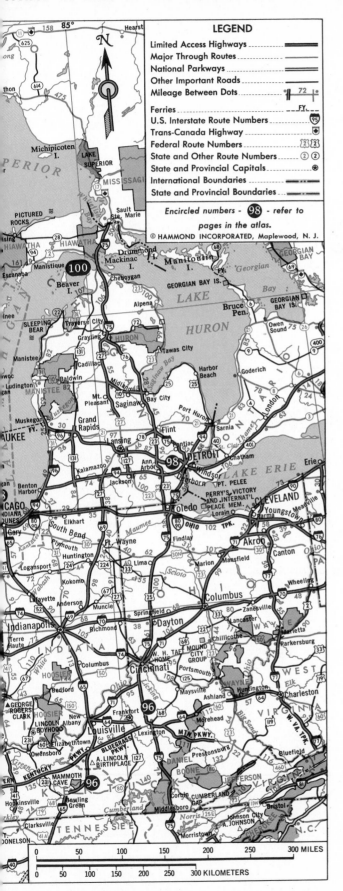

TWO-WEEKS TRIP AROUND LAKE MICHIGAN. For a general introduction see pages 100, 106 and 108, also sightseeing guide pages 114, 116 and 119. Suggested route: Chicago — Milwaukee, Wisconsin, famous for its breweries which offer guided tours, for its fine lakeshore, many parks, the Conservatory in Mitchell Park, its sunken gardens and its zoo — Madison, the state capital, with the campus of the University of Wisconsin, picturesquely located on Lake Mendota — Wisconsin Dells, weird rock formations carved by the Wisconsin River and a popular tourist center — Green Bay, a famous cheese-manufacturing area — north to Sault Ste. Marie where the spectacular locks of the Soo Canal handle the world's heaviest canal traffic — St. Ignace, center of the region's early French history, with Chippewa Totem Village, Castle Rock, Fort Algonquin Museum, French and Indian Museum — boat excursion to Mackinac Island, historic, lovely and unspoiled (no automobiles); ancient post of American Fur Company may be visited — over the 5-mile-long Mackinaw Bridge south to Traverse City, a popular watersport region and major cherry-growing district — Michigan City, Indiana, with International Friendship Gardens — Indiana Dunes National Lakeshore; it preserves a landscape of moving and fixed dunes, and a sandy-soil vegetation — Chicago.

SEVEN-DAY TRIP ALONG THE NORTH SHORE OF LAKE SUPERIOR. For a general introduction see page 102, also sightseeing guide pages 54 and 117. Suggested route: Duluth, Minnesota, with its busy iron ore docks; from the Skyline Parkway a view of the city and lake can be enjoyed — Grand Marais — to the north Superior National Forest with Quetico Provincial Park in Canada comprise a huge, untouched "primitive area" — Grand Portage, with the restored old fort of the Northwest Company, a fur trading center in the days of the Grand Portage Trail — by ferry to Isle Royale, a primitive island with prehistoric copper mines and a herd of moose kept in ecological balance by a pack of wolves — Thunder Bay, starting point for inland canoe trips; Mt. McKay with chair lift is a ski center — Nipigon offers Kama Lookout, 17 miles inland, with magnificent panorama of island-studded Nipigon Bay and of Orient Bay, 28 miles north on Lake Nipigon — return to Duluth by the same route.

EXPLORING SOUTH DAKOTA. For a general introduction see page 104, also sightseeing guide page 119. Suggested excursions: Rapid City with Sioux Museum, Dinosaur Park on Skyline drive, and Reptile Gardens where children ride on huge tortoises — south to Mount Rushmore National Memorial where the giant faces of four presidents are sculptured in the granite of Mount Rushmore — nearby Crazy Horse Memorial honors the great Sioux chieftain who defeated General Custer; the statue will be 565 feet tall when completed — south to Custer State Park where a large buffalo herd can be observed, free on the range — Wind Cave National Park, with caverns of delicate interlacing boxwork; above ground the park maintains herds of buffalo and pronghorn antelope — Hot Springs with Evans Plunge, the biggest natural indoor warm water swimming pool on earth — Badlands National Monument, a spooky world of bare formations of knobs, canyons and ridges; reproductions of antediluvian monsters which lived here in geological times, add to the weird atmosphere — north of Rapid City, Deadwood keeps up the memory of the Wild West; tourists may see the underground workings of the Broken Boot Mine and relax in the historic Number Ten Saloon — Lead, with the Homestake Mine, largest operating gold mine in the Western Hemisphere.

Mammoth Cave and Blue Grass Country

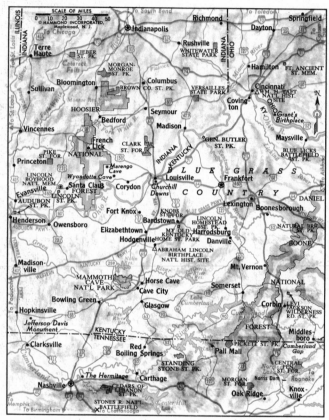

other chambers Jenny Lind, "the Swedish Nightingale," sang to her companions and Ole Bull, famous Norwegian violinist, gave a recital. Therefore Mammoth Cave is not only a natural phenomenon but also an historical monument. In that sense it holds its own very well, although later discoveries like the Carlsbad Caverns in New Mexico are infinitely larger. Another unique feature of the Kentucky cave is the abundance of water: there are, on the five levels of the cave, three rivers, eight waterfalls, one lake and one "dead sea." A boat ride on the Echo River on the lowest level, 360 feet below the surface, is an interesting experience. The ceiling is rather low, and every spoken word echoes back and forth many times before it dies away. The river, 20 to 60 feet wide and up to 25 feet deep, has strange inhabitants. Adapting themselves to their ever dark environment, its small fish no longer have eyes, and their skin is white. There are also transparent crawfish in the cave and crickets and beetles, all of which are blind. Among the cave's stone formations, the so-called Frozen Niagara is noteworthy.

HORSE HEAVEN. If there is an equine paradise to which good horses go after they have passed away, it must be patterned after Kentucky's Blue Grass Country, north of Mammoth Cave National Park and extending eastward, with Lexington at its center. There are well-watered, lush pastures, groves of shady trees, white fences, and both the bluegrass and the water seem to have a special stamina-giving quality. The barns are super-modern — sanitary, spacious, with cork floors and air conditioning. The product of this close collaboration of nature and man is the world's finest thoroughbred racehorse. Not only in the United States but also in Canada and Mexico a substantial majority of all open-stakes races are won by Kentucky-bred horses. No wonder, then, that horses are a tourist attraction; some of the great stud farms are open to the public. Even people without any interest in the turf will find it fascinating to watch the mares with their foals scampering over the velvety pastures, or to walk on broad, tree-lined avenues to spic and span stables, or to see the last resting places crowned with bronze statues of such winners as Equipoise and Fair Play. The grave of Man O'War draws considerably more visitors annually than the tomb of Henry Clay. Famous stud farms, producers of racetrack winners, are Calumet, Coldstream, Beaumont, Walnut Hall, and others, all of them circling Lexington. The great annual event of the Blue Grass Country takes place on the first or second Saturday in May, when America's number one race, the Kentucky Derby, is run at Louisville's Churchill Downs. It is unlikely that there is another spectacle like it, and

"PETER DIRT" AND ECHO RIVER. In the early days of our republic, America's two great scenic attractions were the Niagara Falls of New York and the Mammoth Cave of Kentucky. The latter seemed a bit out of reach, but by stagecoach and on horseback visitors from the Eastern Seaboard and even Europe found their way to the cavern and marveled at its stalagmites and stalactites. During the War of 1812 the cave became a major armament plant; "peter dirt," as they called saltpeter in those days, was gathered there. With the help of oxen and carts, pumps and vats, one of the essential raw materials for gunpowder production was prepared, all underground, and then shipped to Philadelphia by wagon train. After the war the factory became a showplace again, with a long roster of famous visitors. In the so-called amphitheater the great actor Edwin Booth recited Hamlet on a stage of stone; in

THE FAMOUS SIGHTS of KENTUCKY

Many of the world's finest thoroughbred racehorses are raised on the lush pastures of Kentucky's Blue Grass Country.

therefore it is worthwhile attending. Even if thousands of visitors see hardly anything of the race itself, they share in the excitement and the festive mood.

"MY OLD KENTUCKY HOME." That famous ballad was written in 1852 when Stephen Foster and his wife, on their way from Pittsburgh to New Orleans, passed through Bardstown and stopped at Federal Hill, the estate of his cousin John Rowan. The Rowans were wealthy planters, statesmen and diplomats, and life in the splendid but not showy house proved so pleasant that Foster immortalized it in his song. The building is now located in a state park about half way between Mammoth Cave and Lexington, a well-balanced two-story home of brick with large windows and beautifully carved mantels. Local tradition has it that Judge Rowan, Henry Clay and their cronies played many a game of poker there and emptied many a keg of bourbon. Quite near, in a southwesterly direction, is the Abraham Lincoln Birthplace National Historic Site, just out of Hodgenville. A flight of stairs lined by trees and hedges leads to a ridge where the memorial arises in Connecticut granite and Tennessee marble, with Lincoln's motto: "With Malice toward None, with Charity for All" inscribed above the Doric columns. Inside there stands the log cabin that is said to have been Abraham Lincoln's birthplace, the cracks between the logs chinked with clay and the clay-lined log chimney at one end. In December 1808 Thomas Lincoln purchased this farmland, settled there with his wife and daughter, and on February 12, 1809, Abraham was born. Near Harrodsburg the Pioneer Memorial State Park also preserves a Lincoln shrine; Abraham's parents were married there. The reconstructed Fort Harrod and the Pioneer Cemetery honor the first settlers of those "dark and bloody hills." Southeast of Mammoth Cave National Park, the Cumberland Falls are unique. Behind the sheet of falling water, 68 feet high and 125 feet wide, the rock wall recedes, and the visitor can walk through an arch which on one side consists of stone and on the other of water. This cataract shows a moonbow in its spray when the moon is full.

Detroit

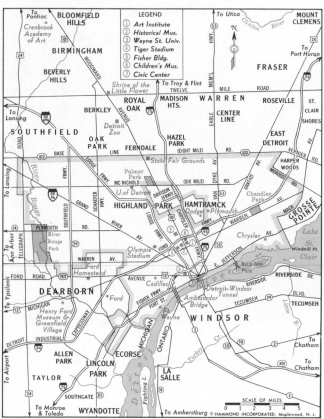

LEGEND
1. Art Institute
2. Historical Mus.
3. Wayne St. Univ.
4. Tiger Stadium
5. Fisher Bldg.
6. Children's Mus.
7. Civic Center

westward to the prairies, the Rockies and the Pacific Coast. By the end of the century the most colorful aspect of the young nation, the frontier, had vanished. Or so it seemed. But at about that time the country discovered that new frontiers were not merely geographical concepts but could be opened, even more promisingly, in other dimensions. The place which made this discovery first was Detroit.

CREATING A NEW WAY OF LIFE. Detroit had grown slowly after the expulsion of the British and had become a pleasant provincial city of shade trees and Victorian mansions. Then suddenly, at the turn of the century, beautiful Detroit turned into dynamic Detroit. For at that time a number of men like Ford, Durant, Buick, Olds and the Fisher Brothers decided that Detroit was the right location for manufacturing the new-fangled automobile. The new movement had all the earmarks of a frontier boom. The leaders became millionaires quickly. The Ford Company was organized in 1903, and in 1908 the stockholders realized a profit on their investment that amounted to ten thousand per cent. It seemed a veritable Comstock Lode. And, just like a western mining town, Detroit became a giant magnet to draw men from all the neighboring states; from the Old World more Poles and Ukrainians flocked there than lived in some of the large cities of Poland and the Ukraine, and tens of thousands of Germans, Italians and Hungarians, Greeks and Syrians also arrived. Almost all of them worked on the automobile, which was not invented in Detroit but was mass-produced there for the first time so that it could be sold cheaply all over the country; it remade the American way of life, and ultimately the life of the world.

CADILLAC AND THE HAIR BUYER OF DETROIT. Since one of America's luxury cars honors the name of the city's founder, Antoine de la Mothe Cadillac, we are tempted to imagine Detroit's father as an aristocrat of the purest blood. He was indeed that, but, in contrast to his swashbuckling grand-seigneur ways, his new town remained a poor and struggling frontier outpost for many years. When it became British, after the French and Indian War, Detroit acquired a horrible reputation. Governor Hudson incited the Indians against the patriots during the American Revolution and paid the redskins a handsome reward when they brought him a scalp but nothing when they brought him a prisoner. The American fighters called him "the Hair Buyer of Detroit." Even after the Revolution had succeeded it took years of negotiations and the Battle of Fallen Timbers to pry the British from Detroit. After that, the frontier moved

TECHNOLOGICAL SIGHTSEEING. The city grew so late and so suddenly that it did not acquire the quaintness of New Orleans which is 16 years younger, or the glamour of Chicago which is a hundred years younger. Consequently the most interesting sightseeing in Detroit is of the technological kind. It shows how our automobiles are made, both actually and historically. Just name the make of car you are interested in — Ford or Dodge, Chrysler or Cadillac — and you are welcome to inspect the plant. Guided tours for visitors are arranged every weekday at frequent intervals. Best known is the tour of the Ford River Rouge plant in Dearborn, which starts at a visitor's center and offers a glance into a sequence of superbly planned manufacturing operations, including the assembly line. Also in Dearborn are the Henry Ford Museum and Greenfield Village, both educational enterprises of the Ford Company. The museum presents the history of agricultural implements, of

98

THE WORLD'S AUTOMOTIVE CAPITAL

manufacturing and transportation, from wooden plows and handlooms to the latest inventions; of particular interest, of course, is the development of the automobile as illustrated in a collection of actual models. Greenfield Village shows a good many of the places where this progress was achieved, like Thomas Edison's Laboratory of Menlo Park, N. J., where the electric lamp was invented; the cabin of George Washington Carver, the great Negro scientist; the office of Luther Burbank, the genius in plant breeding, and the schoolhouse of McGuffey, who wrote the first truly American school books. But there is also a copy of a sixteenth-century cottage from the Cotswold Hills in England, Sir John Bennet's jewelry shop in London, a Cape Cod windmill and many other structures, either in restored originals or in replicas. Among the non-technical sights of Detroit is the Arts Center on Woodward Avenue, with the Institute of Arts (famous for its primitives) on one side of the street and the Public Library on the other. Belle Isle Park, just offshore in the Detroit River, is the city's recreation center, with 20 miles of roads, a swimming beach, a symphony shell for summer concerts and folk dances by Detroit's ethnic groups, an aquarium, a children's zoo and other attractions. Twenty miles north of Detroit, Cranbrook is an artistic oasis, an endowed campus of schools and institutes whose buildings were largely designed by Eliel Saarinen; his Academy of Art has won wide recognition. Also of visitor interest is the Cranbrook Institute of Science which contains a planetarium, observatory and atomarium.

OLD COON'S WOLF STEAKS. In addition to remaking the ways of the world, Detroit claims the achievement of nicknaming the state of Michigan. In Dearborn, opposite the entrance to the Ford estate, a popular old inn was located which belonged to Conrad Ten Eyck, commonly called Old Coon. His steaks were famous, and he himself kidded his guests by forever praising his "wolf steaks." Once a pretty young girl approached the landlord after dinner, looked straight into his eyes and inquired, "Have I really eaten wolf steak?" Seriously he replied, "Of course, you have." "Well," she said "then I am a wolverine now." All the guests laughed, and the word was passed on along the highways and byways; ever since then Michigan has been the Wolverine State.

Greenfield Village — the Wright Brothers' Shop where the first airplane was built.

The Cranbrook Foundation maintains this striking Academy of Art.

99

Mackinac Island and Sault Ste. Marie

Grand Hotel, once presided over by Cornelius Vanderbilt, is one of America's famous hostelries. From its white-columned porch — "the longest hotel porch in the world" — an enchanting vista encompasses the bright town, the busy harbor and the wide waters of the inland sea. Since the island is free of polluted waters, swamps, mosquitoes and hay fever producing pollens, it is an ideal resort. Add to that a wonderful climate, fragrant woods, flowering gardens, white beaches, superb views which in places have a Mediterranean character and such attractions as the Old Fort, Arch Rock and Chimney Rock, Devil's Kitchen and Scott's cave.

A DAREDEVIL PRANK AND A FUR EMPIRE. The island was discovered by Jean Nicolet in his search for China and passed from French to British to American hands. In the War of 1812 the British reconquered it, and the two American warships *Tigress* and *Scorpion* were charged with blockading the island and forcing its surrender by cutting off the food supply. But one dark and blustery night 70 British soldiers rowed stealthily to the *Scorpion,* boarded the ship with scaling ladders in a surprise attack and overpowered the crew. Then they sailed around the island, the American flag still flying, and approached the *Tigress* which was unaware of what had happened. A few cannon shots demolished the second American warship, and the blockade was ended. When, after the conclusion of the war, Mackinac Island was returned to the United States, John Jacob Astor set up shop there with his 2,000 voyageurs and 400 clerks. The island was a convenient bottleneck through which most of the northwestern fur trade had to pass. This was Mackinac's heyday when wigwams and tepees lined the beach three rows deep, housing 3,000 Indians; when millions of pelts were dried, beaten, sorted, counted and repacked there, and the nights resounded with drunken revelry. The buildings of the fur trading post can still be inspected. By the middle of the century the fur trade collapsed, and after the Civil War the summer guests and tourists moved in.

THE SOO — REMOTE BUT BUSY. From the fishing town of St. Ignace whose Indian Village is patterned after the Indian encampment found there by the French explorers in the seventeenth century, you proceed northward to Sault Ste. Marie. This colorful city was once described by Henry Clay as the "remotest in the country, if not on the moon." Yet it is the third oldest surviving community in the United States; Jesuit priests founded a mission there in 1668. It is a great hunting and fishing town, but to the summer visitor the federal St. Marys Locks, also called the Soo Locks, are the most fas-

BEAVER PELTS AND GRAND HOTEL. The bridge which connects the lower and the upper peninsulas of Michigan carries a heavy automobile traffic, but the island to the east of the bridge is strictly car-less. It can be reached only by boat, either from Mackinaw City or from St. Ignace. Rising from the blue waters of Lake Huron, with its gently curved green hills, it looks like a giant turtle; that's what the Indian name Michilimackinac, abbreviated to Mackinac, means. Upon arrival at the harbor which resembles the small British towns in Bermuda, you will find a line of horse drawn carriages waiting to take visitors on an all-island excursion. Or you may board the Victorian hotel bus whose coachman wears a splendid red jacket and whose horses balance their red plumes above arched necks. Of course, such colorful trappings smack of the circus and never fail to evoke pleasant smiles on the riders' faces.

THE GREAT LAKES PAGEANT

MICHIGAN TOURIST COUNCIL (3)

Above: Mackinac Island, once the scene of battles, is now a pleasant resort which maintains a certain old-time elegance.

Above right: The Soo Locks, busiest in the world, offer a close-up view of the big ore and grain ships.

Right: Near the Upper Tahquamenon Falls, Longfellow's Hiawatha built his birchbark canoe.

cinating attraction. The difference in level between Lake Superior and Lake Huron is 22 feet. The connecting rapids, the Sault Ste. Marie proper, can be seen beside the locks, although the locks and the power plant have greatly diminished the volume of the falls. The spectacle here is interesting for more than one reason: it offers a close-up view of the long ore ships that dot the horizon of the Great Lakes as symbols of the steel age; the ship is steered into the locks on the Superior side, the gates close, the water level and the ship sink slowly to the Huron level, the opposite gates open, and the ship glides out quietly. Even more interesting is the ease and efficiency with which the operation is performed; no tolls are levied, no inspectors board the boat, no forms are filled; the purser receives the ship's mail, and the crew members exchange greetings with visiting friends ashore. All over the locks tourists are swarming and watching, at a spot which in a communist country certainly would be labeled strategic and "verboten" to the public. It's a very American sight. The procession of ships is continuous and in

terms of freight carried, the Soo Locks are the most important in the world.

CASCADES IN THE NORTHWOODS. To the west of Sault Ste. Marie an excursion to the Tahquamenon Falls will prove a typical Northwoods experience. The upper falls can be visited by taking a side road from Highway 28 to Soo Junction. There a narrow gauge railway proceeds for five miles to the Tahquamenon River from where an excursion boat rides on to the upper falls past fragrant cedar groves and between 100-foot-high cliffs along the bank where Longfellow's Hiawatha built his birchbark canoes. At the boat landing the low thunder of the falls can be heard, and a three-quarters of a mile trail leads both to the brink of the cascades and the bottom of the gorge. The lower falls may be reached by taking Highway 123 to the mouth of the Tahquamenon River. From there a boat carries visitors over the 18-mile course up the river to the beautiful lower cascades which drop 43 feet in three terraces.

101

Isle Royale and Superior National Forest

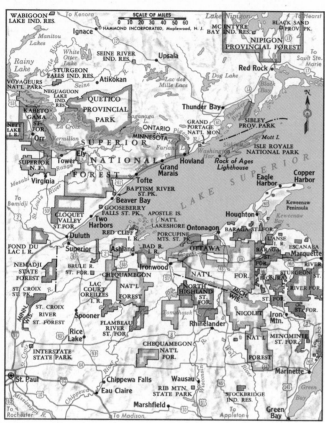

Although archaeologists were intrigued, the miners who flocked there were disappointed. The island deposits could not compete with richer mines on the mainland. Instead of becoming an industrial center Isle Royale has been turned into a National Park, which would suit well the public-spirited Mr. Franklin.

THE BALANCE BETWEEN MOOSE AND WOLVES. Isle Royale can be reached from Thunder Bay, Canada. On the American side it may be reached from Houghton or Copper Harbor, Michigan, or from Grand Portage, Minnesota, the shortest trip. Cars have to be left at the mainland ports, since nothing with wheels is allowed on the island. All excursions are made by hiking or canoeing, or a combination of the two. Limited accommodations are available. Of all our national parks this is one of the wildest. Its beauty is found in its groves of white birches and dark balsams, its wildflowers and mosses, its wooded hills and deep fjords, picturesque bays and excellent harbors, its myriads of small islands and reefs that surround the big "fortress," and its many lakes teeming with fish. In Siskiwit Lake Ryan Island is an island within an island. Among the fauna of Isle Royale the moose is the most spectacular inhabitant. During the winter of 1912 a small herd crossed over the 14 miles of ice from Canada and multiplied until they are now several hundred strong. An investigation by environmental scientists disclosed the interesting fact that the ecological balance is maintained by a pack of wolves which kills the surplus moose but, by a kind of instinctive family planning, does not increase its own number beyond the available food supply.

A SCENIC HIGHWAY BY AN INLAND SEA. The road that crosses the map diagonally along the north shore of Lake Superior, Route 61, is to Midwesterners what the Maine coastal highway is to New Englanders. People unfamiliar with the territory imagine the coast to be low and flat; that, however, is not the case. Thunder Bay, the modern Canadian port, is built at an altitude of over 600 feet, and the white water of the Pigeon River rushes between canyon walls which rise much higher. The river was named for the thousands of passenger pigeons that used to visit this valley before they were exterminated. Five miles to the south, the Grand Portage Trail was traveled for centuries by Indians and 200 years ago by voyageurs and fur traders seeking a way around the falls and rapids. At Grand Marais don't miss the Forest Lookout Tower on a rose-colored rock at a point shaped like an arrow near the fine harbor. Along the highway there are several attractive parks such as Gooseberry Falls State Park. The culinary specialty of the region is smoked fish.

BENJAMIN FRANKLIN'S ISLAND. Like a giant battleship at anchor, the rock Isle Royale stands firmly in Lake Superior, 45 miles long and up to 9 miles broad. It was Benjamin Franklin's obstinate insistence when negotiating the Treaty of Paris that gave Isle Royale to the United States even though its location is closer to Canada. His reasons were quite personal. He had carried out extensive experiments with electricity, a new power that would play an important part in the life of his country, and he knew that copper was a good electrical conductor. Franklin had heard of great copper treasures on Isle Royale. He had his way, and he was right about the future of electricity. The copper, however, turned out to be a matter of pre-history rather than actual wealth. Hundreds of primitive pits had been worked by ancient Indians, who had separated the rock and the metal by alternately applying fire and water.

A CORNER of VIRGIN AMERICA

THE UNTOUCHED WILDERNESS. To the west of the North Shore Drive, Superior National Forest and adjacent Quetico Provincial Park of Canada form one of America's great wilderness areas. It is a region of picturesque forests (virgin toward the north), 5,000 lakes ranging from little ponds to a size of 70 square miles, of crystal-clear cold streams and tumbling rapids, of soft grass and countless wildflowers, and the clean smell of pines. Within the National Forest there is a large primitive area without roads, electric wires, telephone or telegraph. Game in the virgin timber remains undisturbed since planes are not allowed to fly over this area. In a way this country is more untouched now than it was 200 years ago when the fur traders blazed the portages from lake to lake, and the Hudson's Bay Company and the Northwest Company struggled ruthlessly for supremacy. Today it is a peaceful haven for fishermen, and the only way to travel it is by canoe. Canoe trips may start from Tofte or Grand Marais on the North Shore Drive, or from the interesting frontier town of Ely in the western part of the forest. Such trips have to be carefully prepared in advance. More detailed information may be secured from the Forest Supervisor, Superior National Forest, or the Minnesota Arrowhead Association, both in Duluth. The range of possibilities is wide. You may choose a one-day trip from Ely with 13 miles of paddling and 4 miles of portages, or you may take a 17-day trip with 235 miles of paddling and 9 miles of portaging. The latter starts at McFarland Lake in the Gunflint area, which can be reached from Grand Marais, and follows the International Boundary Route. Lake scenery and portages around rapids and waterfalls are picturesque, the currents are varied and the fishing is fine. While crossing Lac La Croix you will view the painted rocks where ancient Sioux or Algonquin artists painted a number of pictures in reddish ocher, representing such varied objects as hands and bear paws, a moose and a goat. Further inland the new Voyageurs National Park embraces an important segment of the canoe routes traveled by early fur traders.

Right: The new Voyageurs National Park is an archipelago of wooded islands in cool, sparkling waters.

Below right: Sunset at Isle Royale. At this national park boats are the only means of transportation.

Below: Autumn beauty along a trail on Isle Royale's Mt. Ojibway

Badlands and Black Hills

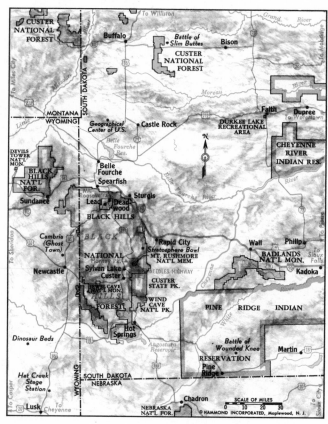

The Badlands are an arid waste, but at dawn and at twilight the bright sunlight and the deep shadows create a fascinating panorama.

DAKOTA CAMELS AND MIDGET HORSES. No greater contrast could be imagined than that between the Badlands and the Black Hills in the southwestern part of South Dakota. The hills are lush with woods and streams while the Badlands, to the east, are an arid waste of 640,000 acres. They are a desolate desert, but a fascinating and beautiful one that should be seen in either the early morning or toward evening when the shadows of its thousands of pinnacles are black, the deep canyons dark and the yellow, reddish and grayish towers sparkle in the sunlight. The landscape has an eerie atmosphere, as if it were part of another world. It does not surprise the traveler who, approaching Rapid City after having passed the wasteland, suddenly distinguishes, on a ridge against the setting sun, the dark outlines of two antediluvian monsters. They are life-size reproductions of the brontosaurus which roamed these lands when they were swamps in geological times. More bizarre animals lived in these parts, and the beds of vanished rivers preserve fossils and skeletons in abundance. The Museum of Geology at the South Dakota School of Mines and Technology has a famous and excellent collection. Among the former inhabitants of the region are midgets like a 2-foot camel, a 9-inch deer and a 20-inch, 3-toed horse. Among the giants there are a clidastes, a 29-foot marine lizard, and a titanothere, half elephant and half rhinoceros. The museum also shows the great subterranean wealth of the area whose rocks contain about 200 different minerals.

FOUR PRESIDENTS ON A GRANITE LEDGE. The Black Hills are a veritable oasis in the hot plains, a cool retreat with shady trees, rushing waters and the clear air of mountains six to seven thousand feet tall. A prime attraction is the Mount Rushmore National Memorial where the great stone faces of Washington, Jefferson, Lincoln and Theodore Roosevelt, carved into the solid granite of a towering pinnacle, look down into the valley. This monumental sculpture by Gutzon Borglum is carried out on a scale of men 465 feet tall. Mountain goats cavort on the rim of Roosevelt's spectacles, and every so often hardy bushes have to be removed from Washington's chin. Modern professional artists usually condemn the monument as "corny," but thousands of

BAD but FASCINATING, not BLACK but GREEN

The Badlands have an eerie beauty all their own, a world of sharp ridges, steep-walled canyons, gullies, pyramids and knobs.

The four faces are sculptured at a scale of men 465 feet tall.

others have found it an inspiring, worthwhile memorial to four great Americans, a work as colossal as the land they served so well and, we hope, as lasting as that land. Geologists believe that the carving will remain intact for a hundred thousand years. The technique is not new, for 3,000 years ago Asiatic sculptors chiseled huge figures into mountainsides in the Near East. For our day such carving is new. An even bigger project is under way near Sylvan Lake, where the sculptor Korczak Ziolkowski is carving a monument of Crazy Horse, the great Sioux chieftain. The equestrian statue will be 563 feet tall when completed. Visitors may see the model and watch the sculptor blasting and chiseling.

THE WHISTLING EARTH. In the southern part of the Black Hills, Wind Cave National Park presents a natural phenomenon different from the usual stalagmite-stalactite cavern. More than 10 miles of passages are covered with fragile, beautiful boxwork where the calcite in the rock remained in delicate, interlacing shapes while the limestone dissolved. This cave was discovered by a deer-hunting pioneer named Bingham, who heard a whistling sound coming from the earth and found a hole in the rock from which a jet of wind was blowing. This puzzling adventure led to the exploration and naming of the cave. The wind current is caused by barometric pressure and the fact that the 10-inch hole is the only natural opening of the cave. The present entrance is artificial. Above ground the park has 27,000 acres of wildlife preserve with a herd of 400 bison.

GOLD IN THE HILLS AND CALAMITY JANE. The cities of the Black Hills are not large, but they are interesting. Lead (pronounced Leed) is a hilltop town that

once had a gold rush and still has the gold. It is the site of the Homestake Mine, America's largest gold mine, in whose underground passages a hundred miles of railroad tracks are in operation. Visitors may inspect the surface installations and see the gray, unimpressive ore, two and a half tons of which produce one ounce of gold. Nearby Deadwood, ambling along a valley road, is one of the great centers of American folk history. Here some saloons of gold-rush days have survived. The old style bar of '76 where buffalo horns and elk heads adorn the walls remains. It was in the No. 10 Saloon that Wild Bill Hickok was shot by Jack McCall. The story of Deadwood's flamboyant past can best be read at Mount Moriah Cemetery which perches precariously high above the town. On this unique hilltop there lie buried some of the most colorful figures of the West. Wild Bill Hickok's grave is fenced in and decorated with a small red sandstone statue whose head, unfortunately, has been chipped off. Potato Creek Johnny lies there, and Preacher Smith who was the victim of a Sioux killer. Next to Wild Bill is the resting place of America's most famous frontier woman, Martha Jane (Canary) Burke, called Calamity Jane. She was a respected member of her society, a mule driver with a marvelous skill in handling the bull whip — she could actually take off a person's ear — a dead shot, and an expert in the roughest language of the Old West. Remembering her fondly, the people of Deadwood buried her in a white dress with a gun in each hand. Presumably she still lies in her grave in that unorthodox fashion. At the southern end of the Black Hills, in the city of Hot Springs, the visitor may view the big, spring-fed indoor pool and the bathtub which prehistoric Indians had carved into the rock to alleviate their aches.

Madison and the Wisconsin Dells

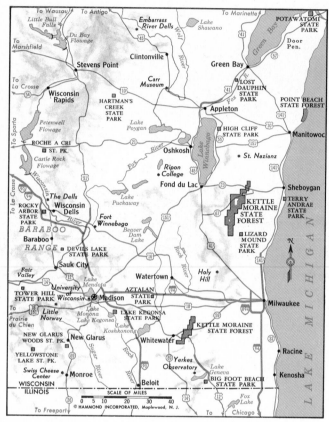

Mendota and Wingra. The seasons are very pronounced. During the summer the gardens sparkle with flowers, and the wooded bluffs and parks, the beaches and boathouses are alive with young people. Mendota's blue waters are dotted with white sails and red canoes. In the fall when the leaves turn scarlet and yellow and pumpkins and apple cider dominate the countryside, the football stadium of the university is the scene of excitement and holiday spirit. During the winter graceful iceboats and noisy snowmobiles swoop over the frozen lakes, tobogganners enjoy the campus slide, and students take off from the ski jump, training for championships. The combination of legislative political activity and scholarly academic work with the facilities of an all-year pleasure resort gives Madison a special place among the cities of America. Ironically, the early settlers of Wisconsin considered the site "beautiful but uninhabitable." It took a land speculator to sell this isthmus wilderness to the legislators. Just west of Madison at Mt. Horeb, "Little Norway" is a memorial for Wisconsin's Norwegian immigrants, and the Swiss Museum Village at New Glarus honors early settlers from Switzerland.

MOUNDS AND ARROWHEADS. From Madison northward, highway U.S. 12 is an excursion route. Sauk City, once America's "Freethinkers Haven," may look like other midwestern towns, but it is an historic spot. On Sauk Prairie the great town of the Saukie Indians was located, one of the most remarkable achievements of native Indian culture. The settlement consisted of about 90 houses, each sheltering several families. Jonathan Carver, who traveled there in the eighteenth century, wrote of these homes that they were "built of hewn plank neatly joined, and covered with bark so compactly as to keep out the most penetrating rains. Before the doors are placed comfortable sheds in which the inhabitants sit and smoke their pipes. . . . They raise great quantities of Indian corn, beans, melons, etc., so that this place is esteemed the best market for traders . . . within 800 miles." In 1832 the Indians fought their last real battle with the whites and were, of course, defeated. One hill that comes to a sharp point is still called Black Hawk Lookout, and country boys find arrowheads in the pastures. Indian mounds are also encountered in this region, particularly to the north of Devils Lake State Park. It is a spectacular spot. The clear, cool oval of the lake has a horseshoe setting of cliffs that tower four to five hundred feet above its surface. There are tumbled piles of rocks, potholes, glacial scratches and petrified sand waves, and the reddish and purple color of the stone is set off by the deep green of the pines. The lake is a frequent goal on field trips of geology students.

INTER-LAKE ISTHMUS. Which American city is most pleasant to live in? Considering different human tastes and individual values, the question cannot be answered statistically, but the city that comes close to winning a prize with many is Madison, Wisconsin. Visitors will easily discover the reasons. On approaching the city the first sight will be the conventional but stately state capitol which stands in the heart of the community on a hill. Its public roof walk offers a fine view of Madison. From the capitol the open half mile of State Street leads to another hill where the university stands. These two landmarks, the capitol and the university, are the two poles that create a lively intellectual and cultural life, for their close and continuous collaboration has won national acclaim. The physical setting is equally attractive; the modern tree-lined city is surrounded by three beautiful lakes with the musical names of Monona,

A SAMPLING of the BADGER STATE

Above: The Wisconsin Dells, an unusual combination of rocks, woods and water, are a popular excursion area.

Left: The Standing Rock is but one of the Dells' many fantastic and seemingly sculptured rock formations.

SCROLLS AND FLUTED COLUMNS. You are now approaching the stretch of the Wisconsin River where, according to a legend of the Winnebago Indians, a giant serpent smashed its way southward, battering and crushing the rocks on both sides and leaving them torn and broken in fantastic shapes. Driving toward the "scene of the serpent," today called the Wisconsin Dells, you will notice road signs that introduce the coming attraction as something like the eighth wonder of the world. That it is not, but it will be worth your while to visit the Dells, to look around from the bridge that divides the Upper from the Lower Dells and to take boat excursions to each of these areas. You will see a river channel carved deeply into solid sandstone, yellow ledges crowned with tufts of green bushes and narrow flumes with steep, rocky walls from whose crevices flowers, ferns and vines protrude decoratively. There are beautiful rock islands, fantastic columns and seemingly sculptured rock formations with names typical of this type of scenery — Fat Man's Misery, Sugar Bowl,

Cave of the Dark Waters, Arrow Head. The lakes are dotted with other sightseeing boats, a varied collection of gaily painted craft often with an Indian in full regalia as guide. The town of Wisconsin Dells, called Kilbourn before 1931, is teeming with tourists during the summer months.

"A GATHERING OF WATERS." This is the meaning of the word Wisconsin, and it expresses the pleasant fact that the modern water sport enthusiast can find lakes in many parts of the state. In addition to the 500 miles of Lake Michigan shore, more than 3,500 lakes have been counted in Wisconsin, the largest being Lake Winnebago with a surface of 215 square miles, and the most fashionable spring-fed Lake Geneva. The latter is surrounded by large estates on wooded hills and is a fishing ground for bass, pike and cisco. The Yerkes Observatory of the University of Chicago is located at Williams Bay on the lake's northern shore.

107

Chicago

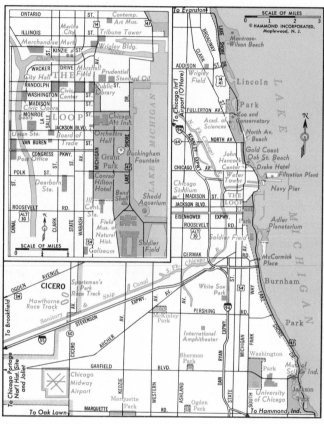

written about Chicago, and that such literary greats as Dreiser, Hemingway, Anderson and Cather expressed their fascination, and that Sandburg heard the young city "laughing the stormy, husky, brawling laughter of youth," and described it as "proud to be hog butcher, tool maker, stacker of wheat, player with railroads and freight handler of the nation."

A BIRD'S-EYE VIEW. Metropolitan cities are always a little overwhelming to the casual tourist, but it is easy enough to get acquainted with Chicago. The 25-mile-long lakefront is the town's splendid reception hall, a multiple row of skyscrapers in a setting of green parks, white beaches and ruffled blue waters. In the lakefront's center the Loop is the principal business district. South of it, the so-called South Side has miles of cool, sandy beaches, tree-lined residential sections, lovely parks, outstanding museums and baseball's White Sox Park. It also has the unpleasant seamy side of ghetto slums, the abandoned stockyards and sooty steel mills. North of the Loop across the Chicago River, the North Side boasts of Chicago's Oak Street Beach, the legendary Gold Coast, a group of great hotels, Lincoln Park, Wrigley Field and the Chicago Cubs. Everything that does not belong to the Loop, the South Side and the North Side is called the West Side, a jungle of factories and an agglomeration of foreign sections.

THE MAGNIFICENT MILE. Michigan Avenue, the high-rise boulevard by the lake, is one of the world's famous streets and is Chicago's best-known. It has been compared to New York's Fifth Avenue because of its cosmopolitan glamour, or to Paris' Champs Elysées because of its monumental layout, or to the waterfront of Rio de Janeiro because of its beach-park-skyline combination. Yet its setting — the quiet, park-fringed lake on one side and the noisy Loop with its steel ribbons of elevated tracks on the other — is truly Chicago. Some of the city's newer buildings are considered architectural masterpieces. These include the Civic Center with a five-story-high metal sculpture by Pablo Picasso, the 100-story-tall Hancock Center and the Marina City Towers whose cylindrical wings rise beside the Chicago River. A landmark is the old "Gothic" Water Tower which survived the great fire of 1871 and the attacks of architects who called it an eyesore. The Water Tower, by the way, is the only Chicago building supposedly plagued by ghosts, but they are of the noisy, good-natured kind called poltergeists. Finally there is the Tribune Tower, home of the outspoken *Chicago Tribune* which modestly calls itself "The World's Greatest Newspaper." Farther south beyond the Public Library, the Chicago Art Institute resembles an Italian Renaissance palace. It contains one of the nation's greatest art

THE CENTER. Chicago's statistics are astonishing. In four generations it assembled more than three million inhabitants, grew into the nation's biggest grain and livestock market, became the country's railroad center with more freight trains than can be counted and developed into the world's leading convention site. It reversed the Chicago River so that its current would no longer flow into Lake Michigan but, eventually, into the Gulf of Mexico. It invented the skyscraper and built scores of them. These had to be placed on huge "floating" platforms of concrete because the soil was "unsuitable" for high-rise construction. Are these reasons for tourists to visit Chicago? They are, especially since there is an unmatched spirit of vitality behind the material phenomena. How else could it happen that 400 novels and innumerable non-fiction articles have been collections, predominantly classical and cautiously modern. Across the street there is the home of the Chicago Symphony Orchestra. Finally Michigan Avenue runs near the campus of the University of Chicago, "the Harvard of the Midwest." Opposite the southern stretch of the avenue, Grant Park is the sightseer's happy hunting ground; Buckingham Fountain and the band shell will attract him on concert nights; Soldier Field has been the scene of great sports events; the Field Museum of Natural History, the Shedd Aquarium and the Adler Planetarium are leading scientific institutions.

THE CENTER'S CENTER: THE LOOP. The name Loop dates back to the 1890's when it was the section bounded by the cable cars. Today it is the part of the city which is circled by the elevated tracks, or simply Downtown Chicago. Crowds are large, bright and busy in this "nerve center of the prairie country." There is a challenge in the air for sightseers too. If you want to watch one of the world's busiest corners, you will find it at the crossing of the two principal thoroughfares of the Loop, State and Madison streets. Marshall Field is one of the nation's best-known department stores and a Chicago landmark. If you are interested in economics, you may walk through La Salle Street, Chicago's Wall Street, to the Board of Trade. Here the grain of the nation is bought and sold at auction. Watching the trading at the grain pit on a day of oscillating prices is a unique experience. Excited men crowd together, shouting and waving their arms and poking their fingers. Split-second decisions often expressed by gestures alone accomplish the buying and selling. Beyond the north-

western corner of the Loop in the near North Side, the Merchandise Mart is one of the world's largest commercial buildings, a monolith by the riverbank. It claims to be big enough to hold the whole population of Chicago. The Standard Oil building when completed will be the third tallest in the world at 1,136 feet. On Wacker Drive, by the Chicago River, is rising the Sears, Roebuck & Co. headquarters building, to be the world's tallest at 1,450 feet on completion.

An unconventional accent on busy downtown Chicago — the Picasso sculpture.

The lakefront is Chicago's splendid reception hall — a row of high rise buildings in a setting of green parks, white beaches and blue waters.

Springfield and Hannibal

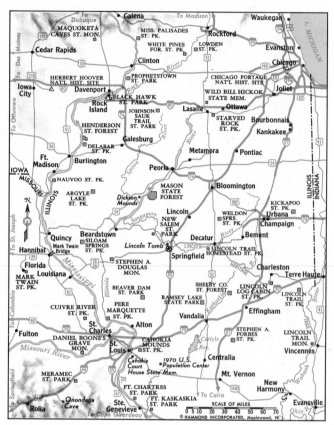

Lincoln Memorial in New Salem, where young Lincoln tried storekeeping and worked as surveyor and postmaster.

A 12-ROOM HOUSE OF OAK AND WALNUT, WORTH $2,800. In April 1837, Lincoln arrived in Springfield on the back of a borrowed horse with all his earthly possessions in two saddlebags. After 28 years of backwoods life the bustling state capital bewildered him, and progress in his new environment was slow. Even when he married Mary Todd in 1842 he was still so poor that the newlyweds lived at the Globe Tavern for four dollars a week. In 1844, however, his practice and income increased. For $1,500 he purchased a story-and-a-half frame house at 8th and Jackson streets. Twelve years later while Lincoln was traveling on the circuit, his wife had a second story of the same solid oak and walnut construction added at a cost of $1,300. For a total expenditure of $2,800 the Lincolns had a fine, sturdy house of 12 rooms, and thousands of visitors inspect this same structure today. It has survived well

and would be a desirable residence even now. The interior arrangements are much as they were during the nearly 17 years while the Lincoln family lived there, when the master of the house sat by the fireplace, reading, or rested on the couch made extra long for his size, and when the Republican Notification Committee was received in the large double parlor.

MARBLE SHAFT ABOVE THE TREES. Four years and two months after the great native son had gone to the White House he returned, and tens of thousands sadly watched the arrival of the funeral train, while 75,000 mourners passed by his bier at the Old State House. On his tomb a white marble shaft was erected, and it rises brightly above the green, wooded hills of Illinois. The city of Springfield considers itself Abraham Lincoln's hometown. Street signs lead the visitor to the various Lincoln memorials, and an impressive collection of Lincolniana has been assembled in the Illinois Centennial Building.

THE VILLAGE THAT VANISHED, LUCKILY. Twenty miles northwest of Springfield, the Lincoln village of New Salem has been reconstructed in a state park. On a ridge by the Sangamon River there stand again the log cabins with their primitive pioneer furniture, the country stores with their wares and the little mills and factories with their simple machinery. The cooper's shop is original while the others are reconstructions. The work has been done with scientific accuracy, and the village gives an excellent picture of the country's

THE MEMORIES of LINCOLN and the HAUNTS of YOUNG MARK TWAIN

Young Lincoln at New Salem: Rail-splitter and law student.

Young Mark Twain enthusiasts recreate the Tom Sawyer-Becky Thatcher story at Hannibal on the Missouri.

way of life when young Lincoln tried storekeeping here, worked as surveyor and postmaster, was elected to the Illinois state legislature, studied law, and had his sad romance with Ann Rutledge, the innkeeper's daughter. After Lincoln had left Salem the town went into a rapid decline, becoming a ghost town and vanishing eventually in the returning growth of the wilderness. Had it prospered, streets, squares and stone buildings would now obliterate the original site. However, it was possible to find the old foundations on the abandoned ridge, and the village of young Lincoln could be reconstructed authentically.

TOM SAWYER'S FENCE. A little over a hundred miles west of Springfield across the Mississippi River, there is Hannibal, Missouri, Mark Twain's boyhood town. He gave a good-natured, amusing picture of it: "... the streets empty — one or two clerks sitting in front of the Water Street stores — chins on breasts, hats slouched over their faces, asleep ... a sow and litter of pigs loafing along the sidewalk ... a pile of 'skids' on the slope of the stone-paved wharf, and the fragrant town drunkard asleep in the shadow of them. ..." Then suddenly "... a Negro drayman, famous for his quick eye and prodigious voice, lifts up the cry 'S-t-e-a-m-b-o-a-t a-comin!' and the scene changes. The town drunkard stirs, the clerks wake up, a furious clatter of drays follows ... and all in a twinkling the dead town is alive and moving. Drays, carts, men, boys, all go hurrying ... to a common center, the wharf. Assembled there, the people fasten their eyes upon the

coming boat as upon a wonder they are seeing for the first time. And the boat *is* rather a handsome sight, too. She is long and sharp and trim ..." Since then Hannibal has changed, of course, but the neat little house that served Sam Clemens as headquarters for his explorations of the Mississippi country is still there, with the whitewashed Tom Sawyer fence on one side and a museum of Mark Twain memorabilia on the other. The furnishings of the house are not those of the Clemens family, but they are early nineteenth-century pieces from Hannibal and create a realistic atmosphere. Across the street, on the second floor of the Becky Thatcher House, the rooms of the Hawkins family, the prototype of Mark Twain's Thatchers, are restored with all their crystal and mahogany magnificence. Even Becky's blue silk dress is still there, and her soft, long, white lisle stockings lie on the chair. It is easy to see here why Becky Thatcher-Laura Hawkins with her out-of-this-world elegance charmed the barefoot boy across the street. At the foot of Cardiff (now Holiday) Hill, where in "Tom Sawyer" the Widow Douglass kept a lamp in the window at night as a miniature lighthouse for the river steamers, there is now a life-size double statue of Tom Sawyer and Huckleberry Finn. Presumably that is the only monument in the Americas in which two fictional characters are honored. The Mark Twain Bridge crosses the river, and the paddle-wheelers that dock at Hannibal are now sightseeing boats. But the banks of the Mississippi with their little bays and coves are as green and lonely as they used to be, and small lads still splash in the river on hot summer days.

111

St. Louis

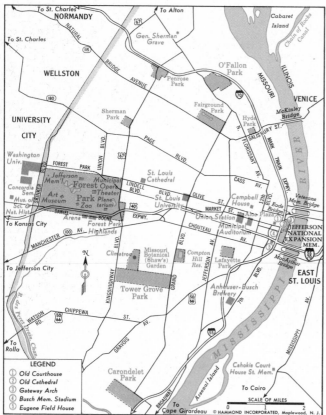

LEGEND
① Old Courthouse
② Old Cathedral
③ Gateway Arch
④ Busch Mem. Stadium
⑤ Eugene Field House

SCALE OF MILES
© HAMMOND INCORPORATED, Maplewood, N. J.

A METROPOLIS FOUNDED BY A 13-YEAR-OLD BOY. St. Louis is not a replica of Chicago or of any other midwestern city. It is different and therefore worth seeing and visiting. America's typical inland cities are self-boosters, but not St. Louis. It does not care whether it takes 6th or 7th place. For in contrast to most of its midwestern rivals St. Louis has a fascinating and important history of its own and its own long traditions, even in such esoteric fields as symphonic music and philosophy. Therefore St. Louis has the mental security and social poise of a grande dame. Calm self-assurance is in the air. The very founding of the city avoided the commonplace. No heavily armed captain-generals as in the South, or farmer-pioneers as in the North, settled it. Well-to-do cosmopolitan businessmen took the step. The great mercantile house of Maxent, Laclede & Co. of New Orleans acquired the fur trade monopoly in the

Missouri Valley and sent a junior partner north into the wilderness. During this expedition on February 14, 1764, his stepson, in temporary command, had the forest cleared at a certain spot south of the mouth of the Missouri and supervised the erection of a trading post which grew into the present metropolis of St. Louis. The boy's name was Auguste Chouteau, and he was only 13 years old.

WESTERN SQUAW, SOUTHERN BELLE, GERMAN FRAU. During the decades that followed, St. Louis became the brain and nerve center for conquering and civilizing the West. Financed and planned by its fur merchants, all western expeditions left from here, and under their guidance the trappers, voyageurs and coureurs de bois opened the trails into the great terra incognita beyond the wide Missouri. At that time St. Louis, in the words of Hamilton Basso, "frolicked away the nights with wild, reckless men who had drunk from the headwaters of the Yellowstone, fought Shawnees and Blackfeet, and been lost in the snow of the Wind River Mountains." Later, when the beaver was almost exterminated, the Astors and most others abandoned the fur trade. But St. Louis stuck to it, and it is still America's leading fur center. In the nineteenth century the French founders were joined by Americans, many of them from the Southern states. The latter injected style and manners into the frontier community and harmonized well with the old French-Creole families. One of their joint contributions to present-day St. Louis lives on in the annual Veiled Prophet Ball and Parade, held each October. Its colorful costumes and floats are a counterpart to the Mardi Gras of New Orleans. Finally, from the 1830's on, there was a great German migration to St. Louis, an event which established gemütlichkeit, beer gardens and Anheuser-Busch as landmarks of the town. Few of the beer gardens have survived, but the huge Anheuser-Busch brewery, the world's largest, is open to visitors. Most of the German refugees of 1848 were intellectuals and liberals, and helped to found and lead the St. Louis movement of philosophy. For a quarter of a century this merchants' town was a world center of philosophic thought. Politically the Germans kept the city on the Union side during the Civil War, and its famous German leader Carl Schurz, who became U.S. senator from Missouri, campaigned with the slogan "Right or wrong, my country. If right, to stay right; if wrong, to be set right." St. Louis' love of music is also a typically German trait. The country's second symphony orchestra was founded there in 1880 and is outstanding today. Music outdoors — always a favorite pastime for summer evenings in Germany — is practiced on a grand scale. The Municipal Opera offers open-air performances in Forest

DOWAGER QUEEN of the MISSISSIPPI

UNION PACIFIC RAILROAD

St. Louis Skyline. The great arch is the symbolic gateway to America's West.

Tropical flowers are grown at the Climatron of the St. Louis Botanical Gardens. Temperature and humidity are controlled within the glass-domed structure.

UNION PACIFIC RAILROAD

Park for residents and visitors during the summer.

GATEWAY CITY. The conquest of the West started here in St. Louis, and the fabulous stainless steel arch by Saarinen commemorates this great historical drama. The arch rises 630 feet above the river, and from its observation platform there is a broad panorama of the Jefferson Memorial Park, the city and the Mississippi. Behind the arch the Old Cathedral, the basilica of St. Louis of France, stands on the exact spot where in 1764 the first mass was celebrated in the presence of Auguste Chouteau. Soon afterward a log cabin church was built there, and in the early 1830's the present limestone structure was erected. In keeping with the genesis of St. Louis, its inscriptions are chiseled into the stone in three languages — Latin, French and English. Three old religious paintings are a gift from France, and one of the church bells has a curious story. A Spanish soldier and landholder, Benito Vasquez, had the bell cast as his present to his church, and he provided 200 Spanish silver dollars which were melted into the bronze to sweeten the bell's sound. Among the newer sightseeing attractions, Aloe Plaza presents one of our continent's famous sculptures, the Meeting of the Waters by Carl Milles. It symbolizes St. Louis' raison d'être, the confluence of the Missouri and the Mississippi. A young woman touching up her hair, representing the Missouri River, is eagerly approached by a young man, representing the Mississippi River, who in a friendly welcome stretches out his hand, offering a flower. They are surrounded by a dozen other bronze figures, sea creatures which spout water.

FAUNA AND FLORA IN THE ZOO AND AT SHAW'S. The St. Louis Zoo is not unusually large, but no visitor to the city should miss it. Its chimpanzee act is sparkling and wonderful, and its lion and elephant shows are entertaining. Shaw's Garden, the Missouri Botanical Garden, has splendid displays of lilies, iris, chrysanthemums, orchids and camellias and is modeled after Kew Gardens in London.

113

Sightseeing Guide

ILLINOIS

EASTERN ILLINOIS. Chicago, America's inland metropolis, is described on pages 108-109. Chicago's tree-shaded lakeshore suburb of Evanston is the seat of Northwestern University. From the Illinois River in Starved Rock State Park near Utica, the steep walls of Starved Rock rise for 140 feet; the unusual name of the rock commemorates a tragic incident. A band of Illinois Indians fleeing from a larger group of enemies sought refuge on the isolated summit. During the siege the Illinois refused to surrender but rather starved to death. The park is also the site of a French frontier fort erected in 1682. Urbana is the home of the University of Illinois with the splendid Krannert Center for the Performing Arts.

WESTERN ILLINOIS. In Galena, near the Mississippi River, the Ulysses S. Grant home is a state memorial now. After the Civil War General Grant lived in the pleasant red brick building which had been given him by his fellow townspeople. South of Galena the Mississippi Palisades State Park offers picnic and camping facilities near rocky bluffs with such names as Twin Sisters and Indian Head. Black Hawk State Park in Rock Island marks the site of the Indian village of the Sac and Fox tribes where Chief Black Hawk lived. The highest point in the park is known as Black Hawk's Watch Tower. Near Peoria the Fort Creve Coeur State Park is the site of a fort built by LaSalle in 1680. New Salem State Park with Lincoln Village, a fine restoration of the New Salem of young Lincoln's time, and Springfield, the state capital with Lincoln's home and tomb, are described on pages 110-111. Père Marquette State Park indicates with a simple cross the spot where Father Marquette, Louis Joliet and five companions began their canoe journey up the Illinois River. This large state park includes hilltop lookouts with broad views of the Illinois river valley, Indian mounds and relics. Near the southern end of the state Giant City State Park is located 10 miles south of Carbondale. There a wall of huge blocks of stone produces the effect of a city skyline; this mysterious structure was erected by an unknown native people. Cairo at the southern tip of Illinois and Cairo in Egypt have two points in common — the fertile soil and the life-giving river.

INDIANA

NORTHERN INDIANA. The industrial city of South Bend is the seat of the University of Notre Dame. On the campus the Church of the Sacred Heart has the country's oldest carillon. Michigan City is a lively lake resort just below the Michigan state line. Its special attractions are the International Friendship Gardens and the Indiana Dunes National Lakeshore. The white, sweeping sand dunes are equally beautiful in the glistening summer sun and when whipped by fall and winter winds. Visitors interested in industrial operations will be attracted to Gary; many of the big steelworks and manufacturing plants conduct guided tours for visitors. There is a certain picturesque grandeur in the towering blast furnaces, the flickering torches, the huge docks, the big ships. In Fort Wayne's Swinney Park is a memorial to a beloved American folklore figure, Johnny Appleseed, who spent a lifetime planting Christian faith and apple seeds throughout Pennsylvania, Ohio and Indiana. On Highway 9 near Rome City, Gene Stratton Porter State Memorial is noted for its Wildflower Woods.

CENTRAL INDIANA. Indianapolis, the state capital, is internationally known for its annual 500-mile auto races held in suburban Speedway on Memorial Day. The great motor speedway has a 2½-mile track, and visitors from all over the world flock to Indianapolis to witness the event. Scottish-American tourists who visit Indianapolis will be interested in the Scottish Rite Cathedral with its huge organ. Another attraction is the old home of James Whitcomb Riley, Indiana's beloved poet. Riley's birthplace is in Greenfield on Highway 40 east of Indianapolis. James Whitcomb Riley Memorial Park surrounds the original Old Swimmin' Hole of Riley's poem.

SOUTHERN INDIANA. Bloomington is the site of the modern campus of Indiana University. Vincennes, the oldest city in the state, has a colorful history; in 1732 it was founded by and named for the Canadian nobleman François de Vincennes, who was burned at the stake by the Chickasaw Indians four years later. The French lost the fort to the British, and the British to the Americans. In 1778 George Rogers Clark conquered it with an army of 350 Virginians, lost it and took it again the following year. His victory is commemorated by a Doric temple on the site of the old fort in George Rogers Clark National Historical Park. When Indiana became a territory in 1800 Vincennes was chosen as its capital. The old Territorial Legislative Hall is a small frame building impressive because of its friendly simplicity. The country furniture, the bare floors, the candles and the quill pens reflect unpretentious pioneer days. The Old Cathedral is also of interest. The Trailblazer Railroad connects the historic sites. French Lick with its three mineral springs is a famous vacation and health resort 45 miles east of Vincennes. Southeast of French Lick the Wyandotte Caves contain an immense limestone cavern. Santa Claus, near the Ohio River, is a busy place at Christmas time when thousands of letters are re-mailed from there with the Santa Claus postmark. Santa Claus Land is a children's park with many attractions for the younger set. Immediately west of Santa Claus is Lincoln Boyhood National Memorial, which includes the grave of Lincoln's mother and the site of the Lincoln family's log cabin. New Harmony on the Wabash was the scene of one of the numerous nineteenth-century experiments in Christian community living which condemned private property. The Rappists, a sect founded by George Rapp, prospered there with farming and small industries. Today New Harmony attracts many annual visitors when the trees are in blossom in June when the Golden Rain Tree Festival is held.

IOWA

EASTERN IOWA. In Dubuque stern-wheeler excursions on the Mississippi are popular. To the north McGregor is the center of a scenic area; from the bluffs there is a broad view of the big river, and the Mississippi forms a number of so-called bayous where beds of exquisite lotus flowers are thriving. Effigy Mounds National Monument preserves ancient Indian mounds in the shape of animals. In the luxuriantly verdant Pikes Peak region such attractions as the Bridal Veil Falls, the Sand Cave and the Pictured Rock Canyon are popular. To the northwest of Decorah there are bluffs and hills, large springs in the valleys and even some ice caves perpetually refrigerated by nature. Of historical interest are the Historical Museum of the Norwegian-American Society, which keeps the colorful traditions of the homeland alive in the New World, and nearby Old Fort Atkinson. The limestone cliffs along the Cedar River are striking in Palisades-Kepler State Park near Cedar Rapids. The seven Amana Villages are an interesting social experiment. In the nineteenth century they were founded by pious German, Swiss and Alsatian immigrants as Christian communities with communal workshops, including kitchens, bakeshops and mills. These villages still preserve many customs of the Old World. The University of Iowa is located in Iowa City. The

NORTH CENTRAL REGION

Fine Arts Building on the campus preserves the studio of Grant Wood, great recorder of the Midwestern scene, recalling the days of his association with the university. The Herbert Hoover National Historic Site is located in West Branch, the birthplace of the late president. The Mesquakie Indians of the reservation near Tama are adept in beadwork and basketwork and sell their handicrafts to tourists. North of Waterloo in Nashua one may visit the small church which inspired a nationally known song: "The Little Brown Church in the Vale."

CENTRAL IOWA. Ames is the seat of Iowa State University and of a research station of the U.S. Department of Agriculture. Des Moines is not only the capital of Iowa but also considers itself the farm capital of the nation. The Iowa State Fair has become so famous that it has been glorified in song hits and on the screen. While the fair usually conjures visions of a giant midway, of auto races and square dances, it is, more properly, a serious competition of the nation's top corn raisers, steer breeders, home bakers and other farming experts. Des Moines is also a great publishing center of newspapers and national magazines and the seat of Drake University.

WESTERN IOWA. The northwestern part of the state is a much frequented resort area. Spirit Lake, the state's largest glacial lake, and the Okoboji Lakes offer swimming, fishing and boating. Council Bluffs, across the river from Omaha, is picturesquely located on the high bluffs above the Missouri. As the name implies, the Indians held their councils there and traded with the French trappers and traders. The city's early history is remembered in the Lewis and Clark Monument. Council Bluffs is also one of the country's centers for growing roses and other flowers.

KANSAS

There may be no spectacular scenery in the conventional sense in the state of Kansas, but a golden ripe wheatfield that reaches to the horizon and a huge meadow sparkling with millions of sunflowers are sights to behold. Tall white grain elevators tower against the blue sky as cathedrals of the plains, and there is no more intriguing work to be watched than the operation of a harvester combine.

EASTERN KANSAS. Kansas City (not to be confused with the Missouri city of the same name) is a major center of grain storage and milling and meat-packing plants. Huron Cemetery, the old Wyandot Indian burial ground, is surrounded by the tall business buildings of the downtown district. Leavenworth, originally founded to protect the Santa Fe traders from marauding Indians, is now one of the country's largest army posts. Tree-shaded Topeka is the capital of Kansas; the State Capitol is noted for John S. Curry's murals of the dramatic John Brown story. The Menninger Foundation is one of the world's leading psychological and psychiatric research centers. Between Topeka and Kansas City is Lawrence, seat of the University of Kansas, which owns valuable collections of Indian arts and crafts. The federal government's largest Indian school, the Haskell Institute, is also located in Lawrence. South of Kansas City, Osawatomie was once John Brown's Kansas headquarters; the log cabin of the abolitionist leader is preserved in a memorial park, and a bronze statue honors his idealistic struggle. The restored first Territorial Capitol of Kansas stands in Fort Riley. In the middle of the nineteenth century Abilene was the teeming terminal of the Chisholm Trail of longhorn and cowboy fame; the old cattle town has been restored and even a prairie dog town survives there. Today Abilene is best known as President Eisenhower's boyhood home. The Eisenhower Center preserves many mementos of the late president's life. West of Abilene the Salina-Minneapolis region is noted for Rock City, a group of huge, weirdly shaped rock formations, and a large Indian burial pit. To the south Wichita is the largest city in Kansas; its cow town on the Chisholm Trail has been reconstructed.

WESTERN KANSAS. In restored Dodge City on the Santa Fe Trail, Frontier Street and Boot Hill with their frontier day relics keep alive the 1880's when the city was the Cowboy Capital of the West. To the northeast Fort Larned National Historic Site contains the military post that guarded the most dangerous stretch of the Santa Fe Trail.

KENTUCKY

CENTRAL KENTUCKY. Natural Bridge State Park is located southeast of Lexington. Lexington and the Blue Grass Country are described on pages 96-97. The Keeneland racecourse near Lexington is visited by thousands of tourists even when no races are in progress. Harrodsburg has the distinction of being the first permanent settlement west of the Alleghenies; Daniel Boone was one of its founders. Old Fort Harrod State Park has a replica of the historic fort, an exhibit of early pioneer life. The play "The Legend of Daniel Boone" is performed there during the summer. The area of the Kentucky River Palisades is a popular excursion goal in Central Kentucky. Frankfort, the capital of the state, lies on both sides of the Kentucky River; some of the finest Bourbon whiskies are distilled in and around Frankfort. Louisville, on the Ohio River, is celebrated for its races at nearby Churchill Downs. (see pages 96-97). The *Belle of Louisville* is a popular excursion steamer. Fort Knox is a military base, although it is usually associated with a huge hoard of gold. A large part of the world's gold is indeed stored there as the U.S. gold reserve. The Lincoln Birthplace National Historic Site and Bardstown where "My Old Kentucky Home" was written are described on page 97. At My Old Kentucky Home State Park "The Stephen Foster Story" is performed during the summer.

SOUTHERN KENTUCKY. Cumberland Gap, in Cumberland Gap National Historical Park in the southeastern corner of the state, is the historic gateway to the West through the wooded Cumberland Mountains. A portion of Daniel Boone's Wilderness Road is preserved here. A toll road leads to the summit of Pinnacle Mountain, which offers a spectacular view. The Cumberland Falls are described on page 97. Between Mammoth Cave and Cumberland Falls the large man-made Lake Cumberland is impounded by Wolf Creek Dam. Mammoth Cave National Park is described on page 96. Jefferson Davis' birthplace at Fairview is marked by an obelisk 351 feet tall.

WESTERN KENTUCKY. Near Henderson on the Ohio River, nature lovers are attracted by John James Audubon State Park and Museum and turf enthusiasts by the racecourse at James C. Ellis Park. The Kentucky Dam, across the Tennessee River, is one of the largest on earth and an important link in the TVA system. A further superlative, Kentucky Lake is one of the world's largest man-made bodies of water; its southern half is in Tennessee. The new Land Between the Lakes recreational area administered by the TVA lies between Kentucky Lake and Lake Barkley and is one of the largest recreation areas in the country. Near Wickliffe, the Buried City of the Mound Builders is an interesting relic.

MANITOBA, CANADA

EASTERN MANITOBA. Whiteshell Provincial Park is a wilderness area of woods and lakes on the Ontario border accessible by highway; it is noted for good fishing. Lake Winnipeg is a huge body of water with several summer resorts on its southern end. Steamboats serve the small shore communities like Norway House, which was founded in 1825 as a trading post of the Hudson's Bay Company near the northern end of the lake. There the Cree syllabic system was invented.

CENTRAL MANITOBA. Winnipeg, the capital of Manitoba, is a pleasant modern city whose Assiniboine Park contains beautiful flower beds, a conservatory, a zoo and various sports fields. Winnipeg is one of several places in Canada which holds annual Scottish Highland games. The excellent Royal Winnipeg Ballet has won international fame, and the Manitoba Theatre Center is a leading institution. The new Cultural Center should also be visited. Twenty miles north of Winnipeg, on the west bank of the Red River, Lower Fort Garry is a historic stone fort built by the Hudson's Bay Company in the 1830's. West of Winnipeg, the city of Portage la Prairie is the site of Fort La Reine, built by La Verendrye in 1739.

WESTERN MANITOBA. On the U.S. border, the International Peace Garden has been established by Manitoba and North Dakota to commemorate the traditional peace and friendship between Canada and the United States. A cairn consisting of rocks from both countries stands on the international boundary. Riding Mountain National Park has been established on the vast plateau of Riding Mountain which rises to a height of 2,480 feet above sea level. On the eastern and northeastern edge it towers more than 1,500 feet above the prairies in a steep escarpment, and it offers a splendid panorama of the fertile plains below. The park's main attractions are its magnificent forests and numerous lakes as well as its deer, elk, moose, bison and bears. The park's largest lake is 7-mile-long Clear Lake whose name is well chosen; its waters are so crystal clear that one can see, on its bottom, the bubbles of the springs that feed it. Highway 10 which crosses the park penetrates far into the north country. It passes through The Pas where a cairn honors the memory of Henry Kelsey, fur trader and daring explorer of the Hudson's Bay Company. It ends in Flin Flon on the Saskatchewan border. Sportsmen who look for the thrill of fishing in a real, faraway wilderness will enjoy this spot. Highlight of the season is the Flin Flon Trout Festival at the end of June.

NORTHERN MANITOBA. In the high north on Hudson's Bay, Churchill harbor was discovered in 1619 by the ill-fated Danish explorer Jens Munck. The Hudson's Bay Company established its first fort there in 1688. The ruins of Fort Prince of Wales on the shore of the bay date from the 1770's; today they are a national historic park.

MICHIGAN

Eleven thousand lakes and the longest shoreline of any state in the "lower 48" make Michigan a popular goal of swimmers, canoeists, sailors, freshwater fishermen and tourists who enjoy the forest and lake scenery.

UPPER PENINSULA. The small but beautiful and historically interesting Mackinac Island, Sault Ste. Marie with the Soo Locks and the Soo Canal and the Tahquamenon Falls in the northern wilderness are described on pages 100-101. Marquette is the center of the Upper Peninsula's recreation area where lakes and streams offer good fishing for a variety of species. Hunting is also varied and includes bear, deer, prairie chicken, grouse and pheasant. Marquette's Presque Isle Park is a scenic spot on a small peninsula in the northern part of the town. Near the Wisconsin border is Iron Mountain, where iron mines may be visited. It is also a popular winter sports center. Sportsmen appreciate also the Keweenaw Peninsula, and in Copper Harbor tourists may make a boat connection with Isle Royale National Park. That park is described on page 102. To the west of Ontonagon, Porcupine Mountains State Park accommodates tourists and fishermen on the shore of Lake Superior. Pictured Rocks National Lakeshore near Munising has interesting rock formations, a 12-mile beach, fishing and hunting.

LOWER PENINSULA, NORTH. Petoskey, on Little Traverse Bay, is a popular resort which celebrates its summer season with an Indian Pow Wow at nearby Cross Village and climaxes its winter events with a gay carnival. The calm and sparkling waters of Grand Traverse Bay make Traverse City a great recreation center. Nature provides a pollen free, temperate climate and broad lake surfaces for deep-sea trout trolling and water-skiing, swimming and canoeing. Clinch Park on the waterfront includes a small zoo, an aquarium, an Indian Museum and a yacht basin. The Leelanau Peninsula, separating Grand Traverse Bay from Lake Michigan, is a delightful scenic spot, and the circular shoreline drive is a well recommended excursion. The region is one of America's principal cherry growing districts; the National Cherry Festival is held every July. Sleeping Bear Dunes National Lakeshore lies on the western side of the peninsula. The country's best known music camp is located in Interlochen, near Traverse City. Music students from all states of the Union attend its summer sessions, and the symphonic concerts presented in the Concert Bowl in sylvan surroundings and led by prominent conductors are the outstanding musical events of the region. At nearby Cadillac the Caberfae Winter Sports Area has 35 ski runs. On the Lake Huron side, the 200-mile shore drive from the top of the Lower Peninsula to Bay City runs through a forest and lake country noted for good hunting and fishing.

LOWER PENINSULA, SOUTH. Travelers interested in interior decoration will find the furniture exhibits in the Public Museum in Grand Rapids a rewarding experience. Wooden shoes, flowing skirts, lace caps and millions of tulips in full bloom, blazing in red, yellow, orange and lavender, are the marks of the annual Tulip Festival at Holland, beginning on the Saturday nearest May 15th. Festivities start with the scrubbing of Eighth Street by Dutch-costumed townspeople, most of whom are of Dutch descent. The cleaning up preliminaries are followed by parades, concerts and exhibits; wooden shoe dances are performed as a special treat. In May the numerous tulip farms of Holland, Michigan, rival those of its namesake in Europe. The adjoining shores of Lake Michigan are studded with white sand dunes and bathing beaches. Lansing, Michigan's capital, is also the seat of Michigan State University. Detroit, the world's automobile capital, Dearborn with the River Rouge Ford Plant and the cultural center of Cranbrook are described on pages 98-99. Ann Arbor, west of Detroit, is the home of the University of Michigan, one of America's great academic centers, with libraries of more than four million books and periodicals and a football stadium for more than 100,000 fans.

MINNESOTA

The sparkling blue of 10,000 lakes and the deep green of

NORTH CENTRAL REGION

immense evergreen and hardwood forests are the features of Minnesota's vacation and wilderness areas.

NORTHERN MINNESOTA. Brainerd on the Mississippi River is the starting point for a tour of the lake country. Its Paul Bunyan Center celebrates the lumberjack giant who left 10,000 footprints (lakes) in Minnesota. To the north Bemidji, on a lake of the same name, is another fishing and hunting center. The climax of the summer season is the Paul Bunyan Water Carnival. Southwest of Bemidji, Lake Itasca is considered the source of the Mississippi River. It is included with 156 other lakes in Minnesota's largest state park, nearly 32,000 acres of woods which shelter herds of deer and other wildlife. The wilderness of the Arrowhead Region, Superior National Forest and the North Shore Drive along Lake Superior to Thunder Bay in Canada are described on pages 102-103, and Voyageurs National Park is mentioned on page 103. Just below the international boundary, 6 miles off the North Shore Drive, the village of Grand Portage has been restored just as it looked when it was the first white settlement in Minnesota. The Gunflint Trail offers a famous wilderness excursion from Grand Marais to Saganaga Lake. Northwest of Duluth is the frontier town of Hibbing, the center of an interesting area where most of America's iron ore is dug from huge, reddish brown, open-pit iron mines in the Mesabi, Vermilion and Cuyuna ranges. Those pits are the biggest man-made holes on earth. The Mesabi mineral wealth, as well as grain from the prairies, is funneled to the twin harbors of Duluth-Superior, where the dock operations are fascinating to watch: the automatic collaboration of ore trains, ore piers and ore ships; the grain elevators, their loading devices and the perpetual going and coming of ore steamers and grain ships, all with the same long silhouette and a flag of smoke from the funnel astern. Among Duluth's attractions are the Aerial Lift Bridge which is raised in toto when a steamship passes below, Minnesota Point Park with its recreation area, the Skyline Parkway and the Enger Observation Tower.

SOUTHERN MINNESOTA. Midway between the Equator and the North Pole, Minnesota's great twin cities are both friendly neighbors and rivals. Minneapolis is more modern, vigorous and progressive while St. Paul is more traditional, dignified and gracious. The residential districts of Minneapolis, permeated with blue waters, trees and flowers, are ideal for open-air living. In the city proper the outstanding sights are the Mississippi River with the Falls of St. Anthony, the Minnehaha Falls of Hiawatha fame, the campus of the University of Minnesota and the nationally famous Tyrone Guthrie Theatre. During the summer, the Aquatennial, a ten-day water festival, is a popular diversion, and during the winter the concerts of the Minneapolis Symphony Orchestra are outstanding musical events. St. Paul, the state capital, is built, like Rome, on seven hills and enjoys a great many lakes and parks. One can drive to historic Fort Snelling on the picturesque high bluffs along the Mississippi. The State Capitol and the botanical conservatory in Como Park are St. Paul landmarks. Ever since 1886 St. Paul has celebrated a nine-day winter carnival with a unique feature. Every year a 4,500-ton medieval ice palace is built in Como Park. Northeast of Minneapolis-St. Paul, the St. Croix River rushes through a rocky gorge 200 feet deep. From Red Wing to La Crescent Highway 61 follows the Mississippi River and offers delightful vistas into the Hiawatha Valley. Rochester is the seat of the Mayo Clinic, a world center of medical treatment and research. Near Harmony the Niagara Cave contains two rivers, a lake and a 60-foot waterfall. In the southwest the

Pipestone National Monument preserves the red pipestone quarries from which the Indians obtained the material for their peace pipes.

MISSOURI

EASTERN MISSOURI. Hannibal, with Mark Twain's boyhood home, is described on page 111. He was born in the village of Florida southwest of Hannibal, and his birthplace stands in a state park. St. Louis, the Dowager Queen of the Mississippi, is described on pages 112-113. Lindbergh's epochal flight in the Spirit of St. Louis was planned largely in St. Louis, and the Lindbergh trophies are exhibited in the Jefferson Memorial in Forest Park. Southwest of the city Grant's Farm, once the property of Ulysses S. Grant, has a zoo, stables and carriages and a deer park. It is operated by Anheuser-Busch.

CENTRAL MISSOURI. Columbia is the home of the University of Missouri; a row of tall, lonely Doric columns, the only remnants of a burned university building, are an impressive landmark on the campus. A few miles west the town of Boonville is the seat of Kemper Military Academy, the oldest military school west of the Mississippi. In the center of the state, Jefferson City is delightfully located on a high bluff above the Missouri River, a splendid setting for the state capital. The impressive capitol of Carthage marble is decorated with murals by Thomas Hart Benton, the great painter of Midwestern and Southern farm scenes. The 130-mile-long Lake of the Ozarks, the largest of Missouri's man-made lakes, is described on page 122.

WESTERN MISSOURI. St. Joseph on the Missouri River was the starting point of the Pony Express in 1860. Mementos of that exciting enterprise may be inspected at the Pony Express Stables Museum. The Jesse James House and several other old homes are open to the public. King Hill, an ancient Indian battleground, is an observation point now. Excelsior Springs is a noted health resort. Kansas City, once a boisterous outfitting town for wagon trains rolling west, is still a traffic center with trunk line railroads keeping up a steady flow of goods, farm products and cattle. Visitors admire the city's landscaped boulevard system which extends for more than 100 miles; also of interest is the Liberty Memorial with its perpetual flame. At the eastern edge of Kansas City, Independence has historic significance as the starting point of the Santa Fe and Oregon trails. Today it is known as the hometown of the late President Harry S. Truman. Near Joplin, in the southwest corner of the state, the George Washington Carver National Monument exhibits the home of Moses Carver, who owned George, and a statue of the Negro boy who became a great scientist. Near Springfield is Wilson's Creek National Battlefield Park, the site of a Civil War battle in 1861. The Ozark Mountain area is described on pages 122-123.

NEBRASKA

EASTERN NEBRASKA. Halfway between New York and Los Angeles, Omaha is America's crossroads city. Originally an outfitting point for wagon trains setting out on the Mormon and Oregon trails, Omaha has spread from the terrace above the Mississippi far into a pleasant countryside of rolling hills. Carter Lake and Levi Carter Park are delightful recreational spots; the Joslyn Art Museum is an art gallery of pink Georgian marble, and the Union Pacific Historical Museum commemorates the first continental railroad whose western advance started from Omaha. The Mormon Cemetery is a grim reminder of pioneer life; it contains the graves of almost 600 Mormons, who perished on their westward trek in the fierce winter of 1846-47. West of Omaha is nationally famous Father Flanagan's Boys Town for homeless boys. An incorporated village, it has a city commission, a chapel, post office, auditorium and farm and trade schools. In Lincoln, the state capital, one of the few modern capitol buildings in the United States raises its 400-foot tower into the blue sky of the prairies. The great white shaft is capped by a dome of gold tile, and on top of the half sphere there stands a 27-foot bronze statue of the Sower, symbol of the plains. On the campus of the University of Nebraska the Nebraska State Historical Society's Museum includes collections of Indian relics, ancient guns and pioneer musical instruments. The Nebraska State Museum offers to naturalists the Hall of Elephants and a large exhibit of fossils, and for art lovers there is the Sheldon Memorial Art Gallery. South of Omaha on the Missouri River, Nebraska City is the home of the Arbor Day founder, J. Sterling Morton. His arboretum in Arbor Lodge State Historical Park is open to the public. South of Lincoln near Beatrice, the Homestead National Monument encloses the first land claim of 160 acres under the historic General Homestead Act of 1862. Some of the homesteaders' original buildings have been restored. White Horse Ranch Museum near Stuart on U.S. Highway 20 is a popular attraction.

WESTERN NEBRASKA. At North Platte on the Platte River is Scouts Rest State Historical Park, Buffalo Bill's Ranch and winter quarters of his Wild West Show. At Valentine near the South Dakota state line, the Fort Niobrara National Wildlife Refuge preserves a large herd of bison, elk, coyote, prairie dogs, bobcats and pronghorn antelope. Agate Fossil Beds National Monument, north of Scottsbluff, contains the fossilized remains of animals which lived 20 million years ago. Scotts Bluff National Monument is a huge tableland of sandstone, a towering pioneer landmark above the Oregon Trail. An automobile road leads to the top; from there a sweeping panorama of the North Platte valley may be enjoyed. A museum depicts the trail history, the westward migration, and the days of the buffalo hunters. Southeast of Scottsbluff, Chimney Rock used to be a road sign for passing wagon trains; its tall, thin chimney is visible for 30 miles. Kingsley Dam on the North Platte River is an earth-filled structure forming Lake McConaughy, the biggest body of water entirely within the state. Facilities for all water sports are available.

NORTH DAKOTA

NORTHERN NORTH DAKOTA. The Turtle Mountains are gently rolling hills embracing lovely small lakes near Dunseith. Commemorating more than a hundred years of peace between Canada and the United States, the International Peace Garden has been established astride the international border. At the Turtle Mountain Indian Reservation the Sun Dance of the Chippewas is an attraction every year in June. To the west of the Peace Garden several wildlife refuges have been established; the largest is the Upper Souris National Wildlife Refuge.

EASTERN NORTH DAKOTA. Devils Lake is the remnant of a glacial sea that has been steadily shrinking; half a century ago the town of Devils Lake was a thriving steamboat landing; now its location is 6 miles inland. Adjoining the lake, Sully's Hill National Game Preserve is a refuge for deer, elk and buffalo. The whole area is popular with campers and picnickers. Fargo, on the Red River of the North, is the farm supply center of a prosperous valley. Its many parks and the campus of North

Dakota State University are attractive. Nearby Fort Abercrombie has been restored.

CENTRAL NORTH DAKOTA. At Beulah a tour into a large lignite coal mine on an underground train and in a miner's outfit is an interesting experience. Bismarck's landmark is the skyscraper State Capitol which rises as a bright and functional column from the plains. On the capitol grounds the statue of Sakakawea (Sacajawea), the "bird woman" of the Shoshoni Indians who guided Lewis and Clark to the west, looks toward the setting sun. The Liberty Memorial Building has a large collection of Indian, pioneer and military relics. At nearby Mandan, Fort Lincoln State Park has been established on the site from which General Custer set out to his "last stand" at the Little Bighorn. On the South Dakota state line at Fort Yates, the Standing Rock Indian Reservation of several thousand Sioux Indians has been so-called because of a sacred gray stone which is shaped like a woman in repose. To the Sioux this standing rock is a holy symbol which they always took along on their tribal migrations. Another Indian sanctuary at Fort Yates is the burial site of Sitting Bull.

WESTERN NORTH DAKOTA. The badlands of North Dakota, which have no connection with those of South Dakota, consist of fantastically shaped buttes of various colors whose tops are level with the big plateau. The Little Missouri winds its way through canyons and land cuts. The badlands can best be seen in Theodore Roosevelt National Memorial Park, which includes a petrified forest and parts of the old Roosevelt ranch. Medora was a thriving cattle center when Teddy Roosevelt operated the Elkhorn Ranch near there in the 1880's. The Rough Riders Hotel still stands on Main Street; its name may have inspired that of Teddy Roosevelt's cavalry outfit in the Spanish-American War. Also in Medora is the Chateau de Mores State Monument, the 28-room chateau of a French pioneer who became a ranching and meat-packing millionaire. South of Medora at Amidon perpetually burning coal mines are a weird sight.

OHIO

EASTERN OHIO. For an all round view of Cleveland, the 42nd-floor observation platform of the 52-story Terminal Tower is recommended. Visitors will be impressed with the colorful harbor and lakefront; the beautiful parks with 14 miles of waterfront can be reached on a parkway circling the metropolis and the Public Square and Mall, where all the government buildings, the stadium and auditorium are located. The Cleveland Institute of Art, Severance Hall, home of the Cleveland Symphony Orchestra, and Case-Western Reserve University are on the eastern edge of the city. American groups of foreign birth or background in Cleveland have been especially active in keeping alive their colorful Old World costumes, dances and songs; thirty such groups have united in creating the International Cultural Gardens, each group contributing the most typical flowers of their homeland. Southwest of Cleveland, Oberlin is the seat of Oberlin College, the nation's first coeducational college. South of Cleveland, Akron is the country's rubber capital; it uses about 40 per cent of all the raw rubber produced on earth, with automobile tires its principal product. The international soap box derby, well-known to every boy, is held in Akron in August. South of Akron, near New Philadelphia, Schoenbrunn Village has been authentically restored as it looked in 1772 when it was a Moravian Indian mission. The first town in Ohio, it was abandoned in 1777. Marietta was the first permanent white settlement in the state.

NORTH CENTRAL REGION

It is the home of Marietta College and the Campus Martius Museum with historic relics of Indian and pioneer days.

CENTRAL OHIO. On a peninsula between Lake Erie and Sandusky Bay, Marblehead and the neighboring archipelago of Lake Erie islands are a popular recreational area. Two famous landmarks dominate the scene: the lighthouse of Marblehead, and Perry's Victory and International Peace Memorial on South Bass Island at Put-in-Bay. Columbus, the state capital, is also the seat of Ohio State University and several other colleges. The Ohio State Museum contains the Coonskin Library, the first collection of books in Ohio. Southeast of Columbus, near the town of Logan Hocking Hills State Park is ideal for hiking, camping and picnicking; streams and waterfalls, spectacular rocks and caves, gorges and boulders dot the pleasant forest land. The Old Man's Cave and Ash Cave areas of the park are best known. Mound City Group National Monument near Chillicothe preserves fascinating remnants of a prehistoric civilization once flourishing there. Surrounded by a three-foot embankment are 23 mounds containing human skeletons and altars; the mounds were built by the Hopewell people, who made utensils of wood, stone and pottery, learned to weave fabrics and used freshwater pearls as ornaments. The most amazing effigy mound in Ohio is the 1,300-foot-long Serpent Mound southwest of Chillicothe. The structure of this weird effigy, the original purpose or meaning of which is not known, is especially impressive from the air.

WESTERN OHIO. Toledo has a famous art museum; in addition to paintings and sculptures, the museum maintains a collection of ancient and modern glass. Dayton is a symbol of the birth and growth of American aviation. It was the hometown of the Wright Brothers, and the small plane that made history on December 17, 1903, was designed and built in Dayton. Ever since then the city has been an aviation center, and today its Wright-Patterson Air Force Base is the foremost experimental arm of our air force. Dayton Art Institute displays pre-Columbian, Western and Oriental art, and Dayton's Carillon Park with Deeds Carillon and various historic relics is a showplace. A general panorama of Cincinnati can best be enjoyed from the top of the 574-foot-high Carew Tower. An observation point in Eden Park offers a broad view. Among Cincinnati's outstanding cultural institutions are the Taft Museum in the old family home, the Museum of Art, the University of Cincinnati and the Cincinnati Symphony Orchestra.

SOUTH DAKOTA

EASTERN SOUTH DAKOTA. Sioux Falls is a meat-packing center. Its Pettigrew Museum displays Indian handicrafts, especially of the Sioux. To the west in Mitchell is the Corn Palace, scene of a week-long fall festival.

CENTRAL SOUTH DAKOTA. Pierre is the state capital and the seat of an Indian school. Northwest of Pierre, the Cheyenne River Indian Reservation is quite picturesque since many of the 4,000 Sioux still live in wigwams.

WESTERN SOUTH DAKOTA. The area comprising the Badlands National Monument, Wind Cave National Park, Rapid City, the Black Hills with Mount Rushmore National Memorial, Lead with the Homestake Mine and Deadwood is described on pages 104-105. Deadwood celebrates the era of Wild Bill Hickok and Calamity Jane with the serio-comic play, "The Trial of Jack McCall," performed summer nights except Sundays. Belle Fourche is the northern gateway to the Black Hills,

an old cattle center where an annual Black Hills Roundup attracts tourists and cowboys early in July. Jewel Cave National Monument, near Wind Cave National Park, is a cavern studded with sparkling calcite crystals justifying the name jewel. Between Jewel Cave and Wind Cave, Custer State Park shelters America's largest herd of bison which roam the range with wild burros and many other native animals. South Dakota is still great Indian country, and in the Rosebud and Pine Ridge reservations in the south central part of the state, some 16,000 Indians live partially in the ways of their forebears. They are excellent horsemen, and since the reservations include good grazing lands, quite a few are self-supporting cattle ranchers.

WISCONSIN

NORTHERN WISCONSIN. When approaching the harbor of the city of Superior boats travel past the group of Apostle Islands, now a national lakeshore, with their spectacular red cliffs. The islands were called The Twelve Apostles by early French fishermen. Superior, the iron ore port, is a twin of Duluth. Ten miles to the south Pattison State Park is located on Highway 35; this scenic spot contains the 165-foot-high Manitou Falls, the highest in Wisconsin. To the south Interstate Park, at the Dalles of the St. Croix River, is a spectacular wilderness. The forest and lake country of northern Wisconsin is one huge vacationland where water sports and winter sports flourish, with Rhinelander a center of the resort area. Rib Mountain State Park near Wausau includes Wisconsin's second highest summit, at an altitude of 1,941 feet. This is principally a winter playground, with toboggan runs, ice hockey fields, ski tows and ski trails. Near the tip of the peninsula between Green Bay and Lake Michigan, Peninsula State Park is a large forest with trails, bridle paths and other recreational facilities. Brown County with the city of Green Bay is a cheese manufacturing area of national fame; numerous small cheese factories sell their excellent Wisconsin cheese in their own stores along the road. In Green Bay, home of the Green Bay Packers and the National Railroad Museum, the Neville Museum preserves relics of early fur trading and lumbering days.

SOUTHERN WISCONSIN. The Wisconsin Dells, Devils Lake State Park and Wisconsin's capital Madison, with the University of Wisconsin, are described on pages 106-107. Just west of Madison, at Mount Horeb in the "Valley of the Elves," Little Norway is an outdoor museum of a dozen log cabins of Norse settlers. In nearby New Glarus the Swiss Museum Village displays replicas of buildings of early Swiss immigrants. Milwaukee supposedly has been made famous by beer, and those interested in the brewing process will find guided tours available at Miller, Pabst and Schlitz. With its magnificent lakeshore, its city-wide system of parks, its conservatory, sunken gardens and zoo, Milwaukee is also one of the country's beautiful cities. A fine symphony orchestra and two art galleries are cultural centers. In the city's surroundings, dozens of inland lakes are within easy reach. In Racine lovers of architecture will be interested in the functional administration buildings of the Johnson Wax Company, designed by the late Frank Lloyd Wright, Wisconsin-born dean of American architects and international leader in contemporary design. Lake Geneva with Yerkes Observatory is described on page 107. To the west Mineral Point is known for a row of Cornish-style houses built by Cornish miners after 1832, when mineral deposits were discovered in the neighborhood. Near Prairie du Chien, northwest of Mineral Point, Wyalusing State Park is a pleasant recreational area of forests and caves, bluffs and green valleys at the junction of the Wisconsin and Mississippi rivers.

South Central Map

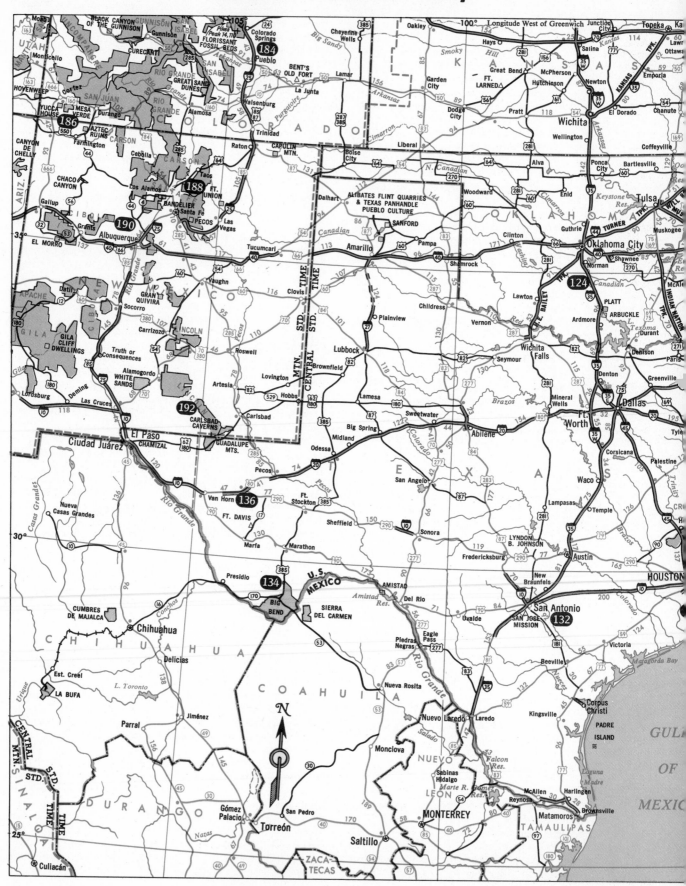

WHAT to SEE in the SOUTH CENTRAL REGION

SIX-DAY TRIP THROUGH THE OZARK AND OUACHITA MOUNTAINS. For a general introduction see pages 122-123, also sightseeing guide pages 114-115, 137-138. Suggested route: Little Rock, Arkansas, with the restored hand hewn oak log Arkansas Territorial Capitol, the Greek Revival Capitol of 1836 and the current one — Hot Springs National Park with Bathhouse Row and Grand Promenade — Fort Smith, Arkansas, once a Wild West town where a single judge sentenced 160 outlaws to death by hanging; court and gallows are a historic site now. This is the gateway to the Ozarks and Ouachita Mountains — Eureka Springs, Arkansas, with 63 springs in a setting of rugged mountains. Christ of the Ozarks is a seven-story statue on Magnetic Mountain. The resort is a center of folk music and square dancing — Branson, Missouri, where floating trips on the White River may be arranged — Springfield, Missouri, a center for hill country crafts — Lake of the Ozarks State Park, a popular fishing area — Van Buren with Big Spring Park; as many as 840 millions of gallons of clear water gush from a limestone bluff every day — Poplar Bluff, Missouri — Little Rock.

EIGHT-DAY TRIP THROUGH THE GULF COAST COUNTRY AND EASTERN TEXAS. For a general introduction see pages 130-133, also sightseeing guide pages 138-139. Suggested route: Beaumont. A granite shaft marks the spot where the first Texas oil well gushed — Port Arthur — Galveston, a cosmopolitan harbor and water sports center with a 32-mile sand beach; sometimes it is called Oleander City because more than a million oleander bushes blossom there with poinsettias and bougainvillaeas. Rides on top of the seawall are popular — Houston. The Manned Spacecraft Center on NASA Road offers exhibits of the Manned Space Program; the Astrodome is a unique air-conditioned stadium — to the east, just outside of town, the San Jacinto Monument, a 570-foot tower, honors the battle of Texan independence; the battleship Texas is docked nearby — San Antonio represents the Spanish Southwest; the Alamo, scene of the 1836 tragedy, is its most famous relic. The governor's palace and La Villita, the Latin Quarter in the city's center, are fascinating, and several Spanish missions near the town may be visited — Austin, the state capital.

SIX-DAY TRIP THROUGH WESTERN TEXAS AND SOUTHERN NEW MEXICO. For a general introduction see pages 134-137, 192-193; also sightseeing guide pages 138-139, 236-239. Suggested route: El Paso, a cosmopolitan and historic city, connected by bridge with Ciudad Juárez on the Mexican side of the border; the old Ysleta quarter and the Mission Nuestra Señora del Carmen of 1682 are relics of Spanish days and the reconstructed Fort Bliss recollects the American conquest of the West. The scenic drive on Mount Franklin, the southernmost peak of the Rockies, is worthwhile — White Sands National Monument with high, spectacular shifting dunes of dazzling white gypsum sand — Carlsbad Caverns National Park contains what are probably the largest limestone caves in the world. There are three floors and the lowest is 1,013 feet deep — Balmorhea State Park with San Solomon Springs, a natural swimming pool of enormous size — across the Davis Mountains to Fort Davis with the W. J. Donald Observatory, operating a large reflecting telescope, and old Fort Davis, a frontier outpost of the nineteenth century — Alpine — Big Bend National Park, a huge, lonely and fascinating wilderness with the Phantom Mountains, the translation of the official name Chisos — El Paso.

Ozarks and Hot Springs of Arkansas

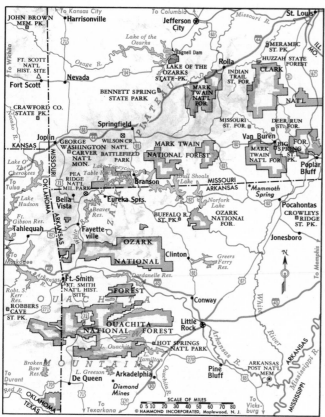

center in the Ozarks, a very ancient mass of hills and plateaus with a north-south span of about 200 miles and an east-west run of approximately 100 miles. The Ozarks are located in southwestern Missouri and northwestern Arkansas, spilling over into the neighboring states. It is a lovely, quiet hill country, a gentle wilderness, a green and pleasant backwoods area with blooming dogwood, redbud and hawthorn, with tall oaks and elms, cold streams and bubbling springs. The region abounds in caves, many of which may be visited. Around the Lake of the Ozarks and to the south, at Table Rock and Taneycomo lakes, there are modern hotels and motels. Branson, Missouri, is the point of departure for the popular Ozark floating trips down the White River, which wends its way with innumerable oxbows between wooded hills and farm country, islands and narrows. On the shallow boat you may fish as you drift along, or just loaf. Nearby at Silver Dollar City is the starting point of the Frisco-Silver Dollar Line, a vintage train that takes tourists through the Ozark woods.

THE GIANT SPRINGS. The east-central edge of the Ozarks is the Big Spring country, where clear cold water rushes and gushes through the earth, bursts through fissures in the granite and porphyry and swirls into sinks, pools, streams and rivers. There are hundreds of such giant springs, but the most impressive and one of the world's largest is Big Spring, located in a park south of the town of Van Buren, Missouri. At the bottom of a dark, 250-foot limestone cliff there is a great basin from which the pale blue flow emerges and rebounds from the boulders; 840 million gallons of water rush over the ledge every day, enough to supply a large city. At the end of a lonely road, this torrent of a spring is an unforgettable sight, whether you see it sparkling in the morning sun or in the blue magic of twilight. Sixty-three springs bubble in the resort town of Eureka Springs, many of them gushing along or near the main street.

FIDDLERS, CALLERS, WALKER HOUNDS. As interesting as the landscape are the people of the Ozarks. They are of English and Scottish stock, mostly mountaineers from Tennessee, Virginia and Kentucky who in the restless years after the War of 1812 migrated to this island of hills and have stayed there ever since. How long they will be able to keep their old ways, with huge hydroelectric dams arising and tourists swarming in, is another question. The frequent presence of visiting anthropologists and folklorists collecting ancient ballads and tape recording the Ozark speech is ominous. At present, folk life is still alive and strong. There are still

GHOST TOWN AT THE LAKE BOTTOM. Some Old World legends describe bewitched towns at the bottom of the sea; if you drift on the surface on a clear day, you may hear the church bells ringing far below and see, in the deep water, the ghostly rows of houses. This is an experience you may also have in the New World at the Lake of the Ozarks. At least you may, while swimming, get your foot caught in the weathercock of a church steeple. When Bagnell Dam was built the people in a number of valleys had to move but, since it seemed too costly and unnecessary to demolish the buildings and trees, the great new reservoir of water, the Lake of the Ozarks, retained its "sunken village" when it was filled with water. The tree skeletons and house ruins are shelters for young bass now. This lake, fed by the Osage River, has the shape of an octopus with a shoreline of 1,375 miles. It is a recreation

A GENTLE WILDERNESS and AMERICA'S NATIONAL PARK PROTOTYPE

some Ozark fiddlers who have whittled their own instruments, who cannot read a note but have a repertory of perhaps 300 tunes, and who can adapt to Saturday dance music any new tune that may appeal to them. And there are square dance callers who can go on without repeating a figure, ordering innumerable patterns from a simple star to a rattlesnake glide, stopping only when the dancers approach collapse. The people are also great hunters and dog breeders. Their coon dogs are killers, trained for the practical purpose of securing raccoon hides, but the smaller Walker hounds are kept and cared for as fox hunters and are used in the world's most gentle variety of fox hunting. Five or six dogs are taken by truck to the neighborhood of a fox's burrow and released at night. The men settle under a tree and do their hunting by ear. Yips, yells and little barks tell them the story of discovering the body smell of the fox, finding or losing the track, confronting the fox, and so on. The fox is never killed.

"TAKING THE WATERS." South of the Ozarks, in the Ouachita Mountains, Hot Springs National Park is an attraction for more than just the sick. Its baths — the waters are heated by vapors rising through cracks in volcanic rock — are applied both as a cure and as a tonic preventive, and their fame goes back to Indian days. According to local traditions the Osages, Ouachitas and Cherokees fought for the possession of the health-giving springs but later came to a sensible accord and declared the spa neutral territory, open to all sick Indians. The first white man to enjoy a mineral bath there is said to have been De Soto, who indeed visited the spot. As early as 1832 the U.S. government set aside as a federal reservation about 1,000 acres surrounding the springs, so that the Hot Springs of Arkansas can claim quite rightly to be the prototype for America's national parks. Today numerous hotels and motels take care of both the sick and the hale who come there in search of restoration and rejuvenation.

Hot Springs, Arkansas, has been a popular health spa since the days of the Indians.

A forest that drowned in Arkansas' Greers Ferry Reservoir.

Everlasting Hills of Oklahoma

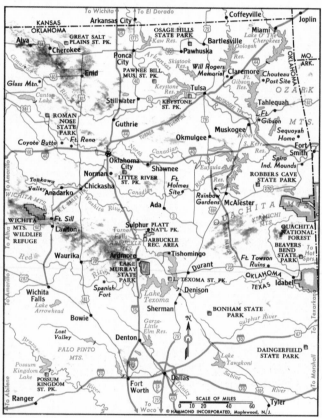

in the backyards of apartment buildings. The whole capital stands on top of a huge petroleum pool.

TULSA: OIL AND INDIAN LORE. Approaching Tulsa from the southwest, you will see one of America's dramatic city panoramas. Beyond the smokestacks and tank installations of a large oil refinery and beyond the sandy carpet of the Arkansas River, there arises high on the ridge of the bluff the skyline of Tulsa. As a low cloud of mist and steam often hovers over the refinery while the air on the hill is dry and transparent, the clear skyline seems to emerge from the cloud like a vision. Although Tulsa considers itself "the oil capital of the world," and is the home of several hundred oil companies and related enterprises and the seat of the quadrennial International Petroleum Products Exposition, it is only of mild interest to the sightseeing traveler. Tulsa's two art institutions, however, will be fascinating to many. The Philbrook Art Center is a splendid private mansion turned into a museum, but the more unusual of the two is the Gilcrease Foundation, just outside the city limits. The latter contains the finest collection of Indian paintings in existence. The art of 45 Indian tribes, beginning as early as the year A.D. 300, can be studied there as well as the paintings of modern Indian artists and of white painters such as Russell and Remington, the outstanding recorders of the Old West. The priceless collection is supplemented by a library of thousands of letters, manuscripts and books. Thomas Gilcrease, the oil millionaire who established this gallery, had a Creek Indian grandmother and lived in Indian Territory as a boy.

A GREAT AMERICAN AT HOME. Northeast of Tulsa, the small city of Claremore is the hometown of Will Rogers, the homespun philosopher and humorist who was probably the best-loved American of his day. By descent he was truly an American. His father Clem, one-eighth Cherokee, served four terms as a Cherokee senator and helped to write the constitution that changed the Indian Territory into the State of Oklahoma. His mother was one-quarter Cherokee, and Will remarked correctly that his ancestors did not come over in the *Mayflower,* they met the boat. After he had won fame as an entertainer and had become a national figure, he returned to Claremore for a visit and bought twenty acres on a hill overlooking the town. There he planned to retire, build a home and "just sit and whittle and gab." He never carried out his plan, for in 1935 on a goodwill mission to Russia his plane crashed in Alaska. Nevertheless, he returned home. The State of Oklahoma built on that hill the Will Rogers Memorial as Will's burial place. From the foyer his statue glances over the countryside in his friendly, casual way. Millions of

OKLAHOMA CITY: PILLARS AND DRILLS. Thousands of Americans have derived their knowledge of Oklahoma from the now classical Rodgers and Hammerstein musical of the same name. Accordingly they picture it as an idyllic farming and ranching area, which indeed it is. But early in the twentieth century another factor appeared that added an accent of its own — oil. Oklahoma City, the capital, in particular bears its imprint. The city is not a tourist attraction in the strict sense of the word, but if you happen to travel in its neighborhood, you will find a visit interesting. Imagine, for instance, the Oklahoma state capitol built in the style of an ancient Greek temple and right in front of the classical columns the lacy steel tower of a modern oil derrick. The contrast is so striking that the derrick is probably the most photographed of its kind. There are derricks in the front yards of private homes and

PLOWS and DERRICKS, BATHS and BUFFALO

Americans have been there and have looked at Will's saddles and lassos, his hat and his typewriter, twisted and battered in the plane crash, and the small red bag "that packed itself." All who visit this shrine like to recall the nail on the head sayings of this "good Injun." One of his own words is chiseled into his statue: "I never met a man I didn't like."

SULPHUR AND BROMIDE. In the southern part of the state is Platt National Park whose attraction is an area of 31 large springs. They include 18 sulphur, 6 freshwater, 4 iron and 3 bromide springs, formerly a part of the Chickasaw Nation territory. Perimeter Boulevard describes an elongated circle in the park which abounds with bright wildflowers.

BISON AND LONGHORNS. Sixty million buffalo roamed this continent when the white man arrived. In 1895 there were 800 left, and there was danger that this great native animal might vanish as had the passenger pigeon. In 1905 President Theodore Roosevelt accepted a herd of 15 buffalo as a nucleus for survival from the New York Zoological Society. He established the Wichita Mountains Wildlife Refuge as a buffalo preserve in southwestern Oklahoma near the city of Lawton. In 50 years the herd had increased to over a thousand, and additional refuges throughout the West and in Canada make it certain now that the American buffalo (properly the bison) will not die out, although it survives in a

half-tame condition. Another equally picturesque American animal saved from extinction here is the Texas longhorn. Survivors of Spanish cows and bulls brought to this continent 300 years ago, the longhorn cattle had run wild, inhabiting the prairies of Texas and the Southwest in great numbers. North of Oklahoma City near the Kansas state line, the Great Salt Plains State Park is unique. From the observation tower near Cherokee there is a wide view of the plains whose salt cover attracts a great variety of wild animals.

Below: The annual American Indian Exposition at Anadarko is managed entirely by Indians.

Below right: Prayer Tower at Tulsa's Oral Roberts University, a church-related college with an ultra-modern campus.

Below left: The Will Rogers Memorial at Claremore honors a great American humorist.

New Orleans

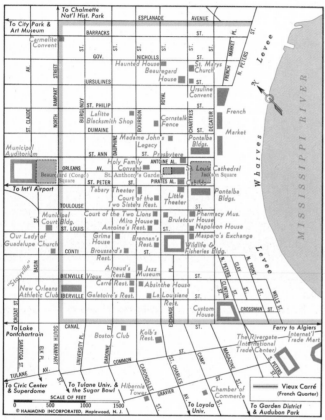

sippi seems a miracle. You visit one of the cemeteries with its above-ground crypts, and you realize that any grave or hole two feet deep filled up with black swamp water immediately. You see the pumping stations at various points of the city and realize that they are necessary to keep streets and cellars dry. You approach the levee and see the steamers tower high above you; the level of the Mississippi may be 20 feet above the level of the town. Obviously only a community which was willing to rebuild again and again could survive floods, conflagrations, tornadoes and epidemics. Yet this dangerously built city became America's gayest.

THE PAST AND THE PRESENT MERGE. The French Quarter is but a small part of the metropolis, but for the traveler it is the greatest attraction. You can see it all on foot. You walk through narrow streets and alleys and look into patios and courtyards where banana and oleander bushes thrive around 150-year-old staircases. Pause for a moment at Pirate's Alley in the shadow of St. Louis Cathedral; look at the stately Pontalba Buildings, the first apartment houses in America; visit the Cabildo, which was the Spanish government house and is now an interesting museum; admire the iron-lace balconies and watch the numerous artists perpetuate the treasured sights in paintings and drawings. You will actually get the feel of history. This is the square on which the French flag was lowered and the Stars and Stripes rose high when the world's greatest real estate transaction was consummated. Until then empires had to be conquered. Here, in 1803, an empire was purchased at 4 cents an acre. At Bourbon Street, on the second floor of the Absinthe House, Andrew Jackson and Jean Laffitte planned the defense of New Orleans in 1815. A small but clever American army beat a large British one brilliantly but unnecessarily, as the peace had been signed two weeks before the battle. You will feel the continuity from the past to the present. There is no restoration as in Williamsburg, which in parts is too spic and span to be convincing. The French Quarter is in good, habitable condition, and if some edges are frayed a little, they are not hidden.

CULTURE AND BURLESQUE, MARDI GRAS AND THE BLUES. During the day Royal Street will intrigue you. It is the antique capital of the United States, where you may furnish a home with a complete set of genuine antiques of any given period. Purchasers like to think that the chandelier they bought had once graced a great Louisiana plantation home, but that is almost certainly not so. Antique dealing is an international business with its main sources of supply in Europe. There are also numerous book and art shops

A FRENCH CITY? Mark Twain called New Orleans "Paris in America." So did Thackeray. Yet many visiting Frenchmen do not perceive any French atmosphere. Architects confirm that the old homes in the Vieux Carré with their patios and iron grillwork are Spanish rather than French. Gastronomes assert that the city's famous cuisine is based on the spices of the Delta and the bounty of the Gulf; it is Creole, not French. Connoisseurs of fine wine discover that New Orleans prefers mint juleps and Ramos gin fizz to the vintages. And entertainment experts find the striptease nightclub shows as American and un-Parisian as apple pie. All that is a tribute to New Orleans. It does not imitate but is fascinating in its own right.

LIVING DANGEROUSLY. That a great and gay metropolitan city should have grown on the lower Missis-

A HERITAGE in the ART of LIVING

Artistic iron railings, often created by master artisans who were slaves, are a tradition in New Orleans.

The New Orleans Mardi Gras is matched only by the carnivals of Nice and Rio de Janeiro.

which lend a cultural touch to the street; fine etchings, old maps and rare books may be bought at reasonable prices. At night the scene shifts to Bourbon Street where for almost nine blocks bars and clubs flourish in profusion. The air is most festive around midnight when cars move slowly, people fill the sidewalks, and rock music resounds from everywhere. You look around and are not at all sure whether that elegant gentleman is a banker or a gambler, whether the pretty young lady in front of you might be a debutante or a call girl; surely all these are represented. The core of every nightclub performance is the striptease which in vigor and liberality has been brought to perfection here. The annual climax of this wine-women-and-song trend is, of course, Mardi Gras. Since its joys are well-known and often described, it is mentioned here only in passing. New Orleans, as everyone knows, is the birthplace of jazz, of "the blues." Jazz parades are still common in the French Quarter, and you are welcome to march along. The Jazz Museum on Bourbon Street owns the world's greatest collection of jazz memorabilia.

THE HEAVENLY FOOD. There is no doubt that New Orleans is America's gastronomic capital. The names of such restaurants as Antoine's, Galatoire's, Arnaud's, Broussard's and Brennan's are nationally and even internationally known; fine food is served in practically every restaurant in town. Even the sandwiches ordered by the dock workers in little eating places are works of art: crusty French bread, hollowed out, contains delicious fillings. The town's specialty is seafood which the bayous and the Gulf furnish in prime quality: crawfish and crabs, shrimps and oysters, and the splendid pompano. Flaming desserts are featured by all the luxurious restaurants. Just before the cherries jubilee, the café brulot or the crepes Sûzettes flare up, the electric lights are dimmed and everybody enjoys the spectacle. A night of merrymaking should end with an old New Orleans tradition, a visit to the French Market on the waterfront where French-style café au lait and fresh doughnuts are served to dock workers and tourists, market vendors and socialites during the wee hours of the morning.

127

Louisiana's Delta Country

LOUISIANA DEPT. OF COMMERCE AND INDUSTRY

The arrival of the shrimp boat is cause for celebration in Morgan City.

RIVERS THAT FLOW THE WRONG WAY. The early explorers of the lower Mississippi were puzzled to discover "tributaries" which did not flow into but away from the big river, ambling southward toward the Gulf of Mexico. The French called them bayous, a variation of an Indian name. The bayous form a cobweb of waterways, a wet and tangled wilderness that remained practically uninhabited until the latter part of the eighteenth century when the Acadians arrived and settled there. The Acadian pioneers would be relatively unknown today were it not for Longfellow's "Evangeline," a literary staple in the American high school diet. Consequently, almost everybody is aware of the heartbreaking odyssey of the French peasants expelled by the English from Nova Scotia, then part of a territory called Acadia, who finally found their way to French-speaking Louisiana. Their country is not exactly a

tourist center in the sense of big hotels and motor courts at every corner, but it will have a two-fold appeal to many. First, the landscape of tangled streams and live oaks, bright green sugarcane fields and somber cypress swamps has an unusual tropical charm; and second, the people are one of America's most interesting ethnic groups.

"RIDING ON A DEW." The Cajuns, their descendants, have become an integral part of the landscape. Gentle, gay, religious and prolific, they have grown deep roots in their new homeland; about 4,000 arrived, and now there are hundreds of thousands of them. They settled along the bayous and made Bayou Lafourche the longest "village" street on earth, lining it on both sides with farmhouses and country stores for 85 miles. They never owned slaves and are content to cultivate their small patches of corn, sugarcane and vegetables, to fish and to trap. Adapting themselves to local conditions they invented the pirogue, a canoe handcarved from a single cypress log and able to "ride out a flood and travel on a dew." The pirogues are difficult to manage but develop incredible speed. The annual pirogue race held on Bayou Barataria over a 5-mile course is a unique event. Fishing is excellent in the bayous, swamps and lakes and, contrary to general belief, the same area is also America's greatest provider of furs because of its enormous muskrat population. In such a setting the Cajuns preserve their old ways, have created a colorful French patois and a rich folklore. Imaginatively they peopled the bayous with strange creatures, for instance

THE BAYOUS of the ACADIANS

The park around the State Capitol of Louisiana is a quiet oasis in the industrially thriving city of Baton Rouge.

Bayou Lafourche is a famous waterway in the lush Acadian country.

the loup-garous, cousins to the European werewolves. These monsters, half wolf and half man, are cursed souls or wicked humans turned vampires. They hold their annual witches' ball, a wild orgy, on Bayou Goula.

EVANGELINE LAND. Center of the bayou country is St. Martinville. There on Bayou Teche, at East Port Street, the Evangeline Oak commemorates the landing of the Acadians. According to local tradition this spot also marks the meeting of Emmeline Labiche and Louis Arceneaux, the Evangeline and Gabriel of the Longfellow epic. Unfortunately, and contrary to the poem, reality had a sad ending. The lover had not been faithful and had taken another wife. Emmeline-Evangeline broke down with grief, lost her mind and died shortly afterward. The heroine's grave is marked with a statue. Nearby in the Longfellow-Evangeline State Park the traditional home of Louis Arceneaux is now an Acadian museum, an interesting relic of pioneer life.

TABASCO AND EGRETS. Starting point for the trip to St. Martinville is the busy town of New Iberia, originally a Spanish settlement. Here "Shadows-on-the-Teche" is a famous plantation manor; so solidly was it built in 1830 that its cypress-wood blinds are still the original ones. The beautiful garden with its marble statues and boxwood, bamboo hedges and thriving flowers faces Bayou Teche and may be visited. New Iberia's other great attraction is Avery Island, a solid circle surrounded by sea marshes. It has been in the hands of the Avery-McIlhenny family since the eigh-

teenth century and has been kept for good reasons. The island contains a rock salt dome more than a mile deep; the mine is leased to the International Salt Company. The island also grows the peppers from which the famous McIlhenny Tabasco Sauce is made. The factory which produces the sharp sauce and exports it to many parts of the world may be inspected. To round out nature's largesse, several oil wells unobtrusively pump the black gold. The McIlhenny mansion lies in 200 landscaped acres called Jungle Gardens which, for a fee, are open to the public. The variety of plants, native and exotic, is stupendous; among the latter, varieties of bamboo range from fern-like dwarfs to Chinese giants 60 feet tall. Chinese lotus grows on the lagoon of the Temple Garden, and the Sunken Fern Garden contains 80 varieties. But the most see-worthy spot of the Jungle Gardens is the southeast corner where Bird City is located. This is a great colony of the American egret or snowy heron, a rookery established in 1893. In those days egret plumes were in such demand for ladies' hats that plume hunters had practically exterminated the species. When, after a prolonged absence, Edward McIlhenny returned home, he found the beautiful birds extinct even on Avery Island. Taking along two young helpers, he prowled through the swamps for days until he found seven young birds in a thicket. He took them to his Willow Pond, and they nested and multiplied. Around the edges of the lake he had "apartments" built of bamboo and perched on stilts. The egrets loved the convenience, and more than 125,000 live there now in the country's largest colony.

Galveston, Houston and San Jacinto

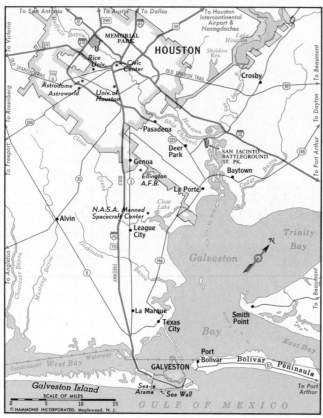

A FORTRESS AGAINST THE SEA. Gently the waves of the Gulf of Mexico ripple over a broad, white, sandy beach where a formidable wall towers 17 feet high like a medieval fortification. Behind that wall the city of Galveston gradually slopes down to the bay side of the island on which it is located. The huge wall was erected as a protection against the sea after the hurricane of 1900 had swept over the city, destroying large parts of it and killing about 6,000 people. Since then the bulwark has withstood several severe tests, and any visitor who happens to be in Galveston during a storm should watch the waves batter the seawall, sometimes throwing sheets of spray 50 feet into the air. But at any time a ride on top of the seawall is an interesting experience. Galveston proper is one of America's most fascinating port cities; its landlocked harbor is connected on the north side with the Gulf by a deep ship

canal. Crowding the docks, dozens of steamers unload their Central American bananas, their Indian jute and Barbadian sugar and take in as cargoes hills of yellow sulphur and mountains of whitish cotton bales. Sailors from every corner of the earth saunter by the curio shops and the consulates of 27 foreign nations. To complete the cosmopolitan atmosphere, most of the town's blacks converse in French patois. Originally they came from Louisiana or the French-speaking West Indies. Galveston is also "the oleander city." In 1841 an oleander shoot was brought to the town from a Caribbean island, and it has multiplied into more than a million oleander bushes which blossom gloriously. Poinsettias and bougainvillaeas thrive with equal vigor. With the Gulf at its front and quiet Galveston Bay at its back door, with five fishing piers and 32 miles of sandy beach, all water sports flourish. Mardi Gras is celebrated in Galveston, and the seawall is an ideal setting for dance pavilions, cafés and nightclubs.

HUNDREDS OF MILLIONAIRES, AND A LEGENDARY SUCCESS STORY. To the west of Galveston Bay there lies the big, modern city which likes to call itself "Houston U.S.A." rather than Houston, Texas. The traveler will find there no eighteenth-century mansions or baroque colonial churches to visit, but clusters of imposing skyscrapers, the headquarters of the oil companies whose gas he buys at the corner station. Some proud resident will tell him that in 1930 Houston had 300,000 inhabitants, 600,000 in 1950, 1,200,000 in 1970 and that it will have a population of 3,000,000 in 1980. The latter figure is not the estimate of an enthusiastic local booster but of Lloyd's of London. You will hear that this inland city, 50 miles from the sea, is one of America's great ports, its link with the ocean being maintained by the ship canal built in 1914. The movement of ocean ships may be watched from the observation platform on Wharf 9. The city was founded as a real estate promotion of the Allen Brothers of New York. In 1837 advertisements praising the new metropolis to the sky appeared in dozens of American newspapers, but when the stern-wheeler *Laura M.* traveled up Buffalo Bayou to Houston, it never noticed the city and traveled past it for three miles. Nevertheless, the land speculation turned out to be a huge success, like almost every other venture attempted there. For Houston symbolizes an America that has been enriched by nature with almost unbelievable lavishness. The Golden Gulf Coast has rich, dark soil on the surface and immense petroleum pools, sulphur mines and salt deposits beneath. It has a hinterland of excellent cotton fields and grazing lands for beef cattle, and it has great natural beauty besides all this. In the residential sections of Houston cypresses, magnolias and live

THE GOLDEN GULF COAST of TEXAS

To travelers approaching Houston at night, the city is a fabulous spectacle.

oaks line the streets, and many mansions have a primeval setting of tangled woodlands draped with wild grapevines and Spanish moss. Roses bloom all year, and bright, subtropical flowers in season. As everybody knows, hundreds of millionaires live in the city, and this wealth has created a number of outstanding institutions. The Astrodome, off South Main Street, is an air-conditioned stadium for major league baseball and football, and the adjacent Astroworld is a super-amusement park. The Jesse H. Jones Hall for the Performing Arts is the home of the excellent Houston Symphony Orchestra, and the widely known Alley Theatre now has its own new building. On NASA Road the Manned Spacecraft Center offers spacecraft exhibits.

THE BATTLEFIELD OF TEXAS INDEPENDENCE.
Twenty-two miles east of Houston a fierce battle was fought in 1836. By modern standards it was microscopic, involving 783 Texans under Sam Houston, about 1,400 Mexicans and three pieces of artillery. But it won independence for Texas, and it was carried out with such vigor and elan that it set the spirit and tenor of the Texan tradition. At a point when the cause of the Texas revolutionaries seemed lost beyond repair, when Santa Anna, the Mexican general, believed he was driving the remnants of the rebellious army into the sea, Sam Houston's men suddenly made a stand where the San Jacinto flows into Buffalo Bayou. On the second day of the battle Houston's men attacked during siesta time and in a furious 18-minute battle annihilated the Mexicans. Santa Anna was picked up in a swampy thicket the following day, and the Republic of Texas was born. Proud and grateful, the Texans of today established San Jacinto Battleground State Park around the battlefield and remembered the great victory of early Texas in the San Jacinto Memorial Monument, with a height of 570 feet. Appropriately it is crowned with the Lone Star of Texas. The tower contains an historical museum and an observation platform that is reached by an elevator. As an additional attraction of the park, the old battleship *Texas* has been anchored in a slip of Buffalo Bayou.

131

San Antonio

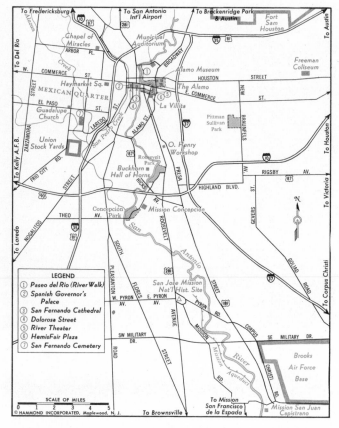

LEGEND
1. *Paseo del Rio (River Walk)*
2. *Spanish Governor's Palace*
3. *San Fernando Cathedral*
4. *Dolorosa Street*
5. *River Theater*
6. *HemisFair Plaza*
7. *San Fernando Cemetery*

SCALE OF MILES
0 1 2 3 4 5
© HAMMOND INCORPORATED, Maplewood, N. J.

VILLAINS AND HEROES. A strange procession trekked laboriously from Mexico City to San Antonio in 1718; the first Captain-General and Governor of the Province of Texas arrived with 1,000 sheep, 548 horses, 200 oxen, 200 cows, but only 72 human beings. The church was represented, of course, and proceeded in its task with admirable vigor, for within 13 years a string of famous missions was established. During the Mexican Revolution San Antonio seceded from Spain, but in 1813 the Spanish General Arredondo recaptured it, smothered some citizens in an airless prison, shot others and mistreated the women. The place where these cruelties occurred is still called "Dolorosa," the Street of Sorrow. During the Texas War of Independence San Antonio witnessed both a triumph and a catastrophe. In December 1835 the Mexican General de Cos surrendered to the victorious revolutionaries,

but on March 6, 1836, the tragedy of the Alamo occurred. One hundred eighty-seven Texans fell heroically in defense of the mission-fortress against an army of more than 5,000 Mexicans. In the 1840's a few thousand German immigrants settled in San Antonio and added to the Spanish flavor beer gardens, sangerfeste and the kaffeeklatsch. After the Civil War the Anglo-American population increased and changed the character of the town. Those were the days of the open range, of the mustangs and the cowboys, of the longhorn herds and the cattle drives, when San Antonio became the lusty capital of a cattle empire, a wide open city teeming with professional gamblers, beautiful women and triggermen. Toward the end of the century the railroads arrived, industries developed and the modern city emerged. During most of its career San Antonio was also an army post, and the large Fort Sam Houston is located within the city limits.

THE CROOKED RIVER. Modern visitors will discover that San Antonio is laid out like an irregular spider web, with most of the sightseeing attractions at or near the center of the web. One of the most pleasant features of the town is the San Antonio River, which meanders along in such a crooked fashion and with so many turns and oxbows that it takes a course of 15 miles to cross 6 miles of city blocks. In a flash of good humor the early Indians of the town coined a name for the river which translated into English means "drunken old man going home at night." The stream has been landscaped very attractively with fountains and walks by the river edge and a unique outdoor theater whose riverbank stage uses a curtain of water. On the site of Hemisfair '68, the Hemisfair Plaza offers the Tower of the Americas mirrored in a lagoon, a skyride, monorail, pavilions and exhibits, all with a Southwestern flavor.

THE TEXAS SHRINE. Of the once mighty fortress-mission of the Alamo only the small gray chapel and some ivy-covered courtyard walls remain. All missions had fallen into decay by the end of the eighteenth century, and by the time of the Alamo tragedy the buildings were roofless ruins filled with debris. But a high rock wall about 3 feet thick was still standing, embracing much of what is now Alamo Plaza. That was the enclosure defended by the Texans who made their last stand in the chapel. The latter remains in its original state except for the new roof and is flanked by the Alamo Museum. In the center of the former fortress area the Cenotaph honors the heroes of the Alamo. The figures of the Texas leaders, Bonham, Crockett, Bowie and Travis appear on the east and west sides. A

OLD SPAIN and MODERN AMERICA

few blocks to the south, La Villita is an interesting restoration of residential houses that were built between 1722 and 1850, the oldest ones erected by the Spaniards. La Villita contains a library, a museum, a theater and interesting shops where the traditional weaving and pottery crafts are kept alive. At the western side of the city's center, on the Main Plaza, San Fernando Cathedral is the oldest parish church in Texas. During the siege of the Alamo Santa Anna occupied the building, flying from its steeple the bloody red flag, signal of "no quarter." The cathedral was completed in 1873, but its rear part is the 1738 original. On the Military Plaza the Spanish Governor's Palace is a long, low white building of ten rooms, with the arms of the Hapsburgs carved into the keystone over the entrance. To the west of the city's center the large Mexican quarter maintains San Antonio's Spanish and Mexican traditions so convincingly that one imagines oneself to be south of the Rio Grande. Among the most colorful fiestas of the Mexican section are The Blessing of the Animals on the 17th of January, the celebration of Dia de Animas, All Souls' Day, at San Fernando Cemetery in November and the Matachines Dances at the Guadalupe Church in December.

SPANISH BAROQUE IN THE WILDERNESS. Artistically and historically, the four missions south of the downtown area are outstanding: Concepción, San José, San Juan Capistrano and San Francisco de la Espada. With fortress-like enclosures, chapels, convents, workrooms and quarters for the Indians, they are fascinating relics of Spanish colonization in America. Thick adobe or stone walls, cloistered arches and front-wall belfries are impressive, and two of the missions can boast of truly artistic treasures. Concepción still preserves some fine ancient frescoes, painted by the monks in dyes prepared from various plants and clays, and San José, the "queen of the missions," is rich in beautiful, rock-carved ornamentations in the decorative Spanish baroque style. The sculptor, Pedro Huizar, who worked there for five years, was the descendant of a great family of artists who helped create the Alhambra at Granada in Spain.

The lovely River Walk along the landscaped San Antonio River.

The Alamo, once a mission-fortress, is now an American sanctuary.

Big Bend National Park

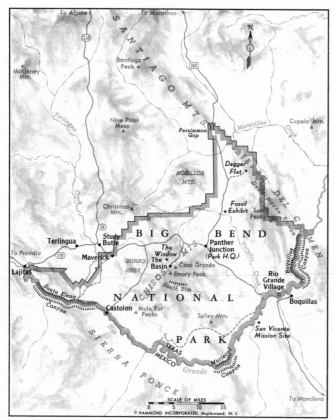

ground. At a height of 5,400 feet the car rolls into a great rocky basin, where overnight accommodations are located. Park headquarters are at Panther Junction. On the rim of the bowl, Emory Peak towers as the tallest of the range, 7,835 feet high. Casa Grande is a castle-like mass of rock, and when the morning mist rises from the valley it looks like a medieval fortress on a mountaintop. The stone wall surrounding the basin is not a complete circle, though. A V-shaped opening called The Window offers a breathtaking view across Burro Mesa into Old Mexico. A horseback ride on the south rim presents a stretch of America that has remained untouched by civilization, with a 100-mile perspective south into Mexico and another 100-mile view north into our country. Three canyons cut by the Rio Grande are located within the park, the Mariscal, Boquillas and Santa Elena. All three may be negotiated on rubber rafts, but only by skillful and daring navigators. Santa Elena Canyon is a 15-mile narrow chasm of wild water between sheer, towering rock walls. Then suddenly the river emerges in the open, pleasant and in broad daylight, an ideal fishing spot.

In spite of its remoteness, the Big Bend country has its share of frontier history. An Indian tribe called the West Texas Cave Dwellers were the first to live here. Later came the Comanches and Apaches. White man discovered Big Bend at an early date. According to tradition Spaniards found here a fabulous silver mine and worked it with Indian slaves. However, the Spanish intruders vanished from the scene, and ever since the search for the Lost Mine has stirred the imagination of treasure hunters.

THE DESERT: AN ACQUIRED TASTE. Easterners and Southerners who live among lush green hills approach the desert with a prejudice, expecting it to be colorless, drab and monotonous. But watching it with an open mind for only a few days at the right season will change their opinion. Gradually they will come under the desert's spell. Looking at a sunset from any hill in the Big Bend desert with the Chisos Mountains, the Dead Horse Range and the Sierra del Carmen in view, they will witness a rare spectacle. As the shadows lengthen, the colors deepen. The yellow cliffs are suffused with pink light, the gray layers turn into magenta, the red bands take on a violet hue. Now the lower tiers of the ranges change first into purple, then into deep black while the highest peaks still flash with the bright colors of the last rays of the sun. A few more minutes, and all outlines merge into the darkness of the night.

After the late spring rains, when the prickly pears and the chollas, the purple-tinged cactus and the strawberry cactus, the yuccas and the amaryllis are in bloom, the desert is a sight to behold. In May the

THE PHANTOM MOUNTAINS. Way down south the Rio Grande makes a "wrong" 90-degree turn toward the northeast on its southward journey from Colorado to the Gulf of Mexico. Here a great, untamed wilderness has been set aside as **Big Bend National Park.** No railroad, airline or superhighway leads into this last frontier, but it can be reached by car quite easily. Traveling over a desert of sand and stone, one sees a row of mountains rise like an island from the plateau, their jagged peaks cutting deep indentations into the blue sky. These are the Chisos Mountains, and the name — meaning phantoms — is well chosen. For in a certain light and time of day they look like a mirage. But the traveler finds it very real as the road winds up a canyon and the cacti and desert plants are gradually replaced by green oaks and clean-smelling pines. Cool springs trickle from rocks, and soft grass covers the

A GLANCE into the LIVING DESERT

The River Road along the Rio Grande leads from Presidio, Texas, to Big Bend National Park.
It crosses an untamed, inhospitable wilderness.

flowering of the century plants at the foot of Casa Grande is an experience to be remembered. For 20 to 25 years — not for one hundred as the name suggests — these agaves have grown to a climax, and overnight the bright and large yet infinitely delicate flower opens. Then the plant begins to die. Lechuguilla belongs to the same family; the Mexican peasants extract tough fibers from it to weave a hundred household items such as ropes for harnesses, pouches and saddlebags. Then there is the living-rock, a strange mimic cactus that looks like the rock in which it lives, gray and full of fissures.

FOUR-FOOT CLAMS AND BEWILDERED CAMELS. At the northern park entrance a rock formation called Persimmon Gap shows that animal life has flourished here since time immemorial. Among the fossil remains are giant oyster and clam shells, one of them 4 feet long and almost 3 feet wide. The head of a crocodile measures 45 feet, and the bones of dinosaurs were discovered at that spot. Since the beginning of historical times the fauna has not changed greatly. Only the large herds of pronghorn antelope that used to live here were either killed by hunters or wandered away when the newly introduced sheep and goats made short shrift of the fine herbs that served as antelope food. Fortunately, with the founding of the National Park the "useful" animals have disappeared. John Muir called the sheep "hoofed locusts" and Freeman Tilden denounced the goats as "long-haired Japanese beetles." The range has been happily returned to the javelina, puma and the kit fox, the white-tailed and the mule deer, to the reintroduced pronghorn antelope and to all the small mammals and reptiles that inhabit the desert. In 1856 a strange cavalcade crossed the Big Bend country, consisting of a patrol of U.S. soldiers and a long file of camels. These Old World animals had been introduced by the army to facilitate transportation in the desert. But the Civil War ended the project, and the camels were released. It would be pleasant to report that they have become part of the American scene, but eventually they all vanished.

135

West of the Pecos

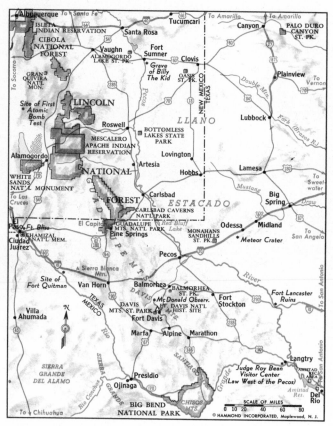

rugged mountain ranges appear, either shutting off a broad valley in a distant purple haze or crowding the highway with steep cliffs, their peaks rising to heights of from 5,000 to nearly 9,000 feet. In some stretches the country seems to be entirely uninhabited, but let there be a Fourth of July celebration or a barbecue or a rodeo, and a surprising number of families appear from hidden valleys and distant mesas. Indeed, the rodeo is said to have originated there. Nobody minds spending untold hours in travel, and to this day many a rancher has to ride 50 miles to reach the nearest post office or to buy a bag of lemons in the general store. This is not really tourist country, and no midsummer visit is recommended. But crossing it in spring or fall, perhaps on the way to Big Bend National Park, is an exhilarating experience.

BALMORHEA: LUSH OASIS. 24,000,000 gallons of water every day — that is one of the occasional surprises of the arid land. It happens at San Solomon Springs, and appropriately the pleasant Balmorhea State Park has been established around this clear flow. A 10,000-acre tract is irrigated by the spring water, with the small town of Balmorhea as a market center.

DAVIS MOUNTAINS: RUGGED BUT FOREST-CROWNED. Southwest of Pecos the rangelands of sagebrush and yucca form undulating foothills where sudden gusts of wind blow dried weeds high into the air in a brief whirling dance. Then the Davis Mountains arise, their ruggedness mitigated by a cover of refreshing green woods. In Davis Mountains State Park you may hike, swim, ride horseback and admire the beauty of upper Limpia Canyon. In season, a startling display of bright wildflowers, including orchids and cacti, will greet you. You may see deer, bear and pronghorn antelope, and although you may not encounter a puma, it is quite true that they live there, too. On one of the higher mountains of the range, Mt. Locke (altitude 6,850 feet), the McDonald Observatory is located. One of the country's large observatories, it is open to the public at certain hours, and occasionally public star-gazing sessions are conducted at night.

AN OASIS AGAIN. Nearby to the southeast, the picturesque town of Alpine lies in a green valley between tall mountains. The shade trees in the streets, the large state parks to the north and south, the many dude ranches and the campus of Sul Ross State University are pleasant, but more interesting to the traveler is the western twang in the town's atmosphere: the high-heeled boots, the Highland Herefords, a famous prize cattle of the region, the cowboys and the cattle barons, the sheepherders and the goat ranchers.

FIFTY MILES TO GET YOUR MAIL. The Pecos River, a tributary of the Rio Grande, was the trail of the Spanish conquistadores. But throughout the centuries it remained a lonely frontier river, one of the roughest the 1880's experienced. "West of the Pecos" became a nationally known phrase implying that no law existed beyond that line. At one time there was even a verb derived from Pecos, either from the river or from the small cow town whose streets were lined with hitching rails. "Pecosin' a guy" referred to a treatment in which a man was shot, his corpse filled with rocks and the body dumped into the river. Of course, more civilized practices have reached the Pecos by now, but the whole western end of Texas is still a vast and lonely country. Plains and mesas roll away to all horizons. The occasional goat or sheep ranches are huge domains because the grazing land is a semi-desert. Every so often wild,

LAST FRONTIER with a TOUCH of the OLD WEST

"Officers Row" at Fort Davis National Historic Site, a memento of Indian and frontier wars.

El Capitan Peak, east of El Paso, in the rugged Guadalupe Mountains.

EL CAPITAN AND THE BUTTERWORTH STAGE. The new Guadalupe Mountains National Park, formerly a huge goat ranch containing some of the most spectacular scenery in the West is being developed but not open to the public yet. The Information Center is east of Pine Springs on U.S. 62. The highway follows much the same route as used by the Butterworth Stage Line in 1858 and passes close to the familiar massive silhouette of El Capitan.

EL PASO: BRIDGE BETWEEN TWO NATIONS. From a mountaintop the great statue of El Cristo Rey looks down upon the city. On the background of a white cross, the Savior's arms point to the north and the south of the U.S.-Mexican boundary, symbolizing the two-nation character of El Paso and the two cultures united in the same religion. El Paso, western cornerstone of Texas, has a history quite different from that of the cattle towns which sprang up overnight. Located at a natural pass through the mountains, El Paso was a crossing point before the arrival of the Spaniards. Cabeza de Vaca found flourishing Indian pueblos in the region of the present-day town as early as 1536. He commented on the Indians' strength and intelligence and marveled at the huge buffalo herds. The town did not take part in the Texas Revolution, and ever since it has been a city of two friendly nationalities. Its at-home-abroad atmosphere has a special charm for the traveler who will also appreciate El Paso's fine winter climate. Ysleta, the oldest town in Texas, is now a part of El Paso. There are few actual sightseeing attractions, but it is an intriguing experience to hear English and Spanish spoken with equal fluency; to take a scenic drive along Franklin Mountain, the southernmost peak of the Rockies; to see reconstructed Fort Bliss, a cavalry outpost of the frontier; to visit Ciudad Juárez across the Rio Grande; to enjoy, on the other side of the river, the adobe stores with their flamboyant displays of chili peppers, varied fruits, sombreros and folk art souvenirs; and to buy, perhaps, a native piece of hand-tooled leather or a handwoven Mexican rug.

137

Sightseeing Guide

ARKANSAS

NORTHERN ARKANSAS. The Ozark Mountains, known for their original folkways, huge springs, float trips, picturesque hills and limestone caverns, are described on pages 122-123. Fayetteville, the largest city in the Ozarks, is the seat of the University of Arkansas. Eureka Springs, near the Missouri state line, is an Ozark spa with 63 mineral springs within its city limits. It is attractively built on a steep hillside and is a center for such native crafts as wood carvings, pottery, quilts and hooked rugs. East of Eureka Springs, Berryville has a museum of hand guns used by Jesse James and Cole Younger, Wild Bill Hickok and Pancho Villa. Bella Vista, on the edge of the Ozarks, is a popular resort with a spring from which two million gallons gush out every day. In north central Arkansas the Norfork and Bull Shoals dams are two of the major dams in the nation. East of Norfork Dam, Mammoth Spring is another fabulous spring with a flow of 840,000 gallons a minute. Fort Smith on the Oklahoma state line is the gateway to the Ozark Mountains in the north and the Ouachita Mountains in the south. The foundations of the fort built in 1817 still stand.

CENTRAL ARKANSAS. The Ouachita Mountains are a pine covered highland popular with fishermen and campers. Wildflowers abound in the Petit Jean State Park near Morrilton. Little Rock, the state capital, is famous for its three capitol buildings. The Territorial Capitol Restoration is a complex of 13 buildings including the frontier cabin capitol. The Old State House is rated as the most beautiful building in Arkansas; it now houses the Arkansas Museum of History and Archives. The present State Capitol, with its gilded dome and walls of white Arkansas marble and granite, is the prosperous successor to its modest forerunners. The rice center of Stuttgart, southeast of Little Rock, is well-known for its duck hunting. Hot Springs, both the national park with its 47 mineral springs and the luxurious resort city which welcomes Northerners in wintertime and Southerners in summertime, is described on page 123. The only diamond mine in the United States is located near Murfreesboro, southwest of Hot Springs. For a fee tourists may go diamond hunting on their own; they may keep everything under 5 carats, but the mine owners receive a percentage from larger finds. One tourist actually picked up a 15-carat diamond. Arkansas Post National Memorial near DeWitt was an important military and trading post under France, Spain, the United States and the Confederacy.

LOUISIANA

NORTHERN LOUISIANA. Shreveport is named after Captain Shreve, who rammed and broke loose the centuries-old log jam on the Red River and opened the river for navigation. The town calls itself queen city of a three-state area, embracing parts of Louisiana, Arkansas and Texas. Visitors are attracted to Shreveport in late April when it celebrates a Holiday in Dixie.

CENTRAL LOUISIANA. Alexandria is headquarters of Kisatchie National Forest, a picturesque region of bayous and lakes, cypresses and live oaks draped with Spanish moss. Natchitoches, the oldest town in Louisiana, was founded about 1714 as a trading post.

SOUTHERN LOUISIANA. New Orleans is described on pages 126-127. The Streetcar Named Desire, made famous by the Tennessee Williams play, is displayed near the French Market. A harbor tour is offered by the boat *President,* and a 32-mile bayou trip is made by the *Voyageur.* Lake Pontchartrain, reached from New Orleans on a palm lined highway, is a very large, almost circular body of water with many miles of sandy beaches. Fontainebleau State Park is located at the lake's northern rim. The lake is crossed by the 24-mile-long Pontchartrain Causeway. Baton Rouge, the capital of Louisiana, is 200 miles from the sea, yet the city is a port for oceangoing vessels, with extensive modern docks flanked by huge industrial plants. A red staff (baton rouge) on a bluff above the Mississippi River supposedly indicated the demarcation line between the territories of Indian tribes, and after the white settlement had been founded a succession of seven different flags flew over the town. The city's outstanding structure is the skyscraper of the State Capitol, the successor to the gothic castle which served as the old capitol. The latter's handwrought iron fence and spiral staircase are much admired. Standing on a bluff above the river, the new state house is seen from everywhere, and its lookout platform, some 30 stories aboveground, offers a grand panorama of the city, the winding river and the broad plains. Baton Rouge is also the heart of the southern magnolia country, and the Capitol is surrounded by some perfectly beautiful specimens. These magnolias are not bushes but trees up to 80 feet tall and perhaps a century old. At the southern edge of the city the campus of Louisiana State University is located. The Bayou Country — in scenery, population, customs, language and folklore unique in the United States — is described on pages 128-129. Its principal points are St. Martinville with the Longfellow-Evangeline Memorial Park and New Iberia with Avery Island. The city of Lafayette has its own 5-mile Azalea Trail, marked for visitors every year in the middle of March. Lake Charles, surrounded by oil fields and rice plantations, is both a modern deepwater port and a recreational area. The Sabine National Wildlife Refuge, a haven for millions of migrating waterfowl, is nearby. Grand Isle, an outpost near the Mississippi Delta and terminus of Highway 1, was once the headquarters for Laffitte and his band of pirates. Many of today's islanders trace their family background to those colorful ancestors. Deep-sea fishing is outstanding there.

OKLAHOMA

NORTHERN OKLAHOMA. Pensacola Dam near Vinita forms the Lake O'The Cherokees and creates a great playground for fishermen and sailors; like most man-made reservoirs, Lake O'The Cherokees has numerous little bays and harbors where people keep boats. The Woolaroc Art Museum stands in a game preserve 14 miles from Bartlesville; buffalo, longhorns and big game animals from other continents are kept in the preserve. The museum collection displays Indian art objects, trophies and costumes, mostly of the Osage tribe. In the Oklahoma Panhandle Black Mesa State Park is a recreational area of mesas and canyons. The Indian pictographs in the park are six feet high, are painted in brilliant blue on sand-colored rock and extend for a whole mile. Near Freedom, 110 miles northwest of Enid, the Alabaster Caverns may be visited; electric light brings out the fantastic shapes and colors of the rocks. As in the Carlsbad Caverns, huge numbers of bats live in the caves, swarm out at twilight and return before sunrise. A 150-foot-high natural bridge is a special attraction near the caverns. Tulsa, the oil center, and the Will Rogers Memorial at Claremore are described on pages 124-125. Sixty miles southeast of Muskogee, the three ancient Spiro Indian Mounds antedate the era of the white man. The origin of these monuments is not certain, but they are estimated to be a thousand years old.

SOUTHERN OKLAHOMA. Oklahoma City with the State Capitol is described on page 124. The National Cowboy Hall of Fame

SOUTH CENTRAL REGION

with displays of fine Western art is located there. Twenty miles to the south, Norman is the seat of the University of Oklahoma. Northwest of Lawton the Wichita Mountains Wildlife Refuge is not only an interesting game preserve of buffalo, pronghorn antelope and elk herds but also a public playground with 90 small and 15 large lakes, all of them man-made and stocked with various species of fish. From the summit of Mt. Scott, which can be reached by car, a wide panorama of hills, blue waters, boulders and rock formations may be enjoyed. The Wichita Mountains Easter Pageant, staged in the wildlife refuge by the citizens of Lawton, draws large numbers of spectators. Near Sulphur, Platt National Park is a preserve of 32 large and many small springs in a setting of streams and wildflowers, woods and distant views of the Arbuckle Mountains. West of the park at Davis the Turner Falls are a lovely cascade. South and east of Ardmore Lake Murray is a rendezvous for fishermen, sailors and swimmers. Nearby the huge man-made Lake Texoma also has excellent facilities for all water sports; the scenery surrounding the lake is beautiful. The ride from Madill to Durant via the mile-long Roosevelt Bridge offers interesting views.

TEXAS

THE COAST OF TEXAS. The countryside around Port Arthur is that of the Deep South, with Spanish moss and cypress swamps. The city itself has palm lined streets and magnolia shaded gardens. But the life blood of the region is oil. Neighboring Beaumont is also an important harbor and oil town; the famous Spindletop Field is close-by. The colorful Gulf port of Galveston, the millionaires' city of Houston and the San Jacinto Battlefield are described on pages 130-131. Corpus Christi is both an industrial ocean port and a Gulf Coast playground. Spearing flounders on the bottom of a shallow bay at night is an exciting Gulf Coast sport; Padre Island National Seashore is a mecca for shell collectors.

EASTERN TEXAS. In Texarkana the state line runs through the heart of the city; the eastern half belongs to Arkansas, the western to Texas. South of Texarkana, Caddo Lake State Park is a huge, fantastic and eerily beautiful maze of bayous, cypress swamps, half-sunken banks and moss draped live oaks. Fish and wildlife abound, and the native Caddo Negroes are noted guides. To the west the town of Tyler is an outstanding rose growing district. South of Tyler at Huntsville the first president of the Republic of Texas, Sam Houston, had his last home, and there he died. Houston's law office, his residence called the Steamboat House and the Sam Houston Memorial Museum welcome visitors.

CENTRAL TEXAS. Waco, a great cotton market, is the seat of Baylor University. In Longhorn State Park, southwest of Waco, the Longhorn Cavern is a large, partly explored limestone cave with lovely crystal formations. Austin is the state capital and the home of the University of Texas with the site of the Lyndon Baines Johnson Library. The building of the French Legation in the Republic of Texas points to a proud era in the history of the state. West of Austin at Johnson City is Lyndon B. Johnson National Historic Site, including his birthplace and his boyhood home. Eighty-five miles from Austin the 1,850-foot-high Bear Mountain offers a magnificent panorama; on the summit Balanced Rock is a huge boulder resting precariously on two granite points. West of Austin, Fredericksburg is a German settlement; its houses with their thick walls, steep roofs and outside stairs have the look of old homes along the Neckar and the Rhine. San Antonio with the Alamo and the

fine old Spanish missions is described on pages 132-133. Nearby Palmetto State Park is a miniature Yellowstone with mud geysers and hot and cold sulphur springs. Ninety miles southeast of San Antonio, Goliad's Presidio La Bahia is a Texas historical shrine, the scene of the Fannin massacre of 1836. The ruins of the presidio and the mission it protected are open to visitors. The Paint Rock Pictographs on a slope of the Concho River about 70 miles south of Abilene are interesting.

NORTHERN TEXAS. Gainesville has become well-known for its nonprofit community circus. Dallas is a streamlined modern metropolis, rich from oil and cotton, literate and sophisticated, the style center of the Southwest. Its Neiman-Marcus store is one of the country's most elegant and expensive shops. Dallas has a fine symphony orchestra and is the seat of Southern Methodist University. Its Fair Park is modern and impressive and is the scene of the Texas State Fair, a tremendous show; its Texas Hall of State is a pioneer museum. Near the cabin of John Neely Bryan, the founder of Dallas, President John F. Kennedy was assassinated. Fort Worth, the friendly rival of Dallas, is equally rich and equally modern but retains a more typically Western atmosphere of friendliness; it is the home of Texas Christian University. Among the city's attractions are a huge new convention center, the Botanical Garden in Trinity Park, the Texas Frontier Centennial Park with its Texas Pioneer Memorial Tower and the impressive cluster of buildings around Amon Carter Square, including the Will Rogers Memorial Coliseum, several museums and a theater. Between Dallas and Fort Worth, Arlington offers a thrilling show called "Six Flags Over Texas." North of Fort Worth, two manmade lakes offer fishing and water sports facilities — Eagle Mountain Lake, at a distance of 14 miles, and Lake Bridgeport, 50 miles away.

TEXAS PANHANDLE. Once a desolate and forbidding ranch country, the Texas Panhandle is now largely a prosperous agricultural region growing grain, cotton and vegetables, with oil bringing additional wealth. Amarillo, the center of the Panhandle, grew from a huddle of buffalo hide shacks to a modern, progressive city. South of Amarillo at Canyon, the Panhandle-Plains Museum exhibits a fascinating collection of relics from the days of the longhorns.

WESTERN TEXAS. El Paso, the ancient crossroads between Mexico and the north, Pecos, Balmorhea State Park with its huge spring, Fort Davis and the Davis Mountains with McDonald Observatory, Guadalupe Mountains National Park and the oasis of Alpine are described on pages 136-137. Big Bend National Park, a fascinating mountain wilderness facing old Mexico across the Rio Grande, is described on pages 134-135.

SOUTHERN TEXAS. Laredo, locale of a popular cowboy song, is the starting point of the Pan American Highway to Mexico City. Across the Rio Grande, Nuevo Laredo is popular with tourists because of its bullfights and night life. South of Corpus Christi, between the Rio Grande and the Gulf, the King Ranch is one of the largest cattle ranches on earth. Managed along scientific lines, the ranch is noted for the development of the Santa Gertrudis breed of cattle. The lower Rio Grande Valley was once largely a desert, but modern irrigation has turned it into a rich farming region producing citrus fruits, cotton and early vegetables. Brownsville, the center of the region, enjoys a strongly Mexican atmosphere, and the annual Charro Days Festival during the week before Lent is a gay fiesta with Latin American overtones.

Northwest Map

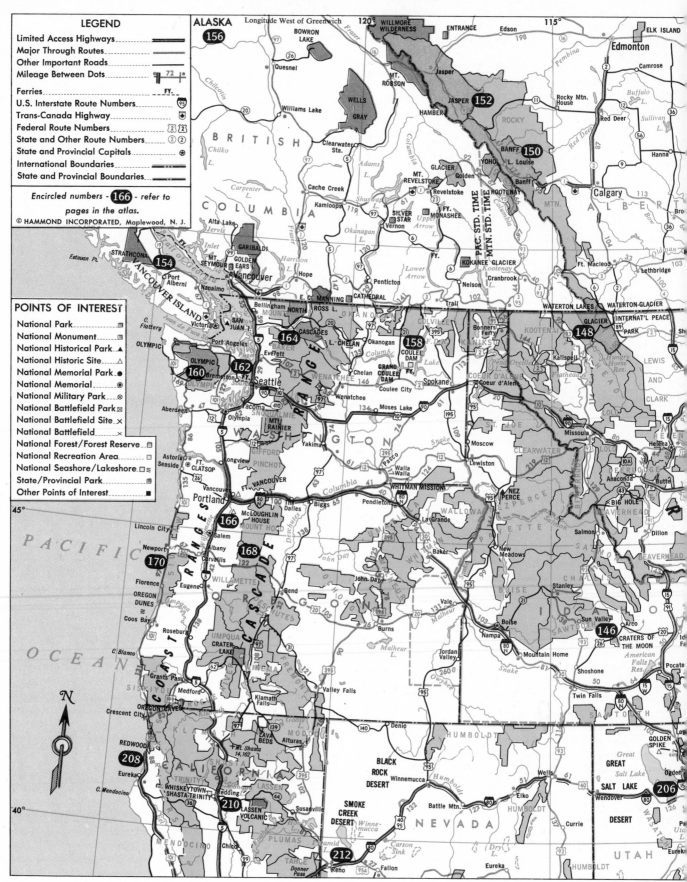

WHAT to SEE in the NORTHWEST REGION

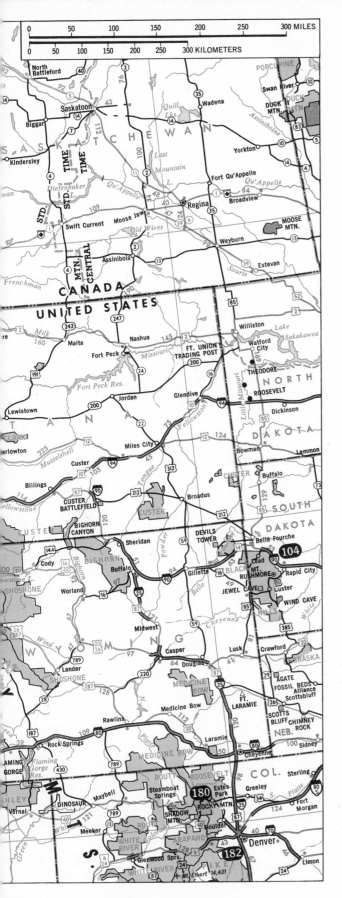

TWO-WEEK TRIP ALONG THE AXIS OF THE NORTHERN ROCKIES. For a general introduction see pages 142-145, 148-151; also sightseeing guide pages 172-177. Suggested route: Jackson, Wyoming, in the old Indian country. For the entertainment of tourists, the Cache Creek Posse chases badmen across the town square nightly at seven — Grand Teton National Park with Jackson Hole, a beautiful valley with picturesque peaks, blue lakes and year-round glaciers and snowfields — Yellowstone National Park, famous for its gorges, geysers, mud volcanoes, bubbling "paint pots" and the Grand Canyon of the Yellowstone River. The park contains many forms of wildlife, especially bears — Butte, Montana. Tourists may visit the Kelley Copper Mine of the Anaconda Company — Missoula, Montana — Glacier National Park, with 50 living glaciers. The Going-to-the-Sun Road crosses the Continental Divide and offers glimpses of the park's elk, deer, bear, bighorn sheep and mountain goats — Calgary, Alberta, Canada. The annual Calgary Stampede, which includes regular rodeo contests and a wild chuckwagon race, is a thrilling performance. A reconstructed frontier village shows a Hudson's Bay Company trading post — At Banff National Park is Lake Louise, possibly the world's most beautiful scenic spot with towering mountains, fabulous valleys and bighorn sheep, Rocky Mountain goats, cougars, coyotes, black bears, grizzly bears, elk, moose, and mule deer — Jasper National Park, another superb mountain park with varied wildlife; the park includes Mount Robson, tallest peak of the Canadian Rockies.

TEN-DAY TRIP THROUGH IDAHO. For a general introduction see pages 146-147, also sightseeing guide pages 172-177. Suggested route: Twin Falls. Its Perrine Memorial Bridge offers grand views of the Snake River — Craters of the Moon National Monument, a weird landscape of volcanic basalt formations — Sun Valley, one of America's most fashionable winter resorts — Coeur d'Alene, on a sparkling lake of the same name, a center of silver, zinc and lead mining — Lewiston on the Grand Canyon of the Snake River. With a depth of 7,900 feet the canyon, now covered by a reservoir, is the deepest gorge on the North American continent — Boise, the state capital. A pioneer log cabin village recreates Idaho's frontier days — Twin Falls.

EXCURSION THROUGH THE PACIFIC NORTHWEST. For a general introduction see pages 154-157, 160-165, also sightseeing guide pages 172-177. Suggested route: Seattle offers Seattle Center with monorail and 607-foot Space Needle — Mount Rainier National Park with the 14,410-foot peak and a fabulous mountain highway to Sunrise at the foot of Emmons Glacier — Olympia, the state capital — Olympic National Park with rain forest and Roosevelt elk — ferry ride from Port Angeles to Victoria, capital of British Columbia, a beautiful garden spot — from Nanaimo ferry ride to Vancouver — from here a one- or two-week cruise to Alaska is recommended.

TEN-DAY EXCURSION THROUGH OREGON. For a general introduction see pages 166-171, also sightseeing guide pages 172-177. Suggested route: Portland, City of Roses, with snow-capped Mount Hood as a backdrop — along the spectacular coastal highway to Newport with Undersea Gardens and Marine Science Center — Sea Lion Caves — Oregon Dunes — Umpqua Lighthouse — Coos Bay, a leading lumber port — east to Crater Lake National Park, a scenic spot of exquisite beauty best enjoyed from the Rim Drive — north to Bend, a ski center with Cascade Lakes Highway — north to Columbia River — Bonneville Dam with salmon ladders — Portland.

Yellowstone National Park

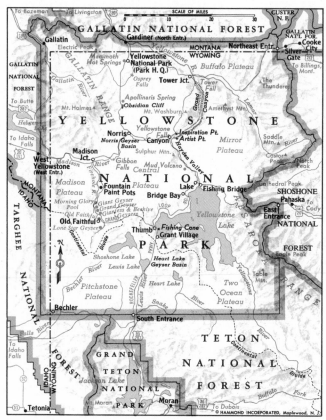

the same fate as their predecessors. Look at Amethyst Mountain in the northeastern corner of the park. A vertical rock section of 2,000 feet shows 12 such successive fossil forests. The trees under which you walk now may in time become the 13th.

The volcanoes are asleep, but the land is still volcanic. Rock deep in the earth retains great heat generated by past volcanic action. It is this heat that makes geysers possible. As water seeps down the hot rocks turn it into steam deep in the earth. The steam tries to escape upward but is stopped by a column of cold water. The pressure increases, some water bubbles over and reduces the weight of the stopper. The steam then rushes out and the geyser erupts.

Old Faithful, which hurls a column of hot water and white steam 90 to 180 feet high into the sky approximately every 65 minutes, has become world famous. Among the others, the Giant and the Giantess throw their spouts to a height of 200 feet, but their eruptions are irregular. Beehive Geyser balances its slender column from a beehive-shaped cone, and Grand Geyser displays a huge fan of spray and steam.

PLANTS AS PAINTERS. The terraces of giant steps painted in brightly sparkling shades of pink and red, tan and blue, brown and gray are another eye-filling phenomenon. Created by the Mammoth Hot Springs, they lie along the northern edge of the park. The colors are the work of tiny algae which thrive in hot water. Where a spring ceases to flow the microscopic plants die, and only the white limestone remains.

The Fountain Paint Pots are a caldron of boiling brown, pink and yellow tints that do not seem to mix properly, and the roaring explosions of Mud Volcano can be heard for a half a mile. Sulphur Mountain and Obsidian Cliff, the hill of natural volcanic glass whose chips were prized by the Indians as arrowheads, are also worth seeing.

CASCADES AND BEARS. If there were no volcanic wonders to be gazed at, Yellowstone Park would still be an outstanding travel goal because its scenery is of superb beauty. Yellowstone Lake, at an altitude of nearly a mile and a half above sea level and with 100 miles of shoreline, is not only the largest American lake at such great height but also one of the wildest or loveliest, depending on the weather and the mood of the day. From Artist's Point or Inspiration Point the Grand Canyon of the Yellowstone River is a symposium of yellow and white, with a pattern of mellowed red, pearly gray and jet black streaks in the rock walls, topped with a border of evergreens. Against this background the whirling and spraying water of the Great Falls drops 308 feet to the canyon floor.

CONTACT WITH THE INNER EARTH. There are three spots on our planet where it is possible to feel very close to the mysterious hot underworld, where you can actually feel its boiling and burning chaos through the soles of your shoes. Two of these places, Iceland and New Zealand, are interesting, but the third, Yellowstone National Park, is fantastic and spectacular. From the sights surrounding you here you can gain a deep perspective into the awe-inspiring story of the earth. Forbidding volcanoes once studded this area, spitting fire and belching black smoke, ashes and lava. They covered the forest with volcanic dust until the trees died, and as the organic matter was replaced by minerals the trunks became petrified. Even the bark, the roots and some leaves turned into stone. For a period the volcanoes slept, and new forests grew on top of the ancient woods. Then the craters awoke again, and the trees experienced

THE WORLD'S GREATEST VOLCANIC OUTDOOR MUSEUM

UNION PACIFIC RAILROAD

Castle Geyser and the other geysers in the park erupt at irregular intervals. Only Old Faithful has a fixed schedule.

UNION PACIFIC RAILROAD

The Upper Falls cascade into the Grand Canyon of the Yellowstone River.

Yellowstone Park is also one of the world's great animal preserves, a veritable outdoor zoo. Thousands of elk, moose, deer and antelope live here. Bands of mountain sheep climb the rocky peaks, a herd of more than 1,000 buffalo graze in the valleys, grizzly bears roam the inaccessible slopes and the hundreds of black bears have become as famous as the geysers. The park service is waging a campaign against the feeding of the bears by visitors who turn the normally self-reliant and good-natured animals into insistent and sometimes dangerous beggars. Lakes and streams are stocked with various kinds of trout, notably cutthroat and brook trout. Almost 800 species of wildflowers bloom profusely throughout the park.

TALL TALES. It is not surprising that so fascinating a region developed a folklore of its own. Handkerchief Pool, they say, would suck your soiled handkerchief out of sight and erupt it a minute later, clean and fresh. Early fishermen liked to cast their lines in Yellowstone Lake near Fishing Cone. Having caught a trout, they dropped the line on the other side into the boiling hot spring, then pulled it out and ate it, all without moving an inch. But the best tale concerns Jim Bridger, Yellowstone's Paul Bunyan. Once, while hunting, he spied a large elk and shot at it. The animal ignored Jim, so he walked on to investigate and bumped head-on into the transparent Mountain of Glass. The elk stood on the other side. Even more astonishing, the mountain acted as a huge magnifying glass; the animal he saw was actually grazing 25 miles away.

Yellowstone Park lies in northwestern Wyoming and extends slightly into Montana and Idaho. With an area of approximately 62 by 54 miles, it is larger than the combined states of Delaware and Rhode Island. John Colter, a member of the Lewis and Clark Expedition, was probably the first white man to see this area in 1807. Later reports by trappers were considered lies until General Washburn's expedition of 1870 established the facts. In 1872 it was set up as the first national park.

143

Grand Tetons and Jackson Hole

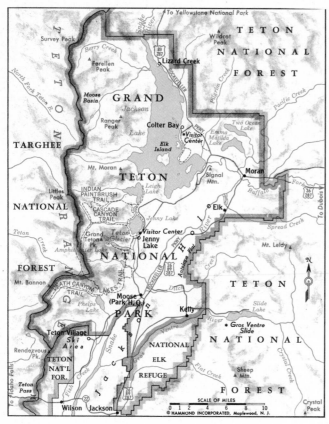

and obtains his first glance of the Grand Tetons across Jackson Lake or drives north and sees the range between some gnarled old trees across Jenny Lake, it becomes quite clear that he moves in a valley of unsurpassed beauty.

At Moose there is a log cabin chapel which has a most unusual altar picture — a simple window with a direct view of the tallest peak of the range, Grand Teton Peak. This picture compares favorably with the finest altar paintings of the old masters. Also at Moose, the ferry that crosses the Snake River is a replica of the primitive ferry which was first operated there in 1892.

THE OLD STAMPING GROUND. Whether or not the Indians and trappers enjoyed the scenic attractions of the spot has not been recorded. It is a fact that they returned there year after year. Jackson Hole — hole because it is a plain surrounded by mountains, and Jackson Hole in honor of a pioneer fur trader — had too severe a winter climate to be inhabited during that season. But when spring came, cavalcades of copper-skinned men and women, Blackfeet and Flatheads, Crow and Shoshoni, began to move into the plain to spend the summer hunting, fishing, trapping and fighting. John Colter was probably the first white man to see these mountains in 1807 or 1808. In 1811 a group of fur traders bound for Astoria in Oregon passed through this region and, as the range seemed an excellent landmark on the road to the West, they called the Grand Teton peaks "Pilot Knobs." At about the same time a party of French trappers stayed there and gave the mountains a more imaginative and longer lasting name. They fancied that the three tallest peaks resembled the breasts of women and called them "Les Trois Tetons," a name that survives to this day. Between 1825 and 1845 Jackson Hole was a paradise for trappers and fur traders, and such famous Western characters as David Jackson, William Sublette, Jedediah Smith, Kit Carson, Jim Bridger and Joe Meek were closely connected with the region's history. Of course, the hole also had its share of outlaws and fugitives from justice. The collapse of the fur trade in 1845 — beaver hats were suddenly out of style — restored the plain to the Indians, and not until the 1880's did the first homesteaders appear, hardy pioneers who braved the terrible winters.

THE CHALLENGE. The plain of Jackson Hole is about 50 miles long and 10 miles wide and stands at an elevation of 6,000 to 7,000 feet. The Tetons extend for 40 miles and include more than 20 peaks over 10,000 feet tall—Grand Teton Peak reaches a height of 13,766 feet. There are many taller mountains in the world, but the sheer granite walls of this range are defiant and

A MASTERPIECE. If a great stage designer, an outstanding artist in his field, were to present a mountain range in all its glory, he would attempt to capture the natural artistry of the Grand Tetons. He would shuffle the huge granite sheets into a well balanced range, short enough so that the human eye could encompass the beginning, the towering center and the end. He would shift the mountains so that the peaks would form a giant saw against the blue sky. He would eliminate the foothills which only clutter the scene and block the view. He would lay a string of clear, blue lakes around the range where the peaks may mirror themselves. And he would provide a huge amphitheater, in this case Jackson Hole, from where the audience could enjoy an unobstructed near or far view of the mountain spectacle. Whether the visitor drives south from Yellowstone Park on the new John D. Rockefeller, Jr., Memorial Parkway

GRANITE SHEETS on a BEAVER PLAIN

seem to have a magnetic lure for mountain climbers. American alpinists have tried their skill at the Grand Tetons for years, and now experts come from all over the world and find the range a worthwhile and rewarding goal. All parties of mountain climbers must register at park headquarters, and no one is allowed to venture into the upper regions alone. An ascent of the Grand Tetons will take two days, and any kind of weather may be encountered. Snow falls in every month of the year.

Less ambitious visitors will enjoy the park's system of good trails for hiking and horseback riding. The Lakes Trail circles Jenny Lake and connects all six lakes at the foot of the range. On a still day the mirrored images of the peaks are perfect. To see a glacier at an elevation of 10,000 feet you may take the Teton Glacier Trail which ends at Amphitheater Lake. To enjoy a waterfall, follow Cascade Canyon Trail leading to the deepest recesses in the mountains. Death Canyon Trail passes through some awesome chasms. If you love wildflowers, the Indian Paintbrush Canyon Trail will lead you through a profusion of blossoms. The Indian paintbrush is the state flower of Wyoming.

Since no automobile roads lead into the mountains themselves, the trails of the park are ideal for an intimate glance at nature. Some bulky moose or a few mule deer may be watched, especially near the Indian Paintbrush Canyon Trail. The visitor will get only an accidental glance at mountain sheep and bears, martens and coyotes, but beavers and ground squirrels may easily be observed. There is also a large elk herd in the park. The animals spend the winter in the National Elk Refuge adjoining the park. When the snow melts they migrate to the higher pastures in the east and north and some bands wander into the Tetons. When the snows return the elks drift back to the refuge.

WHERE ARE THE COWBOYS? Visitors who on their way to Grand Teton or Yellowstone cross Wyoming and Montana, the heart of the cattle country, often complain that they see no thundering herds or swaggering cowboys. The explanation is simple. The biggest ranches are far from the highways, and during the dry summer the herds usually graze on remote hill pastures. But the rodeos are accessible and good fun.

The huge granite "saw" of the Grand Tetons is not one of the highest ranges, but the challenge of its sheer cliffs lures mountaineers from all over the world.

UNION PACIFIC RAILROAD

Craters of the Moon and Sun Valley

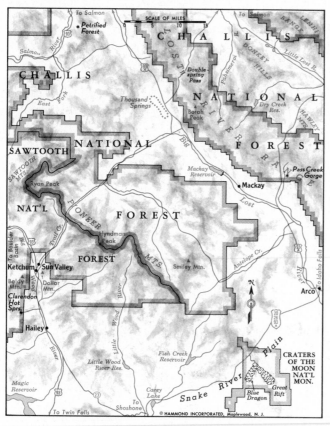

This violent volcanic activity occurred perhaps a thousand years ago, which is quite recent geologically speaking, and the ground has kept on smoking to our own day. The weird terraces and arches, caverns and beds, walls and flows sometimes take on graceful, billowing lines, and formations like the Blue Dragon seem iridescent when touched by the rays of the sun. The perfect molds of tree trunks and tree roots are fascinating. The lava engulfed the tumbling timber, and two actions took place simultaneously. The moisture of the logs quickly hardened the lava in the shapes it had formed around the trunks and roots, and the wood inside burned out. There is one fundamental difference between the landscape of the real moon and the Craters of the Moon in Idaho. The former is sterile, without life and vegetation. The Idaho craters look forbidding enough but, since the hot gases ceased rising through the fissures, the volcanic crust has failed to stem the forces of life. Here and there young aspens raise their heads courageously, and young pines get a firm foothold. Fair-sized chokecherries appear in the cracks where sufficient earth has gathered, and various shrubs make a hesitant appearance. Camping sites are provided at the monument.

TROPICAL TAN IN GLACIAL AIR. If Idaho has its inferno, it also has its paradise. West of the Craters of the Moon lies Sun Valley, the famous resort where nature and man have combined their best abilities. Nature, of course, was first, providing smooth, treeless mountains of various heights, with slopes of varying steepness, with an abundance of light, powdery winter snow which turns pink and purple in the sunset, and with a delightful climate at an altitude of 6,000 feet. Man did not arrive until the mid-1930's when skiing experts, commissioned by the Union Pacific Railroad, searched the West and declared this to be the ideal winter resort. Two hotels, a number of chalets and one of the world's longest chair lifts were built, and Sun Valley has flourished ever since. Today it boasts of 12 ski lifts and dozens of ski runs, ranging from the difficult slopes of Baldy Mountain to the more regular runs of Dollar and Half-Dollar mountains and to the grounds of the ski school where beginners learn the art from a faculty of expert instructors, some of them famous aces. Over the years the resort has maintained its elegant social level, and a number of private chalets have sprung up. There is a fascinating play of contrasts. If you want to acquire a tropical winter tan you may, of course, go to the tropics. But you can acquire it just as easily here by skiing stripped to the waist in the sunshine on the high slopes, or by resting on a kind of chaise longue constructed of your two ski poles and the skis themselves. If you care to swim in an outdoor pool in mid-January while the snowflakes gently drift down from the sky,

THE MOON AND THE CRATERS OF THE MOON. The North American continent supposedly contains every conceivable type of landscape, every formation of rock, soil and water found anywhere on earth. This assertion was even extended to the moon when the Craters of the Moon National Monument was established in southeastern Idaho near the town of Arco. The comparison was checked and found wanting when our astronauts returned with photographs and samples of the moon's landscape. While the national monument is hardly a replica of the moon's surface, it is nevertheless an interesting natural phenomenon. A circular road takes the visitor to a supposedly moon-like area called the Great Rift, a breaking point in the crust of the earth — a well of lava which ejected the black mass slowly, or spat it sky-high in the form of lava bombs which looked like teardrops or pieces of ribbon.

HELL and HEAVEN in the SAWTOOTH MOUNTAINS

you may do so here; the water is, of course, heated. Other popular winter thrills are dog sledding over nearby trails to Trail Creek Cabin, and skijoring, the exciting Scandinavian sport in which a horse with a rider draws the skier behind.

BELLS RING ON MOUNTAIN MEADOWS. The general setting for both the inferno and the paradise is one of grand mountain scenery, of tall peaks, deep canyons and huge, sweet smelling pine forests. Most of Idaho is a wonderful, untouched wilderness first described by Lewis and Clark. There are more than 20 mountain ranges, most of them untamed and untouched, and deep narrow gorges cut into the rocky land. The slopes around the timberline are quite densely populated, though not by human beings. Sheep live there in large numbers and are cared for by an unusual people. Most of the sheepherders are Basques or the descendants of Basques, and so skillful and indispensable are they that newcomers may enter the United States with a minimum of red tape. On the lonely highland pastures the older Basques look like the shepherd-patriarchs of the Old Testament, even to the staff with the hook which seems to have changed little these last 3,000 years. How do they control their wards, especially

when they cannot see them in the rolling hills? The sheep instinctively separate into clans, each small flock following the leader. The latter has a bell tied around his neck, and each bell has a different tone. The result is a perpetual glockenspiel, and if even one note is missing in the harmony, the herder and his dog set out to investigate and retrieve the wayward flock. There is music on those mountain pastures. It's a magic land.

W. S. KELLER — NAT'L PARK SERVICE

Above: The Craters of the Moon National Monument, named in pre-astronaut days, is an interesting volcanic area.

Below: Sun Valley, the country's most glamorous ski resort, provides a tropical tan in glacial air.

IDAHO DEPT. OF COMMERCE AND DEVELOPMENT

Glacier National Park

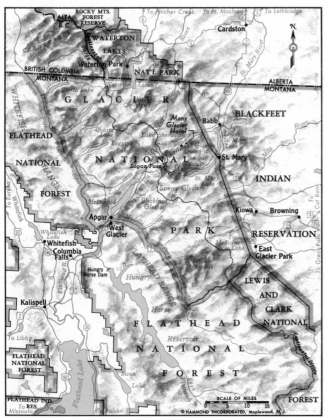

their Museum of the Plains Indians in Browning is one of the finest exhibits of Indian lore, history and art. For the name Blackfeet there are several explanations. One refers to a black salve which was occasionally smeared on the soles of their feet for medicinal and magic purposes; another states that, at the first encounter between white men and the tribe, a group of the latter had marched through a burned-over prairie and their moccasins and and legs appeared black. The Blackfeet were once the scourge of the whole region, feared and hated by the Flatheads and Kutenais, Sioux, Crow and others. Today they are peaceful, and in the town of Browning have adapted themselves to the ways of modern Western man; they operate almost all business establishments. In the countryside they have remained more individualistic. For instance they raise horses although there is little demand for their product. But they do so because they love horses and enjoy trading horses among themselves. Out of this territory Glacier National Park has arisen.

THE SEA BOTTOM THAT CLIMBED TO THE MOUNTAINTOP. The peaks of this park have as much personality as the Cascades and the Tetons; their shape and form is unmistakable. They appear to be in lateral motion as if they were on the march eastward. Seashells and fossils of fish were found on their mountaintops, and ancient layers more than a billion years old lie above younger, 30-million-year-old strata. The phenomena that occurred here have been reconstructed by the geologists. Several shallow seas covered this land in early eras. The mud of the sea bottom hardened into stone and gradually the rocks were lifted to become hills and mountains. Then a huge force arose and began to push the whole mountainous mass eastward for more than 40 miles. In the process the rock strata bent and broke, and the older western layers were shoved on top of the younger eastern layers — sometimes the old sea bottom landed on top of the pile. Next the various glacial periods descended upon the land, and huge glaciers ground and polished the mountains into their current shape. Of the ancient ice fields some 50 rather small remnants are left, but they are impressive enough to give the park its name. Sperry, Blackfoot and Grinnell Glaciers are easily reached. The peaks of the park are not spectacularly tall — Mt. Cleveland with an altitude of 10,448 feet is the highest — but they are magnificently colored. Ribbons of red and gray, green and purple, brown and yellow sparkle and glow in the sun, and their horizontal sweep adds to the impression of lateral motion, of mountains on the move. Of the park's 200 crystal-clear lakes McDonald is the largest and the St. Mary lakes are the loveliest. In their waters silent peaks mirror themselves, miniature icebergs float without motion, wildflower meadows border their shores

OLD INDIAN COUNTRY. The Going-to-the-Sun Road, marvelously engineered and crossing the park from east to west, has a name so imaginative that it seems to have originated in a public relations office on Madison Avenue. In fact the name is ascribed to a Blackfeet Indian leader named Tailfeathers-Coming-over-the-Hill who derived it from a local legend. The Blackfeet had lived high up in the Canadian North but in the 1700's moved south and settled in what is now Glacier National Park and on the adjoining plains. One of their gods came to their villages and taught them the ways of the new land. After his task was finished, he hiked back to the sun god whose abode was a huge mountain which, because of this journey, became Going-to-the-Sun Mountain. The trail leading to it is today's Going-to-the-Sun Road. Descendants of the Blackfeet still live on the reservation adjacent to the park, and

WHITE PEAKS, RED RIBBONS and an INVISIBLE LINE

and tall firs and spruces frame the enchanting view. The waters are stocked with trout and salmon. Most of the attractions, including the rocky fastness of the Continental Divide, can be enjoyed from the Going-to-the-Sun Road. Where the mountain walls leave no space for the road a tunnel has been drilled, and the two picture windows that have been carved into the west tunnel offer views of rarely matched mountain splendor. The road terminates near Apgar at the foot of Lake McDonald. Those who want to get really acquainted with this fourth largest of our national parks should take to the trails. There are more than 1,000 miles of them, either for hiking and climbing or for horseback riding. Horses, guides and trail-riding equipment are more amply available here than in other parks. The hikers and riders will travel through an abundance of wildflowers — the beargrass with its clusters of small, white lily blossoms flourishes in such profusion that it has become a symbol of the park. The visitor will closely observe the mountain wildlife — the black bear, mule deer, bighorn sheep and the Rocky Mountain goat.

NOT GUNS BUT TREES. In addition to nature one may study international relations. For the continuation of Glacier National Park on the Canadian side is Waterton Lakes National Park. Instead of fortifying the frontier with guns and fortresses, both nations decided in 1932 to unite their beautiful parks into one great area of common enjoyment and understanding — the Waterton-Glacier International Peace Park, "forever a symbol of permanent peace and friendship." For such a gesture of goodwill there is no counterpart in the game of international politics, past or present. Waterton Park — named in honor of the English naturalist Charles Waterton — has characteristics similar to those of the American park. There are the same glacier-sculpted amphitheaters with cool lakes, the same red and golden, yellow and purple bands in the mountain slopes, the same hairy mountain goats on the shining peaks. Upper Waterton Lake has a charm of its own, and since the international boundary line crosses it unnoticeably, its wild beauty belongs to Canada and the United States alike.

Bowman Lake is ancient Indian territory and a fine fishing ground for rainbow, brook and cutthroat trout.

149

Banff and Lake Louise

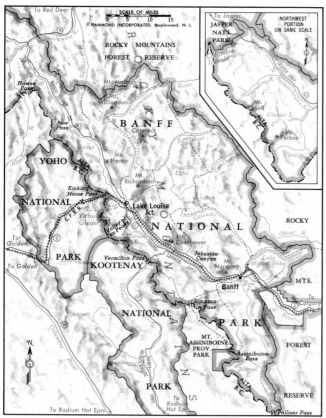

altitude, surrounded by sheer granite walls and snow-fields. In reality you will not be higher than in the American Rocky Mountain parks in Wyoming and Colorado. It is the low timberline in Canada that gives the illusion of greater altitude.

THE SOLITUDE OF UNTOUCHED NATURE. The Alps are a highly civilized mountain chain with a history as old as that of Western man. Fantastic processions trekked over its passes — Hannibal with his elephants, Caesar with his legions, Napoleon and his armies. The Swiss turned their mountains into a playground, dotting them with cable cars, ski huts and hotels. The American Rockies were opened up by mining booms and the great westward migration, events that produced the Rocky Mountain empire with its highways, cities, settlements and ranchlands. But the Canadian Rockies are largely untouched, direct from the hands of the Creator. Their history contains little evidence of man. Not until the end of the last century did the transcontinental railroad push across the wilderness of gneiss and granite, and the few highways appeared much later. There is little silver or gold in their depths, so no noisy mining operations disturb the peace. There is little fertile soil, so few farms have sprung up in the valleys. Comparatively few people live permanently in this huge area, and there is only one city, Banff. If you stand on top of the cliff overlooking Peyto Lake a short stretch west of the main road, you will see the emerald surface with its shoreline and, beyond the lake, both sides of Mistaya Valley. Two monumental rows of snow and granite peaks reach as far as your eye can see, with the farthest summits merging into the clouds in stillness and solitude.

THE MAGNIFICENT PEAKS. Mention the words Lake Louise, Banff or the Canadian Rockies and there will usually be an answering spark in your listener's eye. There are very good reasons for such widespread admiration. The Rocky Mountains are monumental anywhere, but in Canada they produce a particularly large number of jagged single peaks in addition to their long ridges. For this reason the Canadian Rockies are a fruitful field for expert mountain climbers. Their geographic location in the cool north is responsible for much snow, the decorative kind that paints the peaks a gleaming white even in summertime. You will discover the loveliness of glacial lakes and streams. Usually they are neither clear nor deep blue but rather a cool green, the color of delicate jade which will strike you as new and unconventionally beautiful. In the great Canadian national parks you will feel that you are at a great

THE HAND OF MAN. It is a wonderfully reassuring thought that the Canadian Rockies will remain the way they are. The Canadians have turned most of their magnificent mountain ranges into parks and wildlife refuges, of which Banff and Jasper are the best known. Both the Canadian Pacific and the Canadian National railroads cross the district, and there are good highway connections to the east and south as well as roads for adventurous drivers to Vancouver and the West. At two sites of breathtaking scenic beauty the Canadian Pacific has built fine luxury hotels, the Banff Springs Hotel and Chateau Lake Louise. From the terraces of the former there is a wide panorama of the valley of the Bow River; from the latter you look over a slope abloom with Icelandic poppies to Lake Louise. At the water's end, framed by two dark rock walls, Victoria Glacier glistens in the sun. In addition to these opulent and dignified hostelries there are a number of other smaller hotels, lodges and camping grounds.

THE CALL of the CANADIAN ROCKIES

CANADIAN PACIFIC

The panorama of Bow Valley with the city of Banff is one of America's most fabulous views.

A MOUNTAIN ACROSS MAIN STREET. Imagine a business street cut off by a mountainous rock wall on one end and at the other end by a bright rock garden rising from the banks of the Bow River to the stately Government House. This main thoroughfare of Banff is one of its principal charms. Other Banff attractions are boat excursions on the Bow River, fishing on Lake Minnewanka, golfing at Banff Springs Golf Club where ambitious players complain about the scenery. Its grandeur takes their minds off the game. There is also swimming in the various pools of Banff Hot Springs and Upper Hot Springs, which are a year-round attraction. A daily flow feeds a sulphur water pool; the Upper Hot Springs have a temperature of 100 degrees. The fish hatchery and the buffalo paddocks are interesting, and the chair lift rides to the top of Mount Norquay and Sulphur Mountain are recommended. The only road to the north divides at Mount Eisenhower. The left fork leads over the Continental Divide to Kootenay National Park and Radium Hot Springs while the main road proceeds to Lake Louise, about 5,000 feet above sea level. Chateau Lake Louise is the center for hiking or horseback excursions to the Lakes in the Clouds, lakes Mirror and Agnes, and the Plain of the Six Glaciers. Half an hour's drive will take you to Moraine Lake in the Valley of the Ten Peaks, rivaling Lake Louise in beauty and surrounded by ten mountains, many of them higher than 10,000 feet. Along or near the highway to Jasper, Hector Lake, Bow Lake and Peyto Lake are jewels. All are continually stocked with trout and offer fine fishing. The whole region is, of course, also a winter sports area, with championship downhill and slalom courses at Mount Norquay near Banff. The latter is the seat of a famous school of fine arts associated with the University of Alberta.

Wildlife is abundant in all Canadian parks. Cougars and coyotes, grizzlies and black bears, wapiti (the American elk) and moose, bighorn sheep and Rocky Mountain goats roam the ground, and some one hundred species of birds fill the air.

151

Jasper National Park

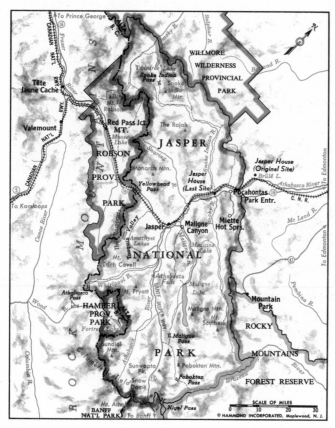

a fascinating glance at the workings of a live glacier. From afar its surface looks smooth and unmoving, but if you ride on its surface, you discover that it is alive with thousands of little streams rushing down the slope and carving small icy ridges and gorges. You can actually hear the busy working of the water. Columbia Icefield is also an interesting example of a worldwide phenomenon that seems to indicate a gradual climatic change on earth — the recession of the glaciers. Every year the ice field recedes about 100 feet, and the distance between the highway and the glacial rim becomes greater.

AN OASIS IN THE HIGH NORTH. The road now follows the Athabasca River which originates at the Columbia Icefield. In the early nineteenth century when the fur trade was flourishing this valley was the scene of a fierce struggle between the two great rivals, the Hudson's Bay Company and the North West Company. This "cold war" was sensibly terminated in 1821 by the merger of the two competitors. An important trading post was Jasper House, which gave its name to the park. The town of Jasper is the seat of the park headquarters and is an all-year resort with well-appointed tourist accommodations. Three miles away, at Lac Beauvert, the luxurious Jasper Park Lodge, owned and operated by the Canadian National Railways, is a log-cabin-style hotel with a central lodge and numerous bungalows which merge naturally into the setting of snowcapped mountains and tall evergreens. At night, when its huge picture windows shine brightly in the silent wilderness, it is a festive vision. At the Jasper railroad station the colorful Raven Totem is a 70-foot pole, carved by the master carver of the Haida Indians.

A FAMILIAR PICTURE. Some spots on earth are so beautiful that their photographs are used over and over again to illustrate poetry, to advertise travel or to sell camping equipment. We become familiar with those corners of the earth long before we even dream of seeing them ourselves. Maligne Lake is such a spot. We may have noticed its picture more than once, but it is incomparably more satisfying to view its blue-gray waters, its wooded bays and its snowcapped peaks. Its bulging white clouds travel over a blue northern sky, and in the foreground, on the little peninsula reaching way out into the lake, the grove of tall, dark green firs sends its slender spires straight up. Not long ago this lake could be reached only by a four-day pack trip on horseback. That is still the most satisfactory way to reach it, but now the excursion can also be made in one day by car and motor launch. The round trip encompasses a hundred miles. Maligne Lake is appreciated not only by sightseers but also by alpinists and fishermen; speckled

GLACIER OF THREE OCEANS. The greatest mass of ice outside of the Arctic Circle lies before your eyes at the southern entrance to Jasper, the most northerly of Canadian national parks in the Rockies. The Columbia Icefield covers 150 square miles and its huge white tongues stretch out in various directions and feed streams that grow into mighty rivers. Their waters flow into the Atlantic, the Pacific and the Arctic oceans. At your feet is the geographical center of the water drainage system for over one-quarter of North America. The glacial tongue you see from the Banff-Jasper Highway protrudes between the Snow Dome and Mount Athabasca, two monumental peaks that frame the ice field like pillars. Snowmobiles will take you up the slope of the glacier for a stretch, and you will enjoy the delightful combination of the sharp, cold air from the ice below and the bright sunrays from above. You will also have

A NORTHERN SANCTUARY along the GREAT DIVIDE

CANADIAN NATIONAL

The jagged wall of the Ramparts rises in the Tonquin Valley. This wilderness spot can be reached on horseback only.

trout is the lake's specialty. One unforgettable spot that can be reached only on horseback is the Tonquin Valley. The jagged skyline of the Ramparts towers above lovely Amethyst Lakes. From Jasper Park Lodge you can see the stately summit of Mount Edith Cavell. High up on its slope Angel Glacier consists of one compact main body and two outspread angel wings. This dramatic spot can be easily reached on a 20-mile automobile road which rises for 2,000 feet over hairpin turns with wonderful vistas. Many miles of trails are also provided for hikers, horseback and bicycle riders. Just off the highway to Edmonton, 38 miles from Jasper, the Miette Hot Springs pour out about 170,000 gallons of mineral water per day at a temperature of 126° F. A modern bathing establishment offers an outdoor swimming pool in which a temperature of 90° is maintained. The outdoor pool is open from mid-May through mid-September. An aerial tramway ride to the top of Whistlers Mountain provides an unforgettable view of the Athabasca Valley, almost 3,500 feet below.

MOUNTAIN SHEEP AND MOUNTAIN LIONS. There is probably no area in the whole United States and Canada where wildlife has been preserved in its original variety as in the national parks of the Canadian Rockies. You can see moose wading through a lake or feeding in a swamp, or a bighorn sheep with its spiral horns. The grizzly bears and mountain lions hunt around the timberline far from human habitations, and in the most remote valleys the wolf and the mountain caribou still find a refuge.

HOW ICEBERGS ARE BORN. West of Jasper on Highway 16, Mount Robson Provincial Park in British Columbia encircles the highest peak of the Canadian Rockies, with an altitude of 12,972 feet. On horseback you can ride through the Valley of a Thousand Falls to Berg Lake on the northern flank of Mt. Robson, and if you are lucky you will see a huge block of ice break off from Tumbling Glacier, splash into the lake and sail off as an iceberg

153

Vancouver and Inside Passage to Alaska

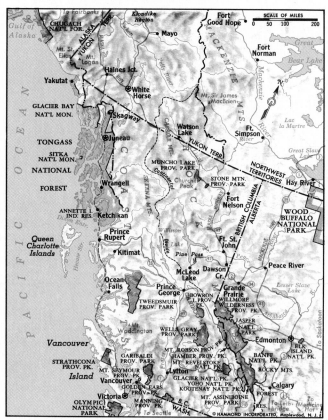

by the same motley crowd of gold seekers that established San Francisco. When word reached the California diggings that gold had been discovered near Lytton, 160 miles up the Fraser River, 30,000 miners sailed northward and started their voyage up the Fraser. They found it a backbreaking task, encountering rapid currents between sheer canyon walls and being forced to make seemingly impossible portages. Hundreds of the newcomers perished. In the ensuing atmosphere of lawlessness and frontier brawls there was a cry for protection by the United States, and for "Fifty-four Forty or Fight." But the boom collapsed and many of the miners stayed, turning to shipping and the lumber trade for a livelihood. They also founded a few small settlements. One of them, Gas Town at the mouth of the Fraser, became Vancouver in honor of the famous British navigator and explorer of the continent's northwest coast. In about two generations it grew into a young, bright metropolitan city in a spectacularly beautiful setting on a great harbor surrounded by snowcapped mountains. To enjoy this vast panorama you can ride by cable car to the top of Grouse Mountain, or in your own automobile to Mount Seymour Park, a short distance from the city over the Second Narrows Bridge. This park is a skiing resort of more than 9,000 acres with ski tows, a ski jump and a ski camp. In Vancouver proper, Stanley Park, near the business center and surrounded by blue waters, is a wonderful combination of forest and flower garden. It is a vantage point for watching ocean liners pass under Lions Gate Bridge, one of the highest suspension bridges in the world. The Stanley Park Zoo has a unique collection of penguins; at the aquarium the porpoise pool is a great attraction. Also highly recommended are the ferry cruises that take sightseers from Vancouver through picturesque, scenic waterscapes. Other local attractions are the Maritime Museum, the British Columbia Building with its Indian relics in Exhibition Park and the new Queen Elizabeth Theatre complex, the mainstay of the Vancouver International Festival of the Arts.

THE FJORDS AND THE ISLANDS. The Inside Passage to Alaska between the continent and the hundreds of outlying islands has often been compared to the coast of Norway. Both have in common the mountains rising out of the water as rounded, forest clad summits or as steep canyon walls, the glaciers and waterfalls, the inlets — called fjords in Europe — and the fishing grounds, which teem with herring and cod in Norway and with salmon and halibut in British Columbia and Alaska. But the shoreline of the Norwegian fjord, unlike the American coast, is indented with smaller inlets where farmer-fishermen have their tiny settlements on small patches of green lowland. The British Columbia-

A REPLICA OF ENGLAND SURROUNDED BY CANADA. Eastern Canadians sometimes refer to the province of British Columbia in this way. They are probably right in reference to Victoria, the provincial capital. That city, with its thriving flowers, its eternal English spring, its retired colonels and its afternoon tea at the Empress Hotel is indeed a piece of England. (As a part of the Puget Sound country it is described on page 162.) But Vancouver, the largest city of the province, strikes the visitor as a cosmopolitan world port. It is quite true that the stately Vancouver Hotel has a certain British dignity, that cricket and curling matches are vastly popular, and that the best restaurants in town specialize in roast beef and Yorkshire pudding. But on the whole the atmosphere is Canadian and international, with interesting oriental overtones in the Chinese, Japanese and Hindu quarters. Vancouver was founded

154

A COSMOPOLITAN HARBOR and a DRAMATIC COASTLINE

Alaska coast is wilder, grander, rockier, more forbidding and very sparsely populated. The few coastal communities are usually perched on a mountain slope and descend to the water's rim. Ocean Falls at the head of Fisher Channel looks like an amphitheater with a street system that includes a great many stairs and elevated planked roads on pilings. The same conditions prevail in other coastal communities. Prince Rupert, British Columbia's most northerly seaport and terminus of the Canadian National Railways, is not even 70 years old and still has a certain frontier atmosphere. The Museum of Northern British Columbia is interesting, and authentic totem poles decorate the parks. The town is the home port of one of Canada's largest deep sea fishing fleets. Ketchikan, Alaska's southernmost port, is a busy harbor teeming with fishing boats. A visit to one of its fish packing plants is worthwhile. The huge white halibuts, some bigger than a man, are cut up with a few expert strokes, then divided, packed and deep-frozen — a fascinating process to watch. Near Ketchikan the Indian village of Saxman has a notable collection of totem poles. Today thousands of tourists depart from Seattle or Vancouver on ferries or cruise ships to Prince Rupert and Alaskan ports. The water is usually calm, and only on the open-ocean stretch between Vancouver Island and the Queen Charlotte Islands is the sea rough at times. It rains a great deal along the coast, and a raincoat is a must.

THE ROAD TO ALASKA. During the Second World War an overland route in addition to the ship and air connections with Alaska seemed desirable. As a result the Alaska Highway was built from Dawson Creek in Canada to Fairbanks in Alaska. The trip by car is long and strenuous, but travel conditions have improved considerably during the last years. Alaska's wildlife includes Dall sheep (a small bighorn sheep) and mountain goats, elk and moose, grizzlies and black bears, caribou and timber wolves, polar bears and walruses, and various species of seals and whales.

Cosmopolitan Vancouver has interesting Chinese, Japanese and Hindu quarters.

AIR CANADA

Aliaska

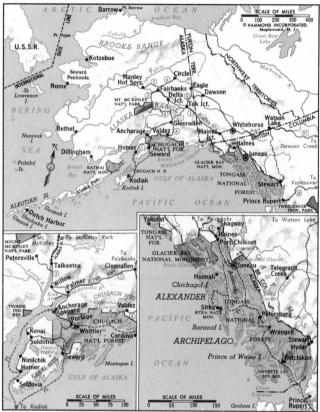

money, and the Russian government was willing to sell Alaska to the United States for $7,200,000, less than two cents an acre. For America it proved to be a fantastic bargain, both economically and politically. If Russia had held on to her possession, a modern Soviet republic would occupy the top of our continent today — an uncomfortable thought. In the wake of the gold rush Alaska became a territory in 1912, and in 1959 it became our 49th state.

THREE APPROACHES. A trip to Alaska by jet would be, of course, the fastest journey, but not the most rewarding one. Far below you see myriads of islands and endless dark forests traversed by icy rivers and mountain walls. From a high-flying plane the country appears uninhabited and uninhabitable. You can travel by car on the Alaska Highway which runs from Dawson Creek in British Columbia to Fairbanks in Alaska. The drive will be strenuous, but it will afford a close look at magnificent scenery replete with a multitude of birds, flowers and animals. But the most spectacular approach is by ship through the Inside Passage, Alaska's marine highway. Modern ships take thousands of tourists to the high North. They wind their way between wooded islands, enter magnificent fjords with calm, clear waters between sheer mountain walls, and call at places like Ketchikan and Juneau, towns that between the tides and the hills, between fishing and lumbering, have developed an original atmosphere of their own. Highlights of such a cruise include the ice-blue Mendenhall Glacier which descends to within 60 feet of sea level near the Juneau airport and which can also be reached by car. Even more spectacular is Glacier Bay National Monument west of Juneau, accessible only by boat or plane. Cruise ships float around the bay for hours, and the startled passengers gaze at magnificent ice peaks and great glaciers. Surrounded by myriads of icebergs, they breathlessly hope that one of the glaciers will calve, i.e., split an iceberg from the mother ice. The cruise liner will drift close to one of the huge glaciers and will give a loud blast with the ship's whistle. With echoes from icy peak to icy peak the sound waves will prod the glacier into calving. With a thundering splash a hunk of ice as big as a 5-story building will split off and drop into the bay, sending up curtains of spray.

AMERICA'S TALLEST PEAK. Mount McKinley National Park, open from June to September, can be reached by railroad from Anchorage or Fairbanks or by car via the Denali Highway. The 20,320-foot-high mountain is not only the tallest on our continent but, measured from the base to the summit, is probably also the tallest on earth. The other world giants rise from far higher levels. It is also unique in remaining

HISTORY'S CLASSICAL BARGAIN. Were Asia and America connected in the high North? Czar Peter the Great decided to investigate and commissioned the Danish navigator Bering to establish the facts. Bering proceeded to the northern Pacific and in 1748 proved that the two continents were separated. He also discovered something else. The American coast teemed with sea otters and fur seals whose pelts brought a fortune in the China trade. Within a generation the Aleutian Islands and the Alaskan shore were overrun with bands of Russian hunters who destroyed or enslaved the natives and on occasion robbed and murdered each other. Finally two trading companies emerged and established a semblance of order, but their large scale hunting operations soon depleted the available resources. By the middle of the nineteenth century the Russian-American venture was losing

OUR ARCTIC FRONTIER

JOHN M. KAUFFMANN — NAT'L PARK SERVICE

The crater in Katmai National Monument. The area contains the Valley of Ten Thousand Smokes and can be reached most easily by plane.

snowcapped two-thirds of the way down its slopes all year long. Only the most experienced alpinists may attempt the ascent, and relatively few have done so. At the southwest corner of Alaska, Katmai National Monument includes the famous Valley of Ten Thousand Smokes, where steam rises from volcanic fissures. The area can be reached only by plane.

IVORY CARVINGS AND TOTEM POLES. While the ancient cultures of Alaska's natives — the Indians, Eskimos and Aleuts — are gradually vanishing, their highly attractive style in arts and crafts survives. Native Alaskan art can best be viewed at Haines-Port Chilkoot, at the northern terminal of the marine highway. Its folk art center exhibits wood and ivory carvings, oil paintings, textiles and ceramics. There the Chilkat Indian dances with their fabulous costumes and masks have been revived and are performed in the replica of a tribal Indian community house. Eskimo craftsmen fashion souvenirs of ivory, and their women make baskets and dolls. The ancient Eskimo game of the blanket toss can be seen each February at Anchorage during the Fur Rendezvous. The world championship competition for sled dog racing is also held on that occasion. Carved and painted totem poles, the records of tribal Indian history, have become the landmark of Alaska and are seen wherever tourists congregate.

To become really acquainted with native life, one has to go to the west and north of the state to places like Nome, Kotzebue and Barrow. Nome is a colorful town where the King Island Eskimos sculpt artistic walrus figures of ivory and make drums and dolls.

Mt. McKinley National Park with Horseshoe Lake is open only from June to September.

W. S. KELLER — NAT'L PARK SERVICE

Kotzebue has been an Arctic trading center since Russian days. Such activities as seal hunting, the butchering of the white whales during midsummer and various dances maintain at least part of the ancient Eskimo culture. The Eskimos of Barrow keep a herd of some 30,000 reindeer, hunt whales, walrus and seals from umiaks (skin boats) and stalk polar bears. The government restricts the number of polar bear kills to 350 per season. The young Eskimos still learn to build ice igloos as a means of protection.

157

Grand Coulee

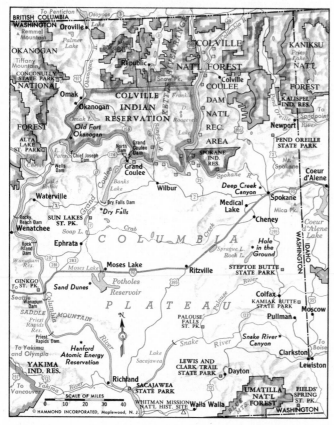

potential waterpower of the river is staggering. Man has taken on the role of equalizer and coordinator and has erected across the Columbia one of the biggest concrete structures ever raised on earth. Grand Coulee Dam, as tall as a 40-story building, is the powerhouse and pulsing heart of Washington's inland empire, bringing into cooperation the soil, the water and the energy to irrigate, turn wheels, produce and create. When all the dams of the Columbia system are built, more energy will be produced here than from all other sources in the United States.

APPLES AND ATOMS. To furnish the life-giving touch to the fertile but arid soil, the Columbia Basin Project uses the ancient, dried-up bed of the Grand Coulee River south of the dam. The old channel has been turned into a storage tank 27 miles long, with two dams sealing off the riverbed. Filled with water from the Columbia, Banks Lake, the equalizing reservoir, can irrigate more than a million acres of desert. It sustains thousands of fertile farms to produce grain, fruits and vegetables in abundance. It maintains and feeds hundreds of thousands of cattle, sheep, hogs, turkeys, chickens. A pioneering venture has been accomplished here but not a homesteading rush in the old western sense. All was done in an orderly fashion, with prices fixed by Congress on a sensible level, and expert advice and guidance for all new settlers. The electric current flows largely into two undertakings, a great aluminum industry which did not exist here before the Second World War and uranium plants. Quite a few of the old lumber towns worried about the diminishing timber supply. But Longview, headquarters of the Weyerhaeuser lumber empire, and Vancouver, the state's oldest city, founded in 1825 by the Hudson's Bay Company, are operating mammoth aluminum plants now. Near where the Columbia turns northward, the Hanford Plant, the Atomic Energy Commission's producer of Plutonium 239, stands in the sagebrush wasteland like the desert castle of an African legend.

INVITATION TO THE TAXPAYERS. In Europe great public works are heavily guarded and considered forbidden territory to the general public. The contrast at Grand Coulee and elsewhere in America is striking. A visitor will be delighted by the friendly and open way in which he is treated. It is obvious — although only to the American mind — that any taxpayer should have the right to see it, wander through it and learn about it. At Grand Coulee, as at most other dams, there are guided tours and interesting lectures about the intakes deep underwater on the upstream side, about the biggest turbine generators yet to be built and the delicate

POWER IN THE DESERT. When you slowly drive over the bridge-road along the crest of Grand Coulee Dam, your first thought will probably be the strange and striking contrast before you. Below, a huge cataract twice the height of Niagara Falls spills torrents of blue water and white, cooling foam into the valley while all around brownish, arid hills stretch their rough wasteland ridges against the sky. The desert landscape is enlivened by tall steel towers and humming high-tension wires strung in various directions. This view illustrates a cooperative venture. Nature has provided a great reservoir of fertile but dry soil and a powerful river, the Columbia, second only to the Mississippi in volume, draining an area of almost 260,000 square miles and delivering more freshwater to the ocean than all other Pacific coast rivers combined. One resource nature did not provide is oil, and there is very little coal. But the

MAN IMPROVES on NATURE

*Grand Coulee Dam is the biggest concrete structure
on earth.*

*The old, dried-up bed of the Grand Coulee is now a
huge water storage tank.*

measuring instruments. During the summer months the
spillway waters are illuminated at night. Toward the
east the dam's impounded current forms Franklin D.
Roosevelt Lake, a 151-mile-long deep blue body of
river water along the shore of which the government
has established a chain of recreational sites. The level
of the lake is controlled so that no backed-up floods
spill into Canadian territory. Around the dam proper a
good deal of greenery may be seen, with the sprinklers
turning day and night. The region is maintained as the
Coulee Dam National Recreation Area and tempts the
vacationer with many outdoor activities, from water
skiing, boating and swimming to the quiet joys of camping in still coves. Facilities, some of which can be
reached only by boat, have been developed along most
of the 660 miles of lakeshore.

THE BALANCE OF NATURE. Has it been disturbed?
Has the interference of man created unexpected problems? The wildlife experts were worried about the
salmon population of the Columbia River. At Bonneville Dam fish ladders lead the mature fish on their
upstream spawning migration around the dam structure,

and special spillways allow the young salmon to avoid
the obstacle on their way to the ocean. But no such
provisions could be made at Grand Coulee Dam, which
has the height of a skyscraper. So thousands of salmon
whose birthplace had been in the cold Canadian headwaters of the river rammed their heads against the
concrete and perished. For a considerable part of the
salmon population the way home was blocked forever.
So the fishery experts conceived a plan in the grand
manner which may at least partially solve the problem.
They trapped masses of Chinooks headed for the Grand
Coulee Dam, transferred them to hatcheries and gently
removed their eggs and milt. The eggs were fertilized
and placed in tributary streams below the big dam. The
baby fish were born and two years later set out on their
journey to the Pacific, many of them tagged. Uneasily
the wildlife men waited for another two years. Would
the ascent of these salmon be a death journey, or would
it conclude a successful resettlement project? To everyone's relief the migrants ignored Grand Coulee and returned to their foster streams. Since more dams are
to be built, it may be conceivable to resettle the whole
salmon population in the lower Columbia valley.

The Olympic Mountains

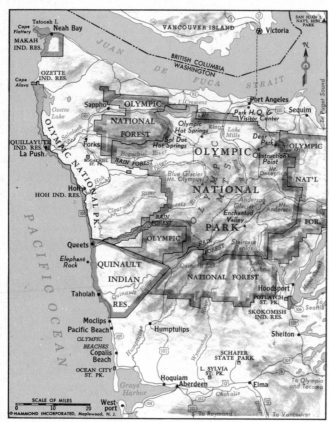

RALPH POOLE — NAT'L PARK SERVICE

The wildflower meadows of the park are famous. The mountains themselves are topped by miles of ice and snow.

ANCIENT GODS IN THE NEW WORLD. There is a legend that Jupiter, discouraged with conditions in Greece, left his holy abode, Mount Olympus near the Aegean Sea, and set out to find a haven elsewhere. He searched for another massive, snowcapped peak that looked out on blue water and finally found it in the northwest corner of America. There was indeed another Mount Olympus, quite similar to the one in Greece, surrounded by a rocky stronghold called the Olympic Mountains and forming the Olympic Peninsula and Olympic National Park. There the ancient god settled happily and has been at work ever since. As Jupiter Pluvius, the rainmaker, he draws as many as 12 feet of rain from the skies onto the western slopes every year, while as Jupiter Serenator, the sunshine producer, he dries the eastern slopes pleasantly and sometimes too effectively.

While this tale has a pleasant Old World flavor, another legend about the Olympic Mountains is of a strictly American nature. It seems that Paul Bunyan's blue ox, Babe, got sick and was carried by its master to the Pacific shore to take the cure on the milk of the western whale. In spite of this tonic, Babe's strength faded away and Paul Bunyan sadly shoveled a grave for the little blue ox. Then suddenly the patient recovered, the funeral was postponed and the open hole remained as it was dug. In time it filled with water, but it is still there, just as the pile of dirt and rock is still lying by the side of the pit. One, the hole filled with water, is called Puget Sound and the other, the pile of dirt and rocks beside it, the Olympic Mountains.

FIVE SHINING RINGS. The unique beauty of this ridgeless mass of piercing peaks is perhaps best described in terms of five vastly different but equally fascinating circles. The first ring is only a three-quarter circle and consists of the blue waters of Hood Canal, Juan de Fuca Strait and the Pacific Ocean. Sailing on these wide waterways and seeing the snowcapped Olympics rising steeply into the sky makes an unforgettable impression. On one side there are the towers of Seattle, Tacoma and other great and busy population centers. On the other side the mountains tower in wild, almost untouched grandeur. Ring number two consists of the Olympic Loop, a 364-mile round trip through the foothills, offering such attractions as a 50-mile ride along the beautiful Hood Canal, a visit to the little city of Port Angeles with its famous salmon and crab grounds and a view of crystal clear Lake Crescent,

160

TALL TALES and ROOSEVELT ELKS

Heavy rain clouds drifting in from the west produce the luxuriant growth of the rain forest.

At the foot of the fortress-like Olympic Mountains, the Hole in Wall area is conspicuous.

which lies in the shadow of Mount Storm King at the northern end of the park. It is the only lake known to contain the Beardslee trout, a big species which often weighs from 15 to 20 pounds.

The next higher circle is a belt of woods which on the western slopes consists of the rain forests. Exposed to the first onslaught of rain clouds drifting in from the west, these wet valleys have produced a uniquely exuberant growth, a forest scene where, from a carpet of thick mosses and huge ferns, trees arise that are the giants of their species. There is a red cedar with a 21-foot-wide trunk, and a Douglas fir 14 feet 5 inches wide, four feet above the ground. Tilden tells of a giant log that fell to the ground many decades ago. On it, 21 hemlock trees took root and grew into healthy, tall specimens, standing in a straight line like a platoon of soldiers. Vines and mosses hang from the branches in flowing streamers as long as 20 feet, and the dim, whitish green light and the complete stillness make the rain forest an eerie, unearthly place. This belt stretches from sea level to a height of about 5,000 feet. Beyond that, the fourth ring above the timberline presents the wildflower meadows which spread a blanket of avalanche lilies, tiger lilies, asters and violets, red columbines and blue lupines, bluebells and many others. Finally there is the circle of glaciers, more than 20 square miles of ice and snowfields which each season receive 200 to 250 inches of snow. Since the Olympics are not volcanic, there is no lava dust to spoil the clean, pure beauty of the scene. One of the largest glaciers is Blue Glacier whose ice seems to be of a blue color; its lower end occasionally breaks off, crashing down into

the valley with a barrage of thunder. The rain and snow statistics should not deter travelers from visiting the park, for the precipitation takes place mostly in wintertime. During the summer there are many weeks of fine, sunny weather, often still delightful in September and October.

ELKS HAVE THE RIGHT OF WAY. There are but a few miles of highways in the national park proper. However, one road in the northeastern section climbs over 6,000 feet through Deer Park to a lookout on Blue Mountain where a magnificent panorama of Juan de Fuca Strait and Vancouver Island may be enjoyed. For the real nature lover there are 600 miles of trails, and the network is extended annually. Most of these trails were already in existence when the rangers arrived. It was only necessary to improve and connect them. They were the runs of the Roosevelt elk, named in honor of Theodore Roosevelt. They are darker than the elk of the Rocky Mountains and also larger, weighing up to 1,000 pounds. Their horns are shorter but heavier. They still like to use their old elk runs, and quite a few trail hikers have had the somewhat exasperating experience of hearing the approaching clop-clop-clop of a band of these big animals, of stepping aside gingerly and seeing four or five Roosevelt elk crashing by. Columbian black-tailed deer, black bear and the more common small animals are plentiful. In an effort to extend the range of some of the rarer American species, a herd of Rocky Mountain goats was brought in from the Canadian Rockies a number of years ago and is now thriving in the Olympics.

161

Seattle and Puget Sound

AMERICA'S GREAT SEASCAPE. The dimensions of Puget Sound country are so gigantic that they cannot be encompassed in one picture by a land based photographic lens. But on a clear day the human eye can absorb much of it from a plane or boat or a high vantage point ashore. The secret of its appeal lies in a rare combination of mountains and forests, islands and bays, cities and ships, and every one of these elements stands squarely in its place, strong, solid and vigorous. Of the three mountain masses that dominate the scene, the two highest are in the Cascades. Mount Rainier is one of America's great peaks, as is Mount Baker, which looks out over the San Juan Islands to the west. While the Olympics across the sound only reach an altitude of 7,954 feet, they rise abruptly out of the blue water in such a broad, fortress-like mass that they are impressive indeed. The waters of Puget Sound stretch for more than

150 miles from Olympia in the south to Blaine at the Canadian border, and for about 200 miles through the Juan de Fuca Strait to Cape Flattery. The sound consists of innumerable picturesque bays and inlets, including Hood Canal. This beautiful, forest-lined natural waterway half a mile broad and 80 miles long has shorelines so straight that it appears man-made. These waters teem with fish: with salmon, sea perch and candle smelts that can in season be scooped up with baskets, and oysters and clams abound. Fishing is an old tradition here. The early inhabitants of this shore, the Makah and Quillayute Indians, found their perpetual harvest of fish so rewarding that they never became hunters. The forests — dark firs, lighter undergrowth and myriads of wildflowers including wild lilacs and wild roses — cover the islands and the slopes like a velvety carpet. The deer of the woods raid orchards, and the bears rob hen houses within sight of villages or even cities. Bushes and trees grow so fast that homeowners forever have to cut and trim the branches to keep their picture window views open.

SEATTLE'S HORIZONS: THE ORIENT AND ALASKA. Into this wilderness great cities have been carved. Seattle is the largest. The others — Bellingham, Everett, Tacoma and Olympia — are all growing communities that someday may merge into a continuous urban half-circle like the cities around San Francisco Bay. Visitors will find it a fascinating experience to walk through the hubbub of downtown Seattle and between modern skyscrapers see stretches of the blue sound, a deep green forest slope, the snowy white peak of Mount Rainier or the crest of the Olympics towering in the distance above low-lying clouds. They will be delighted to discover another big body of water beyond the hills of the city to the east, 25-mile-long Lake Washington where the University of Washington is located. The lake panorama adheres to the Puget Sound pattern. There are islands and inlets, and the tree-shaded shores are connected by a famous floating bridge. Lovers of ships will find a stroll along Alaskan Way on the waterfront with its ferry terminal and totem poles, or a ride over the sound by ferry, steamer or sailboat, most rewarding. The waters swarm with craft of every imaginable type, from Indian skiffs to the boats of the halibut fleet, from canoes to cabin cruisers, from freight scows to big, seagoing log rafts. These last are pulled by tugs so far ahead that the uninitiated visitor's eyes will not connect raft and steamer until he spies the long cable cutting the water. The eye is caught by the freighters, tankers and passenger ships. Some are homeward bound from the Orient, to which Seattle is the closest port in the United States. Others are outward bound to Alaska, for which the city has been the gate-

THE LURE of BAYS and SHIPS

way ever since we bought the northern empire from the Russians. Old-timers on the docks speak with familiarity of Colombo and Calcutta, Yokohama and Macao, Canton and Singapore. But, as to Alaska with its lumber and canning business, they consider it their very own domain and backyard. Today Seattle's shipping is supplemented by the airplane industry. A prime attraction for tourists is the monorail which takes them downtown to the Seattle Center with its 607-foot-high Space Needle. The view from the restaurant on top is superb. Here also are the Pacific Science Center, the Seattle Art Museum and Fun Forest, an amusement park.

ENGLAND ACROSS THE BAY. One of Seattle's most popular excursions by a bright Canadian Princess boat or Washington State ferry is the trip to Victoria, the capital of British Columbia, across the sound on Vancouver Island. That lovely town has been called "as English as Exeter," but the sight that primarily arrests the casual visitor's attention is the abundance of beautiful flowers. Fuchsias and verbenas, violas and heliotrope, Canterbury bells and especially roses are everywhere — in public and in private gardens, in beds, borders and flowerpots, on trellises and even in iron baskets hanging from the streetlamps. The huge rose gardens of the Empress Hotel and the famous Butchart Gardens are real attractions. Victoria's wonderful climate which, according to residents, prolongs the perfect English spring through nine months of the year, accounts for its beautiful flowers. It's the sunniest spot on the sound. Those who like to search for British touches are advised to go to Beacon Hill Park and watch the lawn bowling. Then, toward 5:00 P.M., one may have tea and crumpets at the Empress Hotel, watch majestic dowagers, who reside there in Edwardian magnificence, sip tea from their own precious china and listen to a trio playing Liszt's "Liebestraum." It's a Canadian version of storybook England.

Vision and reality — the distant image of Mt. Rainier seems suspended above Seattle's skyscrapers.

D. MUENCH — SHOSTAL ASSOCIATES

Northern Cascades

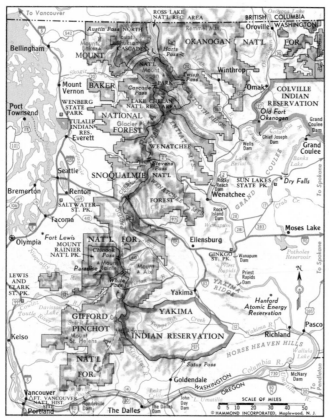

one smaller one and one big island bear his name — Vancouver. The panorama which enthralled the early visitors is still enjoyed by thousands every day. The lofty white peaks, often towering above a layer of low clouds, do not seem to have any contact with the firm, solid earth. As shining pyramids suspended in the sky, they appear as incredible and symbolic apparitions.

A GLANCE FROM THE AIR. Flying over the Cascades on a clear day is a panoramic adventure, the only way to appraise the actual nature of this mountain range. You see the southern Cascades and the southern end of the northern Cascades as a volcanic mass, as a green carpet of rolling wooded mountains interspersed with great, white, extinct volcanoes. There is Mount St. Helens, mirrored in Spirit Lake, which last erupted in 1842. Mount Adams towers to the east, and Mount Rainier, at 14,410 feet the tallest of the range, is uneasily dormant, still steaming a little here and there. Mount Baker sent up clouds of black ashes in 1903.

North of Mount Rainier another, non-volcanic mountain mass emerges and spreads out broadly as it approaches Canada. From a breadth of about 60 miles in the south, the Cascades widen into a seemingly limitless expanse, 120 miles broad, of precipitous ridges, deep valleys and numerous glaciers. It is one of America's last true wilderness areas — almost uninhabited, to a large extent unexplored and with hundreds of mountain peaks unnamed. Its most splendid body of water is Lake Chelan, about 55 miles long and standing at an elevation of 1,079 feet. Since it is 1,606 feet deep, its bottom lies more than 500 feet below sea level. Here newly established North Cascades National Park conserves a large area. This spectacular park offers water sports, camping and climbing on more than 300 miles of trails with access by State Highway 20. Adjoining are Ross Lake and Lake Chelan recreation areas.

A VIEW FROM THE ROAD. If the sea and the air present broad panoramic vistas, the highway and the trail reveal the intimate touches of the Cascades which violently shake mountains on one side and tenderly raise delicate, Lilliputian mosses, ferns and wildflowers on the other. Crossing the mountains on the way to the Pacific Coast, it becomes evident that the Cascades are a sharp climatic boundary. On the eastern side there are the high, dry plains and the pine forest with little underbrush and a soft carpet of needles. There are the great irrigation works, and on the former wasteland patches of orchards, shining in the spray of the sprinkler systems. Here grow the apples, pears, cherries and other fruits for which Washington and Oregon have become famous. On the western slopes the great rain

A LOOK FROM THE SEA. The crew of the British man-of-war *Discovery,* which sailed along Puget Sound in April 1792, were probably the first white men to see the grandiose spectacle of a green, forest clad mountain range out of which huge, pure white peaks rose skyward. The peaks appeared doubly high since the explorers' eyes measured them not from a plateau halfway up but from sea level. It was the captain's chance. In the shining mountains he immortalized, with a lavish hand, his personal friends and himself. He thought of Peter Rainier, the admiral, and named the highest peak Mount Rainier. Mount St. Helens had been previously christened for a diplomat-friend. As they sailed northward, Lieutenant Baker came running to point out another great white dome in the sky. The captain verified the report and promptly named the peak Mount Baker. He also did well for himself, and today one great city,

MAGNIFICENT MOUNTAINS: CANADA to the COLUMBIA RIVER

Mt. Rainier above the fertile Ohop Valley in autumn colors.

forests cover the valleys with an undergrowth that is often jungle-like. The ranchers on the east side and the loggers on the west side would never dream of changing places.

AMERICA'S BRIGHTEST WREATH OF FLOWERS.
There is no all seasons automobile road that actually crosses Mount Rainier National Park, but two highways enter it and climb to appreciable heights, offering equally fine views. One, approaching from the west, leads to Paradise, while the other, from the east, reaches Sunrise, at the foot of Emmons Glacier. In the center of the park and covering about 85 square miles, one of America's tallest mountains raises its glittering peak, with 41 glaciers stretching their white tongues from the icy center downhill in all directions. Nisqually Glacier can be reached over a good trail by a short walk. For those who have the time to spare, a pack trip over the 90-mile Wonderland Trail is a unique experience of primitive and beautiful nature. The trail completely encircles the mountain and provides shelter camps about every 12

miles. However, the two-day climb to the peak is difficult and dangerous because of the crevassed icy flanks, the sharp ridges and the crumbling lava. It should be attempted only by well-equipped experts. You may encounter elk and mountain goats on the trail. One of the park's gifts every visitor can enjoy is Mount Rainier's abundance of wildflowers which thrive in the volcanic soil. In the forest zone, under the tall Douglas firs, red cedars and western hemlocks, the trillium, the anemone and the ghost-like Indian pipe are in bloom. Both in the southern and the northern Cascades the forest highways are often framed on both sides with lush beds of bright blue lupines. Above the timberline the gorgeous flower meadows have two peaks of blossoming. At the end of June the pasqueflowers and avalanche lilies are radiant, and at the end of July the Indian paintbrush, valerian, lupine and many others arrive at full bloom. It was John Muir who remarked that these parks — meadows interspersed with lovely small groves of trees — form a great and beautiful wreath of brilliant flowers around the white peak of Mount Rainier.

Portland and the Columbia River

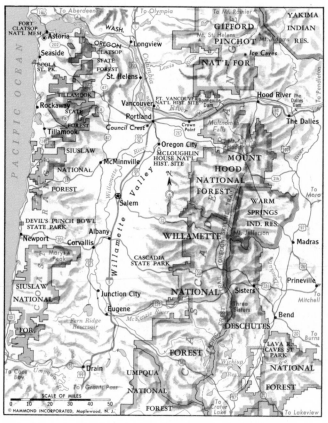

than 1,000 feet high, and the forest is still there. Experts estimate that more evergreen trees — cedars, hemlocks, firs — grow within the limits of Portland than in any other city on earth. Roses thrive everywhere and are a regular adornment of even modest residences. The International Rose Test Gardens and the Japanese Gardens in Washington Park are unusually lovely, and the Sunken Gardens of Peninsula Park are spectacular. To round out the picture, the American Rhododendron Society maintains its test gardens on Crystal Springs Island. Everywhere in Portland something of the quiet, friendly spirit of New England is in the air; the town was indeed founded in 1845 by Yankees from Maine and Massachussetts. Had the flipping of the coin which preceded the official naming of the settlement turned out the other way, the city would be "Boston, Oregon," today. Portland's great hinterland was and is the fertile Willamette River valley, a beautiful, park-like Acadia where farming was started without clearing the primeval forest and rooting out the stumps. From the succession of gold rushes to California, Idaho and the Yukon, the city profited tremendously, selling its Willamette Valley grain and meat at skyrocketing prices. Industries came slowly, expanding during World War II, and the visitor who enters the city from the Cascades will still feel that backwoods, metropolis, pioneer past and industrial future are meeting here face to face.

HEROIC LANDSCAPE. The giant Antaeus of Greek mythology gained rejuvenating strength whenever he touched the earth. That was the way he felt, said President Franklin Roosevelt, whenever he journeyed to the Columbia River Valley. There is indeed an untouched, natural strength in this landscape where history came late and white man arrived only yesterday. The road that follows the river from its mouth at Astoria to the point where the currents turn sharply to the north is one of the continent's great scenic roads with sights full of strength and vitality. In Astoria the spiral frieze of the Astor Column tells of the river's early history. Here horses are used in shallow water to drag in the huge nets with the salmon catches. The road to Portland takes the traveler over wooded hills and through forest and farmland where the lush grass reaches up to the cattle's bellies. But the most spectacular stretch begins east of Portland, following the scenic route that parallels Interstate 80N, where the green horizon is marked with the white domes of Mount Hood and Mount St. Helens, Mount Adams and Mount Rainier. At Crown Point in the Columbia River Gorge the waters cut through the Cascade Mountains, offering a mountain-river-forest panorama not easily forgotten. Multnomah Falls, its waters plunging over the crags down to a pool near the highway 620 feet below, may be admired from below

THE PHOTOGENIC METROPOLIS. A view of Portland in the morning with the cone of Mount Hood glistening in the sunlight; a photo of night descending on the town, the sunset painting the great peak above as rosy as a strawberry sundae; Portland from Council Crest and from Washington Heights; Portland mansions buried under roses and suburban ranch homes shaded by tall evergreens — such pictures frequently appear in magazines and at photo exhibits. But a true impression can be gained only by a personal visit. On a clear day Mount Hood towers above the city more majestically than the great cathedrals of Europe ever towered above their towns. For good measure, on a very clear day Mount Rainier, more than 100 miles to the north, may be seen from many a city street or home window. **166** The residential suburbs lie on hills, some of them more

A VALLEY of the GOOD LIFE

or from a bridge perching halfway up the granite wall. Upstream, the Bonneville Dam offers an interesting experience to those who are fascinated by huge generators and turbines. It is equally interesting to fishermen and lovers of nature who like to watch the ingenious fish ladders which lead around the dam and enable the salmon migrating upstream to bypass the obstacle. Proceeding on our eastward journey, we now enter the drier and sunnier climatic belt east of the Cascades. Here foliage and underbrush are less lush, but the irrigated orchards radiate freshness and life. Beyond the town of Hood River we approach The Dalles, where the Columbia rushes through a narrow 8-mile channel. The chute begins upstream where Lewis and Clark observed, during their epochal journey, a number of Indians standing on rickety, improvised scaffolds and netting or or spearing salmon in the churning waters of the rapids. These fishing rights are still reserved for the Indians.

THE SALMON STORY. The most fascinating inhabitant of the Columbia River and other west coast streams is the Chinook, one of the migrating species of salmon, a creature with a strange fate. Its act of reproduction is also its act of death. Born in the crystal clear brooks and shallows that form the tributaries of the Columbia, they swim downstream at the age of two, spend two years in the ocean and then return in a teeming upstream migration to the very spot of their origin where they spawn and die. The principal movement takes place during the three spring months, and at the Bonneville checking station thousands of Chinooks and steelhead trout have been counted in one hour. It seems that the ladder device functions fairly satisfactorily; nevertheless, the wildlife experts are worried. Of the Columbia Valley streams in which salmon spawned in 1883, many are still blocked by irrigation dams and flumes or are polluted by sewage from factories. Various schemes for the salmon's rescue are being tested. At present it is still possible to experience the joy that Rudyard Kipling felt when with his rod and reel he pulled salmon after salmon from a clear mountain tributary of the Columbia. "I have lived," he wrote.

Multnomah Falls plunge into a pool near the Columbia River Highway.

The graceful Astoria Bridge connects with Washington.

Southern Cascades

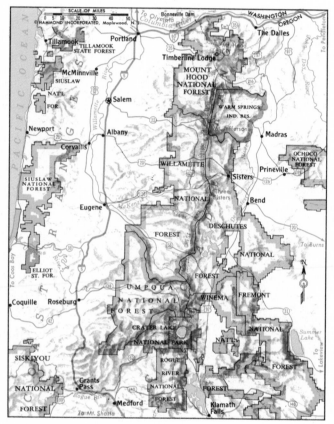

surveyed and inaccessible. Yet man loves this land of thundering landslides and roaring rivers, of 70-foot snowdrifts and jungle-like forests on the Pacific slopes. No range can boast of more mountain clubs. Even at such tourist centers as Timberline Lodge and Crater Lake the call of the wilderness is distinctly felt.

WHITE CLOUD OF STONE. At the northern end of the southern Cascades, Mount Hood raises its white crown of snow into a brilliant blue sky. Its height of 11,235 feet is quite modest if compared with the summits of the Rockies and the Sierras. Yet, as it stands grandly by itself, calm and aloof, rising approximately from sea level, it appears gigantic. The first settlers estimated it to be 18,000 feet high.

The difficult Cooper Spur climb to its top begins at the famous old resort of Cloud Clap Inn which also lies on the 37-mile Round-the-Mountain Trail. The 164-mile Mount Hood Loop Drive presents breathtaking panoramic views. There are other fine roads for motorists, but anyone wishing to become intimately acquainted with these magic mountains should follow their nearly 400-mile-long backbone from the Columbia River to California on Oregon's Skyline Trail, a part of the 2,350-mile Pacific Crest Trail that winds along the Pacific mountain ranges from Canada to Mexico. Here the packtrain rider enjoys the silence of great Douglas fir forests, climbs around snowcapped summits, passes torrential rivers and mirror-like lakes. He marvels at meadows aflame with blossoms and forest floors soft with ferns and green mosses, small creepers and brightly painted fungi. Virtually all of the region is contained in national forest lands, with facilities for mountaineering, skiing and tobogganing.

BLEAKNESS INTO BEAUTY. A ring of huge volcanoes circles the Pacific Ocean — Fujiyama, Japan's sacred peak, Krakatoa off Sumatra, the Andean Cordillera of South America and the Cascades of the northwestern United States. At one time, when their craters belched black smoke and cinders, the Cascades must have loomed bleak and forbidding above the shoreline. Today, when most of them have been extinct for thousands of years, their volcanic nature turns them into monuments of breathtaking beauty. They stand by themselves in massive grandeur and have an unusually regular shape. In addition, they are exposed to the first onslaught of the moist clouds drifting in from the Pacific and receive a heavy snowfall, when they are clothed with dazzling whitecaps.

This range is still truly a wilderness, a last frontier, largely unsettled by human beings, with wide areas un-

NATURE DESIGNS A PARK. The southern Cascades offer beauty spots that are uniquely their own, that cannot be encountered on any other American mountain range. For they possess wonderful parks created not by man but by nature. Encircling Mount Jefferson and the Three Sisters, these sky-meadow parks are carpeted with pink shooting stars and red Indian paintbrushes, blue lupines and graceful columbines. They are dotted with silvery pools and with groves of lush alpine trees, a scene far more exquisite than a mere human landscape architect could create. The most famous of these parks is Jefferson Park, a flower garden two miles square, traversed by crystal clear brooks with banks of velvety moss and with miniature lakes that mirror dark green ponderosa pines and the straight spires of mountain hemlock. The fantastic southern backdrop of the scene, towering massively against the brilliant sky, is Mount Jefferson, which rises suddenly from the floor of

MAGNIFICENT MOUNTAINS: MOUNT HOOD to CRATER LAKE

OREGON STATE HIGHWAY DIVISION

South Sister Mountain rises above Sparks Lake in central Oregon.

the valley in almost perfect architectural design. The blue-black lines of its glacial crevasses separate the shiny ice fields into a dark white pattern all its own. This eldorado can be reached by packtrain only.

THE WORLD'S BLUEST LAKE. The question, "Which is the most beautiful spot on earth?" cannot be answered with definite assurance. But there are world travelers who know our planet well and who have made their decision. It is Crater Lake, whose unearthly beauty touches everyone who sees it. To glance at its blue surface surrounded by tinted cliffs up to 2,000 feet high is an experience that stirs the imagination. The blue of its water is a mystery. It is not simply a reflection of the sky as in other lakes, for its water is always blue under a cloudy sky or on a moonlit night. Nor is it caused by mineral content, as a chemical analysis has shown. The most probable theory makes two factors responsible for the lake's everlasting shades of blue — the perfect clarity of the water and its great depth of almost 2,000

feet. Sightseers feel strongly the fascination of this spot when in a boat. With a sheer, sky-high cliff towering by the shore and water below that is so clear their eyes can penetrate it deeply, they have the impression of floating somewhere in space.

The lake is the product of a geological catastrophe. Once Mount Mazama, a huge volcano, stood here. In an explosive eruption such masses of lava streamed out of its crater that they carried along much of the inner structure of the mountain. The upper cone remained as an empty shell and finally collapsed, creating a round lake approximately 6 miles across. Wizard Island with its crater has been raised by later volcanic activity, and a group of twisted lava pinnacles is called the Phantom Ship. Although without inlet or outlet, the water level remains the same, since evaporation and precipitation balance each other perfectly. To the south 40-mile-long Upper Klamath Lake is a bird sanctuary. Myriads of migratory waterfowl can be observed there, including egrets, cormorants and the giant white pelicans.

169

The Oregon Coast

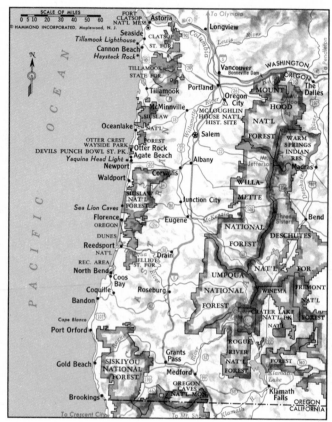

kittles," and this was their "salt cairn." On the southern horizon the Tillamook Head lighthouse, its base 91 feet above the water, rises from a sheer, isolated rock in the sea. A few miles to the south off Cannon Beach lies Haystack Rock, prime example of many similar cyclopic boulders strewn here and there over the broad, white Oregon beach. Haystack is a 300-foot rock, now reached on foot over the hard sand, now completely surrounded by the swishing water of long, rolling breakers, and crowned with a densely populated metropolis of shrieking gulls, terns and cormorants. On the southward journey you will pass through many a small port where the forest and the sea meet. In Tillamook the smell of salt water and of freshly cut cedar is supplemented by the aroma of cheese; it's a dairy center.

AGATES AND SILVERSIDES. The road winds up and down between sea level and the crest of high cliffs. At Otter Crest Wayside Park the seascape is a wonderful blend of rugged promontories, dark green forests and the deep blue Pacific, 454 feet below. The shore along Otter Rock, a seabird rookery, and Devils Punchbowl, a caldron of churning tidal waters, is rich in beach deposits. One can find fossilized wood, jasper, and "Oregon jade," really agate, which gave its name to Agate Beach. Agates are a popular item in the souvenir shops of Newport, whose resort section is located along Highway 101 while the picturesque old fishing town nestles in the hills around Yaquina Bay. The city's Undersea Gardens and the Oregon State University Marine Science Center are open to visitors. An adventurous excursion is available here. To get up at 3:00 A.M. on a summer morning, have breakfast with some skippers in one of the all-night coffeehouses near the wharves, then sail out with the commercial fleet and come home in the afternoon with 2 or 3 silverside salmon which you caught yourself is an exhilarating experience. Or drive to nearby Yaquina Head Lighthouse, climb over the rugged cliffs, enjoy the profusion of wildflowers, watch the cormorants and gulls circling above and the starfish and the sea anemones in the marine garden below, and you will feel that you have spent a few worthwhile hours. There is an unusual and truly American story connected with Newport's history. In 1856 a blockhouse of the U.S. Army was to be erected at the site of an Indian cemetery consisting of hundreds of burial canoes. The Indians agreed to the removal of the canoes but made it clear that they were not willing to touch them themselves. So at the turning of high tide the American soldiers set adrift the canoes carrying the dead warriors. The white men watched the silent flotilla glide past the tall forest from the bay into the ocean and saw the strange craft vanish from their sight in the misty sunset of the Pacific.

HAYSTACK ROCK AND TILLAMOOK LIGHTHOUSE. Talapus, the coyote god of the Indians, walked along this shore, shaped the capes and the bays and determined the limits of the tide. Red warriors followed the coyote god, and the early traders found a trail along the coast. But it took many a generation to change the path into a highway. The latter was not completed until the 1930's. It starts at Astoria, a salmon port with a large Finnish population. The 125-foot-high Astor Column on Coxcomb Hill commemorates the trader-adventurers who established a post here in 1811. The first stop is Seaside, Oregon's best known ocean resort. Here the End of the Trail Monument marks the conclusion of the Lewis and Clark expedition. It commemorates not an heroic but a practical act. Four of the men were directed to "commence making salt with five

SWEEPING CAPES, FOREST-LINED FORTS, TEEMING WILDLIFE

RED-BEAKED PIGEONS AND 12-FOOT SEA LIONS. About 40 miles south of Newport a fascinating spectacle may be observed at Sea Lion Caves, a large multicolored cavern where a herd of sea lions spends the winter and has established its rookery. The inhabitants, Steller's sea lions, are the largest species of their family, averaging 12 feet in length. Originally they appeared in great numbers, but the seal hunters of the nineteenth century almost exterminated them. This Oregon herd is a fascinating remnant. Stairs lead from the highway to observation posts below and make it possible to watch the harem-style family life of the huge seals, which have both the tawny color and the loud roar of lions. Around the cliffs there are swarms of birds just as unusual as the mammals in the cave. Outstanding are the guillemots with their bright red beaks and the thick bodied puffins with their rakish tufts. The latter, excellent swimmers and divers, look so much like small parrots that they are called sea parrots.

CEDARS FOR BLINDS AND A HOTEL FOR SHIP-WRECKED SAILORS. One of the spectacular features of Highway 101 is its large number of tall, graceful bridges. They are especially in evidence at Coos Bay, the region of the Port Orford cedar, which is really a cypress. This straight-grained light wood is greatly in demand for special purposes, particularly for the manufacture of venetian blinds. Bandon is a well kept resort, and to the south Port Orford is the site of a famous Pacific Coast hotel, the Knapp Hotel, which was erected in 1867. Among the inns of America it has a unique distinction. Probably more stranded and shipwrecked sailors gathered there than anywhere else. The coast was dangerous, and the hotel welcomed the adventurers. Hair-raising stories were heard around its fireplace. Jack London loved it and is said to have written his "Valley of the Moon" while staying there. The state line nears, and California is already in the air. On clear days Mount Shasta offers a majestic welcome.

The spectacular Oregon coast at Oceanside west of Tillamook.

Cape Sebastian State Park near Gold Beach combines a lovely landscape with a sparkling seascape.

Sightseeing Guide

ALASKA

Among our 50 states Alaska ranks first in area — it is more than twice as large as Texas — and 50th in population with over 300,000 inhabitants. The southern coast, which has been opened to tourism, has a pleasant summer climate comparable to that of many other states. It rains a good deal, however, which keeps the countryside lush and green. Alaska offers not only magnificent scenery and fine fishing and hunting but also elbowroom, clear air, pure water and the aura of a pioneer society. To stimulate tourism, the U.S. Forest Service is establishing hundreds of recreational areas along the southern coast, attractive spots like the visitors' center at Mendenhall Glacier near Juneau.

Alaska is a huge wildlife sanctuary. Its moose are among the world's largest for an old bull may weigh up to 1,300 pounds, and the Alaska brown bear (or Kodiak bear) is the biggest meat eating land animal on earth with a weight of up to 1,500 pounds. Other native animals are mentioned on pages 156-157. The bison has been introduced, and experiments are carried on to domesticate the musk-ox, producer of superfine wool. The shore is teeming with birds — with ducks and geese, swans and loons, gulls and cranes, puffins and albatrosses. Whales and seals cavort in Alaskan waters; the fur seals have their famous rookeries on the Pribilof Islands. Salmon, halibut, cod, herring, king crabs and abalone are extracted from the sea, and trout, arctic char, northern pike and sturgeon from the rivers.

SOUTHEASTERN ALASKA. Ketchikan in the southern panhandle is a regular stop of the Alaskan Marine Highway; it is an important fishing port with an outstanding collection of totem poles. Sitka was the capital of Russian America and still preserves mementos of its Russian past. St. Michael's Cathedral of the Russian Orthodox Church, built in 1816, recently burned down and is being rebuilt, but icons and similar religious art objects have been saved and are now exhibited in the cathedral's basement. Totem Pole Lane preserves 18 fine poles. The ancient Russian bell foundry furnished bells for the California missions, and these bells are still in use. The sites of the Russian fort and of the battle between the Russians and the Tlingits are preserved in Sitka National Monument. Juneau is the state capital and home of a large fishing fleet. The Last Chance Gold Mine provides visitors with rides on mining cars. Nearby Mendenhall Glacier and Glacier Bay National Monument as well as Haines-Port Chilkoot, the terminal of the inland passage, are described on page 156.

SOUTH CENTRAL ALASKA. Mount McKinley National Park is described on pages 156-157. Anchorage, Alaska's largest city, is the state's commercial center. Not far to the south the Arctic Valley Ski Center has been established on Mount Alyeska; it is equipped with a modern chair lift and features skiing and skijoring, curling, ice hockey and dogsled racing. Fairbanks grew out of the old gold strikes of 1902 and is the terminal of the Alaskan railroad and the Alaska Highway. From there bush pilots fly travelers to any point of the interior. Fairbanks is also the home of the University of Alaska and of Alaskaland, an antique Yukon stern-wheeler which sails daily, gold miners' cabins and Eskimo village. Circle Springs and Circle are the northernmost points to be reached by car on an extension of the Alaska Highway. Kodiak on Kodiak Island, accessible from the mainland by ferry, holds a King Crab Festival every May. The Kodiak bear is one of the most highly prized trophies of big game hunters. Katmai National Monument has been described on page 157; it is located at the base of the Alaska Peninsula off which lie the Aleutian Islands, which have the world's longest chain of active volcanoes.

WESTERN AND NORTHERN ALASKA. The Eskimo areas of Nome, Kotzebue and Barrow have been described on page 157. All three towns offer exhibits and dance performances every summer.

ALBERTA, CANADA

NORTHERN ALBERTA. Wood Buffalo National Park, between Athabasca and Great Slave lakes, is the preserve of America's largest herd of wood buffalo, a species bigger than the plains buffalo. The park is not easily accessible to the public. The Yellowknife wilderness area is accessible only by air; it is an outstanding region for fishing, hunting and roughing it.

EASTERN ALBERTA. Near the golf course of Medicine Hat a cairn marks the site of Police Point, headquarters of the Northwest Mounted Police from 1883 to 1891. Forty-three miles to the south Cypress Hills Provincial Park is a popular playground.

CENTRAL ALBERTA. Edmonton is the capital of Alberta, with impressive government buildings, a museum, planetarium and zoo. It is the seat of the University of Alberta. In the lake country around Edmonton, Elk Island National Park is a fenced preserve for large herds of buffalo, deer, elk and moose; the 75 square miles of the park contain all recreational facilities. Eighty-eight miles northeast of Calgary on Highway 9 the Badlands of the Red Deer valley are a wilderness of geological interest. A section of the badlands, Dinosaur Provincial Park, has been set aside as a tourist attraction, a fantastic region of ravines, flats, coulees and red shale hills. Petrified forests, prehistoric oyster beds and Horseshoe Canyon are decorated with strange formations known as dolomites and ammonites. This was a stamping ground of prehistoric monsters, and fossils are found frequently. Scenically the valley abounds in thrilling vistas which occasionally take on a Grand Canyon splendor.

WESTERN ALBERTA. Waterton Lakes National Park is the Canadian section of the Waterton-Glacier International Peace Park, a famous mountain playground of snowy peaks and lovely lakes. (See also pages 148-49). Northeast of the park in the Galt Gardens near Lethbridge, a cairn commemorates the 1872 opening of the first coal mine in Alberta. Southeast of Lethbridge on the Milk River, Writing-on-Stone Park preserves ancient Indian picture writings on rocks of grotesque shapes. Calgary is the modern trading center of a rich farming and ranching area. The town's Heritage Park and the Horsemen's Hall of Fame are local attractions. The Calgary Stampede, held during the first two weeks in July, is Canada's most famous rodeo; the contest includes an exciting chuckwagon race. On the city's St. George's Island the wild animals of a modern zoo are supplemented by the concrete and plaster forms of huge dinosaurs and saber-toothed tigers which roamed the prehistoric jungles of Alberta. Banff National Park with the city of Banff, Lake Louise and Chateau Lake Louise are described on pages 150-151. Jasper National Park and the Columbia Icefield are described on pages 152-153.

BRITISH COLUMBIA, CANADA

THE COAST OF BRITISH COLUMBIA. Victoria, famous for its

NORTHWEST REGION

colorful flower gardens and its British atmosphere, is described on page 154. Nanaimo on Vancouver Island is an old trading post of the Hudson's Bay Company, with the original loghouse still on the site; a regular boat service connects it with downtown Vancouver. Nanaimo is the gateway to Canada's Evergreen Playground, to the Forbidden Plateau in Strathcona Provincial Park, and to the Campbell River country, which is popular for fishing. On the island's west coast is Port Alberni at the head of the picturesque Alberni Inlet; it can be reached by driving through giant forests. Vancouver is described on page 154; the city is the home of the University of British Columbia. The Inside Passage to Alaska is described on pages 154-155. In Prince Rupert as in Ketchikan, fish canneries and totem poles are the tourist attractions.

INTERIOR BRITISH COLUMBIA. In the eastern part of the province, a number of national parks preserve the most beautiful and spectacular sections of the Canadian Rockies. With Banff and Jasper national parks in Alberta and several provincial parks, they form the greatest mountain park system in America. Mount Revelstoke National Park includes 8,650-foot-high Mt. Revelstoke; its principal attraction is an alpine region of dozens of lovely, clear little lakes, of open stands of slender-spired alpine firs and a carpet of wildflowers. The park contains championship ski runs and a ski jump. Nearby Glacier National Park protects another portion of the superb Selkirk Mountains with their towering summits, jagged ridges and glistening glaciers. Since this is a true wilderness without automobile roads, only hardy hikers and climbers will cherish it. They can reach the park by the Canadian Pacific Railway, and the Trans-Canada Highway passes through the park. On the west slope of the Rockies, Yoho National Park encompasses lofty peaks like Mt. Goodsir (11,686 feet), magnificent cataracts like the Seven Sisters Falls, two ice fields on the Continental Divide and clear lakes like Emerald and O'Hara. The word Yoho is an Indian expression meaning wonderful! Kootenay National Park is a strip of mountain scenery on both sides of the Banff-Windermere Highway; the road leads through bright red walled Sinclair Canyon, past the resort of Radium Hot Springs and Marble Canyon, with a natural bridge and waterfall. Lovers of the untouched wilderness will appreciate Wells Gray Provincial Park to the northwest; it is an undeveloped lake and mountain area of unusual scenic beauty. West of the park Old Barkerville maintains the traditions of an old mining town with a stagecoach ride to the gold commissioner's office and Theatre Royal. Visitors may pan for gold in the creek. In the southwest corner of the province, on the United States border, Manning Provincial Park lies on Highway 3 between Hope and Princeton. Its features are mountain trails, alpine meadows, huge beds of wildflowers and a varied wildlife. All recreational facilities are available, including skiing.

IDAHO

NORTHERN IDAHO. In the Idaho panhandle, Lake Pend Oreille, largest in the state, is a glistening mountain lake whose eastern shore is lined with the cliffs of the Cabinet Mountains. Snow-capped peaks loom in the far distance. The scenery has grandeur, and the lake is an ideal fishing spot. Many fishermen set out from the Pend Oreille Yacht Club at the southern end of the lake to catch landlocked salmon of the blueback variety, or cutthroat, steelhead and Kootenay rainbow trout. Some anglers return with astonishing catches of steelheads, migrants from the Columbia River weighing up to 30 pounds, and

Kootenay rainbows of 32 pounds. Fishing is good as late as November and, at that time, may be combined with hunting for deer and black bear. Hunters stalking game in the nearby mountains will encounter groves of huge cedars almost as tall as the redwoods of the northern California coast. Coeur d'Alene Lake south of Lake Pend Oreille (what an array of imaginative French names!) is one of America's freshwater gems, with a sparkling blue surface and cone shaped evergreen trees dotting the hilly shore. A seven-hour boat trip is available from the city of Coeur d'Alene at the northern end of the lake. Passengers lunch at Heyburn State Park at the southern end. Travelers interested in mining will find Kellogg, east of Coeur d'Alene, a center of extensive silver, zinc and lead mining operations; some of the plants are open to visitors. The Sunshine Mine is one of the largest silver producers in the United States. Leading south from Coeur d'Alene toward Lewiston near the Washington state line, U.S. Highway 95 descends 2,000 feet from the Palouse highlands in 95 spirals, with ten miles of magnificent views. Scattered over 12,000 square miles of northern Idaho are 23 historic sites comprising Nez Perce National Historical Park.

CENTRAL IDAHO. The Grand Canyon of the Snake River, part of the Idaho-Oregon state line, is the deepest gorge on the North American continent; south of Hat Point it reaches a depth of 7,900 feet. At the spot called Hells Canyon the canyon walls are less than 100 feet apart. The perpendicular cliffs of multicolored rocks now fringe the High Mountain Sheep Reservoir; Kinney and Horse Mountain lookouts offer great panoramas, but on land the canyon is still quite difficult to reach. A tributary of the Snake River, the Salmon River, winds its way through the gorges and canyons of central Idaho; for a stretch it can be observed from Highway 95, and some adventurous boatmen brave the river's white water on a downstream trip. But hardly any have dared to undertake the upstream voyage. The awesome Salmon River Gorge can be viewed from U.S. 93 in a setting of wild mountains and forests near the river's source at Challis. Sun Valley, the all-year luxury resort, and Craters of the Moon National Monument are described on pages 146-147. Between the two sightseeing spots the Sawtooth National Forest, part of which now lies in the Sawtooth National Recreation Area, offers pack trips into magnificent mountain country; fishing and big game hunting are popular. Boise, the state capital, was founded in 1863; 24 miles to the east Arrowrock Dam is one of the highest irrigation dams on earth.

SOUTHERN IDAHO. Bear Lake straddles the Idaho-Utah state line and is a popular water sports and fishing resort in both states; 20 miles long, it has numerous delightful beaches of white sand. Lava Hot Springs is a health resort southeast of Pocatello. Mineral springs gush water of 140° F. into outdoor pools. Pocatello is noted for its rodeo held every year in June. American Falls Dam is a huge hydropower and irrigation project on the Snake River. Fort Hall is the headquarters of the Fort Hall Indian Reservation. In midsummer the small town attracts many visitors when the Indians perform their annual Sun Dance and other ceremonials. In the city of Twin Falls the Perrine Memorial Bridge over the Snake River offers magnificent views; 476 feet above the river's surface, it is one of the highest cantilever bridges on earth. To the west one can see the Blue Lakes, lovely bodies of water of deep azure color. Irrigation projects have considerably reduced the scenic splendor of Twin Falls and Shoshone Falls, except early in the year when the spring floods rush over the horseshoe of the Shoshone Falls, plunging into an abyss 212 feet deep. Idaho's contribution to the American cuisine is the Idaho potato.

MONTANA

NORTHERN MONTANA. Fort Peck Dam is a huge, earth filled structure about 250 feet high with a broad highway across its crest. It dams up a man-made lake extending for 189 miles. While its main purposes are irrigation and the improvement of navigation on the Missouri River, it has also created a great recreational area for campers, fishermen and sailors. The Fort Peck Game Range protects mountain sheep and pronghorn antelope, elk, white-tailed deer and mule deer, waterfowl and upland birds. A great number of fossils which were discovered during the construction of the dam are on display in Fort Peck Theater. The town of Fort Peck is an old fur trading post. Great Falls, Montana's largest city, was the home of the great cowboy artist Charles M. Russell, who had his studio in a log cabin. Much of his work is preserved in the Charles M. Russell Gallery and Original Studio. Four and a half miles northeast of Great Falls, on the south bank of the Missouri River, the Giant Springs discharge more than 388 million gallons of water every day. The park surrounding the springs is a popular picnic spot. The Blackfeet Indian Reservation, the excellent Museum of the Plains Indians in the interesting Indian town of Browning, Glacier National Park, one of America's most magnificent scenic spots, and the Going-to-the-Sun Road are described on pages 148-149. South of the park on large Flathead Lake the Flathead Indians have their reservation and communal grazing grounds; their tepees can usually be seen from Highway 93. South of the lake the National Bison Range maintains a huge bison herd; the animals are scattered in small groups over an 18,500-acre refuge.

WESTERN MONTANA. Missoula is the home of the University of Montana. Helena, the state capital, developed from the Last Chance Gulch mining camp, and gold was dug where Helena's main street is now located. On occasion some of the old placer diggings in the neighborhood are still worked successfully. Silver and lead have also been mined there. Historically speaking this is Lewis and Clark country. Everywhere there are plaques and reminders referring to the advance of the explorers, and a mural by Charles M. Russell in the Capitol glorifies the great adventure; the boat which they used on the Missouri River is an interesting relic. The Capitol stands on the summit of a hill and offers a broad panorama of a great valley and distant mountain ranges. Helena is not on but near the Missouri, and a boat cruise on the river to the Gate of the Mountains is a worthwhile excursion. To the west, on U.S. 12, Frontier Town is the replica of an old mining town. Butte has been called the world's greatest mining city; it has hundreds of miles of streets on its surface, but thousands of miles of tunnels underground. Although the town was founded in the gold rush of 1864 and changed to silver mining when the big silver deposits of Silver Bow Creek were discovered in 1874, it was the copper discovery of 1880 that established Butte's fame. The copper ore is shipped to a huge smelter at Anaconda, 26 miles westward. The Kelley Mine in Butte is open to visitors, who are also welcome at the excellent World Museum of Mining. The latter is a part of the Montana College of Mineral Science which attracts to Butte students from every state of the Union and many foreign countries. The climate of the region is pleasant, and the sun shines almost 300 days during the year. Among the scenic attractions are the Continental Divide at Pipestone Pass, south of Butte, and the Lewis and Clark Cavern State Park to the east. This is a large limestone cave with multicolored and weird stalagmite and stalactite formations; guided tours are available. Near the Idaho state line the Big Hole National Battlefield commemorates the fierce fight that took place there on August 9, 1877, during the retreat of Chief Joseph of the Nez Perce Indians. South of Butte Virginia City has been re-created the way it looked when it was the second capital of the territory. This is Virginia City, Montana, not to be confused with Virginia City, Nevada, which has also been revived from its ghost town slumber. Both Virginia Cities recreate for twentieth-century visitors the spirit of western frontier days.

SOUTHERN MONTANA. The Beartooth Highway is a magnificent 60-mile mountain road from Red Lodge to Yellowstone National Park. Splendid vistas of the Beartooth Mountains unfold on all sides, with lookout points provided at frequent intervals. A zoo near Red Lodge exhibits the animals and birds typical of Montana, and in the neighborhood of Cooke City the Grasshopper Glacier is a natural curiosity. On a mountain trail at the northeastern rim of Yellowstone Park, a large ice field a mile and a half long is permeated with layers of millions of frozen grasshoppers imbedded in the glacier. Billings is the center of a great ranching area, and large crowds of tourists are attracted by the annual Midland Empire Fair and Rodeo held in August. One of the local sights, about ten miles from the city near the boundary of the Crow Indian Reservation, is the Pictograph Cave. Visitors may see there the picture writings of an unknown race; excavations and restorations are under way. Three interesting sightseeing spots may be visited south of Hardin. One is the Crow Indian Reservation Agency about 13 miles south of Hardin on U.S. 87. In summertime the driver has the illusion of early trapper days, for the broad lands are studded with groups of tepees. The Sun Dance in July is a great ritual, and late in August the Crow Indian Fair is colorful, a spectacle of fancy horseback riding, ceremonial dancing, racing and arrow throwing. The Crows are outstanding artists in beadwork, and beadwork articles are for sale. A few miles to the south, on the same highway, the Custer Battlefield National Monument honors General Custer and the officers and men of the five companies with him who, on June 25, 1876, were wiped out by the Sioux and Cheyenne. Custer's Last Stand at the Little Bighorn was the climax of the Indian wars which were bitter and bloody in Montana. To the southwest of Hardin, Bighorn Canyon National Recreation Area is worth seeing. From Horseshoe Bend Lookout over the state line in Wyoming one glances down into the winding canyon which has twice the depth of Yellowstone Canyon. The view is breathtaking; from the surface of Bighorn Lake the brightly colored stone walls rise vertically to the top; their sides show dark gashes of immense caverns, and their rims are decorated with strikingly formed rocks.

OREGON

THE COAST OF OREGON. At the mouth of the Columbia River, Astoria, established as a fur trading post in 1811, is the oldest white settlement in the state. An excellent spot to survey its setting is the observation platform on the 125-foot-high Astor Column on Coxcomb Hill. The monument is decorated with a continuous pictorial strip wound around the column in a spiral depicting the colorful story of the fur trading fort, now a fishing port. The city's waterfront is fascinating with its salmon nets

NORTHWEST REGION

hundreds of feet long being manipulated. Oregon's coastal highway, one of America's showplaces, is described on pages 170-171. The sights include Seaside, the bathing resort, Cannon Beach and Haystack Rock, Otter Crest Park, Devils Punchbowl, Agate Beach, the picturesque old fishing town of Newport, the Sea Lion Caves, Coos Bay, the world's leading lumber port, and Port Orford.

NORTHERN OREGON. Portland is one of America's rose cities; the rose festival in June is a great event for Portlanders and visitors. The city is described on page 166. The spectacular Columbia River Highway with Crown Point, the Columbia River Gorge, Multnomah Falls and Bonneville Dam are also described on pages 166-167. Portland's great landmark, the snowcapped Mount Hood with Timberline Lodge, is described on page 168. In the northeastern part of the state the city of Pendleton is a farming and ranching supply center. Every September it is host to the Pendleton Round-up, a three-day rodeo and Indian ceremonial which is one of the gayest and most colorful pageants in the Northwest. There are large camps of real tepees; covered wagons are pulled by teams of twelve longhorns plodding along under their wooden yokes, and in the center of town Happy Canyon invites the celebrants to saloons, gambling houses and dance halls.

CENTRAL OREGON. The Southern Cascades with Mount Hood and Mount Jefferson are described on pages 168-169. South of Mount Jefferson, Cove Palisades State Park is of interest; it was established around the cove, a 1,000-foot canyon now occupied by Lake Billy Chinook where the Deschutes and the Crooked rivers unite. Approaching the McKenzie Pass, the Three Sisters are among the spectacular peaks of the Cascades. The town of Bend is the starting point of the 100-mile-long Century Drive-Cascade Lakes Highway, a loop of scenic roadways south and east of the Three Sisters. Elk Lake, Deschutes River and the Devil's Chair are popular points for sightseeing, fishing and hunting. The drive leads to crystal lakes, glacial meadows and mountain forests. In Bend proper thousands of waterfowl may be watched in Drake Park. Pilot Butte State Park is to the east of Bend; in this park the attraction is a 500-foot-high cinder cone whose summit, accessible by automobile, offers a splendid view of the snowcapped Cascades. Twelve miles south of Bend, Lava River Caves State Park preserves a geologically unique phenomenon — a natural tunnel 5,460 feet long and 35 feet high.

THE WILLAMETTE VALLEY OF NORTHWESTERN OREGON. The fertile and beautiful valley of the Willamette River is Oregon's most densely populated area. South of Portland, Champoeg State Park contains picnic sites and a museum of Oregoniana; in the park is the site of the first provisional government of the territory, established by Americans in 1843 before it was legally determined whether the region would belong to Great Britain or the United States. In Oregon City the McLoughlin mansion of 1846 is now a museum of Oregon relics and a national historic site; its builder, Dr. John McLoughlin, was a director of the Hudson's Bay Company and, for all practical purposes, the ruler of the Northwest Country. The State Capitol at Salem is a fine modern building with a huge symbolic figure representing the Pioneer. To the east are Silver Falls State Park, the Detroit Dam and, on the western slope of the Cascades, Breitenbush Springs, a resort with some 50 mineral hot springs. Eugene is the home of the University of Oregon.

EASTERN OREGON. Enterprise is the gateway to the magnificent Wallowa Mountains, a mountain wilderness with a few civilized spots. At Wallowa Lake a state park provides riding, fishing and all water sports. At the southern end of the lake bighorn sheep may be observed. On the Idaho state line the Grand Canyon of the Snake River is truly wild country; the gorge is deeper than the Grand Canyon of the Colorado River in Arizona. A good view may be had from the lookout tower at Hat Point. On the dry plateau near John Day, the Thomas Condon-John Day Fossil Beds State Park permits a glance into the early eras of the earth; fossils have been unearthed there of huge mastodons and miniature horses, of giant sloths and saber-toothed tigers. In Canyon City, adjoining John Day, the four-room cabin built in 1864 by the poet Joaquin Miller is a museum now. Owyhee Dam creates a 52-mile-long lake and irrigates about 100,000 acres of land.

SOUTHERN OREGON. Crater Lake National Park, one of the continent's truly unique sights, is described on page 169. Oregon Caves National Monument has been established at a chain of great limestone and marble caverns extending underground for miles. Guided tours are available. South of Crater Lake, the region of Upper Klamath Lake attracts students of wildlife. The lake itself is the largest freshwater body in Oregon and its shores are lined with waterfowl rookeries. Particularly interesting are the huge numbers of white pelicans which like to nest at Upper Klamath Lake, nearby Lake Ewauna and the Link River, on which the city of Klamath Falls is located. To the east, U.S. 395 passes through a most picturesque spot near Valley Falls. On the western side there are the rippling waters of Lake Abert; on the eastern side, Abert Rim rises steeply for 3,500 feet like a huge, 19-mile-long sector of the Great Wall of China. The foot of the rim proved a fertile hunting ground for archaeologists, who found there pictographs and arrowheads, fossils and skeletons. Unfortunately, Lake Abert dries out in years of drought. Few tourists travel to the Hart Mountain National Antelope Refuge east of Lake Abert, but occasionally a thrilling sight can be seen from the highway. Over the plain, set off by barren mountains in the distance, a herd of 60 or 70 pronghorn antelope runs by, a picture reminiscent of the African steppe. America's largest herd of pronghorns lives in this refuge.

SASKATCHEWAN, CANADA

SOUTHERN SASKATCHEWAN. Regina, the capital of the province, is a pleasant city surrounded by rich agricultural lands; it has Wascana Centre, including government buildings, a university and a cultural center, in an attractive park and water landscape on Lake Wascana. Regina is also the training headquarters for the Royal Canadian Mounted Police; visitors are welcome. To the west Moose Jaw is an important railroad point, and its grain elevators rise from the plains like huge towers. Saskatoon is a lovely college town, the seat of the University of Saskatchewan. In the southwestern corner of the province six prairie dog towns with more than a thousand animals may be visited just south of Val Marie. Sage grouse, burrowing owls and sometimes black-footed ferrets may also be seen there.

NORTHERN SASKATCHEWAN. Prince Albert, about 100 miles north of Saskatoon, has a flavor all its own. It is a quiet farming community, but the discovery of uranium and other minerals in the north country gives it occasional touches of a boom town. Thirty-six miles north of the city Prince Albert National

Park, a vast region of rocks, woods and water, is still filled with the memories of trappers and fur traders, explorers and Indians. The park's special feature is its wonderful canoeing for it contains hundreds of lakes, and many of them are connected by little rivers and streams. From the dock at Waskesiu Lake canoe journeys of various durations may be undertaken. Lake Lavallée is a famous wildlife sanctuary; its islands are covered with the rookeries of a bird which we usually associate with the Deep South, the white pelican. These quaint "relics of a twilight, antediluvian age" have their extensive nesting grounds in this clear, cool, northern lake. There are also large colonies of double-breasted cormorants. At Montreal Lake just east of the park, a tribe of Cree Indians has a reservation. Superb fishing for fighting freshwater species like northern pike, a special far north variety of pickerel and lake trout is found at Lac La Ronge. Although the lake is located in the wilderness of the far north, the village of La Ronge, at the end of Highway 2, offers modern accommodations.

WASHINGTON

WESTERN WASHINGTON. Puget Sound is described on pages 162-163. Near the Canadian border, the town of Lynden is a bit of Holland in Washington. Dutch customs and language are still cultivated there, and in springtime the town is surrounded by brightly blooming fields of daffodils and tulips. Bellingham is a pleasant city on Puget Sound opposite the San Juan Islands. Nearby Mount Baker National Forest, an all-year recreational area, can be reached by a scenic highway. Seattle, gateway to Alaska, is described on pages 162-163. Two state parks near Seattle are popular: Saltwater State Park and Twanoh State Park across the bay at Bremerton. There, at the U.S. Naval Shipyard, the U.S.S. *Missouri* may be visited; the spot is marked on deck where World War II ended with the Japanese surrender. Olympic National Park is described on page 160. The white peak of Mt. Rainier forms a splendid background to the commercial and industrial city of Tacoma. In Olympia the State Capitol with its sunken gardens and the war memorial form an impressive architectural group near the bay. Twelve miles south of Chehalis, Lewis and Clark State Park is a popular recreation area. Along the coast just below Aberdeen, Twin Harbors State Park has a very large attendance of visitors; it is Washington's only state park on the Pacific Ocean proper. Long Beach, near the mouth of the Columbia River, has a truly long beach; it is 300 feet wide and 28 miles long.

CENTRAL WASHINGTON. The North Cascades National Park, Mount Baker, Lake Chelan and Mount Rainier National Park are described on pages 164-165. Where Lake Chelan touches Highway 97 a popular resort area has sprung up; a boat ride to the northern end of the lake takes visitors into a wilderness of jagged mountains where peaks within the Lake Chelan National Recreation Area are mirrored in the water. Where Interstate Highway 90 crosses the Cascades Snoqualmie Pass is a spectacular stretch of road drilled through rock tunnels and hewn into canyon walls; it is a spot of record snowfalls — up to 400 inches in a year. Near the town of Snoqualmie, the 270-foot-high cataract of the Snoqualmie Falls is a splendid spectacle enhanced by a number of miniature falls on its rocky sides. Mount St. Helens as seen from Spirit Lake is one of America's famous sights; an automobile road leads to the lovely lake, and even the timberline can be reached by car. East of Mount St. Helens, snowcapped Mount Adams rises to a height of 12,307 feet; the area abounds with trout streams. On the northern bank

of the Columbia River west of the Bonneville Dam, Beacon Rock is a 900-foot-high monolith, the world's second largest; a zigzag trail leads to its top. Also on the northern bank of the Columbia River, south of Goldendale, a replica of prehistoric Stonehenge in England stands as a war memorial on a cliff — totally out of place. Samuel Hill, the railroad tycoon, established nearby the Maryhill Museum of Fine Arts; it displays, among other curios, a collection of personal belongings of European royalty. In the Yakima Indian Reservation Old Fort Simcoe has been restored as it looked in 1856. In the village of White Swan the long houses where tribal meetings are held welcome visitors in July. The Yakima ritual of the root-digging-and-salmon-run-thanksgiving is a famous ceremony. Yakima is the center of "the fruit bowl of the nation." To the north, 25 miles east of Ellensburg, in the Gingko Petrified Forest State Park is a 3,000-acre preserve of gingko trees which millions of years ago were buried under volcanic ash and turned into stone; numerous fossilized trees still stand upright as they had grown originally. To the north Wenatchee is the apple capital; it lies in the center of four valleys covered with irrigated orchards. North of the city at Rocky Reach Dam visitors may watch the spillways and fish ladders.

EASTERN WASHINGTON. Grand Coulee Dam and Roosevelt Lake are described on pages 158-159. Near Coulee City, Dry Falls State Park preserves an ancient gorge, now dry, where at one time the Columbia River plunged over a cataract. Spokane, capital of the "inland empire," is a great trading center; nearby are 76 lakes, all within easy reach. Northeast of the city a scenic drive leads to the top of Mount Spokane; Mt. Spokane State Park is a favorite area for summer camping and winter sports. At the bend of the Columbia River near Pasco the Hanford Atomic Energy Reservation contains one of the largest nuclear fission projects. West of Walla Walla the Whitman Mission National Historic Site honors Marcus Whitman and his wife Narcissa, who established an Indian mission and school on the site; they were killed by Indians in 1847.

WYOMING

NORTHERN WYOMING. In the northeastern corner of the state Devils Tower National Monument is a unique kind of mountain. It has the shape of a gigantic tree stump, rising 865 feet above the ridge from which it seems to grow, and even the outside of the rock is grilled like bark. Pleasant woodlands surround the tower, and the visitor center has exhibits which tell its story. To the west Sheridan is noted for its beautiful parks; the Sheridan Rodeo in July is one of the state's most popular festivals. Where Highway 14 crosses the Bighorn Mountains, Medicine Mountain is an attraction on two counts: one is the broad panorama of the Bighorn Basin, the other the Indian Medicine Wheel, a stone wheel measuring 245 feet in circumference, a ceremonial structure laid out by an unknown Indian people. A town which retains a certain frontier flavor is Ten Sleep on U.S. 16 west of the Bighorn range. It is surrounded by sheep and cattle ranches, and scenic Ten Sleep Canyon is nearby. The name is derived from the Indians' method of measuring distances; it means ten days or ten "sleeps" of travel, in this case from Fort Laramie. Cody was founded by William F. Cody, known as Buffalo Bill. He lived there for 20 years and was the driving power behind the Shoshone Irrigation Project and the resultant Buffalo Bill Dam. He is honored in the Buffalo Bill Historical Center, which includes the excellent Whitney Gallery of Western Art. Just outside of Cody U.S. 16 leads through the spectacular five-mile gorge of Shoshone Canyon and scenic Shoshone National Forest.

NORTHWESTERN WYOMING. Yellowstone National Park, the world's greatest volcanic outdoor museum, is described on pages 142-143. The beautiful Grand Teton National Park is described on pages 144-145.

CENTRAL WYOMING. There are several points of interest around the trading center of Casper. North of the city is Teapot Dome, a U.S. Naval Petroleum Reserve which made scandalous political history in the 1920's. To the west Hells Half Acre is an area of twisted caverns, stone figures and spires; one section called Devil's Kitchen has been opened as a park. To the southwest Independence Rock is a stone tower almost 200 feet high and measuring about 1,500 feet in circumference; early travelers of the Oregon Trail carved their names into this rock. Nearby a 218-foot-high dam creates the large Pathfinder Reservoir. Northwest of Casper Hot Springs State Park near Thermopolis is a recreational area.

SOUTHERN WYOMING. The history of Cheyenne, the state capital, is particularly colorful; in the days of Indian attacks, of badmen and vigilantes this was the rip-roaring Wild West. With such traditions Cheyenne's Frontier Days Celebration, held in the last week of July, is one of the country's best Western shows. In the State Office Building the State Museum houses a good collection of Indian relics. Fort Laramie National Historic Site near the North Platte River comprises the remnants of an important trading post and garrison of 1834; of 21 buildings remaining several have been restored. In the days of the Oregon Trail covered wagons stopped there by the dozens, forty-niners on their way to the goldfields sought protection in the fort against the Indians, and the Pony Express maintained a horse changing station there. The Red Desert in southern Wyoming is a little known, colorful wilderness which preserves a remnant of the romantic Old West; herds of wild horses still roam its lonely canyons and mesas. All the mustangs are hardy, and a few are magnificent specimens. Systematic roundups in which the herds are spotted from airplanes threaten to exterminate these picturesque survivors from the days of the conquistadores, but movement for their protection is under way. In the southwestern corner of the state old Fort Bridger is a state historic site which includes the early buildings of the fort and the Pony Express Station. The fort was founded by Jim Bridger, the famous scout, discoverer of the Great Salt Lake and the Paul Bunyan of the Rockies. Fossil Butte National Monument lies just west of Kemmerer.

YUKON AND NORTHWEST TERRITORIES, CANADA

YUKON. The notion that Canada's arctic north is the preserve of explorers and adventurous hunters and fishermen is still widespread. Yet every year more tourists find their way into the northland and discover a fascinating corner of the earth. The scenery of the Yukon Territory is magnificent, especially in the southwestern region where the St. Elias Mountains contain the highest and most majestic peaks in Canada. During the summer, when the temperature rises to 80° F., the valleys are a bright carpet of hundreds of varieties of wildflowers, and the lakes and streams offer an incredible harvest of lake trout, rainbow trout, pike, whitefish, char and arctic grayling. Wildlife enthusiasts will encounter moose and caribou, white Dall sheep, black bears and brown grizzly bears. In the Northwest Territories herds of thousands of bison roam freely in Wood Buffalo National Park, with 17,300 square miles the world's largest national park. A popular travel route starts at the tidewater in Skagway, Alaska, just west of the British Columbia line; from there thousands of tourists ride on the White Pass and Yukon Railway to Whitehorse. This narrow-gauge railroad has a double attraction: it runs through magnificent scenery and follows an historical trail, the "Stampede Route" of the gold rush of 1897-98. Carcross, a way station on the trail, calls itself "the Town that Discovered the Klondike." From the town's bridge the world's largest lake trout was caught, 5 feet 2 inches long and weighing 87 pounds. In Whitehorse, capital of the territory, the Old Log Cathedral, the Indian Cemetery and the stern-wheelers on the riverbank are historic relics in an otherwise modern city. In nearby beautiful Miles Canyon daily boat excursions are provided. The Gold Rush Route, a modern highway, leads from Whitehorse to Dawson in the center of the territory near the Alaskan border; the place offers a fascinating picture of a mining town of gold rush days. The old bars and saloons are still there as well as the beached stern-wheeler *Keno,* the last of the riverboats on the Yukon run. Live stage shows, often similar to those enjoyed by the gold miners, are presented at the Palace Grand Theatre. From this town a well-known "Top of the World Tour" to Anchorage and Fairbanks is offered by Canadian Coachways. South of Dawson, the tributaries of the Klondike River still attract quite a few amateur prospectors who have fun panning for gold. Now and then they actually find a nugget or a flake to take home as a souvenir. All the larger towns can be reached by Canadian Pacific Airways. Smaller connecting airlines and charter air services are at the disposal of hunters and fishermen. Good roads, small hotels, motels and campgrounds are available at most tourist spots.

NORTHWEST TERRITORIES. Still a frontier, the territories are of interest largely to experienced outdoor enthusiasts. However, careful preparation will be necessary before the trip is undertaken. Several gravel roads are available. Highway 1, The Mackenzie Route to Adventure, runs from the border of the province of Alberta to the lake country of the high north across the North Arm of Great Slave Lake. Highway 5 crosses Wood Buffalo National Park just north of the Alberta border. Campground and picnic places are provided and occasionally motels can be found. Resourcefulness and self-reliance are still recommended prerequisites. Both the Yukon and the Northwest Territories have some precious assets which are highly appreciated by modern travelers: the bright summer nights which never fade into total darkness, the undisturbed silence of the countryside and the clear, crisp, unpolluted air.

Southwest Map

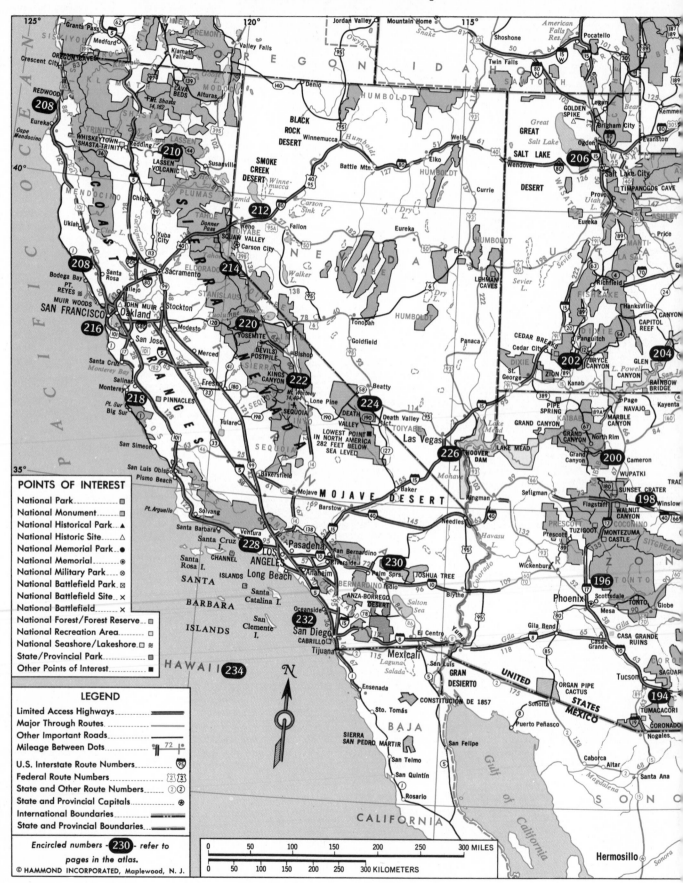

POINTS OF INTEREST

National Park........................□
National Monument........□
National Historical Park...▲
National Historic Site.....△
National Memorial Park....●
National Memorial.........◉
National Military Park.....⊗
National Battlefield Park...⊠
National Battlefield Site....×
National Battlefield.........×
National Forest/Forest Reserve..□
National Recreation Area......□
National Seashore/Lakeshore □ ≈
State/Provincial Park..........■
Other Points of Interest......■

LEGEND

Limited Access Highways.............═══
Major Through Routes................────
Other Important Roads...............────
Mileage Between Dots................⊢72⊣
U.S. Interstate Route Numbers.......⑮
Federal Route Numbers...............㉑㉓
State and Other Route Numbers.......②②
State and Provincial Capitals.......⊛
International Boundaries.............━━━
State and Provincial Boundaries.....━━━

Encircled numbers - ②③⓪ - refer to
pages in the atlas.

© HAMMOND INCORPORATED, Maplewood, N. J.

WHAT to SEE in the SOUTHWEST REGION

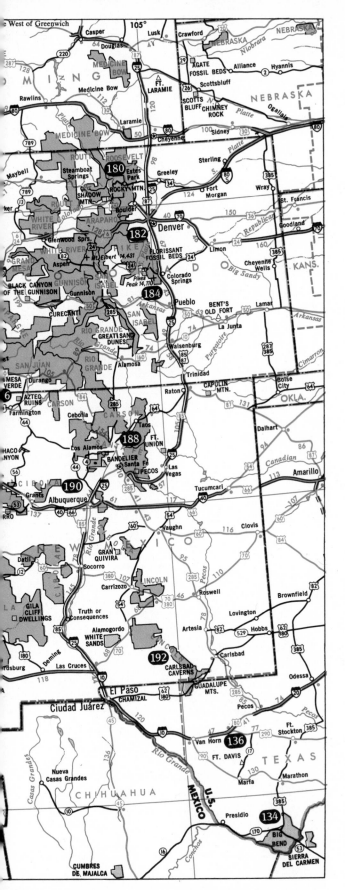

FIVE-DAY TRIP ACROSS THE CENTRAL ROCKIES. For a general introduction see pages 180-187, also sightseeing guide pages 236-239. Suggested route: Rocky Mountain National Park. Its spectacular mountain scenery is made accessible by the Trail Ridge Road which leads over high tundra and crosses the Continental Divide, the Bear Lake Road and the road to Longs Peak, 14,256 feet tall; elk and deer, bobcat and mountain lions, bighorn sheep and bear inhabit the park — Boulder, seat of the University of Colorado —Denver, the mile-high state capital with a gaudy past as a rich mining and cattle town, and with an excellent mountain park system — Colorado Springs, a tourist center with an abundance of scenic attractions: the cogwheel railroad to the top of 14,110-foot Pikes Peak, the incline railway to the summit of Mount Manitou, an authentic ghost town on 21st Street in Manitou Springs, six miles to the north the Garden of the Gods, a group of strange red sandstone formations, the Gold Camp Road, the Rampart Range Road, the Broadmoor-Cheyenne Mountain Highway and other scenic drives — Canon City with the Royal Gorge Scenic Railway and an incline railroad to the bottom of the Royal Gorge. The gorge is spanned by the world's highest suspension bridge — Black Canyon of the Gunnison National Monument near Montrose with the Ute Indian Museum — the Silverton-Durango narrow gauge train offers an old-fashioned scenic ride — Mesa Verde National Park has great pueblos built into the cliffs by prehistoric Indians.

TWO-WEEK GRAND TOUR OF THE SOUTHWEST. For a general introduction see pages 188-191, 194-201, also sightseeing guide pages 236-239. Suggested route: Entering New Mexico from the north, Taos presents a fabulous historic landmark: the five-story pueblo of Taos, still occupied by the Indians whose ancestors built it in prehistoric times. The town is an outstanding art colony — Ranchos de Taos is a Spanish settlement around the mission of St. Francis — Santa Fe, the oldest capital city in the United States, is unique with its adobe architecture and its Spanish atmosphere; with the Governor's Palace of 1609, now a museum; the Cathedral and several ancient missions — Albuquerque which recreates the life of old Mexico in its Old Town. Sandia Peak, reached by cable car, offers a wide view — Gallup, a center of Indian arts and crafts. The Intertribal Indian Ceremonial, celebrated every August with rodeos and dances, is a gathering of numerous tribes — Petrified Forest National Park, located in the dazzling Painted Desert — Flagstaff, Arizona, seat of the Southwest Indian Powwow — South Rim of the Grand Canyon, one of the world's most spectacular scenic spots — Phoenix, a modern city with an Indian heritage. The Desert Botanical Gardens in Papago Park are unique — Tucson with the Arizona-Sonora Desert Museum, presenting living desert plants and animals in their natural habitat.

THREE-WEEK NATIONAL PARK TOUR OF CALIFORNIA. For a general introduction see pages 208-223, also sightseeing guide pages 236-239. Suggested route: San Francisco — via Redwood Highway north to Eureka — east to Whiskeytown-Shasta-Trinity National Recreation Area with Shasta dam, lake and ghost town — Lassen Volcanic National Park, still active — Reno, Nevada, the gambling center — Virginia City, historic mining town, Queen of the Comstock Lode — Lake Tahoe, another spot of exquisite beauty — Yosemite National Park — Kings Canyon National Park and adjoining. Sequoia National Park — via Fresno to the coast on coastal highway past Big Sur to Carmel — Monterey — San Francisco.

Rocky Mountain National Park

THE DISTANT BLUE WALL. Over the western Great Plains a cloudbank seems to loom. Approaching it from the east, the blue vision is transformed and condensed, within an hour's drive, into a very real wall. It has a massive, forbidding, dead-end appearance, as if a huge, impenetrable fortification had been thrown up to divide the continent. The sight of it must have been disheartening to the pioneers. How were they ever to cross that barrier of solid, continuous rock? To them it was indeed a backbreaking task. To the modern traveler the entrance phase is a pleasant surprise, almost a revelation. For as we ride through the foothills, the peaks recede to the left and to the right; between them the road winds up along a raging river, through a canyon and over a pass, and in another hour we are within one of the world's greatest masses of mountains. We are headed for Rocky Mountain National Park in Colorado, the "roof of America," about 50 miles northwest of Denver. In this heart of the Rockies there are 65 peaks higher than 10,000 feet; 42 higher than 12,000 feet; 15 higher than 13,000 feet; and Longs Peak, the park's tallest, reaches a height of 14,256 feet. The first impression of this mountain empire is that of closely packed, towering density, of a massiveness that is unique. The backbone of the country, the Continental Divide, runs through the park. The Mummy Range, a majestic spur of the Rockies lying in the northeast part of the park, includes some of the loftiest peaks and one of the finest glaciers.

THE DRAMA OF THE TIMBERLINE. One of the most spectacular highways on earth crosses the park and makes it possible to enjoy the high mountain country by car — the Trail Ridge Road. Where else on this or any continent can one ride above the 11,000 foot level for 11 miles, and higher than 12,000 feet for 4 miles? Crags, peaks and gorges are everywhere, but the road takes you to many small and large mountain meadows that are carpets of wildflowers, of blue columbines and snow buttercups, paintbrushes and gentians, lilies and hundreds of other flowering plants. Another most interesting sight the Trail Ridge Road has to offer is the spectacle of the timberline. The uninitiated may imagine that the border between the forests and the rocks and meadows is a belt of peaceful and quiet transition. It is not; here in the high Rockies one can see the perennial struggle, the field of battle between the elements and the plants. Freeman Tilden lets the trees speak: " I *will* live. I shall bend. I shall creep on hands and knees. I shall dodge, devise, join hands, and compromise; but I *will* live . . . ." The old and young evergreens, the bushes and the naked skeletons are gnarled, dwarfed and staggering, bent into geometrical half-circles or twisted into absurd forms suggesting old men or bears. One small pine — a boy could carry its trunk on his shoulder — was found to be 258 years old, and some seedlings reached the height of 3 inches in 30 years. A wonderful spot for camera enthusiasts, the timberline, especially for the imaginative ones who have a flair for abstract photography. The Trail Ridge Road is in use from early June to late September while the National Park is open all year. Also the Bear Lake Road and the road to Longs Peak are scenically superb. Of interest to camera buffs is the abundance of wildlife in the park. This is the natural home of the surefooted Rocky Mountain bighorn sheep, and these superb climbers can be observed ascending and descending precipitous slopes with amazing agility. Elk, deer and other animals abound, and beavers patiently working on their dams may be observed along almost every drainage in the park.

THE ROOF of AMERICA

Longs Peak above Bear Lake is America's most frequently climbed high mountain.

THE CHEERFUL MOUNTAINEERS. In spite of the jumbled massiveness of the ranges, and in spite of the struggle for life and the snow flurries that may fall in July, these mountains are friendly. There is a mood of good cheer and adventure in the park; Longs Peak, for instance, is high by any standard, and its summit cannot be reached just by hiking; the last stretch of the trail requires sure footwork. But actually thousands of men, women and children have been on its top. It is the most frequently climbed tall mountain in America. The history of the whole park has the tone of friendliness and enjoyment. The open, forest-rimmed valley now known as Estes Park was first seen by white men when Joel and Milton Estes visited it in 1859. As early as the 1860's groups of settlers and ranchers from the surrounding valleys used to ride with their families to some pristine meadow between the peaks; they set up tents and enjoyed the air, the view, the birds and the fishing, for a week or two. A famous figure of those days was Rocky Mountain Jim, a hunter and trapper who used to trot over the trails on a big white mule. He looked tough, especially after a grizzly bear had scraped out one of his eyes. But the mountains inspired him, and he wrote poetry. Then there was the old hermit who lived in this neighborhood and had his own greeting of welcome to visitors: "May the Lord take a liking to you." He had a distinguished neighbor, the Earl of Dunraven, who loved the Rockies and for his and his friends' pleasure established in the 1870's a ranch of 6,000 acres on the east side of the park, incorporating the former Estes claim. The English lord's enterprise had snobbish overtones, and the mountain settlers saw to it that it was broken up. In 1884 a thin and eager boy arrived on the scene, all by himself, and was strangely fascinated by the shining mountains; Enos Mills was his name. He stayed here most of his life, became a well-known naturalist and writer and was obsessed with one idea and one goal. He had no money but he had friends, and he never gave up the struggle. In 1915 his vision turned into reality: His beloved peaks became the property of the nation, to be preserved forever. In that year Rocky Mountain National Park was born.

181

Denver

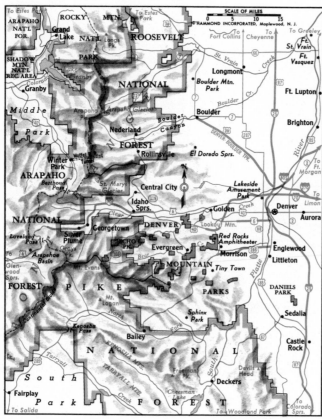

is the special pride of its citizens. It lies southwest of nearby Golden, can be reached in an hour's drive and covers almost 13,500 acres of canyons and mountains, trout streams and lakes, picnic grounds and shelter houses, barbecue pits and softball diamonds. It also includes a good part of the Front Range, some of America's most spectacular scenery. A feature of the parks system is the Red Rocks Amphitheater, which has been carved into the red sandstone. There the Denver Symphony Orchestra plays under the stars on summer nights, or folk dance festivals are held, or an opera is performed. The acoustics are said to be so excellent that the slight thud of a pencil dropped on the stage is heard in the last rows. Within the park system are a highway to the top of Mt. Evans (altitude 14,264 feet), on whose summit is a physical research laboratory where scientists study the nature of cosmic rays, and also Lookout Mountain where Buffalo Bill is buried. Visitors toss coins over the iron railing around his grave for good luck.

PRAIRIES AND MOUNTAINS. One has to see Denver from an airplane on a clear day, the neat gridiron of streets surrounded by the rolling prairies and a backdrop of tall mountains, to understand the various flattering names the city has acquired over the years. Denver is often called "Queen City of the Plains" or "Capital of the Rocky Mountain Empire." If, from a bird's-eye view, bright splashes of sunlight play simultaneously on the tall buildings and the snowcapped ridges of the Front Range, there is indeed something monumental about that panorama. In the city proper the boulevards, the State Capitol and the Neo-Classic Civic Center with the impressive City and County Building, the mall and the esplanades are laid out broadly in the same manner and spirit. The Denver Mint, our biggest gold depository after Fort Knox, is well-known. As can be expected, Denver's museums stress the Western theme. For its collections of American Indian cultures a beautiful new glass tiled museum has been erected. The Denver Public Library owns eight priceless albums of early photographs of the West (1870) by W. H. Jackson, the greatest Western photographer of his day. The Colorado Railroad Museum near Golden has interesting exhibits of railroading in the high Rockies.

A GAUDY PAST OF YOUTHFUL PRANKS. Culturally and economically the Denver of our time is considered progressive, but at the same time quite conservative. Its gaudy past as a cattle and mining town lives on only in numerous tales of the days when the Windsor Hotel served banquets at $100 a plate, a fortune at that time, and the swashbuckling owners of the Denver

1 MILE — 300. This is the magic formula which makes Denver a popular goal for vacation travelers and a good city to live in all year 'round, for the community lies on a plateau one mile high — the exact marker can be seen on the steps of the Capitol — and enjoys 300 sunny days per annum. The climate is fine, and the occasional notices in the Eastern press about unseasonal snowstorms in Denver are misleading. Denver is by no means an arctic waste during the winter. In fact, some winter days are pleasant enough to enjoy a picnic. The favorable weather is supplemented by an abundant water supply, tapping mountain lakes and streams fed by the winter's accumulation of snow. The supply system even siphons water from the Pacific drainage area.

AN AMPHITHEATER HEWN INTO THE ROCKS.
Beyond the city limits, Denver's Mountain Parks system

METROPOLIS of the SHINING MOUNTAINS

Post viciously attacked rival editors and non-advertising merchants. Many a tale centers around H.A.W. (Silver Dollar) Tabor, a mining tycoon who built the Tabor Grand Opera House which once stood on 16th Street. When at the opening in 1881 he spied a picture of Shakespeare in the lobby, he asked angrily, "What has Shakespeare ever done for Colorado?" Promptly the bard was removed and replaced by Mr. Tabor's portrait. In Denver's earliest days the Elephant Corral was a frontier log hotel, so-called because of its size. In its notorious gambling saloon killings were so frequent that the hotel featured funerals with all expenses charged to the house. The hotel undertaker owned the private cemetery where he buried his customers, but he saved the coffins. He was said to have used the same coffin 30 times, the last time for his own burial. The Corral burned down in 1863.

CENTRAL CITY: REVIVAL OF THE GAY 90's.
Denverites have still another means of reviving a lustier past. Every summer for several weeks they take over the picturesque little mining town of Central City, which once was called "the richest square mile on earth." Here, in 1873, President Grant stepped from his carriage to a sidewalk of silver bricks, and the town enjoyed national fame when Horace Greeley wrote glowingly of its fabulous diggings in the New York *Tribune*. With his own hands he had panned gold from a placer mine, unaware of the fact that speculators had shot gold dust into the mine for just that purpose. Later on Central City became a ghost town — the whole region is honeycombed with abandoned mines. In the 1930's the University of Denver inherited the Central City Opera House, and with the help of civic groups an annual Festival of Opera and Drama was instituted. The incomparable scenery — the town dangles precariously on a mountainside — the Broadway stars, Metropolitan Opera singers, the old opera house itself with its gaudy Victorian style and audiences often wearing costumes of the same period, the Glory Hole nightclub, and the Teller House, with "the Face on the Barroom Floor," combine to make the festival a huge success.

Colorado's Georgetown, a silver camp in the 1870's, preserves many charming buildings of that period among them the odd Maxwell House.

The Red Rocks Amphitheater, carved into red sandstone, is part of the spectacular Mountain Parks System of Denver.

Colorado Springs

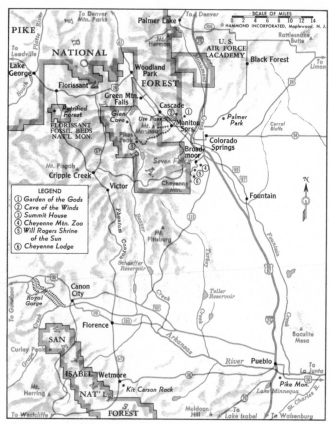

could never be scaled, would be surprised to discover that not only does a cogwheel railroad lead to its summit today but also an automobile road, and that thousands of Americans enjoy the view from the top.

A SUCCESSFUL RESORT. It was inevitable that a city should spring up at the approach to the Ute Pass in the shadow of Pikes Peak. Colorado Springs had the good luck of being planned, from the very beginning, as a resort town. Families wth freshly accumulated mining fortunes looked for a place to build their residential mansions and found the spot ideal. The climate pleased them, and the scenery — the forested foothills, the rugged canyons, the backdrop of Pikes Peak — had the romantic wilderness beauty of the West. Broad streets were laid out and planted with trees and lined with ditches in which clear, cool mountain water bubbled. Air-polluting factories were kept out. This was a time when the word vacation had a somewhat frivolous ring, while taking the cure was considered a respectable activity. The health springs at the neighboring village of Manitou Springs were refurbished, and Colorado Springs now attracted health seekers from all over America. As the climate was considered helpful to TB patients, several sanatariums were established. The patients were outraged when the town's new playhouse opened with a performance of "Camille." Gradually all the scenic beauty spots became accessible, and they are still outstanding attractions. Beyond the river, west of the city, the Garden of the Gods is a municipal park strewn with grotesque rock masses of fantastic shapes. In the late afternoon when the rays of the setting sun suffuse the sandstone columns and figures with a glowing red against an azure sky, this spot is a mecca for color photo enthusiasts. A little beyond, the resort village of Manitou Springs is the starting point for the inclined railway to Mount Manitou (9,455 feet) and for the diesel-powered cogwheel railroad to Pikes Peak. On a clear day the vista from Pikes Peak reaches out over the Black Forest and eastern Colorado to the wheat fields of Kansas 200 miles away. The Summit House, which can also be reached by car on a spectacular highway, is built on a mass of boulders held together by ice. From Manitou Springs, Williams Canyon with the Cave of the Winds is easily accessible. A newer attraction of a different kind is the U.S. Air Force Academy. Modern Colorado Springs is clean, green, bright and attractive, given to golf and polo tournaments, rodeos and flower festivals.

A FABULOUS HOTEL. One of the sights of Colorado Springs merits special mention — the Broadmoor Hotel, located south of the city in a suburb of the same name. Its setting is in the grand manner. The red-roofed group

PIKES PEAK COUNTRY. "Pike's Peak or Bust" was lettered on the canvas cover of many a westbound Conestoga wagon in 1859. The occasion was a gold rush in Colorado. The matter came to national attention again several months later when hundreds of the same wagons, now the worse for wear, recrossed the plains in an easterly direction. This time an additional inscription proclaimed "Busted, by God." Pikes Peak, the disappointing goal of the gold seekers, became so well-known that the whole region was named for it. At 14,110 feet it was not the highest mountain, but its prominent position had made it an Indian landmark for a hundred miles around. It may also have been the northernmost point seen by the Spanish explorers. The first U.S. citizen to describe it was Lieutenant Zebulon Pike in 1806, and as a result the name Pikes Peak was adopted. Pike, who predicted that the wild, great peak

FROM the GARDEN of the GODS to ROYAL GORGE

of white buildings lies in a cluster of green trees by a blue lake against the bold contours of Cheyenne Mountain, which turns purple in the afternoon sun. The hotel cultivates a truly Western atmosphere, not only through its collection of guns and frontier relics and its rodeo grandstand but also by keeping alive the tradition of its flamboyant founder, Spencer Penrose. After leaving Harvard the sunny and extroverted young "Spec" went west and plunged into all sorts of mining ventures, with varying luck. Once when broke he cabled his brother in Pennsylvania for a new grubstake. One hundred and fifty dollars arrived promptly with the warning that the money was to be used as railroad fare to Philadelphia and that Spec was to end his frontier activities. Spec did not answer but appeared in person several months later, handing his brother a check for $75,000. He had invested the railroad money in the Colorado mining boom, he remarked casually, and this was the dividend. When at the Broadmoor, visit the Golden Bee, an old English pub that was bodily transplanted from London.

THE GORGE WITH THE STEEPEST RAILWAY AND THE HIGHEST BRIDGE. Southwest of Colorado Springs, near Canon City, the Royal Gorge, also called the Grand Canyon of the Arkansas River, is one of Colorado's most popular sightseeing spots. The narrow canyon and the sheer red granite walls with picturesque bands of rock strata and the rushing river below are accented by several touches of civilization. The bands of the tracks of the Denver and Rio Grande Western Railroad glisten on the canyon floor beside the river. From the rim to the bottom of the canyon sightseers may ride on an inclined railroad, reputedly the steepest in the world, or they may cross by car or walk over the Royal Gorge Suspension Bridge, said to be the highest of its kind in the world. Its 880-foot main span connects the rim of the chasm 1,053 feet above the river.

The chapel of the Air Force Academy at Colorado Springs reflects a spirit of up-to-date leadership.

Pikes Peak in white and blue, the Garden of the Gods in brown and red.

Mesa Verde National Park

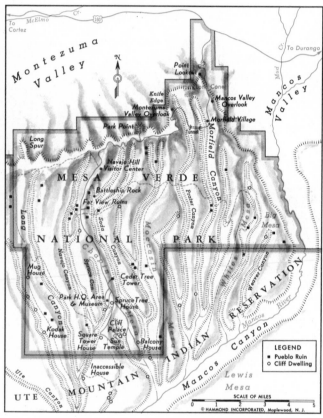

process, however, many more ruined cliff dwellings were discovered. America at large hardly took notice until the famous Swedish archaeologist, Baron Nordenskjöld, visited the cliff dwellings and pronounced them "so magnificent that they surpass anything of the kind known in the United States." That brought action, and in 1906 Mesa Verde National Park was organized. Systematic excavation began and those separate communities were restored, each in a huge cave of its own. Today they are known as Spruce Tree House, Cliff Palace, Far View House and Balcony House. Sun Temple, a strange structure which apparently served as the religious sanctuary for the region, stands on top of the canyon's rim. Many other ruins have been dug out of the debris of centuries, and exploration is still proceeding.

A PREHISTORIC APARTMENT HOUSE. Guided by rangers, tourists may visit several of these ghost towns in the Rock. Some, like Spruce Tree House, are easily accessible while visitors to Balcony House must climb a thirty-foot ladder fastened to the canyon wall high above the valley and squeeze through one or two small connecting tunnels. Best known, perhaps, is Cliff Palace, built high above the canyon floor in a cave 100 feet high and about 300 feet long. Two hundred bedrooms and storage rooms, each provided with a hole for a ladder, were usually square in shape and built of stone on many levels. Daytime activities including the preparation of food were carried on in the courts or the pleasant, loggia-like open space by the rim. There were also the "kivas," 22 of them in Cliff Palace alone. These

Square Tower, the tallest cliff dwelling, 200 feet above the canyon floor.

GERHARD SCHLOTTERBECK

A GHOST TOWN IS DISCOVERED. Rounding up stray cattle in the lonely canyons of Mesa Verde in southern Colorado was a trying job on that December day of 1888. Weary and cold, the two cowboys found a sheltered resting place and began to build a fire. Looking across the canyon wall, their eyes suddenly opened wide. They saw a city of walls, houses, balconies and towers rising from a heap of ruins, all built on the ledge of a giant cave whose upper cliffs overhung the town like a canopy. Excitedly the two men climbed into the ruins and found bones, pieces of fine pottery and other relics, but no life. What had happened to the builders of the towers? Had a war or a siege forced them to surrender? Had an epidemic wiped them out?

Word of the sensational discovery spread, and curious settlers and travelers visited the site, helping themselves to souvenirs and doing a great deal of damage. In this

186

CASTLES of a VANISHED CIVILIZATION

round underground chambers served as ceremonial and religious clubrooms for the men. About 12 feet across, these clubrooms were provided with a "sipapu," a small hole thought to connect with the underworld.

THE TREE CALENDAR. Today we know the story of the cliff dwellers in some detail. This reconstruction of pre-Columbian history became possible through the work of Dr. A. E. Douglass, a scientist at the University of Arizona. He set up a tree calendar based on the fact that trees grow one ring every year, and that the nature of the ring varies according to weather conditions in each particular year. A crosscut of a freshly felled tree from the mesa region offered valuable information for perhaps the last 200 years. A cut from a log used in the construction of a 500-year-old dwelling was compared with the cut of the tree. The characteristics of the innermost rings of the tree were matched with the outer rings of the log. That pushed the calendar back another few centuries. Now a cut from a log in the cliff dwellings was matched, in the same fashion, with the cut from the 500-year-old dwelling. In that ingenious way the tree calendar could be gradually reconstructed for more than 1,900 years, to the first few decades of our era.

THE GREAT SPIRIT WAS ANGRY. It did not rain. For years it did not rain. The corn and the cotton withered, the wild berries shrank. Neither the sorcery of the medicine men nor the dances of the warriors placated the gods. The drought began in A.D. 1276 and lasted for 24 years. It was more than the cliff dwellers could bear. This in addition to unknown social problems forced a decision. Clan after clan left, and gradually the great houses were deserted. No one came back. The emigrants probably wandered in a southerly direction and were absorbed by their blood brothers, the Pueblo Indians.

The question of the origin of the cliff dwellers is equally interesting. Shortly after the birth of Christ the Basketmakers began to inhabit the mesa as farming Indians, living in natural caves. Around the year A.D. 450 they learned to make pottery, use the bow and arrow and build themselves one-family pit houses, consisting of shallow excavations with roofs of poles and adobe. In the late 700's their civilization had become more ceremonious and closely knit, and pueblos were erected as community houses. This new prosperity attracted savage raiders, and soon after the year 1000 the first castles in the canyon walls were erected. They served their purpose for more than 250 years.

PANORAMA OF A CIVILIZATION. To this day ruins of all these stages in their civilization can be observed within the Mesa Verde National Park — the pit houses, pueblos and cliff castles. Two self-guiding loops of the Ruins Road, totaling 12 miles, reach numerous canyon-rim vantage points where many cliff dwellings can be viewed and 10 excavated mesa tops can be visited. Exhibits at five stops explain the points of interest. An excellent museum at park headquarters connects the threads and fills in the gaps so that the visitor sees, in fascinating perspective, the rise and fall of a valiant people.

The Fire Temple, a ceremonial sanctuary built into a cave.

Cliff Palace, with 200 rooms the largest cliff building.

From Santa Fe to Taos

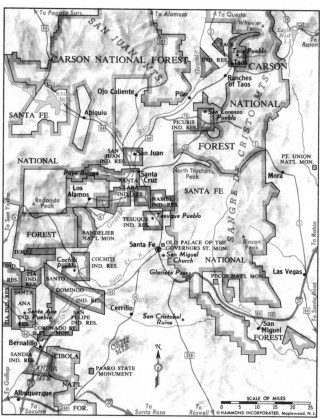

MONOTONY AND BEAUTY. New Mexico is the fifth largest state in the Union. It possesses high mountains and a dramatic mesa and canyon country, but much of it is semiarid grazing land or outright desert. Long stretches may seem monotonous to the newcomer, but if he is willing to look with appreciative eyes he will discover an almost hourly change of color and light that is strangely fascinating. New Mexico's full-blooded Indians harmonize completely with the landscape in their appearance and their way of life, and there is beauty in such harmony. Indian and old Spanish folk art may often seem odd rather than lovely. The wooden spikes surrounding the statue of Our Lady of Guadalupe are primitive, but they are a sunburst of heavenly glory as seen through Indian eyes. Among the relics of local Spanish art there are life-sized effigies of saints which, at first sight, seem almost terrifying. Yet their expression of heartfelt anguish and sorrow reveals unusual depth

and sophistication. The visitor will have a similar experience with the Indian ritual dances. To his eyes they will at first appear colorful and exotic. Later they become monotonous. But it he stays and lets the movements, the drums and the chants sink in without thoughts of hurry, he will appreciate their artistic and religious significance.

THE ROYAL TOWN OF THE HOLY FAITH OF SAINT FRANCIS. This city, called Santa Fe for short, is the oldest capital city in the United States. Ten years before the *Mayflower* cast anchor in Massachusetts Bay, Santa Fe was established in 1610. In the impressive governor's palace 60 Spanish governors ruled a strange empire which stretched from the Mississippi to the Pacific coast and had no real borderline at all to the north. Thousands of converts were made among the Indians. When the latter secretly continued their old rites and were flogged and killed because of witchcraft, the tribes rebelled and drove out the intruders. For 12 years the governor's palace served as an Indian kiva, or council house. In 1692 the Spaniards returned, and their triumphal reentry under General Don Diego de Vargas is to this day the most celebrated event in the town's history. Every year in June the statue of La Conquistadora is carried in a solemn procession through the streets of Santa Fe in fulfillment of a vow made by De Vargas. The city's principal fiesta in September commemorates the same event. In a pageant De Vargas appears again, planting before the palace the royal banner and the Christian cross.

THE BLENDING OF SPANISH AND INDIAN WAYS. The Palace of the Governors is probably the first building the traveler wishes to inspect. It stands on the north side of the Plaza, a one-story white structure with a shady colonnade toward the street and a patio at its center. Adapting the Spanish style to the adobe construction of the Indians, it has seen many changes in its more than three-and-one-half centuries of existence. It was restored to its original appearance in 1909 in accordance with old plans discovered in, of all places, the British Museum. Open to the public, it contains interesting historic and artistic collections. The Plaza, a dusty parade ground in Spanish and Mexican days, was reduced in size when the Americans occupied the city in 1846. The trees, too, were planted by the Americans. Here the Santa Fe Trail ended and, when the wagon trains from Missouri arrived, entering the Plaza in a brisk trot with whips cracking, the sleepy town became alive with excited cries of "Los Americanos! La caravana!" La Fonda, the inn at the southeastern corner of the Plaza, served the freighters and stagecoach drivers as a terminal. It was a rambling,

A BRIGHT and SERENE INDIAN-SPANISH WORLD

colorful caravanseri with stables and corrals. Its remnants stood until 1925, when they were unfortunately razed to make room for a modern hotel. Of Santa Fe's churches the Cathedral of St. Francis is an imposing structure erected in 1869. The Cristo Rey Church contains what is usually considered the finest piece of Spanish-American ecclesiastical art, a perfectly beautiful carved stone altar screen (reredos) of 1761. San Miguel Church was built about 1636 for the Indian slaves of the Spaniards, and Guadalupe Church is a charming, tree-shaded, mission-style structure with Mexican accents. Among the various museums that of Navajo Ceremonial Art is unique. It contains a complete collection of Navajo sand paintings.

THE TALE OF TAOS. Seventy miles north of Santa Fe, the community of Taos (pronounced to rhyme with house) consists of three sections: the old Indian pueblo San Gerónimo de Taos, the Indian farming village of Ranchos de Taos, and Don Fernando de Taos, the principal settlement where the artists' colony is located. Taos lies on a high plateau fringed by tall mountains,

and the approach through deep canyons, some of bare rock, one studded with pines, is a thrilling journey. The air on the plateau is so rarefied and translucent that all colors seem to be glowing. In Don Fernando de Taos the plaza is picturesque without being overly commercialized. Spanish-speaking ranchers shop in the flat-roofed stores, a few white-robed Indians stand in the sun, an artist sketches a figure which caught his eye, and tourists inspect the pottery and Indian blankets. San Gerónimo de Taos is a favorite spot to study the pueblos, the Indian community houses. Two such structures face each other from opposite sides of Taos Creek, and it is a curious thought that you see them today as they stood there in 1540 when the Spaniards came. Four and five stories tall, the straw in the mud adobe gleaming in the sun, they hold many families. Only doors and windows are new — hatchways in each roof were the original entrances. In Ranchos de Taos the massive wall-girdled mission of St. Francis of Assisi is so spectacular with its heavy brown walls and slender white crosses that it is one of America's most photographed and painted churches.

Taos Indian Pueblo. It stands today as the Spaniards found it in 1540.

Spanish conquerors founded Santa Fe a decade before the Pilgrims arrived in Plymouth.

NEW MEXICO DEPT. OF DEVELOPMENT

NEW MEXICO DEPT. OF DEVELOPMENT

Albuquerque to the Great Fiesta

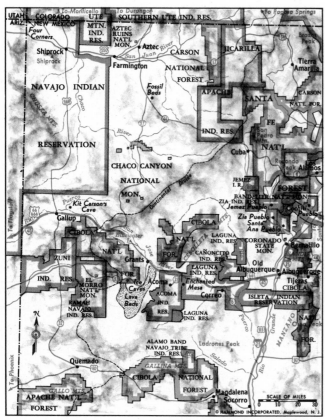

ADOBE HOUSES AND SKYSCRAPERS. There are two Albuquerques in New Mexico, the Old Town of Spanish origin and the New Town, largely an Anglo-American development. Both are connected by Central Avenue. The Old Town is very old; the first Spanish ranches and haciendas were established there about 1598, an early date as far as U.S. history is concerned. In 1706 the city was officially founded by the 28th governor of New Mexico and was named in honor of the Spanish viceroy in Mexico City, the Duke of Alburquerque. The town's enclosed plaza was used to corral cattle at night and later as the marketplace for overland wagon trains. Today all that remains of the past glamour are the fiestas and dances, the solemn church processions and the soft music. The New Town sprang up when the railroads arrived in the 1880's. The first city lots were auctioned off from a railway flatcar, and soon the new

settlement grew into a banking and trading town. The gaudy old saloons with their faro tables and roulette wheels, "The White Elephant" — "The Free and Easy", are gone. Today Albuquerque is a commercial center, especially for the wool and sheep raising industries, and because of its important defense industries is still growing. The city is also the seat of the University of New Mexico, whose principal buildings are erected in the pueblo style adapted to modern needs. The university is known for its research in archaeology and anthropology, a natural result of its location in the midst of ruins and relics of prehistoric Indian cultures.

ACOMA: COMMUNITY ON A MESA TOP. Leaving Albuquerque in a westerly direction on Interstate Highway 40, a side road (State 23) on the left leads to Acoma, one of the most unusual settlements in the United States. Out of the plains a huge rock rises abruptly for 357 feet, and on its flat top of 70 acres the village of Acoma sleeps in the sun. Three parallel rows of 3-story adobe buildings look like Pueblo community houses. But the Indian families do not live on a communal plan, they have separate dwellings. The houses are so old and mellowed that they seem to be a part of the rock. In the earliest days the village could be reached only by a single, tortuous toe and fingerhold trail, and the resulting isolation favored survival. Acoma was considered an ancient community when Fray Marcos de Niza arrived there in 1533 in search of the Seven Cities of Cibola, and some archaeologists consider it the oldest continuously inhabited village in the United States. To the east, the Enchanted Mesa is a golden brown, flat-topped, sheer-walled sandstone mountain 430 feet high. The Indians of Acoma believe it to have been their original home. The story of Acoma's San Esteban Rey Church is charming. Since 1598 the Spaniards had tried to convert the people of Acoma to Christianity but had failed. Then in 1629 Fray Juan Ramírez took over the task and succeeded through the power of true Christian love. He walked alone from Santa Fe to Acoma, taking along nothing but his breviary and cross. When he arrived at the trail leading to the top of Acoma's mesa, the Indians appeared on the rim, throwing stones at him and shooting arrows. But he proceeded unharmed. In the general commotion a little girl was accidentally pushed over the rim and fell onto a pointed boulder 60 feet below. The padre climbed to the spot as fast as he could, knelt down, prayed above her unconscious body and then carried her to the mesa top in his arms. She was smiling and unharmed when they arrived. The Indians accepted Fray Ramírez as their leader, and under his direction a foot and burro trail was hewn into the rock. The building of a church began

FROM an OLD SETTLEMENT to WHERE the TRIBES CONVENE

NEW MEXICO DEPT. OF DEVELOPMENT

GAIL HAMMOND

NEW MEXICO STATE TOURIST BUREAU

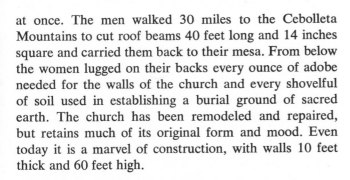

Above: Albuquerque's Church of San Felipe has not missed a Sunday mass since 1706.

Above right: The Tiffany Saloon was once the boisterous social center of a mining town in the hills near Albuquerque.

Right: An adobe house in Albuquerque's Old Town. Spanish ranches were established here early in the 1600's.

at once. The men walked 30 miles to the Cebolleta Mountains to cut roof beams 40 feet long and 14 inches square and carried them back to their mesa. From below the women lugged on their backs every ounce of adobe needed for the walls of the church and every shovelful of soil used in establishing a burial ground of sacred earth. The church has been remodeled and repaired, but retains much of its original form and mood. Even today it is a marvel of construction, with walls 10 feet thick and 60 feet high.

INDIANS DANCE, RACE, AND TRADE IN GALLUP. Interstate Highway 40 leads to the city of Gallup, a rather new community that sprang up as a division point when the railroad arrived in the early 1880's. Throughout the year it is a busy commercial center that does not offer any special attractions to the tourist. But for four days in the middle of August it is a focal point of interest for all sightseers in the Southwest. The Inter-tribal Indian Ceremonial is held there. It began modestly in 1922 when a few Indians were in-

vited to perform their dances at the McKinley County Fair. From that start one of America's greatest and most colorful festivals developed, with thousands of Indians and numerous tribes participating. The street parade of the brilliantly costumed warriors in war paint and feathers is a stunning spectacle. After that, the dances are the prime attraction. Taos Indians perform the Hoop, the Shield and the Horsetail — Laguna Indians the Corn, Butterfly and Eagle — the Hopi the Buffalo and the Clown, and other tribes do numerous other dances. Color effects and choreography are often fascinating. In addition general entertainment includes riding contests, exciting bareback races, the Navajo women's tug-of-war and other games. You may watch Navajo artists making sand paintings, a unique ritual art which assembles grains of sand of different colors in decorative patterns, or you may inspect Indian arts and crafts. As competition is stimulated by prizes and awards, only the finest specimens of pottery, ceramics, basketry, weaving, featherwork and silver jewelry are exhibited.

Carlsbad Caverns and the White Sands

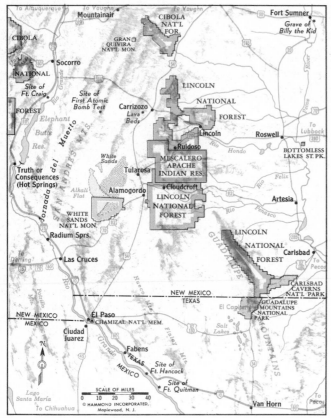

PETER O. SANCHEZ — NAT'L PARK SERVICE

"Stone draperies" at the Queen's Chamber of the Carlsbad Caverns.

THE HIDDEN PALACE. A huge castle with countless chambers and three stories pushed underground — this is Carlsbad Caverns in Southeastern New Mexico. At 750 feet below the surface the main level of the cave is located, at 900 feet the second, and at 1,013 feet the third. How large this underground network is, nobody knows. A 3-mile tour of the first level may be made. Over 30 miles have been explored, but how far into the Guadalupe Mountains the halls and passageways actually extend will have to be discovered by later generations. One might wonder whether the word "palace" is not too fanciful. It is not. In fact it is rather sober and totally inadequate to describe this marvel. Nowhere on earth are there curtains and draperies as elegant and glistening as those hanging to the floor in the King's Palace and the Queen's Chamber. Some, touched by a light from behind, gleam in delicate rose and pink.

Others are partly raised as if expecting the sound of trumpets and the grand entrance of his majesty. The stone of the drapes looks so much like cloth that nature seems to have imitated art. As is befitting a royal castle there are big halls galore, like the Green Lake Room with its green pool, the Papoose's Chamber and the Big Room, the largest open space found underground anywhere on the globe. With a length of three-quarters of a mile, a width of 600 feet and a height that reaches 255 feet, it is many times larger than its nearest competitor. Its ceiling is decorated with millions of stone icicles, the stalactites, ranging in size from a pin to a belfry, and the ground is covered with a forest of stalagmites. Although not permitted, tapping these formations will produce varying musical tones, and brushing lightly over a stalagmite will wipe off one year's growth. The natural color of the limestone formations is white, but mineral matter creates sparkling tints of tan and brown, rose and red, green and purple. A famous surprise of the Big Room are the Fountain Basins, lovely clear pools as wide as 50 feet and as deep as 10 feet. Lily pads of stone with limestone stems grow in the water. Stepping from such a fairyland into the prosaic atmosphere of an underground cafeteria seems a sacrilege. Nevertheless no luncheon guest is known to have complained about the injection of realism. The man-made improvements of the caverns are excellent. A fast elevator takes those visitors who do not wish to climb down through the natural opening, and the indirect lighting system creates fantastic effects.

THE CLOUD OF BLACK SMOKE. The story of the

A THREE-STORIED CAVE and GREAT DUNES of ALABASTER

Entrance to the caverns, probably the world's largest network of underground caves, as yet not fully explored.

The shifting dunes of the White Sands National Monument actually consist of gypsum.

discovery of the caverns is equally amazing. In the twilight of a summer evening a cowboy named Jim White rode through the brush. Suddenly he spied a cloud of black smoke emerging from a mountainside and decided to investigate. As he approached, he made an unexpected discovery. Tens of thousands of bats emerged from a hole, circled upward in a spiraling cloud and disappeared into the gathering darkness. The spectacle lasted for three hours. Then the cowboy threw burning sticks into the hole and knew that he had discovered a large cave. Since Jim later became chief ranger of Carlsbad Caverns National Park, one might assume that he envisioned such a development then. But actually he knew only one fact. He had discovered a fortune. There would be bat guano in the cave in huge piles. It could be had for the asking and could be sold as fertilizer for $30 a ton. And so it was. The company he helped to found took 100,000 tons of the valuable excrement from the cave in the following 20 years. Jim White was also a conservationist who went on exploring the caverns, fell in love with their beauty and became their articulate propagandist. It was largely through his efforts that the discovery became a national monument in 1923 and a national park in 1930. The bats are still there, occupying a cave which is not open to the public. During the day they sleep, hanging head down on delicate claws from tiny fissures in the rock. They venture forth in the evening to catch their insect dinner and return at dawn. They are delicate animals with soft fur and silky, translucent wings. Most of them belong to the species called the Mexican free-tailed bat. Possibly they are a remnant of the fauna that flourished in a remote age of mild, uniform climate. When violent climatic changes developed the bats took refuge in the caves where the temperature always remains the same. Inside the Carlsbad Caverns it is 56° F., summer and winter. During the cold season the bats hibernate, but for the rest of the year no visitor should miss the daily spectacle of the rising black cloud.

SNOW WHITE HILLS, AND THE SURVIVAL OF THE FITTEST. Northwest of Carlsbad Caverns, near the town of Alamogordo, a great basin stretches between two mountain ranges. There billowing dunes of the finest texture and snowy white in color can be seen, a strange but most photogenic display encompassed in the White Sands National Monument. The sand is really gypsum, ground into tiny particles which are forever pushed and moved by the wind so that the dunes and ridges are always shifting and forming new, never repeated baroque outlines. Plants have a difficult time adjusting themselves to this unsteady environment. When the shifting dune rises, the plant has to grow longer to keep its crown aboveground. When the sand recedes, the plant cannot contract and is left with too long a stem — a stem 40 feet long in some cases. Among the few species of plants that can get a precarious foothold on the dunes are those with such unusual names as skunkbush sumac, soaptree yucca, rubber rabbitbrush, shrubby pennyroyal and fourwing saltbush. And the fauna has produced here a miracle of mimicry. The pocket mouse, which has a black coat if found on the black lava beds and a red pelt in the red mountains, has white fur on the White Sands.

193

Tucson and Tombstone

which has attracted national attention because of its work in tree-ring investigation, an invaluable aid to archaeology and anthropology. The Arizona-Sonora Desert Museum is a unique showcase of living desert plants and animals in their own habitat.

INDIANS PAINT THE LIFE OF CHRIST. Just south of Tucson is the Mission San Xavier del Bac, a priceless work of art, a white, asymmetrical building with Spanish baroque and Moorish overtones, like a castle in Spain. Founded in 1700 by the Jesuit Padre Kino, it had a stormy history both as a mission and headquarters of a big ranch to be worked by the Indians. Plagued by Indian revolts and the dissolution of the Jesuit order, the mission was taken over by the Franciscans. Almost immediately it was attacked and plundered by the Apaches, but the Franciscans rebuilt it in its present form between 1768 and 1797. On the outside, the central panel of the front is particularly striking. In contrast to the plain white side panels, it shows in soft red tints the carved shell and arabesque decorations of the baroque period. One but not the other of two identical belfries is crowned with a dome, a shrewd economic move on the part of the padres, for no tax was due the Crown of Spain on an "unfinished building." Indians executed the richly decorated wood carvings and unusual paintings of the interior. A series of panels depicts the life story of Christ and, while they may lack subtlety, they have the vividness of primitive art and are greatly admired today.

A CACTUS FOREST. Seventeen miles to the east of Tucson, Saguaro National Monument is a tract of more than 63,000 acres preserving the finest specimens of America's giant cactus, the saguaro. This fascinating plant sometimes reaches a height of 50 feet and an age of nearly 200 years. In very dry areas it consists of a single fluted column. In more favorable spots it develops side branches up to 20 feet long. The limbs grow in a perpendicular fashion, like the arms of a candelabrum, in a striking design that seems highly modern. It is a corrugated marvel of water preservation. In the event of rain it expands its spiny accordian pleats into a reservoir and shrinks them during a drought. The saguaro forest is a magic place to visit in May when the waxy creamy white blossoms appear at the ends of the columns. By the end of June the red fruit appears, a favorite food of the Papago Indians. These strange plants are an exclusive phenomenon of Arizona and New Mexico.

THE WILDEST WEST. "Welcome to Tombstone and Boot Hill Graveyard. Buried here are the remains of…" At this point you will read a number of names followed

THE OLD PUEBLO. That's what the people call Tucson, pronounced Toosahn, the major city of southern Arizona. Originally it was a Spanish town, and in the Mexican section, El Barrio Libre, there are still many flat-roofed adobe houses built around patios, with flower beds and blossoming trees set into the hard-tramped and clean-swept adobe floors. But on the whole, Tucson is a modern city which does not accent too emphatically its Indian-Spanish past but rather reflects the American West. It fits well into the broad desert valley, surrounded by blue and purple-tinted hills and jagged peaks towering in the distance. To the cowboys and cattlemen it is a marketplace, and also the big town which offers the right kind of entertainment. The annual Fiesta de los Vaqueros is the climaxing event in the rodeo circuit. To several thousand college students it is the seat of the progressive University of Arizona,

THE SPARKLING BORDERLAND

by such remarks as "Killed in Earp-Clanton Battle Sept. 26, 1881," or "Hanged legally for the Bisbee Massacre March 8, 1884," or "Murdered March 8, 1882." In a corner of the graveyard one marker is unusual. It says: "M. E. Kellogg — 1882. Died natural death." These mementos can be seen in the town of Tombstone, southeast of Tucson. One of America's ghost towns, it has been revived so that visitors may get a firsthand impression of the lusty chapter of American history that took place in the Wild West. For such studies, Tombstone certainly is a vantage point. A prospector's disappointment at first, a tombstone of their hopes, some rich silver strikes were made, and mines like the Lucky Cuss, the Goodenough and the Tough Nut poured out their riches. The town was organized, in 1879, a relatively late date, which had rather sinister consequences. By that time many veins in California and other mining areas had run out, and prospectors and gamblers were looking for new fields of action. The initial Australian gold diggings had come to an end, and hundreds of treasure hunters were returning to the States. Finally the older mining communities organized vigilante committees to uphold a semblance of law and order and to rid the towns of their worst characters. Most of these gentry assembled in Tombstone. Add to this calamitous situation the fact that the fierce Apaches under Chief Victorio maintained their headquarters in the neighboring Dragoon Mountains, and one can imagine the life and atmosphere prevailing

in Tombstone during the roaring decade. Among the relics of the period the Bird Cage Theater is the best known. In its time it was operated 24 hours a day, seven days a week. It was a variety theater, bar, saloon, gambling casino and dance hall, and swarmed with adventurers, triggermen and girl entertainers. The name was derived from the birdcage-like boxes in the theater auditorium. Those on one side were often occupied by one of two feuding factions, those on the other side by its rival. The result was bedlam. Today the Bird Cage is a museum. The Wells Fargo Museum and General Store is also interesting.

Above: Chiricahua National Monument near the New Mexico state line is a wilderness of castlelike, sculptured rocks.

Below: Saguaro National Monument is a unique cactus forest; some cactus trees are 50 feet tall and 200 years old.

Phoenix and the Apache Trail

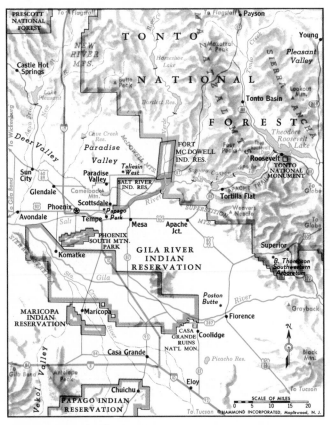

ARISING FROM THE ASHES. Among the first pioneers who settled along Arizona's Salt River was an English globetrotter, "Lord" Darrel Duppa. He was an alcoholic but also a scholar of sorts, and when he noticed that the new community was rising from the ruins of Indian mounds and irrigation ditches abandoned eons ago, he remembered the phoenix, a mythical Greek bird which arose brilliantly from its own ashes. He saw the parallel, and ever since the community has been called Phoenix, an imaginative and meaningful name. Today's modern city, shaded by trees and studded with parks, rises dramatically from the barren desert. Looking down the broad, level streets, one sees stark, lonely mountains closing the horizon — the Four Peaks, Superstition and Camelback. The State Capitol, of Neo-Classic design, has its east entrance appropriately flanked by two pedestals of petrified wood. Its cactus

gardens, with innumerable varieties, are also in keeping with the locale. Papago Park includes the exquisite Desert Botanical Garden. The Arizona Museum and the Heard Museum preserve relics of the country's ancient Indian cultures and mementos of Arizona's pioneer days. Pueblo Grande is the excavation of a pueblo-like adobe structure which was inhabited 800 years ago. Frank Lloyd Wright's Taliesin West is a famous architectural center. Phoenix has two claims to importance: it is the hub of Arizona's saddle and suntan industry, and it is a great agricultural market. Both achievements are based on the dry, sunny climate which blesses Phoenix with more than 200 entirely clear days every year. This figure compares with more than 180 in Los Angeles and about 100 in Miami. The winter climate, sunny and mild by day and pleasantly cool at night, is exhilarating. The summers are hot, but permanent residents comfort themselves with the thought that Phoenix is thoroughly air-conditioned. During the winter season there is popular entertainment galore. In February nearby Scottsdale turns Spanish for the gay Parada del Sol, and in March Phoenix goes Western during the World's Championship Rodeo. The most original annual affair is the Lost Dutchman's Search, also called Superstition Mountain Trek, held every spring. On that day several thousand citizens assault Superstition's slopes and crags with picks and shovels to rediscover America's most famous lost mine.

THE LURE OF THE DESERT. The winter vacation industry is located in the desert near Phoenix. Perhaps this seems strange since we associate few pleasant thoughts with an arid land. Many people don't like the desert when they first see it. Nevertheless it has a way of casting a spell, especially in the morning when the mountains rise sharply into the sky and the wind carries a wonderful fresh scent of herbs, or at night when the columns of the saguaro cactus throw long shadows and darkness and silence fall on the land. Most doubting Thomases change their minds and become very fond of the desert and its moods. Vacationers stay either on a guest ranch which is a luxury hotel with a spectacular view, or on a dude ranch where horseback riding is the outstanding feature. A popular entertainment is the chuckwagon dinner at a picturesque spot in the desert. One can watch the sun go down in a blaze, hear a coyote howling far away, smell the wood smoke of the campfire and eat a hearty steak dinner while the stars begin to glisten close overhead. The feeling of health and exuberance, the bright, comfortable clothes, the campfire tales, the gay music, the square dances, and the good-looking cowboys add up to a worthwhile vacation with a Western flair. Not the least attraction is the potential danger of the desert. No

THE SUNNIEST CITY and the MAGIC of WATER

R. MANLEY — SHOSTAL ASSOCIATES

Petrified wood pedestals at the east entrance of the Capitol of Arizona in Phoenix and an adjacent cactus garden symbolize the state's natural environment.

stranger on horseback may venture into it alone, for if he is thrown, the horse will find its way home, but the rider may be lost.

LETTUCE FOR ALL AMERICA. The other aspect of the Phoenix area is more utilitarian but is nonetheless interesting. After driving for miles through barren cactus and mesa country you suddenly find yourself in the middle of green fields sprouting neat rows of carrots, cabbages, cantaloupes, broccoli, alfalfa and cotton. The reason for this fertility is, of course, irrigation. Nowhere is the magic of water more spectacular than in the potentially fertile soil of the desert. Phoenix is the center and market for a rich farming oasis of hundreds of thousands of acres. The cotton grown here is of an excellent long staple variety. Alfalfa can be harvested six or seven times during a favorable year. During certain weeks lettuce grows nowhere in the United States but in this oasis; it is quite probable that most Americans have tasted the Phoenix variety. Oleander bushes bloom, orange groves thrive, and date palms grow into tall shade trees.

THE ROAD TO ROOSEVELT DAM. An intricate network of ditches and dams, valves and reservoirs harnesses and distributes the available water supply, making possible this astounding fertility. The beginning of the project was the small scale revival of the simple irrigation methods of prehistoric Indians. When a flash

Tonto National Monument near Phoenix preserves two twelfth-century cliff dwellings.

FRED E. MANG, JR. — NAT'L PARK SERVICE

flood destroyed most of the fields in 1891, a modern scientific system was inaugurated on a grand scale. About 75 miles east of Phoenix, Theodore Roosevelt Dam was started in 1906 and completed in 1911, the first of our great reclamation projects and the father of all Western dams. The site was so inaccessible that a 60-mile road had to be cut through the steep mountains — 40 miles were actually hewn into solid rock. This highway is now the spectacular Apache Trail, State Highway 88. Over hairpin curves and along deep chasms, past gorges and caves it winds its way to a long chain of quiet, man-made lakes where flowers bloom and trees grow profusely.

197

Flagstaff and the Painted Desert

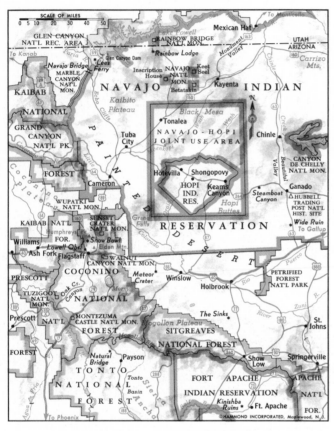

COOL MOUNTAIN TOWN. Snow found sometimes even on the Fourth of July in Arizona illustrates the great variety of scenery and climate which this canyon, mesa and desert state has to offer. The cool area lies on the high Coconino Plateau in the north central part of the state north of Flagstaff. Northeast of the city towers dark green Elden Mountain, and beyond that the San Francisco Peaks rise into the clear blue sky. Humphreys Peak is the tallest with an altitude of 12,633 feet. The Hopi name for the range is "High Place of the Snows," and the snow-filled ravines and slopes offer fine skiing from December through March. In a few isolated places the snow lasts as late as July. Thirteen miles from Flagstaff, the Arizona Snow Bowl boasts of ski tows, practice slopes, ski trails through beautiful pine forests, a ski lodge and various tournaments. Schools in southern Arizona occasionally organize class excursions to

Flagstaff so that the children may discover what snow is. Large herds of pronghorn antelope survive in the open pinelands of this forest-covered plateau. Flagstaff itself is a busy town where Hopi and Navajo women sell silver jewelry and blankets, ceramics and baskets — where dudes from neighboring ranches strut across the street in clothes and boots more Western than those of the cowboys — where Indian ponies clop-clop on the pavement, and where buckboards and wagons bring Indian shoppers from nearby reservations. The town's most exciting days are July 3rd, 4th, and 5th, when the annual Southwest Indian Powwow is held. This is a powwow of 20 tribal nations from 7 states, including a festive all-Indian parade and rodeo, ceremonial dances, chants and an exhibit of Indian folk art in the Museum of Northern Arizona.

THE FAMOUS SIGHTS AROUND FLAGSTAFF. The many points of interest in the neighborhood of Flagstaff will be listed here in clockwise fashion, beginning in the north. The map indicates the roads on which they can be reached. In Wupatki National Monument, one Hopi house of the twelfth century has been restored. The Wupatki ruins are interesting because they cling around natural walls of red sandstone and seem to grow out of the soil. Sunset Crater National Monument contains a pit 400 feet deep and 1,300 feet in diameter. Its sloping sides are bright yellow near the rim and gradually change to orange, red and black — a display of colors which suggested the name Sunset Crater. In Walnut Canyon National Monument remains of some 300 cliff dwellings can be seen in the walls of the gorge. In the apartments, which are believed to have been built early in the twelfth century A.D. and occupied for about 150 years, primitive hoes and other crude instruments have been found. Meteor Crater, a huge pit in the flat desert, is about a mile in diameter and nearly 600 feet deep. Near the rim is a museum which collects and studies meteorites, the only objects on earth to have come naturally from outer space. A ride through Oak Creek Canyon is a wonderful adventure. The road twists along the rushing creek at the bottom of the canyon through miles of dark green pines and light green maples and oaks, sycamores and aspens and between red stone walls rising 2,000 feet above the stream. Montezuma Castle National Monument is an 842-acre tract around what is probably the best preserved cliff dwelling in the United States. There is a large cave in a vertical rock wall into which the grayish pink adobe castle has been built about 70 feet above the ground. Associating the castle with Montezuma was a mistake, but the name survived and is used today. Montezuma Well is a limestone pit with a spring that flows at the rate of 1,500,000 gallons a day. Tuzigoot National

WHITE SNOW and COLORED SAND

Monument is a restored ancient pueblo that differs from the usual type of construction. It was erected of stone, with mud used as mortar. Occupied by several hundred people around A.D. 1200, this community had reached an unusually high degree of culture. Many of the excavated objects are now displayed in the Tuzigoot Museum. They include fine mosaics of shells and turquoise, storage ollas 27 inches tall and tools of stone and bone that are remarkably symmetrical. Prescott is a welcome oasis for the traveler who has just crossed the desert and now deeply inhales the scent of the pine forests, feeling the coolness of the mile-high plateau. Mountain ranges surround the city, and Indians, prospectors, cowboys and sheepherders give the town a Western flavor which is enhanced by historic Pioneer Square, a group of houses dating back to Prescott's early days. The local Frontier Days Rodeo, held every summer since 1888, is the oldest rodeo in the country.

PAINTED SAND AND SAND PAINTINGS. North of the Little Colorado River and clearly seen from Wupatki National Monument, the Painted Desert stretches its dunes and escarpments for 300 miles. There is no other desert like it, for its hills, mesas and terraces glow in warm colors of yellow, red, magenta and mauve. The highly colored shales, sandstones and marls often create in the air above a pink or purple haze, and changing tints of amethyst and lilac, scarlet and russet seem to dance along the mesas. In the slanting light of the early morning, when the shadows are deep, the terraced walls glow blood-red and distant mountain ranges rise in near and clear profiles, the Painted Desert is most spectacular. The Painted Desert Lodge can be reached from the Petrified Forest. Since time immemorial the Indians have used these colored sands to compose their brilliant sand paintings, an art that has been especially developed by the Navajos. Executed by long-trained experts, these circular compositions are painted on the flat ground in various decorative patterns as a ritual of religious significance.

Right: The hills and terraces of the Painted Desert glow in red, magenta, mauve and yellow.

Below right: Sunset Crater National Monument. The display of colors on the slopes is the reason for its name.

Below: Montezuma's Castle is the best preserved cliff dwelling in America.

The Grand Canyon

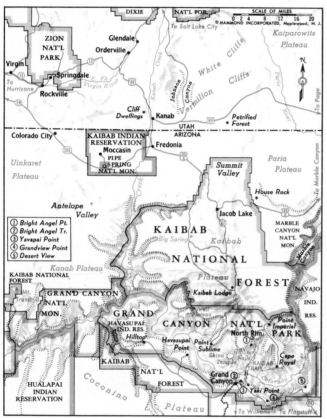

On the map:
- ① Bright Angel Pt.
- ② Bright Angel Tr.
- ③ Yavapai Point
- ④ Grandview Point
- ⑤ Desert View

KALEIDOSCOPE. A huge gorge filled with mile-high mountain ranges and bathed in all colors of the spectrum in an ever changing display — that is the Grand Canyon, Arizona's great chasm. No one will ever see the same spectacle of tints and hues twice, just as no one will see the same sunrise or sunset, spring or fall. No one has successfully described it. Few have tried to paint it. The first one to do so, Thomas Moran, probably came nearest to a true interpretation of this drama in stone. His painting hangs in the Capitol in Washington. The tool which nature employed in creating the canyon is an extraordinary river, the Colorado. At times its current reaches a speed of 20 miles per hour. Every day it carries through the gorge about half a million tons of silt. Therefore it appears colored, and its name Colorado is appropriate. Such a river has tremendous digging power. Hundreds of millions of years ago these

mountains were rolling hills, and, as they gradually rose, the stream had to grind on fiercely just to stay where it was. During the following eons of growth and decay, building and eroding, the external rock formations changed so many times that today the Colorado does not flow down a slope but, strangely, cuts across one. The river did not work alone. It had helpers, from rains and storms and frost to the plants whose roots loosened the rocks.

A JOURNEY INTO TIME. The sudden impact of seeing the Grand Canyon — and there is no gradual way of coming upon it — is one of cosmic awareness. We know that our planet was created in time measures that are beyond human comprehension. Here we have before us a crosscut of the process. The canyon walls expose layer after layer, era after era, distinguishing each stretch of untold millions of years by different color, from brown and red to yellow and green. Some layers are so old that they do not show any fossil life. Others yield petrified remnants of living creatures, ranging in size from huge dinosaurs to tiny sea worms. The near eternity lying between the beginning of this canyon and the day of our visit is before our eyes, and we feel that the great forces around us are still at work. We do not stand here at the end of a chapter but in the middle of one.

CONQUISTADORES, PILGRIMS AND A MIDWESTERNER. Even in the tiny span of white man's history in America, the canyon is an interesting landmark. Those Americans who think that our country got its start at Plymouth Rock, while beyond the Appalachians the "new" America begins, may note with surprise that 13 Spaniards, López de Cárdenas and 12 companions, stood at the rim of the Grand Canyon almost three generations before the landing of the Pilgrims. It is true that in 1540 the Spaniards did not want to erect here a new Kingdom of Heaven, but they did not give up this land either. Others such as Padre Garcés and Padre Escalante, traders and soldiers followed. In time the Spaniards here became Mexicans. Since 1848 they have been Americans, with a tradition as American as any and quite a bit longer than that of any other white group. But the man who explored the river within today's boundaries of the National Park was Major John W. Powell. A professor of geology at the University of Illinois, he was doing field work in the area with a group of students in 1868 when he first thought of exploring the river. Although he was handicapped by the loss of his right arm in a Civil War battle, the project fascinated him. One year later his expedition started out from Green River City, Wyoming, on the 24th of May 1869. Four boats and ten men,

THE GREATEST NATURE SHOW on EARTH

among them the painter Moran, took part. The trip took three months and four days, and none of the survivors ever forgot it. There was no turning back between the precipitous cliffs, and it seems a miracle today that in the river's madly plunging rapids and cataracts only one boat was smashed. The clothes of the explorers were always wet and their food supplies became soaked and rotted. Sometimes the boats had to be lowered one after another, the last man on the upper cliff jumping into the water below, where he was hauled into the boat. On the 29th of August the party arrived at the Grand Wash, tired but happy. "Our joy is almost ecstasy," Major Powell wrote.

GEOGRAPHICAL NOTES. Grand Canyon National Park consists of two distinct sections — the South Rim, accessible by car all year, and the North Rim which can be reached by car only during the summer season from June to September. The distance between the two rims is 12 miles by airplane, 21 miles by trail and more than 200 miles by automobile road. Looking into the canyon is like thumbing through a book; descending to the bottom of the gorge is like reading the book chapter by chapter. It is not only a journey into geological time but also an excursion into plant geography. On the canyon floor the vegetation is Mexican. You then pass through four floral zones, and when you arrive at the North Rim where the great evergreen forests begin, you may study some of the plants of Canada. The descent is usually done on muleback over Bright Angel Trail or Kaibab Trail to Kaibab Bridge, a cobweb of steel over the rampaging river. While the geologists enjoy a heyday, the anthropologists discover hundreds of sites of prehistoric Indian dwellings, the botanists study species of southern cactus and northern blue spruce separated only by canyon walls, and the zoologists ponder a challenging mystery. The 300-acre top of Shiva Temple might have contained living beings shut off, for thousands of years, from normal changes of evolution by the mountain's inaccessible, vertical sides. A group of mountaineering scientists ventured to the summit in 1937, but did not discover any sensational forms of life.

The Grand Canyon has been called "a drama in stone" and "a journey into time." The various rock strata indicate era after era in the millions of years of its development.

201

Bryce Canyon, Zion and Cedar Breaks

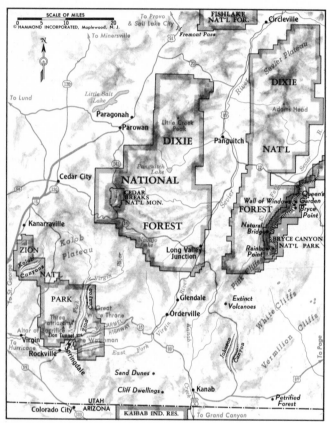

GENTLE PEOPLE AND ECCENTRIC CLIFFS. The first white settlers in southwestern Utah were hardy and gentle Mormon pioneers. When Brother Joseph Black one day discovered the wonderful kaleidoscope of colors flashing around a canyon on the Virgin River, he was overwhelmed. Little Zion, he called it reverently. Brigham Young inspected Black's discovery but thought its name sacrilegious. He declared it to be "Not Zion." His word was law, and the name of the chasm became Not Zion Canyon. The Indians had called it Arrow Quiver, and the maps of the U.S. Army had marked the spot as Mukuntuweap, which name it bore when it became a national monument in 1909. Brother Black's suggestion prevailed in 1918 when it became a national park — it's Zion now. Ninety miles to the northeast Ebenezer Bryce came upon a valley of marvelous statuary in all tints of the rainbow. "What a place to

hunt for a stray cow!" he exclaimed. Although his comment hardly expressed the proper appreciation, his name carried the day. We have not only Bryce Canyon and Bryce Canyon National Park but Bryce Point, one of the most beautiful bright peaks on the rim.

MIRAGE OF AN ORIENTAL CITY. The road leading to Bryce National Park gives no indication of the spectacle to come. Visitors park their cars and walk up to the rim. There they suddenly see a valley of such flaming beauty and radiance that the impact touches them almost physically. Everyone has, of course, a different individual reaction, but it does seem as if a vague vision of a silent, mysterious city of columns, turrets and spires far away in the jungles of the East Indies has become reality. Factually speaking, the valley is not really a canyon but a basin 3 miles long and 2 miles wide, carved into the soft sandstone by rain and snow at an altitude of 8,000 feet. The thousands of strange formations glow in all colors of the spectrum from white, yellow, orange and pink to tan and purple; the predominant color is red. The names given to the various columns and towers may sound trite, but they do express the infinite variety in the shape of the rocks — Queen Victoria and the Pope in the Queen's Garden, the Wall of Windows, the Pipe Organ and Bluebeard's Castle. A trip to the canyon floor is most worthwhile, for to look up between the tall, fragrant pine trees is an entirely new experience. From here the canyon seems to take on different but not less beautiful forms, shapes and colors.

TUNNEL WITH WINDOWS. In Zion National Park the small Virgin River has performed a powerful feat. Into the porous Navajo sandstone it has ground a 15-mile chasm over 2,000 feet deep, with walls as straight in some places as if cut by a knife. The canyon is half a mile wide at its broadest point and only a few feet wide at its narrowest. Here the water may suddenly rise 25 feet in a downpour, grinding the gorge to new depths. One of the most striking features of the rocks is their color scheme. A thick layer of bright red stone is topped by a narrower layer of white rock with a thin layer of red added in places. There are wonderful mountain peaks in the park, most of them adhering to the scheme, like the red Watchman and the forbidding Three Patriarchs. One cliff shows red stone formations in its white layer. Implying a similarity to bloodstains, it was given the rather morbid name of Altar of Sacrifice. Most famous and most photographed of the Zion mountains is the Great White Throne whose solid mass rises to an altitude of 6,744 feet. The pines at its base are green; the rock above is first red, then buff and lastly white. The green of the forest on the plateau contrasts

A PAGEANT of FLAMING ROCKS

Thor's Hammer and Temple of Osiris, Bryce Canyon National Park.

Bryce Canyon seems to be filled with columns and statuary of kaleidoscopic colors.

with the deep blue sky. Another marvel of the park is the Mount Carmel Highway (State Route 15), which enters by way of Pine Creek Canyon. In 3 miles it climbs 800 feet, and in 6 skillfully engineered switchbacks rises to the mile-long Zion Tunnel built into the the side of the canyon wall. Like several famous tunnels in Switzerland, it has "windows" — 6 openings or galleries providing breathtaking views. When the tunnel was built the engineers feared that the debris thrown into the canyon would choke the river, but the little stream took the rubble in its stride and in 3 months had neatly removed the last vestiges.

ZION CANYON BY DAY AND NIGHT. If Zion National Park is a stunning spectacle when the sun shines, it is an enchanted land on a clear, calm, silent night when the wind has stopped and the fragrance of earth and of pines is in the air. When the moon rises

and touches the cliffs and the summits, the brilliant color display reappears in subdued, ghostlike tints. But you can distinguish clearly the reds, pinks and yellows.

A MOUNTAINTOP WHEEL. North of Zion and west of Bryce National Park lies a bowl filled with eroded ridges radiating from the center like spokes of a wheel. It is Cedar Breaks National Monument. As far as colors are concerned, it is perhaps the high point of Utah and Arizona, with white and rose, coral, yellow and orange, rich brown and lavender tints with a brilliance not surpassed anywhere. An especially pleasant feature is the alpine foliage at its height from mid-July to mid-August. Dixie National Forest that surrounds the monument contains a rare species of tree — the bristlecone pine. One pine at Cedar Breaks is about 1,200 years old. Some bristlecone pines in California are the oldest known living things on earth.

203

From the Great Arches to Monument Valley

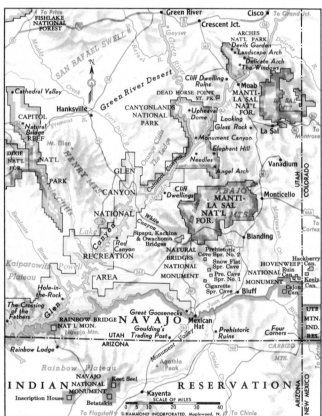

ARCHES ARE NOT BRIDGES. The old saying that Utah is 98 per cent scenery and 2 per cent farmland seems confirmed along the lonely desert highway, known as U.S. Route 163, which turns south off Interstate 70 at Crescent Junction, passes through Monticello and proceeds toward the Arizona state line. The trip might be called an "accrued" adventure. Beginning comfortably enough, it gradually leads into grandiose and lonely Indian lands where only the venturesome travel. The first stop is for lovers of arches — stone formations created in cliffs by wind and weather erosion. There are 88 of them in Arches National Park, east of the road. The largest is Landscape Arch with a length of 291 feet, believed to be the longest natural stone arch in the world. To the north a jumble of huge red slabs is called Devils Garden. Delicate Arch — the cowboys call it Schoolmarm's Panties — has a splendid setting with the Colorado River gorge and the snowcapped La

Sal Mountains in the background. West of Route 163 a rough one-lane road leads to a state park at Dead Horse Point. There you will come upon a vista never to be forgotten — tier upon tier of towering cliffs, overlooking the Colorado River 2,000 feet below and the new Canyonlands National Park — perhaps the most spectacular view in the state.

MAMMOTHS AND URANIUM. The towns along the road — Moab, Monticello, Blanding — are typical Mormon settlements, green oases in the desert, compactly built, with a clean and pleasant atmosphere. If you look down a Moab street and on the red hill beyond the Lombard poplars a cavalcade of cowboys appears, you may think the horses a little too fancy and the riders too swaggering. Your suspicions will be justified for this is a "location" town, and many a Hollywood Western had its origin in these valleys. The story location is genuine; this is the locale of some of the best novels of Zane Grey. The romantic past is complemented by a realistic present. The blasting in the mountains, the trucks rumbling by and the roads being built spell the source of the activity — uranium. The painted cliffs, by the way, contain not only the atomic metal but also fascinating prehistoric pictographs. One, near Moab, shows the drawing of a mammoth that puzzles the scientists. The big animals supposedly became extinct 30,000 years ago, while man is believed not to have appeared here until about 20,000 years ago. Could some remnants of the mammoths have survived until the arrival of the first human beings?

BRIDGES ARE NOT ARCHES. They are carved by water and span a river, either one that is flowing now or used to be there eons ago. Three such natural bridges of immense proportions, as well as several villages of prehistoric cliff dwellers, can be studied at Natural Bridges National Monument, located west of Blanding off State Route 95. Owachomo Bridge is the smallest and considered the oldest of the three. It spans the almost 200-foot Armstrong Canyon at a height of 108 feet. Kachina Bridge, named for the symbols of the Kachina dance of the Hopi which are carved into the rock, is a deep red, massive span of 200 feet, and 200 feet above ground. Sipapu Bridge, which is magnificent in its symmetrical proportions, is the Hopi gateway to the underworld. It is possible to hike between the bridges, and there is also an 8-mile loop road connecting them.

THE LONELY LAND. Proceeding southward on Route 163 the road becomes rough. Past the small town of Bluff a side road leads to the Great Goosenecks, the convolutions of the San Juan River, 1,500 feet below

ADVENTURE in the DESERT

M. WOODBRIDGE WILLIAMS — NAT'L PARK SERVICE

M. WOODBRIDGE WILLIAMS — NAT'L PARK SERVICE

JACK E. BOUCHER — NAT'L PARK SERVICE

Above: A kind of natural watchtower rises above Canyonlands National Park.

Above right: Big Water Camp and Elaterite Butte at the new Canyonlands National Park which is still largely a wilderness.

Below right: Besides this double arch, 87 single arches can be seen in Arches National Park.

the observation point. From now on a jeep or a horse may seem to be a better means of transportation than a car, but the land surrounding you is an American wonderland — Monument Valley. Out of the forbidding red plain the huge skyscraper castles rise into the sky for a thousand feet in a lonely expanse whose horizons are serrated by the distant ranges of Arizona, New Mexico and Colorado. An Indian boy on horseback or an old Navajo hiking may be the only human beings you meet between the "Emperor" and the "Stagecoach," or the "Bear and Rabbit" and "Brigham's Tomb." When the sun is setting and the towering sentinels merge in a violet haze into the darkness, you are witnessing one of the continent's great spectacles. At Goulding's Trading Post at the Arizona border you may see Navajos trading rugs and silver jewelry for groceries, and you may join a pack trip to Rainbow Bridge National Monument.

RAINBOW'S END. You can also travel there by car over a road through the Navajo Reservation of Arizona to Rainbow Lodge or Navajo Mountain Trading Post.

From there a trail leads to the bridge. The riding is rough, but quite a few adventurous travelers brave the desert to reach Rainbow Bridge. Many visitors now cross Lake Powell, contained in the new Glen Canyon National Recreation Area, by boat from Wahweap or Halls Crossing marinas, and then walk about 1 mile up Glen Canyon to the bridge. This natural bridge is the largest on earth with a span of 278 feet and a height of 309 feet. The National Capitol could be placed under it and would not nearly fill the space. The bridge is beautiful as well, with its salmon pink rock, symmetric lines and curved surface above. These qualities suggested the same phenomenon to all who saw it. The Paiutes, the Navajos and the whites gave it the same name in three languages — the Rainbow.

From Kayenta in Arizona you can take U.S. Highway 160 eastward to Four Corners, the only spot in America where four states meet: Utah, Colorado, Arizona and New Mexico. The cowboys claim that on occasion the geographical point of contact is a wonderful refuge; by walking in a small circle you can elude any sheriff.

205

Salt Lake City and the Great Salt Lake

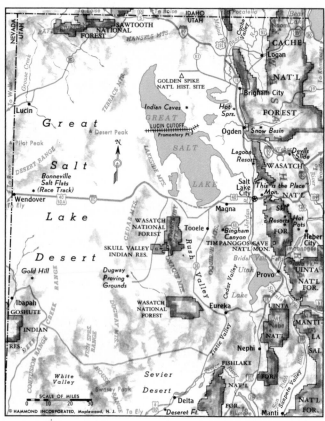

symbols. The first of these is the sea gull. These birds saved the Mormons' first crop which was threatened with destruction by crickets. By devouring the crickets the gulls helped the young settlement to survive. The beehive is the symbol of systematic and energetic activity which made the desert habitable and prosperous. Deseret, a word denoting the state of the Mormons, and Zion, the biblical kingdom of heaven, are the third and fourth symbols. There is little smoking and drinking to be observed, and almost nothing which could be called night life. This quiet state is particularly striking if you arrive from Utah's neighbor Nevada, with its clicking roulette tables and revival of the Old West spirit. However, Salt Lake City is by no means drab. There is a great deal of singing, laughing, dating and dancing, and it claims to possess the loveliest girls of the mid-continent.

"THIS IS THE PLACE." Visitors approach the world capital of Mormonism with a mixture of awe and curiosity. Usually they have a few vague notions about Brigham Young and polygamy. Although only 60 per cent of the city's inhabitants are Mormons, they set the pace, seeing to it that visiting travelers are set straight on the principal issues. Temple Square is Salt Lake City's great attraction, and throngs from all states of the Union move leisurely between the impressive buildings and bright flower beds. If you join a tour, you may discover that your guide is an insurance executive or lawyer who donates his time to the service. From him you hear about the history of Mormonism, the organization of the church, its admirable self-help program and its industrial enterprises which make Mormonism a way of life. We see the Temple with its six spires, its "earth stones," "moon stones," and "sun stones," and learn about the ceremonial and genealogical work carried on there. The building itself, however, is closed to non-Mormons. On the other hand, the Tabernacle is not only open for inspection, but visitors are welcome to hear a free organ concert. This oval auditorium, looking on the outside like a huge turtle, offers seats for 8,000. Its organ is a mammoth instrument of almost 11,000 pipes, ranging in size from five-eighths of an inch to 32 feet. Its construction was started in 1866 using native timber and glue boiled from buffalo hides. The Tabernacle Choir is internationally famous. There are many other interesting historical buildings on and near the square. A ride to the Capitol is worthwhile. From its steps the view of a bright modern city between high, barren desert peaks is fascinating. A circular drive over the foothills will lead to an imposing group of statues, "This Is The Place" Monument. It commemorates the 24th of July 1847, when Brigham Young's wagon emerged from the canyon at this spot.

STRONGHOLD OF THE CENTER. After a night's drive through the desert, the morning begins to engulf us with the glowing light and the blistering heat of the salt flats and the barren hills. But suddenly we are in Salt Lake City. In a bowl surrounded by stark naked mountains there lies a metropolis presided over by a Capitol perching on a rocky bench. Trees line the streets, clear mountain water rushes through all the gutters and thousands of ever revolving sprinklers rain sparkling drops on lawns and flower beds. Here we remember the oriental poets. "To arrive at a lush oasis, after a trek through the Sahara, is a delight." It will take but a few hours to sense the very special atmosphere of this city. Just as it is a physical stronghold circled by mountains, it is also a stronghold of the spirit, independent of and set apart from the civilizations of the Atlantic Seaboard and the Pacific Coast. Everywhere we encounter its four

THE MORMON EMPIRE

The leader looked into the giant desert bowl and decided to establish his heaven on earth there.

BUOYANT WATERS. The Great Salt Lake, located about 15 miles west of Salt Lake City, is known throughout the world. Although it is the largest American lake west of the Mississippi, measuring approximately 70 by 30 miles, it is not its size that made it famous but its salt content. The water of this unique inland sea contains about 4.4 billion tons of salt, representing a salinity 6 to 8 times that of the ocean. Like Israel's Dead Sea, it is fed by a river named Jordan. There are various resorts along U.S. Highway 40 (Interstate 80) where the visitor may discover for himself the lake's buoyancy. He will float with his body partly above water. He will crouch in a sitting position with his shoulders well above the surface. He will learn that it is nevertheless not easy to swim in such a strong brine. Otherwise he may find the big lake somewhat disappointing and desolate, although at certain seasons there is a real magnificence about its green water that the tourist certainly will enjoy. The Lucin Cutoff is an interesting railroad trestle which runs across the lake for 30 miles.

PICKLED BUFFALO MEAT. The Great Salt Lake was discovered in 1824 by Jim Bridger, the merry Paul Bunyan of western America. Floating down Bear River on a bull boat, he arrived at the lake and proceeded to take a drink of water. Instantly he spat it out and announced, "Hell, we are on the shore of the Pacific." This error was corrected a year later. At times Bridger returned, and among his various reports the one of the winter of 1830 is noteworthy. It snowed for 70 days until the whole region was blanketed with a 70-foot white layer. All the wildlife perished, and in spring the shore was strewn with the frozen carcasses of dead buffalo. He rolled them all into the brine of the lake, providing pickled buffalo meat for himself and the Ute Indians for years.

Left: Temple Square is the heart of the Mormon community.

Below: The Mormon Tabernacle offers free organ concerts. Nearby is the monument honoring the sea gulls which saved the crops of the early settlers from a cricket plague.

UTAH TRAVEL COUNCIL

UTAH TRAVEL COUNCIL

Redwood Highway

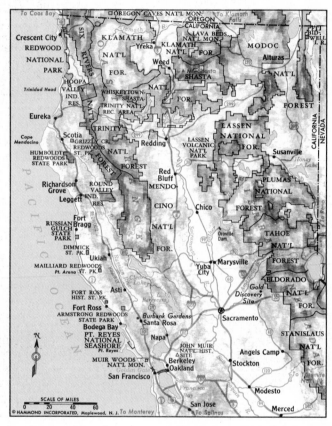

THE UNFORTUNATE FIFTY YEARS. For many millennia the redwood forest stood on the coast between the hills and the ocean in quiet, gigantic majesty. The trees lived on and on. The floor was fertile with the rotting needles of 50,000 years, but because of the semidarkness little underbrush developed. Only delicate small mosses, similar miniature plants and ferns formed a green carpet. This period of peace was suddenly interrupted by 50 years of destruction and chaos. During the late nineteenth century the coast was developed. Wood was needed and great fortunes could be made; the forest could be had for the asking. It was possible to stake a homestead claim and obtain the land from the U.S. Government for next to nothing, but the timber on it was worth millions. So trees tumbled to earth after growing for a thousand years, and one of the most wasteful logging operations started. Only part of the timber was taken out, and it was considered an unproductive waste of time to fight the numerous forest fires. The operators simply let the flames rage and moved to another part of the woods. Finally a group of leading Americans decided that the reckless destruction had to be stopped, and the Save-the-Redwoods League was founded in 1918. The California legislature, the *Saturday Evening Post,* the National Geographic Society and other organizations joined the campaign, and millions of dollars were raised to buy and preserve the most beautiful groves. The Save-the-Redwoods League is still very active, constantly expanding the existing preserves and adding new ones.

NOT THE BIGGEST BUT THE TALLEST. While there are scattered groves to the north and south, the heaviest concentration of redwoods is in Humboldt County. Some of the finest groves are in the state parks and in Redwood National Park. The tallest trees in the world are here, including one giant in the national park which measures 367.4 feet. In a way this giant sets a pattern. The coastal redwoods are taller than but not as big around as the sequoias of the Sierras, nor are they as ancient. None of them is believed to be more than 2,000 years old. The general impression of these redwood groves is also very different. The sequoias of the mountains tend to stand farther apart, letting in more light, and when the rays of the sun strike the compact armor of the red bark and the green of gnarled branches, each single tree is a great work of art in itself. In contrast, the coastal redwoods keep close company, and it is this unity which turns their groves into cathedrals. The light is as subdued as in a gothic church, the floor as soft as a carpet. At sunset the evening dampness curls here and there like smoke from incense vessels. Even the birdcalls are distant and hushed. There is a great and unique experience to be enjoyed, prefer-

THE LONG, DARK GREEN BELT. There are celebrities among the highways of America: the Trail Ridge Road in Colorado, the Grand Canyon Rim Road, the Coastal Highway in Oregon, the Blue Ridge Parkway, the Skyline Drive in Virginia and others. All of them glorify the mountains. But there is one famous road devoted to a forest — the Redwood Highway, U.S. Route 101, which runs along the redwood belt, a strip of land extending from southwestern Oregon to the Santa Lucia Range south of Monterey in California. The redwood belt is 450 miles long but only 1 to 40 miles wide. The tree *Sequoia sempervirens* flourishes at no other place in the world. The moist and foggy climate of the coast is its natural habitat. It is a species quite different from the *Sequoia gigantea* of the high Sierras.

A CATHEDRAL of TREES

ably on a Saturday or Sunday. On the other days the parade of lumber trucks — some of them carrying a single giant log — is a bit disturbing. All along the highway dishes, bowls and vases of redwood burls may be bought. Whatever you may think of travel souvenirs, you will find many pieces among them that are beautiful and unique products of a truly American local art.

RUSSIAN RIVER AND ITALIAN WINE. Proceeding southward toward San Francisco, the groves occur more rarely. One, in the Muir Woods National Monument, lies near the entrance of the Golden Gate. In Sonoma County we are on historic ground. This part of California was once a Russian colony. Russian soldiers camped here, and their Aleut slaves were sent out in their kayaks to hunt the precious sea otter. There is another contact with world history here. Fort Ross, the Russian stronghold restored now as a state park, was founded

in 1812, the year Napoleon entered Moscow, and it was equipped with French cannon Napoleon left behind on his retreat. In 1841, when practically all sea otters had been destroyed, the Russians gave up their California outpost, but the Russian River and the Russian Gulch still remind us of a strange interlude in our history. The commander's house and the chapel, which burned in 1970, had been restored. In this same neighborhood a more peaceful enterprise draws our attention. The countryside is dotted with lush vineyards and old stone wineries. Practically all of them welcome visitors. The Italian-Swiss Colony at Asti is a modern winery and may be inspected. Here visitors learn of a happy marriage of redwood and wine. The redwoods furnish ideal material for the storage casks. Don't forget to include a visit to the tasting room, and name your preference. You may have all the wine you want just for the asking. In Asti even the church looks like a wine barrel.

Right: California wines are now competing in quality with European wines. The Beringer Winery in St. Helena looks like a small chateau.

Below right: Sonoma is the most northerly of the Spanish missions in California.

Below: The coastal redwoods are not the largest but the tallest trees on our planet.

Lassen Peak and Mount Shasta

May 1915, a fiery mass of glowing lava spilled over the rim of the crater, became a huge, black tongue as it crawled over the snow, and melted the icy ground. Consequently a torrent of mud swept down the valley of Lost Creek and into Hat Creek across the divide. The slimy flood carried along rocks and logs, uprooted trees and boulders weighing up to 20 tons and filled a lonely ranch house, fortunately without loss of life. One boulder was reported to have sizzled in the water all day. It took a week to change from hot to warm. Three days later a few additional mud flows occurred, accompanied by a new phenomenon.

MOWING DOWN THE TREES IN ROWS. A terrific blast of steam and hot gases mixed with dust and ashes blew from the crater into the valley, mowing down the big forest in neat, uniform rows, all the treetops pointing away from the crater like a grainfield cut with a scythe. It also appeared as if some woodworking machinery had been applied. All the tree trunks had their bark sandblasted on the upper side, and the stumps seemed nicely finished and polished. Strangely, no fires occurred. After this spectacular outbreak, the periodic eruptions diminished in force.

HONORING A BLACKSMITH. Whether or not anyone in Denmark knows that one of America's famous peaks has been named in honor of a Danish blacksmith seems doubtful. Yet it is so. Peter Lassen, who was born in the Scandinavian kingdom in 1793, came to this country as a young man, worked in smithies in the East but soon drifted into Mexican California and established a ranch in the shadows of a great peak. In 1849 he was not tempted by the gold rush but stayed at his home and acted as guide for the many wagon trains bound for the Sacramento Valley. His mountain became a landmark. The riders of the covered wagons called it Lassen Peak. Today the area is a part of Lassen Volcanic National Park. Visitors find the climb to the white cloaked summit quite easy and the 150-mile view rewarding. There are other dormant volcanoes in the park, among them the smaller Cinder Cone which had its last eruption in 1850-51. In its crater, which is difficult to reach, a ribbon of painted volcanic sand contrasts sharply with the dark lava. Other signs of volcanic activity are the bubbling hot springs of Boiling Springs Lake and a sulphuric basin of mud pots, warm springs and steam vents called Bumpass Hell. Bumpass was a farmhand who in 1865 broke through the thin crust, scalded his leg and named the place. The Chaos Crags were once hard lava plugs standing upright. The terrific explosions and avalanches tore them down and

SWEATSHOP OF THE GODS. Looking up from the broad Sacramento Valley toward the Cascades and seeing one of the peaks belch a huge cloud of coal black smoke five miles into the air, the cloud finally taking on the ominous shape of a mushroom, would be considered surprising indeed. Yet that happened not so long ago in May 1914, when Lassen Peak erupted. This region had previously shown signs of mild volcanism. In 1843 Frémont reported volcanic activity in Mount Baker and Mount St. Helens. Even the name the Indians had given the harmless looking peak long before it became Lassen Peak contained a warning. They called it "Sweatshop of the Gods." But on Decoration Day in 1914, when the first eruption occurred, without previous rumbling or quaking, the awakened volcano made world news. Within two weeks the crater expanded from 25 to 1,500 feet, and it rained ashes as far as Nevada. A year later, in

ONE HALF WILD, the OTHER FULLY TAMED

SHASTA-CASCADE WONDERLAND ASSOCIATION

In spite of its quiet beauty, Mt. Lassen might erupt again. The volcano seems to follow a 76-year cycle of eruption.

spread them in wild and indescribable disorder over a 2-mile stretch of ground. Lassen Park Road passes through the helter-skelter of the Chaos Jumbles. The various volcanic eruptions caused lava flows and avalanches which in turn blocked several creeks and created a number of beautiful mountain lakes. In some cases whole groves of trees were submerged. In Snag Lake you can still see, through the crystal clear water, the remains of trees standing on the bottom. Lake Helen is a beauty spot, and on its shore two tantalizing signs attract attention. One says, "Dozens of rainbow trout will come for crumbs tossed in this lake." The other announces, "Closed to fishing."

COULD THIS VOLCANO SUDDENLY ERUPT?
This question is often heard by the park rangers, and the only answer they can give to the slightly worried visitors is a shrug of the shoulders. Nobody knows, but tourists are advised to return, with cameras cocked, in 1979. No eruption is guaranteed, but geologists believe that this volcano operates on a 65-year cycle. The last outbreak occurred in 1914.

ANOTHER VOLCANO COOPERATES. Thirty miles northwest of Lassen Park, the huge and splendid 14,162-foot-high Mount Shasta looks over the rich, checkered farmlands of the Sacramento Valley, its 5 glaciers furnishing an ermine cloak for its summit. Mount Shasta, too, is a dormant volcano, and to this day a number of steam vents and fumaroles around its peak emit hot gases. But so sure are the scientists of its continued good behavior that this scene of ancient eruptions has been turned into one of man's huge technical projects. Shasta Dam has been built there, its height of 602 feet and its width of 3,500 feet at its crest making it one of the nation's largest. Thus the once fiery volcano and the once violent Sacramento River combine forces to create electric power, irrigate desert lands and control floods. The 7,800-foot-high Mount Shasta Ski Bowl is a winter sports center with a double chair lift.

211

Reno and Virginia City

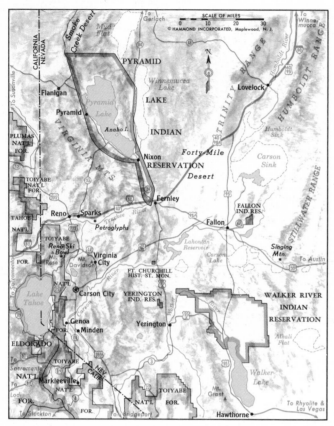

Virginia City, Nevada. The nearby Comstock Lode created some of America's richest families.

GAMING, NOT GAMBLING. The minute you cross the state line into Nevada, you realize that gaming — the word gambling is frowned upon here as not being quite appropriate — is a statewide industry. You know, of course, about Reno and Las Vegas, but the neon signs begin at the border, and there is hardly an eating place without roulette tables and slot machines. If you are a puritan, you hurry on without stopping, but most visitors don't mind investigating the casinos, although they might not gamble at home. The Nevadans' viewpoint is this. Their state is largely a desert; outside of mining there is practically no industry and there is little land fertile enough for agriculture. At the same time a far-flung network of highways and an adequate school system have to be maintained. The money has to come from some source, and legalized and continuously supervised gaming is better than underground

gambling. At any rate, it is strictly a Nevada affair.

THE DIVORCE CAPITAL. Although Reno's slogan, "the Biggest Little City in the World," is meaningless as far as Reno's attractions are concerned, your first visit there will be a curious and intriguing experience. You will like the tree lined Truckee River and the bright appearance of the city. You will watch the young women downtown and wonder whether they are all divorcées. You will walk through the clubs which operate around the clock, marvel at the democratic atmosphere and smile at the signs and inscriptions: "Be careful with your money." "All this is very solid and respectable." "This club is operated by a family of Vermont farm boys." "Come and see our historical collection of the Old West in back of the blackjack tables, it's very educational." And if you watch an elderly lady with a lapful of silver dollars operating three clattering slot machines simultaneously, with a face as serious and concentrated as if she were working on an assembly line, the effect is both comical and pathetic. Whatever you may think, Reno is a genuine corner of America and worth seeing.

THE BUCKET OF BLOOD SALOON. Not far from Reno is one of America's historic shrines. It is neither a battlefield nor the birthplace of a hero, but it is the area where the Old West "happened" in its gaudiest and most fantastic form — Virginia City, Nevada. In 1859 a certain ore which the prospectors had disregarded and called "black stuff" was assayed. It yielded over $3,000 worth of gold and almost $5,000 worth of

SILVER DOLLARS in YOUR POCKET, the OLD WEST in the AIR

silver per ton. The Comstock Lode had been discovered, later proving to be the greatest strike ever made anywhere on earth. Fortunes made in Virginia City built great West Coast cities, constructed continental railroads, financed the first cable across the Atlantic and reduced the debt of the War Between the States. A city with such a past must be fascinating, and it is. Part of it is a ghost town which in outsiders always creates an eerie interest. Part of it has a pleasant residential Victorian atmosphere. Part of it is a revival of the old western spirit, and it certainly is fun to visit the Bucket of Blood Saloon which has done business on C Street since 1876, and the Crystal Bar with its ancient chandeliers in red and green, dressed up with prisms in splendid tiers. Piper's Opera House, where a voluble audience acclaimed the most famous actors and actresses of its day, is still open during the summer. Mark Twain once worked at the *Territorial Enterprise* newspaper office. The town's gallows frame is still in position. In addition to the flamboyant history there is the spectacular scenery. The city lies on the eastern slope of Mount Davidson, with a choice seat in the theater-in-the-round that is formed by high, rocky mountains. Two thousand feet below, the Carson River winds its way between green pastures and tall cottonwood trees. Further on you see the white dunes of the Forty Mile Desert. The snowcapped blue mountain chain that massively closes the horizon in the crystal clear air is the Humboldt Range, 100 miles away.

THE BREATH OF THE ERRING WOMAN. There are other see-worthy sights in the western section of Nevada. Carson City, the smallest state capital in America, is a lush oasis in the desert, a fertile, well watered spot, a lovely park above which the white dome of the Capitol arises. The city was named for pioneer scout Kit Carson. Every year at the end of October there is an eye-catching celebration in honor of Nevada's admittance to statehood. In front of the State Museum, which exhibits full-scale mining operations, the antique woodburning Glenbrook locomotive of 1875 can be inspected. The State Museum has a spectacular exhibit of mining operations. Mount Rose is a winter sport center, and the Reno Ski Bowl offers slopes of varying steepness. But the most unusual sight, and one of breathtaking beauty at sunset or in full moonlight, is Pyramid Lake, a large body of water 30 miles long and up to 10 miles wide. Deep blue, surrounded by sharp edged hills and studded with islands of tufa that jut steeply from the surface, it offers a view that cannot be duplicated, especially when the rays of the setting sun paint rocks and islands red, orange and purple. In season Anaho Island is a white seething mass of pelicans. It is the greatest rookery in the West and, fortunately, a national bird refuge. When the cui-ui fish run, the mouth of the Truckee River swarms with fishing pelicans, and the awkward and weird looking birds fit well into the eerie landscape. Beyond Anaho Island a pyramid rises 475 feet above the water. The Paiute Indians have a legend about the huge boulder at whose foot steam rises from several hot springs. Once upon a time a handsome girl fell into erring ways, so the Great Spirit clapped a giant basket over her, and she turned into rock. But her breath is still clearly visible.

Reno's casino district has a perpetual fiesta atmosphere.

Pioneer Theater Auditorium, a modern touch in the Old West.

RENO NEWS BUREAU (3)

Lake Tahoe

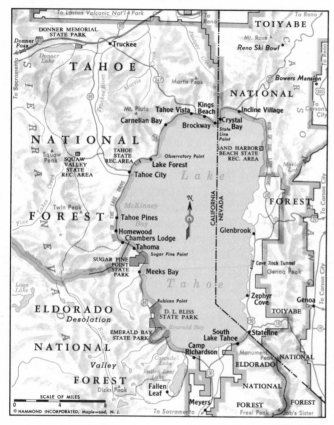

Sister, Mt. Rose, Monument Peak and Pyramid Peak, all over 10,000 feet. In the morning the ranges are brilliantly photographed on its still surface. In the evening, when the low clouds hover over the lakeshore, the mountains rise into the clear sky above the clouds like a mirage. Evergreen forests with a carpet of heather, Indian paintbrush, primroses and other wild flowers descend to the banks. It is possible to pick up a handsome 15-inch sugar pinecone to be used as a Christmas decoration. There are sandy beaches, summer resorts, state parks, public camping grounds and estates of millionaires. The scenery can be enjoyed from excursion boats or from the road circling the lake, and sportsmen will find the trout fishing good. South Lake Tahoe is the largest community; Meeks Bay has a fine bathing beach, and on the Nevada side visitors may try their luck at roulette in simple gambling halls or luxurious casinos. The lake is almost surrounded by Tahoe, Eldorado and Toiyabe national forests.

BIRTHPLACE OF SKIING IN THE U.S. According to sports chroniclers, the first skiing and ski racing took place in the mountains around Lake Tahoe about a hundred years ago. To pass the time when they were snowbound, Scandinavian miners cut down spruce trees, fashioned the trunks into 12-foot skis and revived the art of skiing, which had been popular in Norway for generations. After this auspicious start, however, more popular skiing resorts sprang up elsewhere in less rugged terrain. Only lately has the Lake Tahoe region come into its own again. It did so on a grand scale, and some

Lovely evergreen forests with a carpet of wildflowers descend to the banks of the lake.

DAZZLING, BRILLIANTLY SO. Lake Tahoe is both the model and paragon of American mountain lakes. It has an old Indian name of pleasant sound. It lies in the crisp mountain air at an altitude of 6,225 feet and is more than 22 miles long and about 12 miles wide. It is very deep and contains so much water that it could flood the whole state of Texas to 7 or 8 inches, according to Californian estimates. Mark Twain glowingly expressed the most startling aspect of the lake: "Down through these great depths the water was not merely transparent but dazzling, brilliantly so; we could see trout by the thousands winging about in the emptiness under us."

It is this combination of clarity and depth that accounts for the water's deep colors. The lake is surrounded by mountains towering some 4,000 feet above it, among the tallest summits being Freel Peak, Job's

214

GREATER NORTH LAKE TAHOE CHAMBER OF COMMERCE

"THE FAIREST PICTURE the WHOLE EARTH AFFORDS"--MARK TWAIN

now consider that it has the greatest concentration of skiing resorts in the world. This late second start had a considerable advantage, because experience gained elsewhere was taken into account when the new centers were created. Skiing, it seems, never became popular in America until the chair lift was invented. Europeans would trudge up the mountains in order to slide down, but not Americans. Lazy? No, just traditionally machine-oriented. So the Sierra Nevada side of the lake is a chair lift country now and operates in the manner of mass transportation. Squaw Valley, the site of the 1960 Winter Olympics, for instance, has 24 chair lifts that take 20,000 skiers per hour to bunny slopes and professional race courses. They climb to such a height that they almost seem to speed into the blue horizon. Swinging out high above the snow covered forests, valleys and gorges, the ride on these lifts is an unparalleled thrill. In summertime the cable car operates for sightseeing, and no traveler should miss the ride.

AN AMERICAN CAVALCADE. The Lake Tahoe country is also historic ground. It has no connection with wars or revolutions, but with that stirring and particularly American brand of history which concerns the settling of a great continent. Two monuments recall the westward trek that passed this way. The Pony Express Monument at Meyers, near the southern tip of Lake Tahoe on U.S. Highway 50, and the Donner Memorial, northwest of the lake on Interstate 80. The latter commemorates the stark tragedy of the Donner Party, which was snowbound at that spot during the winter of 1846. Of the more than 80 members of the party only about half survived the nightmare of hunger and cold. In the despair of starvation, the living ate the corpses of their dead companions.

On the other hand, the bronze relief south of the lake honors a cheerful American enterprise, the Pony Express of 1860 which carried letters at $5 a piece from St. Joseph, Missouri, to Sacramento in 8 days. Eighty pony riders were "in the saddle all the time, night and day, stretching a long, scattering procession from Missouri to California, forty flying eastward and forty toward the west, and among them making four hundred gallant horses earn a stirring livelihood." "Each messenger," Mark Twain wrote, "rode a splendid horse . . . kept him at his utmost speed for ten miles, and then, as he came crashing to the station where stood two men holding fast a fresh, impatient steed, the transfer of rider and mail bag was made in the twinkling of an eye, and away flew the eager pair . . ." U.S. Highway 50, now the southeastern part of the lake's circle drive, saw much more thrilling history. In the early 1850's it was an almost unmarked, barely passable immigrant trail. In 1858 the first wagon rolled over an improved roadbed. Then the Comstock Lode was discovered, and the boom hit the road. Huge crude wagons, each loaded with as much as 8 tons of ore, rattled along, drawn by teams of 10 mules. Hay for the animals cost about 6 cents a pound, and the franchise holders who maintained the road and the bridges charged whatever the traffic would bear. The toll for a 6-horse team and wagon was $36 for the whole length of the course.

Lake Tahoe is a jewel of rare splendor.

Squaw Valley, the famous Olympic winter sports resort, is a beauty spot at any season.

GREATER NORTH LAKE TAHOE CHAMBER OF COMMERCE

GAIL HAMMOND

San Francisco

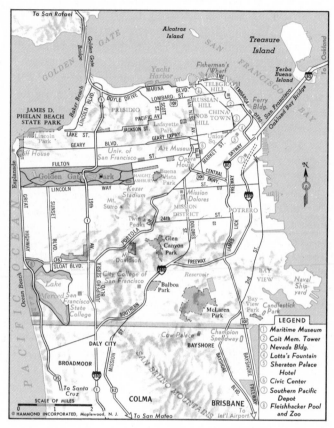

To San Rafael

Alcatraz Island

Treasure Island

To Oakland

Yerba Buena Island

GOLDEN GATE

SAN FRANCISCO BAY

Yacht Harbor

Fisherman's Wharf

THE

TELEGRAPH HILL

RUSSIAN HILL

CHINA TOWN

NOB HILL

Ferry Bldg.

Oakland Bay Bridge

San Francisco

Golden Gate Bridge

Baker Beach

DOYLE DRIVE

MARINA

LOMBARD ST.

VAN NESS AV.

EMBARCA.

JAMES D. PHELAN BEACH STATE PARK

PRESIDIO

SCOTT ST.

PACIFIC AV.

LINCOLN BLVD.

JACKSON ST.

Lafayette Park

GEARY EXPWY

Union Sq.

LAKE ST.

Lincoln Park

Cliff House

GEARY

BLVD.

Univ. of San Francisco

Art Museum

Opera House

MARKET ST.

CENTRAL

SKWY

FULTON

Esplanade

Golden Gate Park

LINCOLN WAY

HAIGHT ASHBURY

Buena Vista Park

Mt. Sutro

Kezar Stadium

Mission Dolores

MISSION DISTRICT

SKWY

FREEWAY

PACIFIC OCEAN

GREAT HIGHWAY

SUNSET BLVD.

19th AVE.

Twin Peaks

24th

ST.

DOLORES

JAMES LICK

3rd

ST.

POTRERO

Ocean Beach

PORTOLA DR.

Glen Canyon Park

Mt. Davidson

FREEWAY

BAY VIEW

Naval Ship-yard

JUNIPERO SERRA BLVD.

SLOAT BLVD.

City College of San Francisco

Reservoir

Bay-View Park

Candlestick Park

Lake Merced

San Francisco State College

Balboa Park

SOUTHERN

McLaren Park

BAYSHORE

101

To Santa Cruz

DALY CITY

Cow Palace

Champion Speedway

BAYSHORE

BAYSHORE FREEWAY

BROADMOOR

BAYSHORE

BLVD.

MISSION ST.

COLMA

SAN BRUNO MOUNTAINS

BRISBANE

To Int'l Airport

SCALE OF MILES

© HAMMOND INCORPORATED, Maplewood, N. J.

To San Mateo

LEGEND
1. Maritime Museum
2. Coit Mem. Tower
3. Nevada Bldg.
4. Lotta's Fountain
5. Sheraton Palace Hotel
6. Civic Center
7. Southern Pacific Depot
8. Fleishhacker Pool and Zoo

FABULOUS GEOGRAPHY. The world's most beautiful cities, such as Hong Kong, Rio de Janeiro and San Francisco, are built on hills by the sea, with rockbound, bay studded harbors and small islands set into the surrounding waters like jewels. In Hong Kong and Rio the hills are mountains, while San Francisco's peaks stay well below the 1,000-foot altitude. But the Golden Gate city is washed by choppy waters on three sides, and the bracing smell of the sea is everywhere. Its panorama may be enjoyed from such famous lookout points as the Coit Memorial Tower on Telegraph Hill, Twin Peaks in the center of town, or the traditional Top of the Mark in the Mark Hopkins Hotel, 20 stories above Nob Hill. In addition, there are any number of streets where you look ahead casually and in the distance see a dark island resting in the sunny water of the bay, or a steamer from the South Seas slowly approach-

ing the wharf. You distinguish the silhouettes of the Golden Gate Bridge and the 4½-mile-long San Francisco-Oakland Bay Bridge and realize how their man-made beauty harmonizes perfectly with their nature-made surroundings. Part of the local geography is the weather, and that, too, is unique. With the absence of heat waves and cold waves, it has been described as a perpetual invigorating fall climate. To be sure, there is a good deal of rain, and the thick, regular fog is not popular either. But the more frequent, local type of fog has picturesque qualities of its own and is an important ingredient of the San Francisco atmosphere. In low-hanging drifts it roams around the bay and between the hills, its serpentine motions covering and uncovering section after section. One end of the Golden Gate Bridge may stand out in super clarity, the other may be hidden completely in a white blanket.

ORIENT AND OCCIDENT. Not only is San Francisco's location fascinating but also its global geography. While its culture remains thoroughly American, there are touches of the Orient everywhere. Its Chinatown is the largest Chinese settlement outside of Asia, and Americans of Far Eastern extraction are found among the people on every street. Wonderful oriental food may be eaten here, and oriental spices and teas may be purchased. In New York the museums and the wealthy homes are filled with pieces of European art. In San Francisco masterpieces of oriental art abound in museums and stores. Treasures in jade and china, tapestries and sculptures of the East may be bought here as easily as in Hong Kong. Every American should know both New York and San Francisco; such a double acquaintance will give him a center-of-the-world feeling. Our country is a giant who with one hand touches the civilization of the Occident, with the other that of the Orient.

FISHERMAN'S WHARF AND THE CABLE CARS. The best sights are free in San Francisco. You may enjoy the spectacle of the city's hills and bays, with the ever changing lighting effects of towering cloud formations, bright sunshine and meandering fogbanks. You may park your car under Union Square and stroll through the shopping center where elegant stores, smartly dressed women and bright flower stands will catch your eye. In Chinatown you will have the feeling that you are not merely witnessing a show staged for the tourists but are in a genuine Chinese settlement. On a sightseeing tour — a Chinese-American graduate student may be your guide — you will learn a great deal not only about Chinese-American life but also about China's

TWENTY-ONE HILLS by the GOLDEN GATE

DOROTHY BACHELLER

The span over the Golden Gate is probably the country's most famous bridge.

San Francisco's maritime traditions, which reached from the Orient to Alaska, are still very much alive.

DOROTHY BACHELLER

religious cults. Two blocks to the west Nob Hill arises, once crowned with the million-dollar mansions of various bonanza kings. The palaces have been largely replaced by hotels and apartment houses, but a certain air still prevails. Some of the hills may be climbed in small, half-open cable cars, a 100-year-old institution close to the hearts of all San Franciscans, who refuse to have them scrapped for more modern means of transportation. If you are interested in history, don't miss the Mission Dolores where, in the midst of a howling wilderness, the first mass was celebrated 5 days before the Declaration of Independence. The present building was started in 1782, and the Indian workmen did not use a single nail but tied the beams of the arched roof with leather tongs. A more worldly landmark is the Sheraton Palace Hotel which once catered to the wealthy and famous and is still one of the world's fabulous dining spots. You will enjoy luncheon at the Cliff House while watching the sea lions frolicking among the rocks near the shore, or have a seafood meal at Fisherman's Wharf and observe the brightly painted fishing boats riding into port to unload their squirming cargoes. At Trader Vic's you'll eat wonderful Polynesian food. San Francisco's museums are varied, among them the Maritime Museum on the waterfront, where you may interrupt your study of Pacific shipping history with a swim from a sandy beach below. In the Wild West Museum of the Wells Fargo Bank in the Nevada Building the most honored exhibit is, quite appropriately, a shiny red stagecoach which crossed the Sierra Nevada. There are many more attractions — Golden Gate Park, the Opera House where the United Nations organization was born, Lotta's fountain which was given to the city by a charming actress of the gold dust era, and way-out cabarets and discotheques. You will enjoy not only the sights but also the atmosphere. Out of a violent and vibrant past of gold rush, earthquake and phenomenal growth, a spirit of true friendliness has emerged. "No cold theological eye here," says George West, "no lifted eyebrow, no cautious hand withheld."

217

The Monterey Peninsula

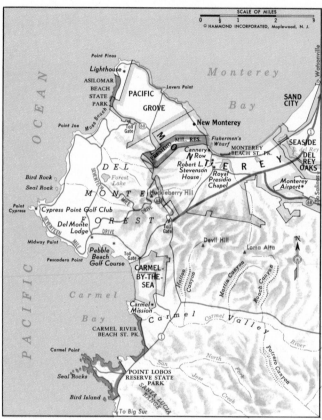

many modern visitors the lacy, windswept landscape looks Japanese.

PADRES AND ARTISTS IN CARMEL. In 1602 three Carmelites visited the southern corner of the peninsula and were impressed by a hill which reminded them of Mount Carmel in Palestine. The Lord's mills turned slowly in Old Spain. In 1771 the mission was established at Carmel, with the same eye for scenic beauty and inspiring views that guided the building of missions and monasteries in Europe and Latin America. Today the rambling Carmel Mission is restored, and the visitor from the East who cherishes the simplicity of the small, white New England churches will enjoy a fascinating new experience. In the colorful halls, with their lovely objects of art and the leather bound volumes of a library established in the virgin wilderness, he will feel something of the magnificent Hispanic empire of the mind.

Akin to the padres in their appreciation of scenic beauty are the artists who appeared at this lovely spot after the turn of the century and founded the now famous city of Carmel, also called Carmel-by-the-Sea. The initiated complain that the true artist-residents (among them some famous names) have been joined by so many dilettantes, charlatans and idlers that the village has been turned into a Walt Disney-type Montmartre. Whether or not that is true seems debatable. To most visitors, Carmel-by-the-Sea is still a splendid resort, with dark green pines on roads and walks, a main street that leads to a broad, sloping beach, with clusters of brilliant blossoms everywhere, with art stores that display fine creations from France or Sweden or the South Seas, with art galleries and an open-air theater and an annual Bach Festival.

THE ENCHANTED FOREST. This real estate venture of the Del Monte Properties Company, just north of Carmel, has been called "the Monaco of America" and "the last stronghold of feudalism" in the western hemisphere. Four thousand carefully selected citizens live among the grandeur of the forest ridges, the primeval groves, the costly homes and the famous golf courses whose setting is so breathtaking that the golfers complain about it. They don't play their best golf there — the scenic beauty distracts them. Mere sightseers have to pay a toll for the privilege of entering this sanctuary. But its main road, the Seventeen Mile Drive along the peninsula's shore, offers sights worth many times that modest tax. There is Del Monte Lodge with its Pebble Beach Golf Course where championship games are played. Midway Point with its lone cypress is one of the world's most painted and photographed tree, rock and ocean ensembles. On the compact granite mass of Seal Rock hundreds of sea lions sun themselves, play

POINT OF THE SEA WOLVES. Flat, dark green umbrellas on top of gnarled, contorted trunks is the way the Monterey cypresses grow. Nowhere else on earth do they exist but on this coast. Singly or in small groups they rise from precarious slopes or hidden fissures in the cliffs that jut out into the sea. The rocks beneath the trees appear ghostly gray in a fogbank, bright yellow in the sun of noon and glowing red at sunset. The most spectacular of these cliffs was named Punta de los Lobos Marinos, Point of the Sea Wolves, because of the sea lions playing among the rocks. Unfortunately the Spanish name was anglicized into a rather meaningless Point Lobos. Robert Louis Stevenson roamed these cliffs, and according to some scholars Point Lobos became the Spyglass Hill of Treasure Island. "The finest meeting of land and water in existence" — that was his verdict. Perhaps he sensed an affinity to the Orient. To

OUR SPANISH HERITAGE

and cavort unmindful of the nearby human visitors. Here it becomes clear why the German language calls these animals "Seehunde," for sometimes their barking fills the air as if a thousand hounds were let loose. Bird Rock, a stony island near the shore, swarms with a seething mass of sea gulls and pelicans, cormorants and other birds. Finally we reach the northern toll gate and arrive at Pacific Grove, a prim, neat, tavernless city that was founded as a Methodist retreat. The town retains its spiritual independence of both the Bohemian life of the artists and the grand-style living of the rich.

MONTEREY AND TORTILLA FLAT. At the northern end of the peninsula history is again in evidence. Monterey was the capital of Spanish California before the United States had been founded. With its interesting old adobe houses of Spanish days — the Royal Presidio Chapel, the Casa Abrego, the old whaling station and the Old Custom House — it has sometimes been called the western Williamsburg. The Robert Louis Stevenson House, originally built by a Mexican customs official, contains in its thick-walled, high-ceilinged rooms many interesting mementos of the author's stay in Monterey in 1879. One rectangular adobe building houses the first American theater in California. The State Museum illustrates the way of life of the Spanish days: a primitive burro cart with wheels of solid wood is exhibited next to a belle's evening dress imported for $1,000 from Paris to Monterey via Cape Horn. The town's liveliest spot is Fishermen's Wharf where Japanese abalone divers and Italian skippers mingle with tourists from many states. The wharf's seafood restaurants are widely known. Fishing — sardines, albacore and abalone — and canning were once the city's major industries. The street called Cannery Row is the setting of two of John Steinbeck's famous novels, "Tortilla Flat" and "Cannery Row." No longer a line of factories, it is now a complex of art shops and restaurants.

From the days of the old Spanish Presidio, a cannon overlooks Monterey Bay.

Yosemite National Park

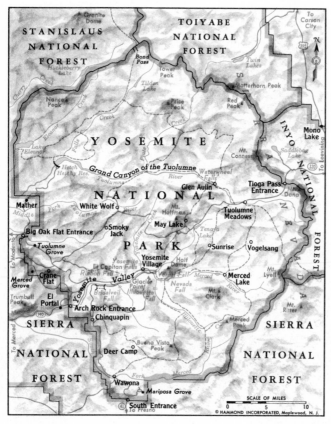

own eyes. Savage suspected a redskin hidden behind every boulder and expressed his feelings as quoted above, but the young physician of the expedition, L. H. Bunnell, recognized the extraordinary beauty of the spot and began to sing its praises. Soon parties which included writers and artists found their way to Yosemite, and when the arduous horse trail was widened into a primitive wagon road travelers came by the hundreds. A quickly constructed railroad, now defunct, brought thousands, and the modern highways now open the park to millions. As early as 1864 Abraham Lincoln signed an Act of Congress giving the region to the state of California as a reservation.

THE MISSION OF JOHN MUIR. Yosemite's most famous promoter was John Muir who, although a well educated naturalist, spent years in the wilderness of the high Sierras as a shepherd. He has been called "the Thoreau of the West," and in his harmony with nature and disdain for material comforts he was a Thoreau. Quite unlike Thoreau, he was also an articulate and effective missionary and prophet, and in countless articles spread the exciting news throughout the country. He invited Ralph Waldo Emerson, the Concord philosopher, to join him. "You are yourself a Sequoia," he wrote, "stop and get acquainted with your brethren." The famous man came but was not as vociferous in his praise as Muir had hoped. He spoke little, "yet it was a great pleasure to be near him, warming in the light of his face." Another celebrity did not hesitate to express his views. Horace Greeley inspected the valley, and far away in the East his New York *Tribune* praised Yosemite as "the marvel of the continent."

ELEVEN NIAGARAS. The heart of the national park is the 7-mile-long Yosemite Valley, a grassy, park-like floor walled in by towering cliffs, domes and pinnacles. Its most celebrated spot is the rock over which the Yosemite Falls tumble their white torrents in spring or their graceful, swaying ribbons in the drier summer months. The Upper Fall leaps 1,430 feet, which equals 9 Niagaras, to which the Lower Fall, with 320 feet, adds 2 more Niagaras. With the intervening cascades, the total leap covers almost half a mile. Among the other falling waters Ribbon Fall has a sheer drop of 10 Niagaras — 1,612 feet. Nevada, Vernal, Illilouette and Bridalveil falls have their own beauty.

V INTO U. The process by which nature created this abundance of falls is interesting. In an early geological era, when volcanic upheavals crushed the crust of the earth and raised the peaks that are today the Sierra Nevada, an antediluvian river cut the first V-shaped groove into the rock. Three times in the following

EARLY FAME. Of all the great scenic spots in the country none won recognition, protection, admiration and international fame as quickly and enthusiastically as the Yosemite Valley. It seems that the only visitor who expressed a critical opinion was one of the valley's discoverers, Major James Savage. "It's a hell of a place," he reportedly said.

There was a reason. Savage owned a trading post on the western slope of the Sierra Nevada, 15 miles away. There he exchanged trinkets for the "yellow sand" the Indians of the five neighboring tribes brought him, and to improve his customer relations he married 5 squaws, one from each tribe. In spite of this precaution there were raids on his property, so he organized the Mariposa Battalion which proceeded under his leadership toward the valley of the Yosemite Indians. On the 25th of March 1851, the men saw the great valley with their

VALLEY of FALLING WATERS

20,000,000 years glaciers invaded the valley and slowly transformed the narrow V into an ever broader and deeper U, employing as grinding tools masses of loose rocks and boulders embedded in the moving ice. But while the mainstream deepened to a lower and lower floor, the side streams could not keep pace. They too ground their grooves, but not as speedily and forcefully, and upon meeting the main valley had to throw the waters over the cliff. They still do, presenting America's most unique collection of cascades.

FOUR GIBRALTARS. Among the peaks of the valley a few have achieved great fame. Half Dome is best seen from Sentinel Bridge in the very center of the valley's activities. The missing half was ground out by ancient glaciers as neatly as if turned by a machine tool. Another majestic mountain is El Capitan on Northside Drive a few miles from the western (Arch Rock) entrance, open all year. It is probably the greatest single rock on earth, quite capable of accommodating four

rocks of Gibraltar. Glacier Point, high on top of the canyon rim but easily reached by automobile, offers a breathtaking panorama. In the northern part of the park is Hetch Hetchy Reservoir that serves San Francisco; it is carved out of the Grand Canyon of the Tuolumne River, a canyon almost as beautiful as Yosemite Valley.

While Yosemite Valley proper is crowded with visitors, lovers of lonely nature can still find many untouched square miles of high country within the park limits. In the words of John Muir, "smooth, silky lawns and wildflower gardens on high slopes; at their feet lie newborn lakes, blue and green. They are sometimes dotted with drifting icebergs like tiny Arctic Oceans, shining, sparkling, calm as stars." The park's three Sequoia groves are wonderful sights, but they do not compete with the Big Trees in Sequoia National Forest. In spite of extensive campgrounds, the park is crowded during the summer. Free modern buses are provided in part of the park to reduce private car traffic.

Right: The height of Yosemite Falls equals eleven Niagaras.

Below right: To the left, El Capitan is probably the largest rock on earth. It could hold four Gibraltars.

Below: Sunsets often suffuse the mountains of the valley with an "Alpine glow."

CECIL W. STOUGHTON — NAT'L PARK SERVICE

GAIL HAMMOND

GAIL HAMMOND

Sequoia and Kings Canyon National Parks

A London botanist inspected some sample branches and named the new genus Wellingtonia in honor of the British hero. Outraged, an American botanist renamed it Washingtonia. Finally the Hungarian botanist Endlicher created today's name Sequoia in honor of the Cherokee Indian chief, and a French scientist made the final distinction between the coast redwood, *Sequoia sempervirens,* and the Big Tree of the Sierra Nevada, *Sequoia gigantea.* Gradually the public began to accept the facts, particularly when the popular John Muir wrote his glowing accounts of these unique American trees. The details revealed astonished the world. Tree ring counts of felled trees indicated that many were about 3,000 years old, and among the still standing giants some might have reached their 4,000th year. The tree blooms during the winter when the ground is covered with 10 or perhaps 20 feet of snow. The seeds are tiny, about one-fourth of an inch long and set in small cones. The roots spread as far as 150 feet. The wood does not seem to rot and may be used after the log has been lying on the ground for centuries. The bark is practically fireproof.

THE DEFEAT OF THE LUMBERJACKS. Of course, the timber interests also heard of the Big Trees in the Sierra Nevada and soon began to move in on them. The struggle was terrific. The first felled trunks splintered into a million bits, so elaborate beds had to be built to cushion the fall, and scaffolds 20 feet high were erected as working platforms for the hewers and sawyers. Felling a single tree took 2 weeks. Most of the lumber was wasted, and what finally reached the Pacific ports cost as much as the lumber shipped from Maine around Cape Horn. For a number of years the battle lasted, then the conservation forces won out. But to this day it is well worthwhile seeing the main scene of destruction, Converse Basin. It is located in Sequoia National Forest, north of the General Grant Grove

The "Mark Twain Stump" at Sequoia National Park where many of the Sequoia trees are over 3,000 years old.

PAUL BUNYAN TALES? When Americans in the East heard of trees nearly 300 feet tall, 30 feet wide and 3,000 years old they did not believe it. These trees, the tales went on, were sometimes hollowed by lightning and fell to the ground. In one such hollow shell a man by the name of Tharp had set up housekeeping in 1858 in a living room 58 feet long and 8 feet high, and in another fallen tree a U.S. Cavalry patrol was stabling 32 horses. Had a California-style Baron Münchhausen been revived? When as late as 1876 a Big Tree trunk, shipped in sections because of its bulk, was sent to the Centennial Exposition in Philadelphia, it was ridiculed as an easily detected hoax.

THE SCIENTISTS' VIEW. To be sure, scientists had known of the existence of the Big Trees earlier, but with academic reticence did not broadcast their knowledge.

222

THE WORLD'S BIGGEST TREES

GAIL HAMMOND

These beautiful, colossal trees grow from tiny seeds, about one-fourth of an inch long, set in small cones.

GERHARD SCHLOTTERBECK

Many of the trees in Sequoia National Park, over 3,000 years old, are among the oldest living things on earth.

Section of Kings Canyon National Park, and can be reached easily. Here giant stumps 20 or 30 feet high dot the ground, and logs and branches are strewn around pell-mell. Only one tree was left standing. But the life cycle continues. Quite a few young sequoias now raise their crowns above the undergrowth. They will form a fine grove 2,000 years from now.

THE CRUSADING JOURNALISTS. The Save-the-Big-Trees movement was largely the work of western nature lovers. The journalists took up the cause, and Colonel George W. Stuart, editor of the weekly paper of Visalia, California, campaigned so vigorously that in 1890 Sequoia National Park was created. The small General Grant Grove Section, located to the northwest of Sequoia National Park, was expanded into Kings Canyon National Park in 1940. In the Sequoia Park the number of Big Trees is estimated at nearly a million, the most impressive group being the Giant Forest, and the most famous sequoia, the General Sherman, is the biggest and surely one of the oldest living things. Like a 27-story tower it is 272 feet high, 36 feet wide at the bottom and 17 feet wide at the height of 120 feet. The General Grant Tree in Kings Canyon National Park is equally impressive, with a width of 40 feet at the base and a height of 267 feet.

TITANIC LANDSCAPE. Besides the sequoias, the 2 great parks of the Sierra Nevada offer to the visitor many of America's most sweeping views, a landscape of

true grandeur that includes about 75 peaks more than 11,000 feet tall, and 11 that exceed 14,000 in height. Among them is Mount Whitney, the giant of them all, whose towering peak, 14,494 feet in the sky, looks eastward into the desert of Death Valley, 282 feet below sea level. The wonder of it all is that not only experienced alpinists may reach that highest spot in the "lower forty-eight," but almost anybody may do so, on horseback or on foot. A trail leads right to the peak. In the sister park, Kings Canyon is a mountain scene of giant proportions, without the cascades of Yosemite but on a grander scale.

Those visitors who come by car will receive an impressive sampling of all this beauty. But the great adventure of the Sierra Nevada is the foot or burro trip from Sequoia to Yosemite National Park on the John Muir Trail, which winds its way along the ridge of the great range, crossing five sky-high mountain passes. The trail rarely drops below and frequently rises above 8,500 feet.

INYO COUNTRY: FORGOTTEN CALIFORNIA. Between Kings Canyon and Sequoia national parks and the Nevada state line there lies a wild and beautiful stretch of America — the land of the Inyo Mountains. To the south in Owens Valley where water is diverted to Los Angeles some activity can be observed, but the rest of Inyo Country consists of mountains in lonely grandeur, tree lined lakes and a few gold rush ghost towns abandoned and in ruins.

223

Death Valley

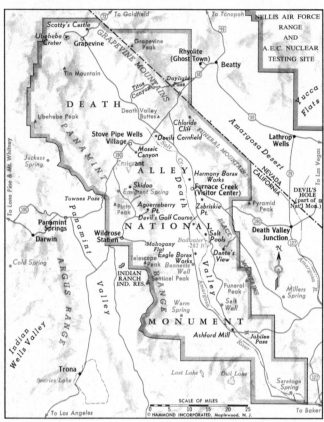

red granites, yellow dunes and various sandstones which appear green and blue, pink and red. Yet this drama of color is not at all like that of the Grand Canyon, for Death Valley is not the product of erosion. Instead of being delicate and lacy, the pattern here is bold, strong and barbaric. It hardly ever rains — the annual precipitation is less than 2 inches — and in the dry, incredibly clear air distances seem to melt. The high mountains which surpass 11,000 feet to the west appear to be within a stone's throw.

FUNERAL MOUNTAINS AND SARATOGA SPRING. The place names of this valley are as original as the whole region is unique. Skidoo and Mahogany Flat, Chloride Cliff and Telescope Peak speak for themselves. On the west is the Panamint Range, and to the east the names of the Grapevine Mountains and the Funeral Mountains express a grim good humor. On the southern end of the valley a swampy, desolate marsh is named after a fashionable spa in the East — Saratoga Springs. Two well-known hotels are Furnace Creek Inn and Stove Pipe Wells. The latter is built around some ancient waterholes which have saved many human lives. As the flying sands tended to obscure the spot, it was marked with a stovepipe. One famous lookout is Dantes View. It has an altitude of 5,475 feet and is named for the great poet's Purgatorio. If that implies a glance into the deepest depths and to the highest heights, it is well chosen. For from here both the lowest and what was the highest point in the United States before Alaska's statehood can be seen — the Badwater salt pools just below our feet and Mount Whitney far away in the high Sierras. However, an exceptionally clear day is the prerequisite for such an experience.

GROUND AFIRE. That is the translation of "To-mesha," the Indian name for this valley which stretches its parched floor for 140 miles between the barren ranges of east-central California. Its two famous distinctions are rather on the unattractive side. It is one of the hottest spots on earth — the thermometer has reached 134° F. — and it contains the lowest point in North America, with an altitude, if that seems the right word, of 282 feet below sea level. Therefore one might ask why such a scene of desolation was made a national monument and why it is listed here as an American travel attraction. The answer is simple. During the summer months Death Valley is indeed unbearable; during the winter it is one of the most fascinating spots on this planet. Then it has a delightful climate, and it presents an ever changing spectrum, with shiny white salt beds and jet black volcanic masses, gray clays and

THE LIVING DESERT. The name Death Valley implies the absence of all life. That, however, is erroneous. Every few years Death Valley is in bloom, and desert holly and creosote bush, paper-bag bush and cigarette plant, brittlebush and several others blossom profusely and ripen their seeds speedily. These plants possess a special tenacity for survival, and their seeds remain dormant but creative for long periods. For their cycle does not last one year but five to ten, depending on the rainfall. Animal life is actually abundant, although it functions mostly at night. Flocks of Nelson's bighorn sheep as well as white-tailed antelope squirrels live in the mountains. There are kit foxes and desert coyotes, and a great variety of colorful lizards, from horned toads to chuckwallas. Rattlesnakes are rarely encountered. In Saratoga Spring and Salt Creek the tiny Death Valley fish survive from the day when the whole region consisted of a lake. These "desert sardines" belong to an

DANTES VIEW and TWENTY-MULE TEAMS

order which occurs both in salt and in freshwater. Finally, another unusual member of the local fauna should be mentioned although it was not placed here by nature but by man. Small herds of wild burros roam the hills and canyons. They cannot claim the noble ancestry of the wild mustangs whose progenitors were steeds of Arabian blood which had escaped from the Spaniards. The first wild burros were runaways, too, but merely from the grueling routine as a prospector's helper.

"A SINGLE-BLANKET JACKASS PROSPECTOR."

To the white man Death Valley remained terra incognita until 1849. Indians had occasionally ventured into the desolate area but had hardly ever lived there. Then, during gold rush days, an impatient wagon train of emigrants, the Bennett-Arcana Party, broke away from the Salt Lake-Los Angeles Trail in search of a short cut, got lost in the canyons and wastes of the Death Valley and suffered incredible hardships, especially thirst. Two of their number, Manly and Rogers, went ahead for help. On their return they found that panic had turned to apathy. As Manly and Rogers led them to safety the weary emigrants gave the region its present name. During the following decades prospectors combed the area, and some gold, silver and copper deposits were discovered. Many a searcher and wanderer died there, including Shorty Harris, who on his gravestone called himself "A Single-Blanket Jackass Prospector." Between 1882 and 1927 borax was mined intermittently and carried out on 20-ton trailer-wagons drawn by 20 mules. The coachman had to be an artist to handle the 125-foot check line. One old-timer who prospered was Death Valley Scotty, who built himself a $2,000,000 castle at the northern end of the valley near Ubehebe Crater. For years it was rumored that he retired periodically to his gold mine in the desert to replenish his cash funds. In fact, the establishment was maintained by Scotty's millionaire partner who enjoyed the hoax. The castle is worth seeing and also offers accommodations for guests. In its unlikely surroundings it is, as Freeman Tilden puts it, "as unobtrusive as a symphony conductor's bandaged thumb."

Death Valley includes the lowest point in America, 282 feet below sea level; it is also one of the hottest spots on earth.

CECIL. W. STOUGHTON — NAT'L PARK SERVICE

Las Vegas, Hoover Dam and Lake Mead

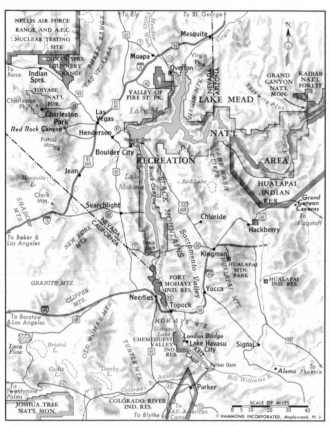

method elevated Las Vegas to a kind of cinema dream in about ten years. U.S. Highway 91 just south of the city limits is known as The Strip; there an ever-growing number of luxury hotels draws crowds from all the states. Originally a winter resort, Las Vegas operates now on an all-year basis, with powerful air conditioning counteracting the heat of the summer. Many gambling casinos are open 24 hours a day, and the swankiest are said to allow higher stakes than are permitted anywhere else in the world. Chips of various denominations are used like money in town, and tales of lucky windfalls create an air of excitement. The fact that Los Angeles is only 300 miles distant often attracts members of the motion picture and television colony to Las Vegas — another addition to the town's glamour. Las Vegas proper is a friendly, tree-shaded town which celebrates its western past every spring, with a parade, rodeo, street and dance festival called Helldorado. The whole population turns out dressed and bearded in western pioneer style. As a community Las Vegas is both old and new. The gushing springs which mark the site were known as good watering places even in Spanish days. But the settlers, ranchers and prospectors came and went, and the modern town was not founded until 1905, as a project sponsored by railroad interests. It has prospered ever since.

THE HIGH DAM. In a circular, one of the luxury resorts of Las Vegas refers to itself as "The Old West in New Splendor." This label might be much more appropriately attached to the airplane view one can enjoy 35 miles southeast of Las Vegas. In a mountain region so bleak and forbidding that two generations ago only a few adventurous prospectors had penetrated it, there is now a huge, deep blue lake created by the bright concrete structure of Hoover Dam. This giant producer of electricity, irrigation and recreation in its wilderness setting is a great American monument. Built in the early 1930's, the task was of Cyclopean proportions. At first the Colorado River had to be diverted, and for that purpose 4 tunnels were blasted through Black Canyon. Then the grooves into which the dam was to fit were chiseled into the canyon walls. For the floodwaters from the spillway, 91 tunnels were bored. All these operations involved the removal of millions of tons of solid rock. Then the dam began to rise, and the artificial lake created by the backed up waters of the Colorado submerged a thousand-year-old pueblo along the Virgin River. Completed, the barrier rose to a height of almost 727 feet, the largest dam on earth for 20 long years. Nobody who merely rides by car over its crest can appreciate the size of the enterprise. The powerhouses at the base may seem like toy buildings, yet they are huge plants sending torrents of electric cur-

THE HIGHEST STAKES. There are, no doubt, people who travel to Las Vegas because of its dry, sunny winter climate, but the vast majority visit the famous resort in southern Nevada because of the special brand of gambling offered there. Not that its black jack or roulette games are different from those played at Reno or Monte Carlo, but Las Vegas has evolved a kind of vacation establishment that seems to have a special appeal to a great many people — a combination of hotel, restaurant, nightclub and gambling casino. The last department brings in the big and steady profits. Consequently the other sections can offer deluxe accommodations with valet service and swimming pool, fine meals by outstanding chefs, and nightclub entertainment by the brightest stars of the entertainment world at a relatively reasonable cost. Even the motels operate as luxurious sleeping, eating and gambling units. This

NEVADA SUPERLATIVES

GAIL HAMMOND

Lake Mead, a man-made reservoir 115 miles long, is a colorful water sports playground.

rent to California, Nevada and Arizona. The turbine houses and other departments are open for inspection, and visitors will find them not only functional but also designed in a modern style adapted to the Indian patterns of the Southwest. Much of the irrigation water is carried to the deserts of southern California.

A MAN-MADE SEA. The waters of the Colorado River are muddy, but after they have deposited their silt at the bottom of Lake Mead they take on a deep indigo blue which contrasts strikingly with the red, green and yellow streaks in the rocky cliffs and steep ranges lining the shores. For 115 miles the lake winds its way up the Colorado nearly to the Grand Canyon, forming picturesque arms and bays, inlets and capes, promontories and islands. Las Vegas Wash, Boulder Beach and Katherine Landing are the chief water sports centers where swimming, boating and water skiing flourish. But sailing is most popular in this spectacular rock and water setting, and the lake's fleet of yachts and sailing vessels of all types is always increas-

ing. Daily lake cruises leave from Lake Mead Marina. In the Lake Mead National Recreation Area, which also includes Lake Mohave south of Hoover Dam, a number of campgrounds are available. Wilderness camping is popular at the northern end of Lake Mead. In the canyons of the area desert bighorn sheep and wild burros may be seen on the lakeshore.

THE VALLEY OF THE FLAME. To the west of Lake Mead, the Valley of Fire State Park is traversed by State Route 40, leading from Interstate 15 eastward. In a fabulous crescendo of colors and eerie stone formations it reaches its climax in the Valley of the Flame, a narrow pass high above the northern arm of Lake Mead. There rock colors of incredible intensity, petroglyphs of a people long vanished and the remains of petrified trees combine to create an impression of unearthly splendor. Another spectacular road branches off U.S. Highway 66 (Interstate 40) in Arizona north to a forest of Joshua trees and a panoramic view of the Colorado River and the Grand Wash Cliffs.

227

Los Angeles

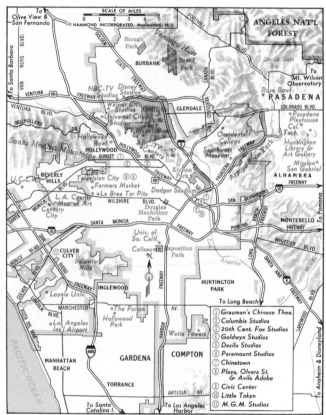

Map legend:
① Grauman's Chinese Thea.
② Columbia Studios
③ 20th Cent. Fox Studios
④ Goldwyn Studios
⑤ Desilu Studios
⑥ Paramount Studios
⑦ Chinatown
⑧ Plaza, Olvera St. & Avila Adobe
⑨ Civic Center
⑩ Little Tokyo
⑪ M.G.M. Studios

like Old Mexico, but it was built in the 1930's. The town's most valuable Spanish heritage is its name and, although the words Los Angeles have been cut quite arbitrarily out of a resounding El Pueblo Nuestra Señora la Reina de los Ángeles de Porciúncula, the modern name has a pleasantly exotic Spanish flavor, is easily recognized as meaning "the angels" and therefore suggests a paradisical place.

MAKE-UP AND MAKE-BELIEVE. There are two schools of thought about Los Angeles, and the visitor will find it fascinating to explore their teachings. One school — its strongest rampart is found in San Francisco — maintains that Los Angeles is an impossible monstrosity, an improvised catchall. "If you tilt the country sideways," Frank Lloyd Wright is quoted as saying, "Los Angeles is the place where everything loose will fall." It has been called the capital of smog, of bad taste, of quacks and faddists, of weird cults and strange sects, a nightmare in technicolor where the Hollywood gossip columns are the most important news of the day, where promoters flourish and intellectuals despair, a perpetual convention, a giant circus and the Coney Island of the Pacific Coast. There is and always was a tendency toward makeshift. "Even the trees and plants did not belong there," said Frank Fenton. "They came, like the people, from far places, some familiar, some exotic, all wanderers of one sort or another." The other school, while admitting a grain of truth in all these statements, points out that the end is not yet and that Los Angeles may eventually emerge as the country's most truly American metropolis. For it was not settled, in its modern version, by Europeans who brought along their Old World heritage, but mostly by Midwesterners of the second generation who had not yet had time to develop a cultural heritage of their own. Consequently their judgment in matters of art and style, philosophy and taste often proved deficient, but at the same time they did not bring along any prejudices. They created an unmatched opportunity for experimentation. The city's new Music Center turned out to be magnificent, and the Los Angeles Philharmonic Orchestra is now one of the country's leading orchestras. A short drive to the east, Disneyland offers highly enjoyable family fun.

FRESHWATER, SEAWATER. The hundreds of thousands of solid citizens who are neither quacks nor faddists point to their city's fantastic material achievements. From the viewpoint of physical geography, Los Angeles was built at an extremely unfavorable location. It had no natural harbor, and it had no water resources in the form of fair sized rivers or lakes. So, at a spot which Richard Henry Dana in "Two Years Before the

NO PAST, ALL FUTURE. If you step into your car at Los Angeles Harbor and drive straight north until you reach the Los Angeles city limit sign, you will have driven more than 50 miles through the largest city in area in the United States. If you travel through Los Angeles County, which is the metropolitan area as a whole, you'll find it almost half as big as the state of Vermont. Sprawling over a pleasant plain between the mountains and the sea, practically all of it is new, and an air of expansion and progress hovers over the city and its suburbs, which form a confused melee of administrative units and subdivisions typical of uninhibited growth. Hardly anything is left of the old Spanish days. Not even the plaza is today where it had been laid out in 1781. The Plaza Church, the Avila Adobe, a private museum, and one or two other adobe houses are the only remnants of the pueblo. Olvera Street looks

SPRAWLING, MUCH INSULTED, BIZARRE and BEAUTIFUL

DELTA AIR LINES

Above: The Civic Center is one of the country's great cultural enterprises, a symbol of the new spirit of Los Angeles.

Right: Disneyland is a unique and enjoyable playground. The replica of a Mississippi steamboat is one of its lively exhibits of Americana.

TRANS WORLD AIRLINES

Mast" described as perfectly desolate, its citizens proceeded to build a huge artificial harbor capable of holding our whole Pacific fleet. And to provide a sufficient water supply, the entire flow of the Owens River was diverted about 240 miles from the Sierra Nevada to the city. In addition, the Colorado River was tapped in the 1930's, and today a gigantic agglomeration of dams and pipelines furnishes streams and torrents of water for more than a million households, for sprinkler systems and swimming pools, and for irrigation canals that have transformed arid acres into bright orange groves and lush vegetable gardens. Another civic project of similar magnitude is the system of freeways, modern automobile highways which, however, do not solve the traffic problem of a city which owns more automobiles per capita than any other place in the world.

ROSE BOWL AND BLUE BOY. In addition to purely material achievements, Los Angeles and its suburbs have exerted a wide influence with their flair for entertainment. Hollywood has left its imprint on America and on the world, and at least some of its motion pictures have been masterpieces. The Universal Studio Tour is highly entertaining, and the CBS and NBC TV-Tours are also popular. Pasadena's Tournament of Roses and the annual Rose Bowl Game on the first of January have become an American tradition. The Pasadena Playhouse and Hollywood Bowl are widely known to lovers of drama and music. The Huntington Library and Art Gallery in San Marino with its first-rate collection of arts and letters — Van Dyke's "Blue Boy" is the center of attraction — lures both casual visitors and scholars from many parts of the country. On the physical rather than the cultural side it must be stated that the young people of Los Angeles are good to look at. Year-round sunshine and unlimited quantities of orange juice and fresh fruit have indeed produced a healthy and handsome race, including thousands of lovely girls and the world's best tennis players.

229

Arrowhead and Palm Springs

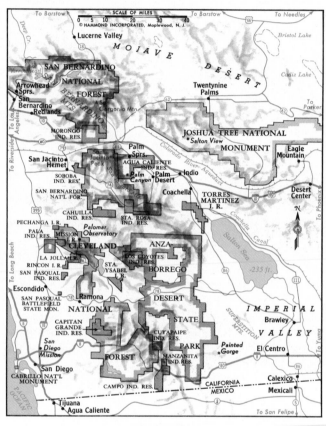

model, but the village has turreted and gabled buildings, Tyrolean leather shorts and dirndl dresses, Bavarian vocalizing and genuine Swiss yodeling. The San Bernardino Mountains are the stand-in for the Alps. The resort is pleasant and relaxed, with an accent on health and youth. Los Angeles is only 70 miles away and sends enough young people to create a gay and informal atmosphere.

DATE PALM OASIS. Not far away in a southeasterly direction and about a hundred miles from Los Angeles another Indian spa has achieved spectacular national prominence. In fact, Palm Springs has become a winter mecca for America's rich. The palm in the name refers to the date palm which thrives here and is a pleasant local specialty. As long as only Indians and a few health seekers used its hot springs it remained an insignificant little hamlet, but in the 1930's the motion picture colony discovered the assets of Palm Springs, created its bright mood and attracted various industrial and financial leaders. The sleepy village was turned into a unique resort of modern, multicolored ranch houses, luxury hotels, smart shops on Palm Canyon Drive and even deluxe mobile home parks. There are about 4,000 swimming pools, an extremely high number per capita. As a winter vacation spot Palm Springs is perfect. The very thought of spending some January weeks on an oasis in the desert appeals to the imagination, and the dry climate, about 80° F. at noon with cool nights, promotes a state of physical well-being. It has fabulous golfing facilities, was President Eisen-

To the Mormons Joshua Trees pointed the way to the Promised land as Joshua did in the Old Testament.

AN ARROW ON THE MOUNTAINSIDE. Once upon a time the Cahuilla Indians migrated westward, guided by a fiery arrow sent by the Great Spirit. They wandered many a mile until the arrow affixed itself in a mountain, pointing to boiling springs and a fertile valley below. Here the Indians settled. The arrowhead of the Great Spirit can still be seen in the form of quartz and granite outcroppings, overgrown with whitish weeds and covering seven and a half acres. The Indians healed their sick in the mineral waters, still an attraction at the modern spa of Arrowhead Springs which arose from the Cahuilla settlement. There are steam caves where you may enjoy a 10-minute sweltering session at 160° F., take a mineral mud bath at 100° F., a popular tonic for body and soul, or swim in the hotel pool which is fed by hot and cold mineral springs. A resort with so genuine an American past hardly needs a European

230

DOROTHY BACHELLER

TWO ANCIENT INDIAN SPAS THRIVE on SUN and GLAMOUR

GAIL HAMMOND

East of Palm Springs the lonely Mojave Desert stretches to far horizons.

PALM SPRINGS CONVENTION AND VISITORS BUREAU

Palm Springs, once an Indian spa in the desert, has become the ultra-modern winter resort of the very rich.

hower's favorite winter playground and is now considered the golfing capital of the West. The San Jacinto Mountains, with their sculptured ridges rising more than 10,000 feet into a glassy blue sky, is not only a decorative background to the fashionable desert town but also provides plenty of water, usually a rarity in the arid valley. Surprisingly, Palm Springs is also a ski resort. A cable car takes skiers to the top of San Jacinto Peak's snowy slopes. In the valley rodeos, fashion shows and parties keep the visitors occupied, and the weekend fiesta called the Desert Circus is a star studded event. Dude ranches provide horseback rides into the mountains and chuckwagon picnics in the spirit of the Old West. Famous hotels in Palm Springs are the Palm Springs Biltmore, the Sheraton Desert Inn and the Racquet Club.

INDIAN CHECKERBOARD. There is another fascinating touch in Palm Springs. It is one place where the original Americans have not been crowded out. Half the town belongs to the Indians. The town map is a checkerboard, and every other block is the property of the Cahuilla Indians of the Agua Caliente Reservation. Since the Indians cannot sell their real estate and are legally only allowed to lease it for periods of not more than 5 years — a stipulation enacted to protect the Indians from exploitation — they cannot take full advantage of the city's real estate boom. Nevertheless, they receive a tidy annual sum from rentals. They also operate the resort's mud baths. The latter were once quite famous but no longer play an important part in Palm Springs, since their sulphuric smell is not appreciated

by many. The Indians don't care. Unchanging in a rapidly changing community, they are the fixed pole in the new resort life.

THE BIBLICAL TREES. Northeast of both Arrowhead Springs and Palm Springs, the Mojave Desert stretches to far horizons. Adjacent to the San Bernardino Mountains, the Joshua Tree National Monument has been created. Its 558,183 acres protect from extinction and help to a healthy survival the spectacular Joshua tree, a landmark of southeastern California which is becoming rare elsewhere. This plant, which reaches a height of 40 feet, belongs to the lily family. When in bloom a grove of Joshua trees is a sight to behold. At the end of their angular branches magnificent clusters of creamy white blossoms glisten in the sun. The biblical name is said to have originated with the Mormons, who considered them road signs on their western trek. To the pious explorers the outstretched branches of these trees obviously pointed to the Promised Land, the Kingdom of Zion.

INLAND SEA ON THE WANE. The Salton Sea is an unusual lake south of the San Bernardino chain. Lying about 235 feet below sea level, it is too salty for most fish, but mullet may be caught in some quantity and mullet spearing is a local sport. Geysers and hot springs surround the lake. In 1905, when the Colorado River inundated the Imperial Valley in a catastrophic flood, the Salton Sea filled up to a length of 45 miles. At present it is receding, and some day it may entirely disappear.

San Diego: Birthplace of California

① Old Town Plaza, Presidio Park & Serra Mus.
② Ramona's Marriage Place
③ U. S. Naval Training Center & Marine Recruit Depot
④ U. S. Naval Air Sta. (North I.)

SCALE OF MILES
0   5   10   15   20

© HAMMOND INCORPORATED, Maplewood, N. J.

tempts at reconstruction were made, but the buildings were demolished again by the earthquake of 1918. At that point man gave up the struggle, and the ruins remain. It is an uncanny place at night. At times the old bells are said to ring by themselves without any pull of the bell ropes, and on a still night, the people say, you can hear them clearly.

THE SKY ATLAS. Inland to the east, a famous observatory stands on Mt. Palomar, at an altitude of 6,138 feet. In the grandiose mountain scenery visitors sometimes find that the Palomar Observatory looks small and inconspicuous. But once inside the dome, they realize that they are standing in a huge, 12-story cavern. The 200-inch telescope with its 16-ton mirror is not an oversized spyglass but an intricate camera. One interesting project is being carried out with the 48-inch telescope camera called "Big Schmidt." It is a sky atlas of several thousand photographs presenting to students of astronomy a body of maps of three-quarters of the heavens.

SPANISH LABEL, AMERICAN CONTENTS. The nomenclature of southern California is so predominantly Spanish that some visitors are surprised to discover how completely American the country is. To be sure, San Diego possesses some mementos of the Spanish past. There is, for example, Cabrillo National Monument, north of the Point Loma Lighthouse, which honors the Portuguese navigator in the service of Spain. In 1542 he discovered the harbor, stayed for a week, and took possession of the land for the Spanish crown. He was familiar with Montalvo's then popular story which asserted that "on the right hand of the Indies there is an island called California, very near to the terrestrial paradise." Cabrillo believed that he had arrived at that near paradise, and ever since the name of his discovery has been California. Naming a country after a piece of fiction seems unorthodox, yet the later development of California justified the explorer's fling at symbolism. From the foot of the Cabrillo monument a fascinating spectacle can be observed in season: migrating schools of whales pass by. The old town plaza, the center of the original city, is still lined with a few adobe houses of Old Spanish flavor, among them the Casa de Estudillo. The house is open to the public and exhibits relics of the days of Spanish California. Several structures in Balboa Park, the city's 1,400-acre recreation center, are in the style of the Spanish Renaissance. Among these are the California Building, the Museum of Natural History and the Fine Arts Gallery, which prides itself on owning paintings by some famous Spanish masters including El Greco, Murillo, Goya and Zuloaga. Also in Balboa Park, the San Diego Zoo is one of the world's biggest; it is largely cageless, and visitors

ROMANTIC RUINS. San Juan Capistrano, San Luis Rey, San Diego de Alcalá — these names along the coast road from Los Angeles to the south are reminders of the Spanish mission days when trails were laid out, orange groves planted, medicinal herbs cultivated, libraries collected and Christian tenets preached before the United States was born. San Juan Capistrano, playground of the swallows, was the most beautiful of all California missions, with seven domes and an arched roof, a tall belfry visible for 10 miles and stone carvings by a Mexican sculptor. The superstitious said that it was too elaborate for a house of God. At any rate an earthquake destroyed most of it only 6 years after it had been completed. In 1865 the church was being rebuilt with adobe bricks when torrential rains descended and reduced the work to a puddle of mud. More at-

TRAIL of the MISSIONS and HARBOR of the FLEET

seem to see the wild animals in their natural habitat. A subtropical jungle may be crossed on a moving sidewalk. Honoring San Diego's maritime past, the *Star of India*, a 100-year-old sailing vessel, is moored north of the B Street Pier. The Junípero Serra Museum is devoted to the history of the California missions. Six miles up the valley of the San Diego River, the San Diego de Alcalá Mission is a restoration of the ancient buildings, the first mission on the coast and the starting point of the chain established by Padre Serra.

DRAMATIC PORT. San Diego harbor, 20 square miles of water sheltered by islands and promontories and studded with picturesque bays and inlets, is the city's primary sightseeing attraction. As the great Pacific naval base of the United States, it offers to the cruise boat tourist a most impressive panorama of our naval power. Displayed in a 12-mile curve are aircraft carriers towering high above the water, rocket-launching vessels, landing ships and troop carriers. Submarines, destroyers

and destroyer escorts are measured by whole flotillas. The cruise boats wind through this huge maritime exposition, including the billion-dollar mothball fleet. The shores are lined with naval installations and training centers which turn out sailors, flyers, leathernecks and the frogmen of the underwater demolition squads. San Diego is also a great fishing port for tuna and albacore. Its modern tuna clippers venture out as far as Panama and the Galápagos Islands.

THE SHORT THERMOMETER. The people of San Diego are proud of their climate. In their city, they say, only short thermometers are needed — a scale of thirteen degrees is enough. The average summer temperature is 68°, the average winter temperature 55°. The climate and the industrial opportunities attract a constant stream of newcomers to San Diego. Its beaches are outstanding, particularly in La Jolla, which combines fabulous scenery with lovely homes, bright gardens, smart shops and cultural interests.

Right: Cabrillo National Monument honors the Portuguese navigator who in 1542 discovered the harbor of San Diego.

Below: Torrey Pines Mesa is a lookout spot on a bluff by the sea north of La Jolla.

Hawaii

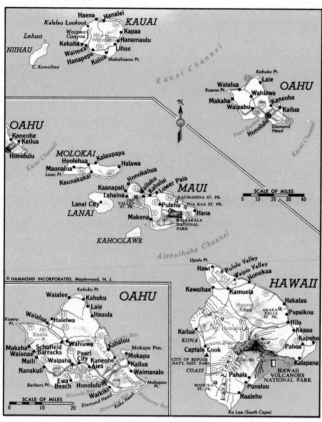

were carried out until the fourteenth century. Captain Cook discovered the islands for the white man in 1778. He paid with his life a year later when the warrior hero Kamehameha the Great united the islands. In 1810 the latter proclaimed the Kingdom of Hawaii. In 1893 the kingdom became a republic, and in 1898 it was annexed as a territory by the United States at the urging of Hawaii's American sugar planters. It has been the 50th state of the Union since 1959. During the nineteenth century the planters imported thousands of orientals as plantation laborers, and Europeans were attracted by the climate and the pleasant life. Consequently Hawaii's population consists today of minorities only. Polynesians, Japanese, Chinese, Filipinos, Koreans, Spaniards, Portuguese, North Americans, Germans and Scandinavians. The diversity is fantastic, but all live together peacefully, and little racial prejudice exists. The pure Hawaiians form only a small minority, but their spirit of friendliness and their joy in life lives on, pervades all strata and is felt and enjoyed by all visitors. The relaxed Aloha, the lively girls with a bright hibiscus flower in their shiny black hair, the hula dances that tell the ancient stories of the islands, the leis of orchids that are placed on your shoulders as a greeting, the soft Hawaiian words still used in songs and phrases, the feast called luau, and the fabulous scenery of tall black mountains in a turquoise sea — all this makes our 50th state a delightful vacation spot. Many celebrities have written about its splendor: Mark Twain, Robert Louis Stevenson, Jack London and James Michener.

OAHU. This island is the seat of the state government and the site of Honolulu, Hawaii's only metropolis. Its resort section is world famous Waikiki. The latter's location with Diamond Head in the background is most striking, but some visitors are disappointed by the narrowness of the beach and the high rise hotels that crowd in on the bay. However there is no lack of lonely beaches elsewhere, and most young people love Waikiki's gay commotion. In Honolulu Iolani Palace, the former royal residence, was the home of the state legislature until 1968 and is now a museum. King Kamehameha's statue is a reminder of the state's colorful history. Nearby attractions are Sea Life Park at Makapuu Point, with a porpoise theater and a whaling cove, the breathtaking view from the sheer cliffs of Nuuanu Pali, and the Ulu Mau Village, the reconstruction of an ancient Polynesian community. West of Honolulu, the site of the Japanese attack of 1941 at world famous Pearl Harbor may be reached by a sightseeing boat. On the leeward coast, Makaha is known for its wonderful surfing beach and the international surfing championships are contested there. The Hawaiians had been surfers from time immemorial. The Yankee missionaries

UA MAU KE EA O KA AINA I KA PONO. Imagine a state of the Union with a motto in a most outlandish tongue, with a state bird called nene and a state tree called kukui. Such names stir the imagination. The motto means "the life of the land is perpetuated in righteousness." The nene is a rare wild goose, and kukui the candlenut tree. To have among our homogeneous family of states one that is totally different in geography, history and population and exceeding all in natural beauty is a stroke of good luck for all traveling Americans. Hawaii's history alone is fabulous. About 1,200 years ago Polynesian seafarers set out from their homes in southeast Asia in quest of adventure in double-hulled canoes loaded with pigs and chickens, seeds and roots. They discovered a group of uninhabited picture book islands and settled there. But the sea was in their blood, and two-way trips between Tahiti and Hawaii

OUR MAGIC ISLES

GAIL HAMMOND

While Oahu's Waikiki resort is a bit crowded, other beaches like the one pictured here still offer wide spaces and privacy.

who arrived in 1820 strongly frowned upon the sport, however, because for the natives it had implications of religion and sex. So surfing almost vanished from the islands until it was vigorously revived in the twentieth century.

HAWAII. This largest of the islands is topped by two giant mountain peaks, Mauna Kea and Mauna Loa, both almost 14,000 feet tall. In winter their summits are snow covered and offer skiing in the midst of lush tropics. Mauna Loa erupted spectacularly in 1950, throwing up 600 million cubic yards of lava. In Hawaii Volcanoes National Park the huge crater of Kilauea is circled by the 11-mile-long Crater Rim Drive, a modern highway that leads through jungles of lush tree ferns, stands of barren cinder cones and lava flows that may still be warm. The Jaggar Museum at the park's headquarters presents movies of eruptions which have been frequent in the last decade. In 1959 the crater shot up flaring lava fountains of record height. The city of Hilo is one of the world's flower capitals and is surrounded by fields of orchids. Lava caves and orchid blossoms are the attraction of Kong's Floraleigh Gardens, and a lovely Japanese garden is maintained at the bay front in Liliuokalani Park. A most unusual and beautiful plant, the silversword, grows only on the floor of craters in Hawaii and Maui. Once in a lifetime it sends up a magnificent stalk of yellow or purple flowers, then dies.

MAUI. Haleakala National Park surrounds the 10,023-foot peak whose name means House of the Sun. Its dormant crater has at its bottom "an iridescent kettle

Missionaries from New England played a leading role in civilizing the Hawaiians in the nineteenth century.

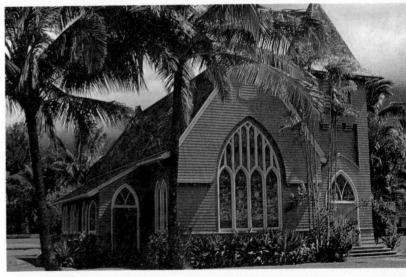

GAIL HAMMOND

of optical illusions, changing colors minute by minute." In Iao Valley State Park on the western end of the island, the "Needle" is a beautifully shaped pinnacle. The west coast of Maui's northern sector includes some Yankee history. Whaling ships from New England anchored there to get provisions, brandy and women. The jail in the town of Lahaina, still standing, was usually filled with drunk sailors sleeping off their hangovers. At the pier near the old Pioneer Inn, the square-rigger *Carthaginian* is a whaling museum.

235

Sightseeing Guide

ARIZONA

NORTHERN ARIZONA. Monument Valley is described on pages 204-205. In the Navajo Reservation north of the Petrified Forest is Canyon de Chelly National Monument, an impressive canyon with ruined cliff dwellings. Monument Canyon, Spider Rock and Canyon del Muerto, an unusual gorge with deeply undercut walls, may be seen here. The Navajo Reservation, three times as big as Massachusetts, is the largest reservation in the United States and contains some of the continent's most grandiose scenery. Navajo National Monument includes several elaborate cliff dwellings. Northwest of the Grand Canyon Pipe Spring National Monument contains an historic Mormon fort. The Grand Canyon of the Colorado, America's greatest natural spectacle, is described on pages 200-201.

CENTRAL ARIZONA. Petrified Forest National Park, about 25 miles east of Holbrook, disappoints some people because they expect the petrified trunks to stand erect. The giant logs, which actually lie on the ground, are strikingly colored and up to 250 feet long. They lie in six separate "forests" and are the greatest display of petrified wood on earth. The Painted Desert consists of eroded shales and limestones, spectacularly colored. The Painted Desert Lodge can be reached from the Petrified Forest (see page 199). Flagstaff and the three San Francisco Peaks are described on page 198. On the same page are Wupatki Nat'l Mon., Sunset Crater Nat'l Mon., Walnut Canyon Nat'l Mon., Meteor Crater, Oak Creek Canyon and Montezuma Castle Nat'l Mon. Tuzigoot Nat'l Mon. and Prescott are described on pages 198-199. Castle Hot Springs, near U.S. 89, 60 miles northwest of Phoenix, have a daily flow of 400,000 gallons. Phoenix, state capital and winter resort, and the Apache Trail with Roosevelt Dam are described on pages 196-197. Tonto National Monument, south of Roosevelt Dam, preserves two cliff dwellings of the fourteenth century which were then nearly impregnable. Near the city of Globe the Southwestern Arboretum is a lovely outdoor museum of native plants and flowers. Signal Peak (7,875 feet) in the Pinal Mountains offers splendid 100-mile views in every direction. Coolidge Dam, the first multiple dome dam, and the man-made San Carlos Lake in the heart of the old Apache country are 25 miles southeast of Globe on U.S. 70. West of Coolidge Dam, Casa Grande Ruins Nat'l Mon. is an impressive 600-year-old adobe tower.

SOUTHERN ARIZONA. Tucson, the famous desert resort, is described on page 194. Tucson Mountain Park is a large recreational area with many trails and good roads. The Mission of San Xavier del Bac and the Saguaro National Monument are described on pages 194-195. South of Tucson the Tumacacori National Monument preserves the ruins of a mission built about 1800 to replace an earlier Jesuit mission established by Padre Kino. At the Mexican border is Nogales, a lively and colorful frontier town. Of interest to tourists is the café operated in a cave, once a mine and later employed as a prison for Geronimo, the Apache chief. Southeast of Tucson, Tombstone and Boothill Cemetery are described on page 195. In the southeastern corner of the state the region of Bisbee and Douglas is a rich mining country; the open-pit copper mines look like giant amphitheaters. Bisbee is built on such a steep mountain slope that there is no mail delivery in town; no mailman can be expected to trudge up and down that many stairs. Near the New Mexico state line Chiricahua National Monument is a wilderness of weirdly shaped rocks. On the international border south of Highway 85 Organ Pipe Cactus National Monument lies in an uninhabited area. Twenty-foot cactus columns without branches stand straight up like organ pipes,

and their lovely white flowers tinged with lavender bloom in May. Arizona's only native palm trees grow on the sides of the narrow red granite Palm Canyon in the Kofa Mountains 60 miles northeast of Yuma. On the California line, Yuma is the center of a highly prosperous, irrigated valley surrounded by jagged mountains. The All-American Canal, carrying irrigation water from the Colorado River to California, can be seen from U.S. 80 in California.

CALIFORNIA

NORTHERN CALIFORNIA. Tule Lake National Wildlife Refuge just below the Oregon state line is a large preserve for wild fowl; in certain parts of the refuge hunting is allowed during open season. Lava Beds National Monument is a forested area of lava beds, collapsed lava tubes and cinder cones. Merrill Cave includes an ice river and a frozen waterfall. Castle Crags State Park, south of Dunsmuir on Interstate Highway 5, features a row of giant domes, crags and spires up to 6,000 feet high. Snowcapped Mount Shasta, Shasta Dam and Lake form a great recreational area with fabulous scenery (see page 211). Old Shasta is a ghost town preserved as a historical monument about five miles west of Redding; it is an interesting relic of gold rush days. Lassen Volcanic National Park is described on pages 210-211. Highway 70 runs through the scenic Feather River Canyon for 50 miles, sometimes proceeding on the canyon floor and sometimes ascending along the walls and bridging the canyon above the foaming river; the Feather River country is a famous hunting area. On the northern coast of California, Eureka is a fishing and lumber port and a center for the display and sale of fine, locally manufactured gifts of redwood and myrtle wood. Pacific sea life can be watched at the aquarium and seal pool called Shipwreck. Restored Fort Humboldt is a state historical monument. The nearby Redwood Highway, U.S. 101, crosses Redwood National Park, which is described on pages 208-209. Russian Gulch State Park along the rugged Mendocino coast is a redwood preserve offering surf fishing from its promontories. From Fort Bragg, a lumber town with a lumberman's museum, a little railroad called the Skunk travels through two tunnels. Mendocino is an old lumber town, an artists' colony and a skin diving center. Clear Lake, picturesquely surrounded by wooded hills and dotted with islands, is the center of a recreational area which includes other smaller lakes. Fort Ross State Historic Park is described on page 209. Near Santa Rosa are the experimental gardens of Luther Burbank, the genius of flower and plant culture and propagation (he is buried in his garden), the home of Jack London in the Sonoma valley — now a state historical park, and the Sonoma Mission — the last and most northerly of the chain of Spanish missions. It also became a military post, erected to stop the expansion of the Russian colony into California. The Bear Flag of the short-lived Republic of California was raised before the mission in 1846. A mile from Sonoma early California vineyards were planted by a Hungarian count; the wine cellars, the oldest in the state, are still in use. The whole district around St. Helena and Napa is one of America's leading wine producers (see page 209). Muir Woods National Monument is a redwood sanctuary in the shadows of San Francisco honoring John Muir, the great naturalist. Across the Golden Gate Bridge from San Francisco, Sausalito, Tiburon and Belvedere are residential towns, avant-garde and affluent. San Francisco is described on pages 216-217. Mount Diablo stands by itself on the plain east of Oakland surrounded by Mount Diablo State Park, a forested recreation area with an automobile road leading to the summit. In Oakland the First and Last Chance Saloon was the favorite haunt of Jack

London. The Skyline Boulevard offers a fine view of San Francisco Bay. North of Oakland, Berkeley is the seat of the original campus of the University of California. The 307-foot-tall campanile is its landmark.

CENTRAL WESTERN CALIFORNIA. The Lick Observatory of the University of California is located on top of Mount Hamilton east of San Jose; the view from the summit is magnificent. On the coast north of Santa Cruz, Big Basin Redwoods State Park includes some truly gigantic trees 330 feet tall. Santa Cruz is a seaside resort and a center for surfing and rock fishing. On Highway 101 the San Juan Bautista Mission is the largest of the mission chain; several other interesting nearby adobe buildings from Spanish days are open to the public. Monterey and Carmel are described on pages 218-219. Each October monarch butterflies from Alaska, western Canada and California fly to the butterfly trees on Lighthouse Avenue in Pacific Grove and cluster there for the winter. To the south the beautiful Big Sur coast is the home of many writers, painters and musicians. The Hearst Castle at San Simeon, now a state historical monument, is one of the most magnificent residences in America and is open to the public. Near Highway 101, the San Miguel Mission contains paintings by Indian artists. Southeast of Monterey Pinnacles National Monument is spectacular. Tall, dark red rock spires tower against the blue sky. The various canyon caves are said to have been hiding places of early-day bandits. Today they are the favorite haunts of spelunkers.

CENTRAL EASTERN CALIFORNIA. Lake Tahoe is described on pages 214-215. Sacramento, the capital of California, is famous for the gold rush days of 1849. Gold was discovered nearby on the land of John Sutter, and Sutter's Fort has been restored as a museum filled with pioneer relics. Sacramento was also the terminus of the Pony Express, and in the Pony Express Museum visitors may inspect the saddlebags and spurs, the prairie schooners and ore wagons of the early 1860's. Southeast of Sacramento, Calaveras Big Trees State Park is the northernmost important stand of sequoias. It is also a popular skiing and tobogganing resort. Mark Twain's hilarious story of "The Jumping Frog of Calaveras County" made the name of the county and of the park famous. Columbia Historic State Park preserves the ghost town of Columbia as it looked during the gold rush. During the summer plays are performed in the town's old theater. Sonora was a Mexican settlement, and Chileans discovered the Big Bonanza, but control of the mine soon slipped into the hands of Yankees. Chinese Camp was the scene of a fierce tong war, the first in California. Yosemite National Park is described on pages 220-221. East of Yosemite Park, Devils Postpile National Monument is a basaltic lava flow in the form of tightly grouped columns. Fresno is a bright, clean city with tree-lined streets, the center of the upper San Joaquin Valley, which on fertile, irrigated soil produces an abundance of wonderful fruits. Tourists may inspect the Roma winery and the Sun Maid raisin packing plant. A popular recreation spot for the people of Fresno is lovely Huntington Lake to the northeast in the Sierra Nevada. Kings Canyon and Sequoia national parks are described on pages 222-223. The lonely but beautiful Inyo-Mono country between the Sierra Nevada and Death Valley is mentioned on page 223. Death Valley National Monument is described on pages 224-225.

SOUTHERN CALIFORNIA. San Luis Obispo has a fine mission now restored; it was the first one to use tile roofs to foil the Indians who liked to set the thatched roofs afire. Pismo Beach is noted for the rare and delicious Pismo clams. Santa Barbara is a lively, popular seaside resort; its mission is considered the most beautiful of the California chain. The city's many old adobe dwellings keep alive the Spanish heritage; downtown, El Paseo is lined with fine shops. Nearby in the Santa Ynez valley, Solvang is a charming Danish village. Los Angeles, Pasadena and Hollywood are described on pages 228-229. On the Palos Verdes peninsula, the world's largest oceanarium, Marineland of the Pacific, can be enjoyed. In Buena Park, not far from Disneyland, Knott's Berry Farm and Ghost Town is a popular attraction. A visit to the colorful Los Angeles Farmers' Market is also highly recommended. Long Beach is one of the leading seaside resorts of the West Coast. It has a fine bathing beach, and its protected outer waters are popular with fishermen. The former Cunard liner *Queen Mary* is moored there as a maritime museum and shopping center. North of Long Beach are other well-known resorts: Redondo Beach, Venice, Santa Monica, Malibu Beach. Santa Catalina Island, with its submarine gardens and glass bottom boats, its Bird Park and Skyline Drive is a popular excursion goal. San Juan Capistrano Mission, San Luis Rey Mission with its Indian paintings, Palomar Observatory with the greatest lens ever made and San Diego, harbor of our Pacific fleet, are described on pages 232-233. Mission Bay is a 4,600-acre aquatic playground; it includes Sea World, where seals, porpoises, and even a killer whale perform, and where Japanese pearl divers demonstrate their skill. Across the border, Tijuana attracts visitors with bull fighting, jai alai, horse and dog racing and its Mexican atmosphere. Near the Mexican border El Centro looks like a tropical Latin city; palm trees and patios, flower beds and overhanging second stories give it a romantic accent. It is the center of the irrigated desert of the Imperial Valley, abundant producer of lettuce, melons, dates and grapefruit. In the desert country of southeastern California the Anza-Borrego Desert State Park protects colorful plant life and interesting wildlife; the Salton Sea, Joshua Tree National Monument, the mountain resort of Arrowhead Springs and the fashionable desert resort of Palm Springs are described on pages 230-231. East of Lake Arrowhead, Big Bear Lake is a popular water sports resort at an elevation of 7,000 feet; both lakes are connected by the spectacular Rim of the World Drive.

COLORADO

CENTRAL COLORADO. Rocky Mountain National Park is described on pages 180-181. Estes Park is a lively resort at the eastern entrance of the Rocky Mountain National Park. On the southwestern edge of the park lies Shadow Mountain National Recreation Area. Here are Grand Lake, a popular center for trout fishing, sailing, trail riding and hunting, and glacial Lake Granby. Boulder, to the southeast, is the seat of the University of Colorado. Denver, the state capital, is described on pages 182-183. Central City is described on page 183. The summit of Mount Evans, over 14,000 feet above sea level, is reached by the highest auto road in the country. Climax, southwest of Denver near Leadville, has the highest location of any community in the United States, and the world's largest molybdenum mine is located there. Once it was the state's silver capital. West of Leadville, Aspen has developed into a nationally known cultural and winter sports center. During the summer it offers concerts in the amphitheater on the Aspen Meadows as well as lectures and dramatic performances. Its sports facilities include jeep pack trips. During the winter it maintains one of the greatest ski complexes in America, with splendid facilities; dog sledding is available. Vail, to the north, is also a major haven for winter sports enthusiasts. The great resort of Colorado Springs is described on pages 184-185. The tourist resort of Manitou Springs, once visited by the Indians because of the mineral springs, is the starting point of the cable car to the summit of Mt. Manitou. The beautiful modern campus of the U.S. Air Force Academy is also located near there. Cripple Creek, southwest of Colorado Springs, is a ghost town with old-time relics, old-style dramatic performances and similar attractions. The Royal Gorge, a spectacular canyon with modern touches, is described on page 185.

WESTERN COLORADO. Dinosaur National Monument, straddling the Colorado-Utah state line, is listed under Utah. Colorado National Monument, not far from the Utah state line near Highway 50, is a mountainous country of pine forests traversed by deep, winding canyons and studded with towering monoliths of odd shapes. Petrified forests, dinosaur fossils, Indian picture writing and a refuge for buffalo are additional attractions. Two splendid roads lead to the monument: from Fruita the Rim Rock Road, and from Grand Junction the Serpents Trail Road. Grand Mesa, east of Grand Junction, is one of the world's largest flat-topped mountains (altitude 10,500 feet). It has a recreation area with sparkling, snow fed lakes; from Land's End on the western rim the unexcelled panorama covers hundreds of miles. South of Grand Mesa, the Black Canyon of the Gunnison National Monument includes the most spectacular ten miles of the Gunnison River Canyon. The granite walls, most of them black, drop to a depth of more than 2,000 feet. Higher up the Gunnison River is Curecanti National Recreational Area with its many attractions.

SOUTHERN COLORADO. Yucca House National Monument, located near the meeting point of Colorado, Utah, Arizona and New Mexico, preserves the remnants of a prehistoric Indian village. Mesa Verde National Park is described on pages 186-187. The Durango-Silverton-Ouray region is a wonderful sightseeing and vacationing area; the mountain scenery is grand, and the roads have some thrilling stretches, particularly the so-called Million Dollar Highway which runs midway on a canyon wall south of Ouray. Everywhere there are relics of the old mining days, ghost towns and abandoned mines. The small railroad from Durango to Silverton is a scenic ride that is a great favorite of all tourists. At Ouray the Camp Bird Mine, whose gold vein produced the fortune of the Walsh-McLean family of Hope Diamond fame, may be visited upon application at the office. In Ouray the scenic jeep trips are thrilling. Great Sand Dunes National Monument, north of Alamosa, embraces a sea of shifting sand dunes; they are the country's largest, reaching a height of 700 feet. The Sangre de Cristo Mountains loom in the east.

HAWAII

The Hawaiian Islands are located 2,400 miles southwest of California; they form an archipelago 2,000 miles long. The original Hawaiian language is spoken today only in tiny enclaves, but it survives in names, songs and sayings.

OAHU. Honolulu is described on pages 234-235. Other attractions are the Aquarium across from Kapiolani Park, Diamond Head (early sailors mistook the volcanic crystals for diamonds), the Aloha Tower, the Bishop Museum (the world's most outstanding collection of Hawaiiana and Polynesiana), the University of Hawaii with its East-West Center, the Coral Gardens of Kaneohe to be seen from glass bottom boats and the cultural center of the Mormons at Laie. Laie is also famous for its Saturday luaus, celebrated every last Saturday of the month except in December. Visitors join the Hawaiians in pulling a leaf trimmed net for the fish to be used in the luau

(roast pig, poi and fresh vegetables and fruit are the other ingredients), and Hawaiian and Samoan dances are performed. West of Honolulu, at Pearl Harbor, excursion boat guides point out the spot where the battleships *Utah* and *Arizona* were sent to the bottom by Japanese war planes. In Honolulu a visit to a pineapple cannery is recommended.

HAWAII. This mountain isle with two volcanoes of almost 14,000 feet, Mauna Kea and Mauna Loa and Hawaii Volcanoes National Park are described on page 235. Nature and history meet here; the footprints of a barefoot army which passed here can be clearly distinguished. In a sudden volcanic eruption the warriors perished, but they left their mark. On the Kona (west) coast, the City of Refuge, a national historical park, was established in the twelfth century to provide a refuge in the case of war for women and children of both feuding parties, a truly civilized arrangement. Nearby on Kealakekua Bay a monument commemorates the death of Captain Cook. To the north, the town of Kailua Kona is the site of Hulihee Palace, furnished by Hawaiian royalty, and now a museum, and of the first Christian church on the islands. In the northeast is the Parker Ranch, one of the world's largest ranches, which may be toured by visitors. South of Hilo is the renowned black sand beach of Kalapana.

MAUI. From the rim of the crater Haleakala you see, 3,000 feet below, 25 square miles of brightly colored cinder cones. Here, in Haleakala National Park, according to an ancient Hawaiian legend, the demigod Maui captured the sun and held it prisoner so that his people could enjoy more daylight hours. On the eastern coast, the photogenic Seven Sacred Pools are of exquisite beauty. Continuing northward, you will find Puaa Kaa Park, "place of the rolling pigs," and Kaumahina Park pleasant picnic sites. On the northwestern sector of the island is Lahaina, which is described on page 235. The town's Lahainaluna School, founded in 1831, is said to be the oldest one west of the Rockies.

KAUAI. A drive north from Lihue, the island's capital, will take you to Wailua River, and a 3-mile ride on a launch to the Fern Grotto and Hanalei Bay. A helicopter will fly you to the otherwise inaccessible Na Pali coast, a virgin stretch of breathtaking beauty, of 4,000-foot cliffs and crashing surf. On the western side of the island the road leads to 3,000-foot deep Waimea Canyon and ends at Kalalau Lookout, with another view of the Na Pali coast. Several luxury hotels have been built in this section.

MOLOKAI AND LANAI. The small island of Molokai has only one large village, Kaunakakai. In the center, Palaau Park offers a fine view of the peninsula at Kalaupapa. The even smaller Lanai is Hawaii's pineapple isle, with offices of the Dole Company in picturesque Lanai City. The shoreline abounds with excellent beaches for swimming and surfing, and with shady picnic grounds. Many miles of the western shore are a "shipwreck coast" where all sorts of debris washes ashore; there beachcombing is an exciting sport.

NEVADA

EASTERN NEVADA. Those who would like to see a typical cattle town teeming with ranchers and cowhands, with mooing herds in the stockyards and with crowded bars and spinning roulette wheels, should visit Elko during the fall roundups and at the time of the county fair. A Basque festival is celebrated in Elko each summer. The sheep raising industry is largely in Basque hands. Lehman Caves National Monument near the Utah state

SOUTHWEST REGION

line is an underground cavern with rock formations in striking shapes. Illumination brings out the varied colors of the columns and walls. In a state park 11 miles south of Pioche, Cathedral Gorge is a bastion of colored rock arches and spires. At sunset a few sections resemble a medieval cathedral with double towers. Lake Mead, Hoover Dam and the spectacular Valley of Fire are described on pages 226-227. At Overton near the northern end of Lake Mead a museum exhibits the tools and artifacts which were found and excavated at Lost City, a thousand-year-old pueblo now at the bottom of the lake. At the Hoover Dam exhibition building free introductory movies and a scale model of the Colorado River Basin may be seen. Las Vegas, the all-year resort, is described on page 226. Northeast of Las Vegas, Rhyolite on Highway 95 is one of the better known ghost towns.

WESTERN NEVADA. Pyramid Lake, Reno, Virginia City and Carson City are described on pages 212-213. Lake Tahoe and the Reno Snow Bowl at Mount Rose are described on pages 214-215. On the north shore of Lake Tahoe the Ponderosa Ranch has been recreated; it used to stretch from the desert to the big pine country.

NEW MEXICO

NORTHEASTERN NEW MEXICO. At Capulin Mountain National Monument a road leads to the summit of a recently extinct volcano rising over a thousand feet above the plain.

NORTH CENTRAL NEW MEXICO. The picturesque pueblo town of Taos, Ranchos de Taos and the state capital, Santa Fe, are described on pages 188-189. Twenty miles west of Santa Fe Bandelier National Monument preserves ancient Pajaritan cliff dwellings. San Ildefonso Pueblo is noted for its beautiful pottery. In the Cerrillos region south of Santa Fe the Gem Turquoise Mines have been operated by such divergent interests as prehistoric Indians and the Tiffany people. The pueblo nearest Santa Fe is Tesuque; its people are adept in pottery making and painting in watercolors. Also near Santa Fe are the Puye cliff dwellings, a prehistoric Tewa pueblo, and Pecos National Monument, which includes the ruins of a Pecos pueblo of the fourteenth century and the ruins of a seventeenth-century mission church. A 7-foot-long plumed serpent can be seen carved into the cliff of the Tshirege Ruins in Pajarito Canyon, 20 miles northwest of Santa Fe. In Las Vegas, New Mexico, relics of the Santa Fe Trail can still be inspected. The ruins of Fort Union, which held such outlaws as Billy the Kid and the savage Indian chief Geronimo, are now a national monument nearby. Albuquerque, the University of New Mexico and Acoma Pueblo near the Enchanted Mesa are described on pages 190-191. Southeast of Albuquerque is Gran Quivira National Monument, where the ruins of a pueblo and a Spanish mission stand.

NORTHWESTERN NEW MEXICO. Aztec Ruins National Monument was an apartment house of 500 rooms with a great kiva in the twelfth century. Chaco Canyon National Monument preserves 12 large pueblo ruins, among them the Pueblo Bonito wth 800 rooms. Gallup and its Indian festival are described on page 191; 42 miles south of Gallup, Zuni Pueblo with its red sandstone houses and ancient mission church is the home of the Zuni Indians, noted makers of turquoise jewelry. Nearby El Morro National Monument is a natural sandstone tower on which travelers have long carved their names. This is the famous inscription rock; the earliest legible inscription is of a Spanish explorer in the year 1605.

SOUTHERN NEW MEXICO. The huge Elephant Butte Dam has transformed some 180,000 acres of desert into fertile farmlands producing long-staple cotton, sugar beets and vegetables. Boating and fishing for bass, catfish or crappie are popular on the reservoir. Truth or Consequences was formerly Hot Springs, a health resort offering mineralized mud baths. To the west Gila Cliff Dwellings National Monument preserves the homes of people who lived here from A.D. 100 to the 1300's. Ruidoso is a popular resort in the Sierra Blanca Mountains, and at Cloudcroft golf may be played at an altitude of 9,000 feet. White Sands National Monument is described on page 193. To the east Roswell is the home of the New Mexico Military Institute; every October the Eastern New Mexico State Fair and Roswell Rodeo attract thousands of visitors. Thirteen miles to the southeast Bottomless Lakes State Park embraces a chain of lovely lakes; they were formed by cave-ins and are as deep as 600 feet. The famous Carlsbad Caverns National Park is described on pages 192-193.

UTAH

NORTHERN UTAH. Bear Lake is a popular water sports area both for Idaho and Utah; white sand beaches line this 20-mile-long lake. On Highway 39 the traveler from Ogden to Woodruff rides along the Ogden River at the bottom of Ogden Canyon. The towering canyon walls sometimes seem to close in on the road. The Ogden Snow Basin is a winter sports area. Salt Lake City and the Great Salt Lake are described on pages 206-207. At Promontory north of the Great Salt Lake is Golden Spike National Historic Site, which commemorates the completion of the first transcontinental railroad. Approaching Salt Lake City from the Nevada state line, the highway crosses the grassless Great Salt Lake Desert. Its Bonneville Salt Flats are 100 square miles of hard, level white salt, with barren mountains on the horizon. This is an eerie region, especially if you see the mountain peaks standing upside down, or hills and lakes floating in the sky; such visions are, of course, mirages, and are quite a frequent occurrence. The flats are an ideal automobile racing course, and several speed records have been established there; salt mining operations are also carried on. Kennecott's open-pit copper mine is located in Bingham Canyon 20 miles southwest of Salt Lake City. There are observation platforms for visitors. The nearby Timpangos Cave National Monument offers guided tours through three small caves; its curious helictites are a strangely twisted form of stalactites. Provo, on Utah Lake, is a steel center and the home of Brigham Young University; the city is picturesquely surrounded by mountains, canyons and waterfalls. Dinosaur National Monument is an area of rich fossil beds, rugged canyons, weirdly shaped cliffs and Indian pictographs on the cave walls.

SOUTHERN UTAH. Southwest of Moab is Canyonlands National Park, a wilderness of arches, gorges, pinnacles and buttes; only two unimproved roads cross the park. Arches National Park, Dead Horse Point, Moab, Natural Bridges Nat'l Mon., the Great Goose Necks, Monument Valley and Rainbow Bridge Nat'l Mon. are described on pages 204-205. Hovenweep National Monument lies partly in Utah and partly in Colorado. It consists of prehistoric cliff dwellings and pueblos. In south central Utah, Capitol Reef National Park is a spectacular red sandstone "reef" topped with white sandstone domes which includes strange rock formations, canyons, natural bridges, Indian pictographs and petroglyphs. Three fabulous sightseeing attractions of southwestern Utah are described on pages 202-203: Zion National Park, Bryce Canyon National Park and Cedar Breaks National Monument.

239

Mexico, Bermuda, West Indies

MEXICO

Her Character. Mexico is foreign in the most fascinating sense of the word; as a travel experience it is utterly different from both the United States and the countries of the Old World. Here the Indians of Middle America erected monumental structures, created great works of art, learned to write and calculated a correct calendar long before the white man arrived. After the conquest the Spaniards built stately baroque cathedrals and splendid palaces and imposed on the country their language and political institutions. Out of the Indian and Spanish heritage a new and truly Mexican culture emerged with its own folklore, art and music, its world renowned ballet and its colorful architecture that sometimes retains Aztec Indian touches even on the most modern buildings. The country's geography is unique. The mountain walls along the Pacific coast and those in the east contain some of the world's tallest snow covered peaks, which abruptly descend into subtropical valleys. The high plateau between the mountains, with an altitude varying from 4,000 to 8,000 feet, is the very heart of Mexico and has a pleasant climate all year long. Modern airlines, highways, hotels and motels make travel enjoyable.

Access To Mexico. The country's capital can be reached by rail from St. Louis via Laredo on the *Aztec Eagle,* a modern express train. A rail voyage from New York to Mexico City takes three days and three nights. If you drive your own car, five highways are at your disposal, all of them leading to the capital. Highway 15 starts at Nogales south of Tucson, Arizona, and runs along the Pacific coast; it has a branch road, Highway 2, from Tijuana opposite San Diego, California, and Mexicali. Highway 45 is the central route, starting at Ciudad Juárez opposite El Paso, Texas. Highway 57, the Constitution Route, begins at Piedras Negras opposite Eagle Pass, Texas. Highway 85 is the Pan American Highway; it starts at Nuevo Laredo opposite Laredo, Texas, and runs through spectacular mountain scenery. Highway 101 begins at Matamoros opposite Brownsville, Texas, proceeds along the east coast and joins Highway 85 to Ciudad Victoria. Far more tourists, however, arrive at the capital by plane; the flight takes 1¾ hours from Houston, 4¾ hours from New York, 4 hours from Washington, 3½ hours from Chicago and 3½ hours from Los Angeles. Mérida in Yucatán is most easily reached by plane from Miami, Florida, in 1¾ hours. No passport is necessary — only a tourist card which is issued without charge.

What To See In Mexico. The Palace of Fine Arts with frescoes and murals by Orozco, Rivera, Siqueiros and others; the National Palace with frescoes by Diego Rivera; paintings and drawings by Rivera and the excellent Rivera collection of pre-Columbian sculpture at Anahuacalli Museum, also called the Diego Rivera Museum; the impressive cathedral, the largest in North America; Chapultepec Park with the magnificent Museum of Anthropology (see below), the Museum of Modern Art, the Museum of Natural History, Chapultepec Castle with interesting memoirs of Mexico's imperial days, zoological and botanical gardens and an amusement park; the Franciscan monastery of St. Matthew in Churubusco; Xochimilco floating gardens and flower canals with boat rides and mariachi music; the City of the Gods at Teotihuacán (see below); the Basilica of Guadalupe, a national shrine; a day trip to Amecameca southeast of the capital at an altitude of 8,000 feet and with a fine view of snowcapped Popocatepetl, 17,887 feet tall; a performance of Mexico's famous Ballet Folklórico at the Palace of Fine Arts and a bullfight at the Plaza México, the world's largest bullring.

North Of The Capital. Guanajuato: Once a center of great wealth derived from silver mining, it preserves its palaces and churches, cobblestone streets and fountains as a picture of colonial Spain. San Miguel de Allende: A national monument of colonial architecture and a charming small mountainside town of walled homes and gardens; tours are conducted on Sundays at noon. An important art center, it is the home of Instituto Allende, a well-known art school.

West Of The Capital. Morelia: Curved pink stone facades and artistic ironwork on mansions and churches conserve the glories of former centuries. An aqueduct of graceful masonry arches reminds us of Mediterranean prototypes. Pátzcuaro: Prime objects for photographers are the fishermen who spread their picturesque butterfly nets in Lake Pátzcuaro. Market day on Friday is a colorful event. Guadalajara: A modern city with a colonial atmosphere, horse drawn carriages, strolling mariachis and romantic serenades. The cathedral and the governor's mansion are worth seeing. Nearby Tlaquepaque is known for its pottery and native music; the neighboring Lake Chapala, the art colony of Ajijic and the town of Tequila, home of the Mexican drink, are often visited.

South Of The Capital. Puebla: The distinguishing architectural feature of its many churches is the use of red bricks and Talavera tiles. The city has numerous art treasures. Cuernavaca: The city is a prime tourist attraction reached from Mexico City by a new superhighway. Cortés relaxed here, as did Emperor Maximilian and his court. The Palacio de Cortés is decorated with murals by Rivera. Quaint old streets are lined with colonial buildings and fine shops, and there are also gardens, lakes and pyramids. Visit the 11 o'clock mass at the cathedral, featuring mariachi music. Taxco: One of Mexico's most picturesque hillside towns, Taxco has ancient fountains, charming small plazas and tile roofs, the lovely church of Santa Prisca and a lively Indian market. It is built on a silver rich mountain range and is studded with dozens of silver shops. Oaxaca: This very old, pre-Columbian city is located between jungle and mountains in a splendid subtropical valley. Among the city's famous churches are the cathedral, the Church of Santo Domingo, with a fabulous polychrome interior and the genealogical tree of the Virgin, and the Shrine of La Soledad. The archaeological excavations at Monte Albán and Mitla are interesting (see below). On Saturday the city market swarms with Indians from the neighboring villages; native specialties are shiny, black glazed pottery, serapes (shawls), straw mats, idols of obsidian and jade, and gold jewelry.

Yucatán Peninsula. Mérida: A white city with horse drawn coaches, odd effigies that depict street names and wandering violinists and guitar players, Mérida is the gateway to the fabulous Maya monuments of Chichén-Itzá and Uxmal (see below). Cozumel: This island on the east coast offers crystal clear waters and coral reefs for skin divers; its fine beaches are not yet overrun by tourists. The same is true of Isla Mujeres, north of Cozumel.

The Pacific Coast. Acapulco: One of the Americas' most outstanding international resorts, Acapulco lies on an oval bay surrounded by mountains and has fine hotels and a cosmopolitan clientele; the high divers of La Perla Club are a local attraction. Puerto Vallarta: A picturesque town buried under blossoming bougainvillaea, Puerto Vallarta is a seaside resort on the Bahía Banderas (Bay of Flags). With its white, palm fringed beaches, it is one of the most magnificent sites on the coast. Horseback

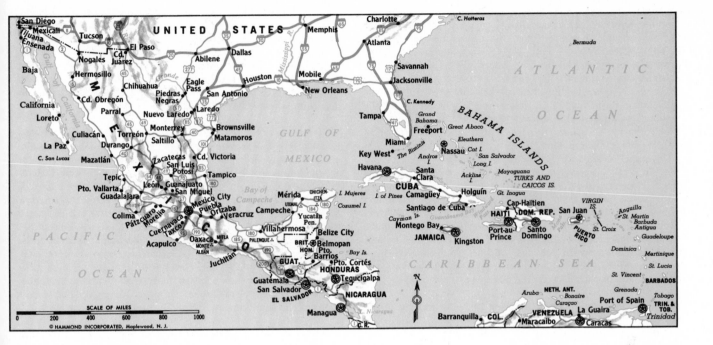

SCALE OF MILES
0   200   400   600   800   1000
© HAMMOND INCORPORATED, Maplewood, N.J.

hunting trips for jaguars, ocelots, deer and iguanas are popular. The local crafts center is outstanding. Mazatlán: Fishing for marlin, sailfish, bass and snapper is excellent at this scenic resort; all water sports are available, and hunting for peccaries, deer, jaguars and game birds is popular.

BAJA CALIFORNIA. La Paz: The town can be reached by air or by ferry from Mazatlán. It is a favorite resort of big game fishermen who go after marlin, bonito, dolphin and yellowtail. Cortés once visited the place. Other deep-sea fishing resorts are Cabo San Lucas at the southern tip of Lower California, Ensenada and Loreto.

THE INDIAN HERITAGE. An excellent overall impression of the culture and art of the pre-Columbian Olmecs, Zapotecs, Mayas, Toltecs and Aztecs can be gained by visiting the National Museum of Anthropology at Mexico City's Chapultepec Park; it is one of the world's most outstanding museums, a magnificent display of Mexico's archaeological and ethnographic history.

The best preserved actual sites are the following: thirty miles north of the capital, the "City of the Gods" at Teotihuacán is an awe-inspiring reminder of Indian greatness, with the pyramids of the sun and the moon in its center. From October to May a sound and light spectacle is performed on the site, re-creating the past by illumination, words and music. The English version starts at 7 p.m.; buses leave from the Monument of the Revolution.

From Oaxaca, southeast of Mexico City, two interesting archaeological sites may be visited. To the west Monte Albán was the ceremonial city of the Zapotecs, outstanding gold workers and city planners who leveled a mountain to build their sanctuary. East of Oaxaca the burial city of Mitla shows the fine art of the Mixtecs; they created friezes as delicate as lacework.

The monuments of the Mayas — pyramids, temples, palaces, arches, vaults and friezes artistically carved, beautifully conceived and proportioned — are found on the Yucatán Peninsula near the capital of Mérida. Chichén-Itzá to the east and Uxmal to the south are best known. Palenque, between Mérida and Veracruz, is perhaps the most impressive of the Maya cities. The fabulous bas-reliefs and the royal crypt in the Temple of Inscriptions are especially worth seeing. It is fascinating to imagine that these magnificent structures, now standing in the semidesert or in an outright wilderness, once were the centers of populous cities with thousands of Indians swarming over streets and squares. Yucatán should be visited during the winter when the climate is warm, dry and pleasant.

BERMUDA

BERMUDA. The oldest self-governing British crown colony consists of a group of seven large islands and hundreds of smaller islands which cover 21 square miles. It preserves its own atmosphere of quiet beauty, velvet soft beaches and clear water coves, cliffs and coral reefs, charming houses with pastel walls and white roofs buried under blossoming oleander and hibiscus, bougainvillaea and frangipani. Bermuda Easter lilies and Bermuda grass are known around the world. The use of cars is restricted, and bicycling is popular. There are no gambling casinos but elegant hotels and nightclubs are available. Fine, low key shops sell British and French imports in Hamilton, the capital, in the old town of St. George and on the neighboring island of Somerset. A fine view of the archipelago can be enjoyed from the top of Gibbs Hill Lighthouse. Sightseeing attractions are St. George, a seventeenth-century town, with Fort St. Catherine, the old State House and the carriage museum; the aquarium and Devil's Hole; Leamington and Crystal caves, and the Marine Gardens seen from glass bottom boats. Many visitors find the trials of the Supreme Court at Sessions House interesting.

WEST INDIES

BAHAMAS. About 700 lovely tropical islands and almost 2,500 tiny islets called cays are scattered over 100,000 square miles of ocean in a 600-mile arch. Clear water ranging in color from light green to dark blue, miles of uncrowded, white and pink beaches and pleasant resorts make the Bahamas a favorite vacationland. In Nassau, the capital, the lovely old houses and churches have an English accent. A splendid view of the city and harbor can be enjoyed from the top of the 126-foot-tall water tower on Bennett's Hill. The Queen's Staircase, 65 steps hewn into the rocks, leads to Fort Fincastle. Fort Charlotte with its dungeons commands the western entrance of the harbor. Other places to see are the straw market, the Ardastra Gardens with their pink flamingos, the interesting Sea Gardens and the Seafloor Aquarium with trained porpoises and giant turtles. Lovely Paradise Island with its casino and the Versailles Gardens are connected with Nassau by a new bridge.

The other islands do not boast of historical treasures but offer an ideal, unspoiled environment for all water sports. The more important ones are Abaco, noted for its pine forests, wild horses, native boat building, Andros, which has many clubs and lodges and the U.S. Underwater Test Center, Bimini, famous for yachting and big game fishing, Eleuthera, with the old settlements of Governor's Harbor and Rock South, and Grand Bahama, which has five 18-hole golf courses, huge hotels, marinas, glass bottom boats, gambling casino and the International Bazaar, centered on Freeport.

BARBADOS. This small island measuring 21 by 14 miles is an independent member of the British Commonwealth; it cultivates an English accent and a quiet and relaxing atmosphere. George Washington and his half-brother Lawrence visited Bridgetown, the capital, in 1751. St. Michael's Anglican Cathedral, where they attended services, was destroyed by a hurricane but rebuilt of coral rock in 1780. From St. John's Church a fine view of the Bathsheba coast may be enjoyed. From July to March many beautiful Barbados homes are open to the public once a week; the admission fees preserve historic landmarks. The harbor police with their bell-bottom trousers and big straw hats and the snappy police band are a favorite object for photographers.

DOMINICAN REPUBLIC. The Dominican Republic shares with Haiti the island of Hispaniola. It is a landmark in the history of the New World, for here Columbus founded America's first colonies. His tomb and his cross can be seen at the cathedral, the Basilica de Santa María La Menor, which boasts of outstanding carvings and a treasure room. In the center of old Santo Domingo Columbus' son Diego built the Alcázar de Colón, which has been splendidly restored. The Viceregal Museum, filled with fine Spanish antiques, is nearby. Other attractions are the Tower of Homage, the first stone fortress to be built in America and now a prison, the National Capitol erected of pink stone and University City, the home of the University of Santo Domingo, which was founded in 1538. The country's rice paddies, sugar plantations, coffee and tobacco plantings look prosperous, and the bright tropical flowers and splendid tropical birds — from flamingos to parrots — add a touch of beauty. There are also fine beaches and resort hotels.

HAITI. The western third of Hispaniola, Haiti is probably the most colorful and original of all Caribbean countries. Voodoo is still taken seriously there, and loads are carried on the backs of burros or on the heads of gaily robed Negro women. The people are poor, but they are neatly dressed, gentle and courteous; they speak a soft French patois. They have also a flair for art, and in the markets one can buy fine original mahogany carvings for very little money. Several of the art galleries in Port-au-Prince have international status. The Troupe National Folklorique can be seen at the Théâtre du Verdure, an open-air playhouse, and voodoo rites can be observed in the hills. These, of course, are staged for the tourists. In the capital the elegance of Paris and the crudeness of the jungle seem to meet. On the northern coast the Cap-Haïtien region boasts of two relics of the country's fantastic past: the magnificent ruins of the Sans Souci Palace of King Henri Christophe, an illiterate ex-slave, and the Citadel, a huge mountain fortress that was built by 200,000 laborers in 13 years. It was never attacked.

GUADELOUPE AND MARTINIQUE. These French islands are two fine Caribbean vacation resorts with broad beaches of white coral or black volcanic sand, with volcanic peaks and tropical forests, mountain lakes and waterfalls. On Guadeloupe Columbus' landing place in 1493 and the Carib rock engravings at Trois-Rivières are interesting. On the spectacular west coast of Martinique the ruins of St. Pierre, the former capital, are a tourist attraction. In a sudden eruption of Mount Pelée in 1902 the city's population of some 30,000 people perished in three minutes; only one prisoner in an underground dungeon survived. This Pompeii of the New World is a unique sight; the Mount Pelée Museum displays mementos of the catastrophe. Trois-Îlets is the birthplace of Empress Josephine, Napoleon's first wife. French imports, especially perfumes, are bargains.

JAMAICA. An independent country within the British Commonwealth, Jamaica has been a famous resort for generations. It is a beautiful, mountainous island. The daily train from Kingston to Montego Bay runs through a fabulous wild landscape. The beach resorts of the North Shore, particularly Montego Bay and Ocho Rios, are internationally known for their deep blue, delightfully warm waters, which offer unsurpassed swimming, snorkeling and water-skiing. In Kingston, the capital, the Institute of Jamaica has interesting collections referring to the country's past and present; at the Hope Gardens the display of orchids is spectacular. Spanish Town, west of Kingston, is a historic relic with a fine Folk Museum. Across Kingston harbor Port Royal, once the bustling haven of buccaneers, is today a quiet fishing town and a tourist resort.

NETHERLANDS ANTILLES. These islands consist of two groups 500 miles apart. Aruba, Bonaire and Curaçao are located along the coast of Venezuela, and St. Maarten, Saba and St. Eustatius are east of the Virgin Islands. Willemstad, the capital (on Curaçao), looks as if it has been transplanted from Holland with its 200-year-old pastel colored houses, Dutch gables, spic and span streets and an atmosphere of comfortable prosperity. It is a great shopping center for the world's luxury goods at bargain prices. Oranjestad on Aruba is a typically Dutch trade fair deluxe. Both islands are sites of huge oil refineries. Bonaire, an unspoiled playground, is famous for its flamingos and its pink conch shells. St. Maarten, half French and half Dutch, has recently become popular as a winter resort.

PUERTO RICO. An autonomous commonwealth associated with the United States, Puerto Rico is a fascinating island. Its historic traditions are far older than those of the continental United States. The Dominican Convent was begun in 1523, and Ponce de León's remains were interred in the adjacent church from 1559 until 1908, when they were moved to the Cathedral. El Morro, the ancient castle begun in 1539, is both impressive and beautiful. La Fortaleza, built in 1533 as a fort, is the governor's residence, and Fort San Jerónimo houses the Museum of Military History. All of Old San Juan reflects colonial Spain, while the Condado area with its luxury hotels is reminiscent of Miami Beach. Visits to the racetrack, a cockfight or a rum distillery are popular. Twenty-seven miles east of San Juan, Luquillo Beach is a splendid playground in the shadow of a mountain range. The tropical rain forest called El Yunque is nearby. El Conquistador at Las Croabas is one of the world's most luxurious hotels, with hilltop views of both the Atlantic and the Caribbean, an Olympic swimming pool, a marina, cable cars and a casino. At Parguera, near the island's southwest corner, Phosphorescent Bay is a fascinating phenomenon; a boat ride on a night without moonlight produces showers of sparks.

TRINIDAD AND TOBAGO. Trinidad is the most cosmopolitan island of the Caribbean. In the nineteenth century the British imported farm laborers from Asia, so that today the population includes Hindus and Chinese. There are also many of African extraction as well as Portuguese, Spaniards, Lebanese, Syrians, French and British — all living together peacefully. Their churches, mosques, temples and bazaars are fascinating. The island has spectacular mountain and sea scenery, with peaks of 3,000 feet, teak forests and bamboo groves. At the Caroni Bird Sanctuary thousands of scarlet ibis may be observed. Trinidad's famous asphalt lake has paved many a European boulevard. Trinidad's sister, Tobago, has a striking similarity to the Robinson Crusoe island as it is described in the novel. The beaches are excellent, and the coral gardens at Buccoo Reef are worth exploring. On Little Tobago, north of Tobago, the Bird of Paradise Sanctuary is unique. Hummingbirds abound.

VIRGIN ISLANDS. The American-owned, formerly Danish Virgin Islands have a charm of their own. White beaches, crystal clear water and mountains with fabulous views make them ideal vacation resorts. As a duty free port area they offer the world's finest luxury goods at prices far below those on the mainland. At the harbor of St. Thomas, a 1,000-foot cable car takes you to the top of Flagg Hill for an unforgettable panorama of little islands floating on the coral sea. The Street of 99 Steps which lead up the hill are actually 102; the old Danish cemetery displays brightly painted tombstones of conch shells, and the dungeons of Fort Christian are a historic landmark. A tower above the harbor supposedly was Bluebeard's castle. St. Croix is also a major resort. The wharf area of Christiansted is a national historic site including several old Danish buildings. The Lutheran Church, the archways along the main street, the ruins of sugar plantations, the numerous windmills and the Whim Estate, the restored establishment of a rich, slave-holding planter are interesting. Buck Island Reef National Monument preserves a fine coral reef off the north coast. On St. John, the Virgin Islands National Park and Caneel Bay Plantation, a famous resort, are tourist attractions. At Trunk Bay, snorkelers will enjoy a unique underwater trail.

Trunk Bay at St. John in the Virgin Islands where a unique underwater trail for snorkelers is maintained.

243

National Parks

If you plan to visit one or more national parks, you may wish to write for a descriptive folder; addresses of Park Superintendents are indicated below.

UNITED STATES

UNITED STATES

ACADIA — Bar Harbor, Maine 04609
ARCHES — Moab, Utah 84532
BIG BEND — Big Bend National Park, Texas 79834
BRYCE CANYON — Bryce Canyon, Utah 84717
CANYONLANDS — Moab, Utah 84532
CAPITOL REEF — Torrey, Utah 84775
CARLSBAD CAVERNS — Box 1598, Carlsbad, New Mexico 88220
CRATER LAKE — Crater Lake, Oregon 97604
EVERGLADES — Box 279, Homestead, Florida 33030
GLACIER — West Glacier, Montana 59936
GRAND CANYON — Grand Canyon, Arizona 86023
GRAND TETON — Moose, Wyoming 83012
GREAT SMOKY MOUNTAINS — Gatlinburg, Tennessee 37738
GUADALUPE MOUNTAINS — c/o Carlsbad Caverns National Park, Box 1598, Carlsbad, New Mexico 88220
*HALEAKALA — Box 456, Kahului, Maui, Hawaii 96732
*HAWAII VOLCANOES — Hawaii Volcanoes National Park, Hawaii 96718
HOT SPRINGS — Box 1219, Hot Springs, Arkansas 71901
ISLE ROYALE — 87 North Ripley St., Houghton, Michigan 49931
KINGS CANYON — Three Rivers, California 93271
LASSEN VOLCANIC — Mineral, California 96063
MAMMOTH CAVE — Mammoth Cave, Kentucky 42259
MESA VERDE — Mesa Verde National Park, Colorado 81330
*MOUNT MC KINLEY — Box 9, McKinley Park, Alaska 99755
MOUNT RAINIER — Longmire, Washington 98397
NORTH CASCADES — Sedro Woolley, Washington 98284
OLYMPIC — 600 East Park Avenue, Port Angeles, Washington 98362
PETRIFIED FOREST — Holbrook, Arizona 86025
PLATT — Box 201, Sulphur, Oklahoma 73086
REDWOOD — Drawer N, Crescent City, California 95531
ROCKY MOUNTAIN — Estes Park, Colorado 80517
SEQUOIA — Three Rivers, California 93271
SHENANDOAH — Luray, Virginia 22835
VOYAGEURS — c/o Midwest Region Office, NPS, 1709 Jackson Street, Omaha, Nebraska 68102
WIND CAVE — Hot Springs, South Dakota 57747
YELLOWSTONE — Yellowstone National Park, Wyoming 82190
YOSEMITE — Yosemite National Park, California 95389
ZION — Springdale, Utah 84767

CANADA

BANFF — Banff, Alberta
*CAPE BRETON HIGHLANDS — Ingonish Beach, Nova Scotia
ELK ISLAND — Lamont, Alberta
*FUNDY — Alma, New Brunswick
GEORGIAN BAY ISLANDS — Honey Harbour, Ontario
GLACIER — Revelstoke, British Columbia
JASPER — Jasper, Alberta
*KEJIMKUJIK — Maitland Bridge, Annapolis County, Nova Scotia
KOOTENAY — Radium Hot Springs, British Columbia
MOUNT REVELSTOKE — Revelstoke, British Columbia
POINT PELEE — R. R. 1, Leamington, Ontario
PRINCE ALBERT — Waskesiu Lake, Saskatchewan
PRINCE EDWARD ISLAND — Stanhope, Prince Edward Island
RIDING MOUNTAIN — Wasagaming, Manitoba
ST. LAWRENCE ISLANDS — Mallorytown Landing, Ontario
*TERRA NOVA — Glovertown, Newfoundland
WATERTON LAKES — Waterton Park, Alberta
WOOD BUFFALO — Fort Smith, Northwest Territories
YOHO — Field, British Columbia
*park located off map area

UNITED STATES
CANADA · MEXICO

SCALE OF MILES
100 200 300 400 500 600 700 800

245

Highway Mileage Chart

	Albuquerque, N. Mex.	Amarillo, Tex.	Atlanta, Ga.	Baltimore, Md.	Bangor, Maine	Birmingham, Ala.	Boise, Idaho	Boston, Mass.	Buffalo, N.Y.	Butte, Mont.	Charlotte, N.C.	Chicago, Ill.	Cincinnati, Ohio	Cleveland, Ohio	Dallas, Tex.	Denver, Colo.	Detroit, Mich.	El Paso, Tex.	Fargo, N. Dak.	Houston, Tex.	Jacksonville, Fla.	Kansas City, Mo.	Little Rock, Ark	Los Angeles, Calif.	Louisville, Ky.	Memphis, Tenn.	Miami, Fla.	Milwaukee, Wis.	Minn.-St. Paul, Minn.	New Orleans, La.	New York, N.Y.	Oklahoma City, Okla.	Omaha, Nebr.
Albany, N.Y.	2114	1825	988	321	366	1091	2584	170	283	2344	750	807	707	466	1702	1844	536	2168	1462	1824	1117	1268	1360	2930	827	1217	1468	894	1223	1476	147	1569	1295
Albuquerque, N. Mex.	•	289	1429	1884	2433	1276	980	2232	1781	1040	1669	1285	1405	1516	650	432	1580	270	1310	844	1662	791	901	805	1328	1032	1986	1390	1223	1145	2056	545	892
Amarillo, Tex.	289	•	1143	1595	2144	985	1279	1963	1524	1237	1380	1071	1123	1319	361	422	1295	417	1056	604	1373	577	612	1091	1039	743	1697	1144	979	859	1756	263	648
Atlanta, Ga.	1429	1143	•	671	1215	155	2292	1070	876	2158	259	707	467	692	820	1431	726	1429	1343	841	315	823	541	2254	428	366	665	804	1114	517	863	880	1006
Austin, Tex.	774	485	938	1571	2221	783	1749	2012	1571	1814	1187	1140	1133	1383	197	907	1372	592	1307	161	1085	727	507	1385	1042	646	1403	1224	1161	519	1771	480	884
Baltimore, Md.	1884	1595	671	•	632	800	2440	400	366	2151	421	690	497	348	1393	1625	510	2025	1367	1452	794	1062	1102	2669	602	951	1143	772	1100	1153	192	1339	1153
Bangor, Maine	2433	2144	1315	632	•	1407	2900	233	652	2642	1049	1174	1094	827	2019	2189	892	2573	1828	2107	1426	1630	1718	3238	1198	1594	1773	1271	1589	1747	450	1902	1639
Billings, Mont.	1024	1001	1875	1924	2406	1782	607	2213	1754	237	2037	1234	1528	1579	1352	579	1503	1291	621	1595	2190	1065	1474	1300	1564	1532	2547	1171	831	1853	2062	1195	857
Birmingham, Ala.	1276	985	155	800	1407	•	2201	1210	932	2018	415	661	499	742	660	1327	743	1288	1308	673	427	716	386	2073	362	247	765	748	1069	359	988	741	926
Boise, Idaho	980	1279	2292	2440	2900	2201	•	2722	2268	452	2433	1726	1963	2082	1637	867	2011	1267	1228	1825	2615	1446	1833	887	1993	1913	2901	1763	1446	2140	2568	1489	1267
Boston, Mass.	2232	1967	1070	400	233	1210	2722	•	458	2442	821	974	861	640	1815	2012	707	2401	1631	1874	1201	1436	1492	3037	964	1340	1539	1060	1387	1556	211	1733	1467
Buffalo, N.Y.	1781	1524	876	366	652	932	2268	458	•	1988	733	520	428	186	1406	1537	249	1950	1177	1502	1080	980	1066	2586	537	924	1431	610	937	1248	367	1249	990
Butte, Mont.	1040	1237	2158	2151	2642	2018	452	2442	1988	•	2266	1468	1783	1813	1586	815	1737	1310	858	1829	2427	1302	1711	1158	1790	1769	2784	1408	1068	2077	2317	1413	1086
Charleston, W. Va.	1594	1325	519	391	1018	589	2197	781	439	2327	303	483	202	268	1119	1369	357	1670	1119	1201	671	796	752	2341	266	615	1043	561	880	936	566	988	905
Charlotte, N.C.	1669	1380	259	421	1049	415	2433	821	733	2266	•	765	475	578	1055	1609	664	1688	1419	1139	388	987	776	2474	467	637	746	854	1180	781	613	1119	1180
Chattanooga, Tenn.	1356	1067	118	662	1282	145	2140	1063	775	1972	320	590	343	592	807	1317	605	1439	1234	838	441	694	456	2197	275	317	788	686	995	514	854	811	886
Cheyenne, Wyo.	545	533	1468	1656	2147	1374	766	1954	1501	711	1644	967	1192	1320	880	101	2515	809	823	1143	1899	657	1053	1182	1187	1127	2240	1019	821	1376	1782	702	491
Chicago, Ill.	1285	1071	707	690	1174	661	1726	974	520	1468	765	•	294	345	936	1018	269	1466	657	1092	1017	505	652	2106	304	548	1377	87	418	929	828	826	465
Cincinnati, Ohio	1405	1123	467	497	1094	499	1963	861	428	1783	475	294	•	244	984	1171	251	1505	956	1081	783	600	625	2226	108	487	1133	385	717	820	635	901	700
Cleveland, Ohio	1596	1319	692	348	827	742	2082	640	186	1813	578	345	244	•	1219	1351	168	1754	999	1335	971	789	884	2427	351	737	1322	433	760	1060	486	1096	818
Columbia, S.C.	1655	1366	215	509	1140	371	2558	910	806	2278	94	759	527	664	1045	1687	733	1644	1416	1040	294	1045	749	2486	512	607	645	898	1226	713	694	1137	1205
Columbus, Ohio	1472	1220	563	392	994	592	2023	757	332	1789	503	311	108	140	1080	1228	186	1619	968	1205	867	668	762	2292	218	618	1213	404	737	959	546	937	765
Dallas, Tex.	650	361	820	1393	2019	660	1637	1815	1406	1568	1055	936	984	1219	•	784	1182	624	1110	243	1029	498	330	1410	876	468	1327	1063	964	500	1642	212	672
Denver, Colo.	432	422	1431	1625	2189	1327	867	2012	1537	815	1609	1018	1171	1351	784	•	1305	668	901	1028	1790	613	962	1162	1143	1058	2100	1039	845	1284	1788	616	537
Des Moines, Iowa	1032	786	916	1013	1520	854	1397	1328	866	1189	1085	330	584	688	704	674	614	1160	491	948	1255	207	581	1788	585	627	1598	358	254	1028	1165	566	139
Detroit, Mich.	1580	1295	726	510	892	743	2011	707	249	1737	664	269	251	168	1182	1305	•	1716	926	1307	1039	750	859	2419	363	726	1387	357	690	1077	626	1068	744
Duluth, Minn.	1380	1141	1193	1179	1585	1150	1540	1392	933	1109	1244	487	787	836	1113	1000	757	1506	251	1357	1518	608	996	2088	795	980	1870	406	152	1382	1315	968	518
El Paso, Tex.	270	417	1429	2025	2573	1288	1267	2401	1950	1310	1688	1466	1505	1754	624	668	1716	•	1453	753	1641	946	961	793	1513	1092	1994	1557	1351	1119	2175	682	1027
Fargo, N. Dak.	1310	1056	1343	1367	1828	1308	1228	1631	1177	858	1419	657	956	999	1110	901	926	1453	•	1364	1684	636	1045	1935	951	1061	2008	573	239	1479	1485	900	436
Fort Wayne, Ind.	1395	1181	633	528	1026	606	1882	845	394	1624	629	156	154	199	1035	1179	159	1559	819	1147	943	604	691	2224	207	568	1287	251	580	962	670	907	629
Fort Worth, Tex.	616	340	859	1367	2038	696	1615	1847	1438	1543	1087	968	1011	1248	31	759	125	588	1110	261	1061	534	371	1441	919	512	1398	1082	964	531	1667	212	701
Grand Forks, N. Dak.	1387	1133	1287	1415	1897	1385	1305	1705	1254	913	1496	734	1033	1076	1187	978	1003	1530	77	1441	1751	713	1122	1990	1028	1138	2085	650	316	1039	1552	984	513
Grand Rapids, Mich.	1462	1248	781	631	1017	736	1903	840	381	1645	857	167	306	278	1160	1207	148	1755	834	1278	1106	663	829	2355	364	694	1439	262	601	1124	763	1003	659
Great Falls, Mont.	1227	1224	2097	2113	2595	2026	610	2375	1923	158	2458	1423	1717	1768	1586	803	1692	1497	744	1831	2412	1301	1698	1316	1991	1768	2757	1322	988	2086	2247	1419	1035
Greensboro, N.C.	1762	1473	352	328	1316	507	2408	718	640	2292	93	749	469	485	1148	1626	571	1764	1425	1232	481	1030	824	2537	492	687	839	836	1167	874	520	1174	1156
Hartford, Conn.	2169	1869	966	297	332	1108	2634	101	387	2376	711	908	753	582	1755	1901	648	2288	1565	1791	1092	1327	1396	2947	866	1242	1440	995	1324	1464	113	1632	1373
Houston, Tex.	844	604	841	1452	2107	673	1825	1874	1502	1829	1139	1092	1081	1335	243	1028	1307	753	1364	•	924	744	439	1554	981	572	1242	1163	1211	358	1678	458	917
Indianapolis, Ind.	1313	1034	539	565	1136	492	1853	931	486	1674	586	188	104	300	921	1057	277	1425	840	1031	852	491	571	2131	114	444	1197	276	601	839	716	778	591
Jackson, Miss.	1062	777	400	998	1635	243	2063	1446	1115	1968	668	747	678	924	411	1219	931	1040	1271	433	597	613	257	1864	573	210	920	826	1062	182	1232	587	882
Jacksonville, Fla.	1662	1373	315	794	1426	427	2615	1201	1080	2427	388	1017	783	971	1029	1790	1039	1641	1684	924	•	1138	821	2427	766	672	345	1123	1440	568	979	1195	1349
Kansas City, Mo.	791	577	823	1062	1630	716	1446	1436	980	1302	987	505	600	789	498	613	750	946	636	744	1138	•	409	1620	523	467	1491	564	461	846	1214	357	208
Las Vegas, Nev.	587	876	2015	2478	3074	1861	688	2841	2396	877	2268	1876	1996	2221	1238	901	2140	716	1656	1445	2249	1416	1488	288	1939	1631	2628	1902	1708	1733	2630	1140	1401
Lincoln, Nebr.	834	590	1005	1211	1697	938	1240	1550	1048	1080	1211	576	758	876	635	613	845	1017	459	885	1360	222	631	1662	745	689	1713	557	289	1068	1304	430	58
Little Rock, Ark.	901	612	541	1102	1718	386	1833	1492	1066	1711	776	652	625	884	330	962	859	961	1045	439	821	409	•	1698	531	139	1161	727	833	434	1283	350	623
Los Angeles, Calif.	805	1091	2254	2669	3238	2073	887	3037	2586	1158	2474	2106	2226	2427	1410	1162	2419	793	1935	1554	2427	1620	1698	•	2161	1823	2737	2145	1996	1916	2823	1353	1698
Louisville, Ky.	1328	1039	428	602	1198	362	1993	964	537	1790	467	304	108	351	876	1143	363	1513	951	981	766	523	531	2161	•	365	1078	392	712	719	759	808	707
Madison, Wis.	1312	1091	842	834	1318	805	1685	1127	664	1330	909	144	443	493	1007	975	417	1508	506	1194	1178	493	747	2101	449	636	1507	78	267	1065	990	875	423
Memphis, Tenn.	1032	743	366	951	1594	247	1913	1340	924	1769	637	548	487	737	468	1058	726	1092	1061	572	672	467	139	1823	365	•	1017	632	852	399	1142	482	671
Miami, Fla.	1986	1697	665	1143	1773	765	2901	1539	1431	2784	746	1377	1133	1322	1327	2100	1387	1994	2008	1242	345	1491	1161	2737	1078	1017	•	1632	1771	878	1327	1518	1671
Milwaukee, Wis.	1390	1144	804	772	1271	748	1763	1060	610	1408	854	87	385	433	1063	1039	357	1557	573	1163	1123	564	727	2145	392	632	1463	•	334	1034	922	905	501
Minn.-St. Paul, Minn.	1223	979	1114	1100	1589	1069	1446	1387	937	1068	1180	413	717	760	964	845	690	1351	239	1211	1440	461	833	1996	712	852	1771	334	•	1251	1246	818	364
Mobile, Ala.	1277	988	369	1040	1672	235	2270	1439	1167	2148	628	896	734	977	627	1399	978	1263	1411	510	405	846	437	2037	597	350	687	983	1402	140	1232	787	1021
Montréal, Que.	2161	1876	1268	597	363	1324	2592	321	383	2309	1018	841	821	577	1759	1881	576	2331	1502	1883	1384	1326	1435	2995	828	1302	1732	941	1263	1637	395	1662	1320
Nashville, Tenn.	1247	972	251	732	736	201	2002	1126	717	1907	422	452	289	532	700	1192	544	1320	1092	810	577	556	359	2047	180	220	916	542	853	536	929	702	761
New Orleans, La.	1145	859	517	1153	1747	359	2140	1556	1248	2077	780	929	820	1060	500	1284	1077	1119	1479	358	568	846	434	1916	719	399	878	1034	1251	•	1353	684	1065
New York, N.Y.	2056	1756	863	192	450	988	2568	211	367	2317	613	828	635	486	1642	1788	626	2175	1485	1678	979	1214	1283	2823	759	1142	1327	922	1246	1353	•	1519	1293
Norfolk, Va.	1962	1673	592	249	881	753	2561	543	561	2342	321	874	600	531	1433	1892	699	2009	1531	1460	661	1193	1097	2795	693	958	1013	961	1287	1101	441	1535	1311
Oklahoma City, Okla.	545	263	880	1339	1902	741	1489	1733	1249	1413	1119	826	901	1096	210	616	1068	682	900	458	1195	357	350	1353	808	482	1518	905	818	648	1519	•	477
Omaha, Nebr.	892	646	1006	1153	1639	926	1267	1467	990	1086	1180	465	700	818	672	537	744	1027	436	917	1349	208	623	1698	707	671	1671	501	364	1065	1293	477	•
Philadelphia, Pa.	1915	1694	771	99	541	897	2450	303	360	2226	521	758	571	425	1540	1726	578	2091	1415	1589	889	1121	1197	2741	682	1057	1230	853	1176	1239	91	1436	1219
Phoenix, Ariz.	449	727	1888	2310	2882	1697	1020	2703	2348	1141	2126	1753	1854	2061	1021	826	2027	401	1726	1158	2053	1238	1337	389	1776	1470	2388	1833	1671	1527	2479	989	1325
Pittsburgh, Pa.	1636	1379	737	230	819	763	2156	576	220	1927	523	459	278	127	1260	1427	287	1803	1116	1364	893	850	914	2194	398	786	1237	550	877	1113	363	1145	918
Portland, Oreg.	1461	1737	2735	2847	3295	2658	435	3039	2671	653	2880	2131	2413	2519	2057	1285	2425	1709	1590	2282	3070	1901	2284	994	2437	2367	3414	2069	1721	2591	2959	1926	1700
Providence, R.I.	2232	1932	1037	368	276	1176	2757	44	456	2444	777	976	811	642	1818	1964	705	2351	1633	1855	1155	1390	1459	2999	935	1318	1503	1066	1389	1529	176	1695	1441
Québec, Que.	2333	2048	1426	765	228	1496	2764	390	533	2470	1176	1002	1027	738	1911	2043	738	2492	1764	2045	1542	1488	1597	3157	1058	1475	1897	1089	1420	1810	544	1806	1482
Rapid City, S. Dak.	831	799	1575	1605	2089	1498	952	1982	1493	552	1714	915	1231	1278	1108	401	1225	1080	536	1352	1932	743	1164	1399	1238	1245	2284	858	576	1573	1764	873	534
Reno, Nev.	1036	1324	2471	2641	3147	2416	427	2978	2512	842	2649	1970	2187	2323	1695	1040	2249	1167	1639	1888	2560	1665	2030	476	2213	2083	3021	2003	1797	2199	2818	1529	1500
Richmond, Va.	1877	1586	545	144	773	697	2473	543	473	2254	292	786	512	443	1333	1754	611	1937	1443	1353	646	1105	984	2709	575	845	994	877	1204	1057	330	1345	1223
Sacramento, Calif.	1117	1406	2611	2781	3287	2556	545	3118	2652	982	2789	2110	2327	2463	1835	1180	2389	1267	1779	2020	2700	1805	2170	387	2353	2223	3161	2143	1937	2339	2958	1669	1640
St. Louis, Mo.	1057	783	553	804	1379	503	1701	1188	723	1536	738	291	338	540	651	863	513	1167	812	801	881	254	357	1862	267	294	1222	371	553	699	961	523	453
Salt Lake City, Utah	612	908	1976	2110	2616	1857	363	2419	1965	428	2121	1443	1661	1784	1262	512	1719	880	1215	1453	2237	1118	1444	730	1656	1570	2603	1502	1246	1773	2278	1112	953
San Antonio, Tex.	719	512	1023	1649	2299	861	1704	2099	1651	1749	1254	1223	1230	1470	275	947	1448	568	1378	197	1141	773	578	1380	1124	711	1439	1313	1234	575	1863	477	943
San Diego, Calif.	815	1087	2172	2668	3240	2043	963	3061	2637	1212	2450	2118	2241	2446	1291	1201	2416	742	1943	1491	2320	1605	1695	122	2143	1829	2618	2191	2046	1864	2851	1349	1716
San Francisco, Calif.	1132	1420	2563	2884	3371	2409	654	3182	2728	1069	2835	2183	2424	2527	1773	1267	2482	1196	1873	1955	2787	1893	2032	403	2425	2162	3193	2203	2001	2278	3054	1692	1720
Savannah, Ga.	1683	1380	254	640	1269	409	2546	1048	971	2345	240	951	660	818	1017	1717	914	1653	1597	1029	154	1112	795	2482	647	657	506	1038	1352	641	830	1156	1298
Seattle, Wash.	1511	1800	2843	2733	3205	2703	529	3095	2629	615	2992	2031	2451	2511	2136	1377	2444	1785	1505	2354	3115	1904	2273	1177	2427	2362	3451	2045	1673	2645	2944	1975	1657
Shreveport, La.	836	547	637	1296	1940	477	1844	1736	1308	1796	892	867	879	1127	186	981	1078	813	1212	239	829	567	216	1631	751	322	1180	970	1386	316	1486	366	776
Sioux Falls, S. Dak.	1082	838	1196	1215	1699	1116	1295	1499	1045	895	1370	525	890	870	844	655	794	1217	230	1110	1539	390	799	1817	897	858	1861	507	221	1265	1353	644	187
Spokane, Wash.	1336	1559	2531	2515	2990	2420	391	2804	2390	318	2584	1716	2159	2176	1928	1067	2085	1617	1208	2164	2818	1617	2018	1249	2167	2082	3191	1751	1386	2383	2671	1651	1513
Springfield, Ill.	1086	861	652	753	1316	602	1688	1134	675	1507	749	196	302	489	766	832	443	1284	857	915	946	295	464	1982	282	390	1317	280	481	796	914	637	421
Tampa, Fla.	1738	1449	464	986	1620	552	2753	1383	1263	2551	583	1187	948	1166	1106	1928	1201	1746	1807	1007	194	1280	939	2607	865	782	248	1268	1578	644	1176	1264	1493
Topeka, Kans.	801	551	898	1133	1701	787	1433	1510	1051	1279	1058	568	688	862	509	557	841	947	604	759	1203	71	479	1549	593	538	1562	633	532	929	1288	342	168
Toronto, Ont.	1815	1530	975	465	683	1031	2246	462	99	1972	832	495	540	296	1391	1540	235	1951	1161	1542	1275	985	1094	2654	598	961	1530	582	913	1347	486	1303	979
Tucson, Ariz.	454	674	1746	2380	2887	1605	1191	2686	2235	1245	2005	1739	1842	2037	951	845	2005	317	1746	1070	1958	1255	1278	512	1749	1417	2311	1819	1677	1436	2517	941	1341
Tulsa, Okla.	658	374	832	1230	1791	680	1569	1597	1143	1498	1066	702	753	953	277	691	930	791	840	522	1123	247	291	1458	687	426	1461	792	779	706	1374	110	399
Vancouver, B.C.	1660	1949	2992	2882	3303	2852	674	3168	2878	764	3141	2247	2541	2504	2259	1526	2505	1934	1654	2503	3264	2053	2422	1328	2576	2511	3600	1612	1822	2794	3023	2121	1803
Walla Walla, Wash.	1208	1527	2570	2566	3045	2430	260	2938	2449	390	2670	1871	2187	2234	1858	1104	2181	1476	1248	2049	2833	1631	2000	1092	2194	2162	3204	1814	1458	2369	2720	1708	1384
Washington, D.C.	1904	1591	640	39	673	767	2440	440	372	2153	383	687	497	362	1403	1640	516	2040	1357	1448	754	1057	1058	2739	605	917	1105	784	1105	1150	226	1330	1149
Wichita, Kans.	620	359	978	1293	1832	830	1663	1673	1206	1327	1186	711	817	1012	386	512	969	744	731	629	1309	202	472	1384	744	549	1206	792	650	840	1436	168	309
Winnipeg, Man.	1658	1444	1587	1570	1803	1541	1443	1812	1377	875	1622	857	1151	1227	1328	1065	1149	1621	215	1611	1896	851	1260	2033	1161	1428	2212	786	462	1713	1683	1208	643

DISTANCES ARE APPROXIMATE AND HAVE BEEN COMPUTED OVER MAJOR THROUGH ROUTES

Climate Data

	Philadelphia, Pa.	Phoenix, Ariz.	Pittsburgh, Pa.	Portland, Oreg.	Rapid City, S. Dak.	Reno, Nev.	Richmond, Va.	St. Louis, Mo.	Salt Lake City, Utah	San Antonio, Tex.	San Diego, Calif.	San Francisco, Calif.	Savannah, Ga.	Seattle, Wash.	Spokane, Wash.	Tampa, Fla.	Washington, D.C
Albany, N.Y.	233	2536	457	2999	1784	2798	472	1016	2251	1962	2894	3009	981	2928	2623	1331	367
Albuquerque, N. Mex.	1915	449	1636	1461	831	1036	1877	1057	612	719	815	1132	1683	1511	1336	1738	1904
Amarillo, Tex.	1694	727	1379	1737	799	1324	1586	783	908	512	1087	1420	1380	1800	1559	1449	1591
Atlanta, Ga.	771	1888	737	2735	1575	2471	545	553	1976	1023	2172	2563	254	2843	2531	464	640
Austin, Tex.	1681	993	1411	2301	1257	1759	1479	876	1386	78	1334	1787	1160	2274	1974	1168	1563
Baltimore, Md.	99	2310	230	2847	1605	2641	144	804	2110	1649	2668	2884	640	2733	2515	986	39
Bangor, Maine	541	2882	819	3295	2089	3147	773	1379	2616	2299	3240	3371	1269	3205	2990	1620	673
Billings, Mont.	1992	1258	1693	890	323	982	2040	1307	570	1513	1354	1208	2029	835	553	2314	1919
Birmingham, Ala.	897	1697	763	2658	1498	2416	697	503	1857	861	2043	2409	409	2703	2420	552	767
Boise, Idaho	2450	1020	2156	435	952	427	2473	1701	363	1704	963	654	2546	525	391	2753	2440
Boston, Mass.	303	2703	576	3039	1982	2978	543	1188	2419	2099	3061	3182	1048	3095	2804	1383	440
Buffalo, N.Y.	360	2348	220	2671	1493	2512	473	723	1964	1651	2637	2728	971	2629	2390	1263	372
Butte, Mont.	2226	1141	1927	653	552	842	2254	1536	428	1749	1212	1069	2345	615	318	2551	2153
Charleston, W. Va.	481	2042	233	2619	1457	2389	309	538	1865	1363	2409	2615	536	2618	2265	884	355
Charlotte, N.C.	513	2126	523	2880	1714	2649	292	738	2121	1254	2450	2835	240	2992	2584	583	383
Chattanooga, Tenn.	757	1808	618	2668	1420	2359	545	433	1829	1022	2146	2515	373	2598	2290	586	611
Cheyenne, Wyo.	1727	924	1427	1211	300	995	1708	910	457	1068	1257	1209	1722	1279	1032	1992	1658
Chicago, Ill.	758	1753	459	2131	915	1970	786	291	1443	1223	2118	2183	951	2031	1716	1187	687
Cincinnati, Ohio	571	1854	278	2413	1231	2187	512	338	1661	1230	2241	2424	660	2451	2159	948	497
Cleveland, Ohio	425	2061	127	2519	1278	2328	443	540	1784	1473	2446	2547	818	2511	2176	1166	362
Columbia, S.C.	604	2086	599	2995	1726	2697	362	742	2166	1250	2448	2771	142	2985	2676	492	412
Columbus, Ohio	472	1929	184	2478	1239	2269	473	413	1716	1372	2307	2475	720	2445	2117	1058	390
Dallas, Tex.	1540	1021	1260	2057	1108	1695	1333	651	1262	275	1291	1773	1017	2136	1928	1106	1403
Denver, Colo.	1726	826	1427	1285	401	1040	1754	863	512	947	1201	1267	1717	1377	1067	1928	1640
Des Moines, Iowa	1088	1449	799	1819	637	1638	1105	349	1089	983	1835	1851	1217	1766	1574	1403	1041
Detroit, Mich.	578	2027	287	2425	1225	2249	611	513	1719	1448	2416	2482	914	2444	2085	1201	516
Duluth, Minn.	1254	1830	954	1771	688	1956	1273	676	1395	1389	2188	2084	1435	1677	1385	1681	1179
El Paso, Tex.	2091	401	1803	1709	1080	1167	1937	1167	880	568	742	1196	1653	1785	1617	1746	2040
Fargo, N. Dak.	1415	1726	1116	1590	536	1639	1443	812	1215	1378	1943	1873	1597	1505	1208	1807	1357
Fort Wayne, Ind.	595	1842	302	2287	1071	2126	614	356	1572	1269	2200	2339	814	2187	1872	1099	528
Fort Worth, Tex.	1593	1044	1305	2078	1235	1663	1364	701	1239	268	1358	1734	752	2148	1903	1138	1434
Grand Forks, N. Dak.	1492	1803	1193	1645	613	1694	1520	889	1649	1455	1920	1928	1674	1459	1162	1884	1434
Grand Rapids, Mich.	738	1975	442	2308	1092	2147	750	478	1626	1412	2364	2389	966	2208	1893	1281	643
Great Falls, Mont.	2181	1273	1882	779	558	1000	2209	1533	585	1736	1370	1226	2351	701	413	2561	2108
Greensboro, N.C.	420	2219	430	2973	1807	2742	452	831	2224	1347	2543	2928	333	3085	2677	676	290
Hartford, Conn.	201	2592	474	3039	1823	2818	445	1070	2351	1976	2932	3091	937	2939	2624	1287	340
Houston, Tex.	1589	1158	1364	2282	1352	1888	1353	801	1453	197	1491	1955	1029	2354	2164	1007	1448
Indianapolis, Ind.	639	1750	355	2307	1122	2074	620	239	1544	1176	2134	2331	766	2312	1959	1005	567
Jackson, Miss.	1153	1456	972	2506	1453	2104	944	505	1685	614	1789	2203	603	2601	2263	678	1000
Jacksonville, Fla.	889	2053	893	3070	1932	2697	646	881	2237	1141	2320	2787	154	3115	2818	194	754
Kansas City, Mo.	1121	1238	850	1901	743	1665	1105	254	1118	773	1605	1893	1112	1904	1617	1280	1057
Las Vegas, Nev.	2537	338	2274	1016	1129	446	2514	1677	449	1319	337	583	2256	1193	1070	2325	2429
Lincoln, Nebr.	1213	1293	918	1712	569	1460	1270	473	931	930	1658	1683	1259	1790	1461	1465	1207
Little Rock, Ark.	1197	1337	914	2284	1164	2030	984	357	1444	578	1695	2032	795	2273	2018	939	1058
Los Angeles, Calif.	2741	389	2194	994	1399	476	2709	1862	730	1380	122	403	2482	1177	1249	2607	2739
Louisville, Ky.	682	1776	398	2437	1238	2213	575	267	1656	1124	2143	2425	640	2427	2167	865	605
Madison, Wis.	908	1748	602	2034	780	1925	930	361	1387	1282	2139	2145	1095	1956	1673	1306	835
Memphis, Tenn.	1057	1470	786	2367	1245	2083	845	294	1570	711	1829	2162	657	2362	2082	782	917
Miami, Fla.	1230	2388	1237	3414	2284	3021	994	1222	2603	1439	2618	3193	506	3451	3191	248	1105
Milwaukee, Wis.	853	1833	550	2069	858	2003	877	371	1502	1314	2191	2203	1038	2045	1751	1268	784
Minn.-St. Paul, Minn.	1176	1671	877	1721	576	1797	1204	553	1246	1234	2046	2001	1352	1673	1386	1578	1105
Mobile, Ala.	1140	1648	1106	2705	1601	2316	914	644	1881	707	1918	2400	506	2710	2455	522	1031
Montréal, Que.	480	2603	603	2830	1756	2825	725	1073	1295	2024	2942	3029	1225	2774	2486	1571	601
Nashville, Tenn.	838	1690	568	2457	1295	2227	625	295	1674	949	2051	2409	508	2495	2173	908	697
New Orleans, La.	1239	1527	1113	2591	1573	2199	1057	699	1773	575	1864	2278	641	2645	2383	644	1150
New York, N.Y.	91	2479	363	2959	1764	2818	330	961	2278	1863	2851	3054	830	2944	2671	1176	226
Norfolk, Va.	348	2437	400	3012	1859	2734	88	930	2352	1575	2733	3059	507	3024	2775	859	195
Oklahoma City, Okla.	1436	989	1145	1926	873	1529	1345	523	1112	477	1349	1692	1156	1975	1651	1264	1330
Omaha, Nebr.	1219	1325	918	1700	534	1500	1223	453	453	943	1716	1720	1298	1657	1513	1493	1149
Philadelphia, Pa.	•	2430	294	2921	1703	2724	240	881	2188	1772	2769	2951	736	2862	2624	1083	136
Phoenix, Ariz.	2430	•	2085	1273	1238	762	2332	1492	688	978	358	794	2046	1510	1419	2134	2331
Pittsburgh, Pa.	294	2085	•	2599	1395	2427	312	599	1902	1521	2493	2645	745	2511	2267	1045	229
Portland, Oreg.	2921	1273	2599	•	1237	566	2924	2113	807	2190	1115	669	3051	173	366	3225	2904
Providence, R.I.	267	2655	539	3135	1891	2941	506	1137	2419	2039	3013	3168	1006	3007	2692	1352	402
Québec, Que.	635	2765	735	2994	1937	2987	869	1251	2457	2168	3120	3190	1368	2934	2646	1720	762
Rapid City, S. Dak.	1703	1238	1395	1237	•	1224	1771	984	686	1263	1466	1454	1828	1183	870	2011	1624
Reno, Nev.	2724	762	2427	566	1224	•	2737	1906	531	1744	565	227	2703	760	779	2798	2666
Richmond, Va.	240	2332	312	2924	1771	2646	•	842	2264	1579	2638	2964	499	2936	2687	842	107
Sacramento, Calif.	2864	902	2567	544	1364	140	2877	2046	671	1758	509	87	2792	717	834	2896	2806
St. Louis, Mo.	881	1492	599	2113	984	1879	842	•	1381	927	1906	2133	841	2102	1868	1030	804
San Francisco, Calif.	2188	688	1902	807	686	531	2264	1381	•	1341	784	755	2236	869	738	2416	2123
Savannah, Ga.	1772	978	1521	2190	1263	1744	1579	927	1341	•	1306	1779	1227	2265	2113	1229	1641
Salt Lake City, Utah	2769	358	2493	1115	1466	565	2638	1906	784	1306	•	526	2381	1292	1343	2457	2737
San Antonio, Tex.	2951	794	2645	669	1454	227	2964	2133	755	1779	526	•	2792	858	921	2943	2886
San Diego, Calif.	736	2046	745	3051	1828	2703	499	841	2236	1227	2381	2792	•	3063	2772	352	604
Seattle, Wash.	2862	1510	2511	173	1183	760	2936	2102	869	2265	1292	858	3063	•	288	3250	2752
Shreveport, La.	1394	1221	1161	2226	1309	1885	1183	582	1460	389	1549	1990	831	2344	2129	923	1246
Sioux Falls, S. Dak.	1283	1481	984	1580	343	1472	1311	632	941	1119	1865	1696	1473	1526	1213	1683	1212
Spokane, Wash.	2624	1419	2267	366	870	779	2687	1868	738	2113	1343	921	2772	288	•	2942	2500
Springfield, Ill.	841	1533	551	2121	955	1872	810	99	1374	1062	1900	2133	906	2133	1825	1154	765
Tampa, Fla.	1083	2134	1045	3225	2011	2798	842	1030	2416	1229	2457	2943	352	3250	2942	•	947
Topeka, Kans.	1214	1250	921	1863	727	1645	1176	321	1086	794	1534	1847	1183	1833	1658	1351	1128
Toronto, Ont.	460	2262	320	2626	1410	2465	572	748	1954	1683	2613	2678	976	2600	2312	1424	477
Tucson, Ariz.	2377	123	2486	1396	1246	912	2286	1457	820	881	422	921	1970	1666	1523	2063	2360
Tulsa, Okla.	1304	1113	1010	2037	932	1713	1288	412	1194	554	1475	1790	1106	2026	1830	1213	1214
Vancouver, B.C.	3008	1656	2657	319	1329	906	3082	2250	1015	2411	1438	995	3209	146	288	3396	2881
Walla Walla, Wash.	2659	1222	2318	281	956	622	2643	1832	596	1992	1214	849	2821	273	157	2977	2479
Washington, D.C.	136	2331	229	2904	1624	2666	107	804	2123	1641	2737	2886	604	2752	2488	947	•
Wichita, Kans.	1361	1040	1070	1854	729	1542	1318	460	1020	634	1410	1730	2821	1842	1642	1386	1283
Winnipeg, Man.	1615	1941	1316	1523	751	1854	1643	1105	1430	1602	2260	2088	1808	1444	1156	2014	1541

	AVERAGE TEMPERATURE IN °F				AVERAGE RAINFALL IN INCHES			
CITY	JAN	APR	JUL	OCT	JAN	APR	JUL	OCT
Albany, N.Y.	23	46	72	51	2.5	2.8	3.5	2.8
Albuquerque, N. Mex.	35	56	79	58	0.4	0.5	1.2	0.8
Amarillo, Texas	36	56	78	59	0.6	1.5	3.0	2.2
Anchorage, Alaska	12	37	58	36	0.8	0.4	1.9	1.9
Atlanta, Ga.	45	60	79	62	4.4	4.5	4.7	2.4
Augusta, Maine	20	43	70	49	3.5	3.3	3.4	3.4
Birmingham, Ala.	47	63	82	66	5.0	4.5	5.2	3.0
Boise, Idaho	29	50	75	52	1.3	1.2	0.2	0.8
Boston, Mass.	30	48	74	55	3.9	3.8	2.9	3.1
Buffalo, N.Y.	25	44	70	51	2.8	3.0	2.6	3.0
Butte, Mont.	15	38	63	42	0.4	0.9	1.2	0.7
Charleston, S.C.	50	65	81	66	2.5	2.9	7.7	2.8
Charlotte, N.C.	43	60	79	63	3.5	3.4	4.8	2.7
Cheyenne, Wyo.	25	43	70	48	0.6	1.7	1.9	0.9
Chicago, Ill.	26	49	76	55	1.9	3.0	3.4	2.8
Cincinnati, Ohio	34	54	77	58	3.7	3.5	3.5	2.2
Cleveland, Ohio	28	47	72	53	2.7	3.4	3.3	2.4
Dallas. Texas	46	65	85	68	2.3	4.0	1.9	2.7
Denver, Colo.	29	46	73	51	0.6	2.1	1.5	1.0
Detroit, Mich.	27	48	74	54	1.9	3.1	2.7	2.6
El Paso, Texas	43	63	82	64	0.5	0.2	1.6	0.9
Fargo, N. Dak.	6	43	71	47	0.5	1.7	3.5	1.1
Great Falls, Mont.	22	44	69	48	0.7	1.0	1.3	0.8
Honolulu, Hawaii	73	74	79	78	3.8	1.3	0.4	1.8
Houston, Texas	54	69	83	71	3.8	3.2	4.3	3.8
Jacksonville, Fla.	56	69	83	71	2.5	3.6	7.7	5.2
Juneau, Alaska	25	38	55	42	4.0	2.9	4.5	8.3
Kansas City, Mo.	32	56	82	60	1.4	3.6	3.2	2.9
Las Vegas, Nev.	44	65	90	67	0.6	0.2	0.5	0.3
Los Angeles, Calif.	56	62	73	67	3.1	1.2	.01	0.4
Memphis, Tenn.	42	61	81	63	6.1	4.6	3.5	2.7
Mexico City, D.F.	54	64	62	59	0.2	0.5	4.9	1.4
Miami, Fla.	67	74	82	78	2.0	3.9	6.8	8.2
Milwaukee, Wis.	21	44	69	50	1.8	2.5	3.0	2.1
Minneapolis, Minn.	12	44	72	49	0.7	1.9	3.3	1.6
Montréal, Que.	16	43	71	49	1.2	2.8	4.0	3.2
New Orleans, La.	55	68	82	70	3.8	4.6	6.7	2.8
New York, N.Y.	33	51	77	58	3.3	3.4	3.7	3.1
Oklahoma City, Okla.	37	60	83	63	1.3	3.1	2.4	2.5
Omaha, Nebr.	22	52	79	56	0.8	2.6	3.4	1.7
Philadelphia, Pa.	32	52	76	56	3.3	3.4	4.2	2.8
Phoenix, Ariz.	50	67	90	71	0.7	0.3	0.8	0.5
Pittsburgh, Pa.	29	49	72	53	3.0	3.1	3.9	2.5
Portland, Oreg.	38	52	67	54	5.4	2.1	0.4	3.6
Rapid City, S. Dak.	24	45	72	50	0.4	1.9	2.3	1.0
Reno, Nev.	30	48	68	49	1.2	0.5	0.3	0.5
Richmond, Va.	39	58	78	59	3.5	3.2	5.6	3.0
St. Louis, Mo.	32	55	78	58	2.0	3.7	3.3	2.9
Salt Lake City, Utah	27	50	77	52	1.4	1.8	0.6	1.2
San Antonio, Texas	52	68	84	71	1.7	2.8	2.1	2.5
San Diego, Calif.	55	62	70	66	2.0	0.8	.01	0.5
San Francisco, Calif.	51	56	59	61	4.0	1.3	.01	0.7
San Juan, P. Rico	74	77	80	80	4.7	3.7	6.3	5.8
Seattle, Wash.	38	49	65	52	5.7	2.4	0.8	4.0
Spokane, Wash.	25	47	71	49	2.4	0.9	0.4	1.6
Tampa, Fla.	61	71	82	75	2.1	2.8	8.6	2.8
Toronto, Ont.	25	45	72	51	1.3	2.3	2.9	2.4
Vancouver, Br. Col.	37	48	64	50	6.6	2.8	1.4	5.4
Washington, D.C.	37	56	78	59	3.0	3.2	4.2	3.1
Winnipeg, Man.	0	38	68	43	.01	0.8	2.7	1.2

Vacation Travel by Air

COMMERCIAL AIRPORTS

Every major vacation and sightseeing spot in the United States, Canada and Mexico can be reached by air, and such arrangements as reduced excursion tickets and the family fare plan (the husband pays for a full fare ticket while his wife and children fly at considerably reduced rates) make air travel financially attractive. The arrangements for reduced rates are subject to frequent change, both as to cost and as to the days of the week on which they are valid, so please consult your travel agent in order to receive the most advantageous treatment. Car rentals are available at most airports; a combined airplane and car vacation can be highly practical if the traveler's time is limited and if he wants to avoid long stretches of driving.

With huge jet planes and an ever increasing flight speed, airplanes have become a medium of mass transportation; the largest number of tourists fly in "coach;" first class tickets are considerably higher, and considering the short flying time between almost any two points in the U.S. the advantages of the first class seem to be worthwhile only if money is no object. Ground service has been improved; reservations are easy and instantaneous, and upon arriving at the airport the porter checks in your suitcases without weighing them as soon as you step out of the taxi. Upon arrival at your destination your baggage can be picked up from circular conveyor belts. More refinements are being tested.

Package offerings are usually advantageous. Combinations of air travel, accommodations and sightseeing are offered for such tourist centers as Florida, the West Coast and Hawaii by both airlines and tour operators. Again your travel agent is the most reliable counselor in a field where changes are frequent.

Vacation Travel by Train

UNITED STATES
CANADA · MEXICO
RAILROADS
(PASSENGER SERVICE)
SCALE OF MILES
0   50   100   200   300
SCALE OF KILOMETERS
0   50   100   200   300

Capitals of Countries .... ☆
State and Provincial Capitals .... △
International Boundaries .... ▬▬▬
State and Provincial Boundaries ...... ▬·▬·▬
AMTRAK Routes ....
NON-AMTRAK Routes ....
Other Routes ....

© HAMMOND INCORPORATED, Maplewood, N. J.

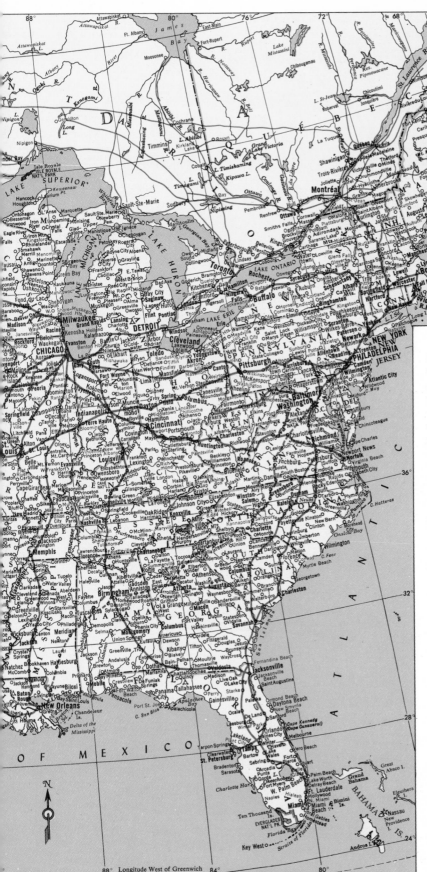

Amtrak is a government corporation which has been placed in charge of all passenger train traffic in the United States. Its task is to revitalize a medium of transportation that in the face of airplane and automobile competition has drastically declined in importance during recent years. Best known among its first successes are the twelve daily 2½-hour metroliner rides between New York and Washington. There are now many daily trains from New York to Boston and four trains make the journey to southern Florida daily in 23½ hours; they stop at Walt Disney World. The very popular new Auto Train carries automobiles between Washington and central Florida overnight while their drivers and passengers ride in cars with dining facilities and movies.

For extended vacation travel the Private Train Tours are popular. For 19 to 24 days the passengers live in special trains en route and in hotels at the sightseeing spots. These tours cover Mexico and the Southwest, the Rocky Mountain country and California, the Northwest and the Canadian Rockies, a grand circle of the western national parks, and the Northwest, the Inside Passage and Alaska. Most trains on these scenic routes have vista domes and dome lounges with glass roofs which make it possible to enjoy the splendid mountain scenery.

The two Canadian railroad systems — Canadian Pacific and Canadian National — are strongly geared to tourist and vacation travel. In Canada's principal vacation areas they own hotels, lodges and chalets. They also own fleets of steamers and in the beautiful Puget Sound region make railroad-steamboat tours available to southern Alaska and elsewhere. Canadian railroads cross some of the most magnificent parts of our continent.

Index

252